Inside Sociology

Michael Hughes
Virginia Polytechnic Institute and State University
Carolyn J. Kroehler

Mc
Graw
Hill

Boston   Burr Ridge, IL   Dubuque, IA   Madison, WI   New York
San Francisco   St. Louis   Bangkok   Bogotá   Caracas   Kuala Lumpur
Lisbon   London   Madrid   Mexico City   Milan   Montreal   New Delhi
Santiago   Seoul   Singapore   Sydney   Taipei   Toronto

The McGraw·Hill Companies

Higher Education

INSIDE SOCIOLOGY

Published by McGraw-Hill, a business unit of The McGraw-Hill Companies, Inc., 1221 Avenue of the Americas, New York, NY, 10020. Copyright © 2007 by The McGraw-Hill Companies, Inc. All rights reserved. No part of this publication may be reproduced or distributed in any form or by any means, or stored in a database or retrieval system, without the prior written consent of The McGraw-Hill Companies, Inc., including, but not limited to, in any network or other electronic storage or transmission, or broadcast for distance learning. Some ancillaries, including electronic and print components, may not be available to customers outside the United States.

This book is printed on acid-free paper.

2 3 4 5 6 7 8 9 0 DOC/DOC 0 9 8 7 6

ISBN: 978-0-07-352804-5
MHID: 0-07-352804-8

Editor in Chief: *Emily Barrosse*
Publisher: *Phillip A. Butcher*
Sponsoring Editor: *Sherith H. Pankratz*
Freelance Developmental Editor: *Craig S. Leonard*
Senior Marketing Manager: *Daniel M. Loch*
Managing Editor: *Jean Dal Porto*
Senior Project Manager: *Diane M. Folliard*
Associate Designer: *Marianna Kinigakis*

Cover Designer: *Marianna Kinigakis*
Manager, Photo Research: *Brian J. Pecko*
Associate Production Supervisor: *Jason I. Huls*
Senior Media Project Manager: *Nancy Garcia*
Composition: *9.5/12 Sabon by TBH Typecast, Inc.*
Printing: *45# New Era Matte,*
R. R. Donnelley/Crawfordsville, IN

Credits: The credits section for this book begins on page 353 and is considered an extension of the copyright page.

Library of Congress Cataloging-in-Publication Data

Hughes, Michael (Michael D.)
    Inside sociology / Michael Hughes, Carolyn J. Kroehler.
        p. cm.
    Includes bibliographical references and index.
    ISBN-13: 978-0-07-352804-5 (softcover : alk. paper)
    ISBN-10: 0-07-352804-8 (softcover : alk. paper)   1. Sociology.   I. Kroehler, Carolyn J.
    II. Title.
HM585.H835 2007
301—dc22
                                                                            2005054049

The Internet addresses listed in the text were accurate at the time of publication. The inclusion of a Web site does not indicate an endorsement by the authors or McGraw-Hill, and McGraw-Hill does not guarantee the accuracy of the information presented at these sites.
www.mhhe.com

About the Authors

Michael Hughes is Professor of Sociology at Virginia Polytechnic Institute and State University (Virginia Tech). He received his Ph.D. in sociology from Vanderbilt University in 1979 and has taught introductory sociology over the past 34 years. He also regularly teaches courses in minority group relations, deviant behavior, the sociology of mental illness, and data analysis. From 2000 to 2004, he served as editor of the *Journal of Health and Social Behavior.* He has held positions as research fellow at the University of Michigan's Institute for Social Research (1992–1994) and research associate at Vanderbilt University (1980–1982). With Walter R. Gove he is the author of the book *Overcrowding in the Household.* His research interests in mental health and mental illness, race and ethnicity, and crowding and living alone have resulted in over 60 professional articles published in a variety of journals. In 2004–2005, he served as president of the Southern Sociological Society.

Carolyn J. Kroehler is a professional writer and editor who has received her sociological education "on the job." Before her work on *Sociology: The Core,* she contributed to criminology and criminal justice textbooks. She edited and helped with the writing of a guide to academic success for college students, *Straight A's: If I Can Do It, So Can You.* At the Virginia Water Resources Research Center, she wrote public education and technical materials about water quality and other environmental issues, including a book on drinking water standards. Her writing experience also includes several years in a college public relations office and writing and editing for the *Lancaster Independent Press.* She earned her Ph.D. in botany at Virginia Tech and has published in the *Canadian Journal of Botany, Plant and Soil,* and *Oecologia.*

Mike and Carrie live in Blacksburg, Virginia, with their children Edmund and Camilla.

Dedication

To Sally and Lamar Hoover,
who launched Carrie on her writing and editing career.
CJK and MH

Contents

Chapter 6 Inequalities of Race, Ethnicity, and Gender   152

Chapter 7 The Family   183
seven

Preface

A course in sociology should broaden students' horizons, sharpen their observational skills, and strengthen their analytical capabilities. *Inside Sociology* aims to make the introductory course manageable for instructors and students alike, with a tight, readable text. It includes all of the major topics of the discipline, introducing the functionalist, conflict and symbolic interactionist perspectives in the first chapter and applying them throughout the book. It uses compelling chapter openers and lots of real-world examples to make sociology come alive. Its feature boxes, "Doing Social Research" and "Social Inequalities," draw readers in with information about blogging, campus rape, exporting toxic trash, unequal childhoods, model minorities, and more.

Inside Sociology is intended for instructors who desire an especially short, relatively inexpensive introductory text. This text covers the essential content in our text *Sociology: The Core,* seventh edition, in 10 brief chapters. These chapters can easily be covered in a course, along with other materials instructors might wish to add.

Pedagogical Aids

Each chapter opens with an **outline** of its major headings. **Key terms** are set in boldface type and defined in the text; they also appear in the **glossary** at the end of the book. Each chapter concludes with a set of **review questions,** and each box includes **discussion questions.** The data presented in the **figures and tables** are as user-friendly and accessible as we could make them and include original analyses generated from publicly available data sets. **Photographs and cartoons** help to illustrate important concepts and principles. An extensive list of **references** makes it possible for motivated students to find out more.

Ancillary Materials

Inside Sociology is accompanied by a number of supplementary learning and teaching aids.

For the Student

Reel Society 2.0

Available as a separate package option, this professionally produced movie on CD demonstrates the sociological imagination using actors in campus life scenarios. Each viewer takes on the role of one of the characters and influences key plot turns by making choices for them. Through it all, a wide variety of issues and perspectives are addressed relating major sociological concepts and theories to students' lives. Please go to www.mhhe.com/reelsoc for further details.

For the Instructor

The Instructor's Manual, Test Bank, Computerized Test Bank, and PowerPoints are available to instructors on the **Instructor's Resource CD** (IRCD).

Instructor's Manual

The Instructor's Manual provides chapter summaries, chapter outlines, learning objectives, teaching suggestions and discussion questions, student exercises and projects, and suggested films/videos.

Test Bank

The Test Bank offers multiple-choice, true-false, and essay questions for each chapter in the text. The Test Bank is available as a Word file and as a Computerized Test Bank on the Instructor Resource CD.

Videos

Please contact your McGraw-Hill sales representative to learn about videos that are available to adopters of McGraw-Hill introductory sociology textbooks.

Acknowledgments

We would like to thank the McGraw-Hill team that helped produce *Inside Sociology:* publisher Phil Butcher, sponsoring editor Sherith Pankratz, development editors Kathy Blake and Craig Leonard, project manager Diane Folliard, and designer Marianna Kinigakis.

Many thanks also go to Mike's colleagues at Virginia Tech who, through many and varied discussions and suggestions, have made substantial contributions to this work: Carol Bailey, Alan Bayer, Cliff Bryant, Toni Calasanti, Peggy DeWolf, Jay Edwards, Skip Fuhrman, Ted Fuller, Ellington Graves, Kwame Harrison, Bradley Hertel, Terry Kershaw, Jill Kiecolt, John Ryan, Don Shoemaker, Bill Snizek, Bob Turner, Anastasia Vost-Yuan, and Dale Wimberly.

Finally, we would like to thank our children, Camilla and Edmund, for their patience, and our families and friends for their support.

Michael Hughes
Carolyn Kroehler

Chapter 1

Developing a Sociological Consciousness

The Sociological
Perspective

The Development
of Sociology

Theoretical
Perspectives

Conducting Research

E ach of us is a social
being. We are born into
a social environment; we
fully develop into human
beings in a social environ-
ment; and we typically live out our lives in a social environment.
What we think, how we feel, and what we say and do all are shaped
by our interactions with other people. The scientific study of these
social interactions and of social organization is called **sociology.**

Why are some people wealthy and others poor? What causes
war? Why do people violate social rules? How do revolutions occur?
What causes mass hysteria? We know from ancient folklore, myths,
and archeological remains that humans have long had an interest in
understanding themselves and their social arrangements. Yet it has
been only in the past 175 years or so that human beings have
sought answers to these and related questions through science.
This science—sociology—pursues the study of social interaction
and group behavior through research governed by the rigorous and
disciplined collection of data and analysis of facts.

Many of us are not only interested in understanding society and human behavior. We also would like to improve the human condition so that we might lead fuller, richer, and more fruitful lives. To do this we need knowledge about the basic structures and processes underlying our social lives. Sociology, through its emphasis on observation and measurement, allows us to bring rigorous and systematic scientific thinking and information to bear on difficult questions associated with social policies and choices, including those related to poverty, health, immigration, crime, and education. Many people interested in these issues do not realize that more than concern is needed to solve problems. Action must be informed by knowledge.

Sociological research often is applied to practical matters. For example, the U.S. Supreme Court relied heavily upon social science findings regarding the effects of segregation on children in reaching its historic 1954 decision declaring mandatory school segregation unconstitutional (Klineberg, 1986; Jackson, 1990). Social and behavioral sciences also are central to the world's health and science agenda. Although we must still contend with bacteria and viruses, nowadays we get sick and die primarily because of our individual and collective behaviors. A 2002 study showed that human behaviors including smoking, drinking, practicing unsafe sex, and eating improperly are major contributors to death and disease around the world (Ezzati et al., 2002). Other major factors in global mortality and disease stem from societal problems: air pollution, unsafe drinking water, poor sanitation, and inadequate nutrition.

Sociologists may do basic research, seeking to better understand social interaction and group behavior, or they may design studies deliberately to evaluate public policies or to inform us about social conditions, including assessments of criminal justice programs, the social consequences of unemployment, and the effects of family structure on children and their future. The collection of census and other national statistical data, which is the foundation of many federal and state policies on health, education, housing, and welfare, is based on sample survey and statistical techniques developed by sociologists and other social scientists. Sociology, then, is a powerful scientific tool both for acquiring knowledge about ourselves and for intervening in social affairs to realize various goals.

The Sociological Perspective

The sociological perspective invites us to look beyond what we take for granted about our social lives and examine them in fresh and creative ways (Berger, 1963). There are many layers of meaning in the human experience. Networks of invisible rules and institutional arrangements guide our behavior. We continually evolve, negotiate, and rework tacit bargains with family members, friends, lovers, and work associates. As we look beyond outer appearances at what lies beneath, we encounter new levels of social reality. This approach to reality is the core of the sociological perspective.

In this section we will see how sociology uncovers new levels of reality, discuss the sociological imagination, and define microsociology and macrosociology.

New Levels of Reality

Tally's Corner, a classic study by social scientist Elliot Liebow (1967/2003) in a downtown Washington, D.C., African-American neighborhood, shows us how sociology can reveal new levels of social reality. In the early 1960s, our nation's concern about poverty led Liebow to involve himself in a unique study of low-income urban black men. Of course, most African Americans are not poor; today, for example, nearly 80 percent live above the poverty line (Proctor and Dalaker, 2002), and African-American men are typically employed and live respectable, conventional lives (Duneier, 1992). Nonetheless, most of the problems of poverty that Liebow observed 40 years ago are still with us today, and his findings continue to provide insight into this major U.S. social problem. Perhaps more importantly for us, his study provides an excellent example of how sociological research allows us to go beyond outward appearances and simplistic explanations.

Liebow conducted his study by hanging out on a corner in front of the New Deal Carry-out Shop, where he won the trust of 20 or so African-American men. The men Liebow got to know came to the corner shop, not far from the White House in a blighted section of the city, to eat, to enjoy easy talk, and in general to pass the time. The following excerpt relates what Liebow observed one weekday morning (Liebow, 1967/2003:19):

> A pickup truck drives slowly down the street. The truck stops as it comes abreast of a man sitting on a cast-iron porch and the white driver calls out, asking if the man wants a day's work. The man shakes his head and the truck moves on up the block, stopping again whenever idling men come within calling distance of the driver. At the Carry-out corner, five men debate the question briefly and shake their heads no to the truck. The truck turns the corner and repeats the same performance up the next street.

The white truck driver viewed the African-American streetcorner men as lazy and irresponsible, unwilling "to take a job even if it were handed to them on a platter." Like many middle-class Americans then and today, he believed that inner-city African-American men live only for the moment with little thought for long-term consequences. The truck driver assumed that all the streetcorner men were able-bodied men with no means of support—and no desire to take the work he offered them. Like many Americans, he assumed that the job problems of inner-city men resulted from the men themselves—from their lack of willingness to work.

Liebow's relationship with the men at the New Deal allowed him to look beyond the stereotyped images of African-American men to find another level of reality. Liebow found that most of the men who turned down the truck driver's offer had jobs but, for various reasons, were not at work that particular morning. A few did not have jobs, but with reason; the man on the porch, for example, had severe arthritis. Liebow discovered that streetcorner men and middle-class men differed not so much in their values and their attitudes toward the future as in the different futures they saw ahead of them. Middle-class men have incomes high enough to justify long-term investments, and they hold jobs that offer the promise of career advancement. Like middle-class men, the men on the corner wanted stable jobs and marriages. However, in their world, jobs were only intermittently available, almost always menial, often hard, and invariably low paying. The day jobs offered by such as the driver of the pickup truck usually involved back-breaking labor at heartbreakingly low wages. Even the jobs held by the men that day did not offer them much hope for the future. As Liebow observed, "A man's chances for working regularly are good only if he is willing to work for less than he can live on, sometimes not even then" (Liebow, 1967/2003:32).

Social policy based on the truck driver's interpretations would be directed toward changing the motivations of streetcorner men and encouraging them to develop those values and goals that lead to occupational achievement. But such social programs would have no chance of succeeding; the men were already willing to work and did not need to have their values and goals redirected. What they needed were jobs that provided wages they could live on.

This conclusion was supported by a study by sociologist Stephen M. Petterson in the late 1990s (Petterson, 1997). Petterson found that, far from being unwilling to work, jobless black men were willing to work—and had worked in the past—for lower wages than were white men. As Liebow had found 30 years earlier, joblessness is not necessarily related to a lack of willingness to work for low wages, and social programs designed in ignornace of that fact are doomed to failure.

In seeking an explanation for the behavior of the men he observed, Liebow looked beyond the individual men and the outward appearances of streetcorner life. He turned his investigative eye upon the social arrangements that are external to individuals but that nonetheless structure their experiences and place constraints on their behavior.

The Sociological Imagination

A basic premise underlying sociology is the notion that only by under-standing the society in which we live can we gain a fuller insight into our lives. Sociologist C. Wright Mills (1959) termed this quality of the discipline the **sociological imagination:** the ability to see our private experiences, personal difficulties, and achievements as, in part, a reflec-tion of the structural arrangements of society and the times in which we live. We tend to go about our daily activities thinking only about school, job, family, and neighborhood. The sociological imagination allows us to see the relationship between our personal experiences and broader social and historical events.

The job difficulties recently experienced by many young Ameri-cans provide an example. The restructuring and downsizing of cor-porate America in the early 1990s compounded the effects of economic recession. This economic malaise had a devastating effect on the employment ranks of the nation's youth: According to the Department of Labor, nearly 1 million fewer young people were employed in 2003 than in 2000 (http://www.bls.gov/cps/cpsatabs .htm). Clearly, the work values and attitudes of 1 million young Americans did not change so drastically that by 2003 they were unwilling to work. Mills's (1959) point is that in situations of this kind, we cannot simply look to the personal character of individuals to explain changes in their employment circumstances. Rather, we need to focus on our economic and political institutions for a defini-tion of the problem, for an understanding of its causes, and for a range of possible solutions. The sociological imagination allows us to place the private job frustrations of many Americans into the con-text of the structural factors operating in the larger society and the workplace.

In sum, the sociological imagination allows us to identify the links between our personal lives and the larger social forces of life—to see that what is happening to us immediately is a minute point at which our personal lives and society intersect.

Microsociology and Macrosociology

Sociologists seek to extend Mills's insight by distinguishing between the micro, or small-scale, aspects of the social enterprise and the macro, or large-scale, structural components. When we focus on the micro elements, we examine behavior close-up and observe what hap-pens as people interact on a face-to-face basis. Sociologists term this level *microsociology*—micro meaning "small," as in the word *micro-scope*. **Microsociology** entails the detailed study of what people say, do, and think moment by moment as they go about their daily lives. In short, microsociology deals with everyday life: a woman and a man initiating a conversation on a bus, several youngsters playing basketball on an inner-city playground, guests at a baby shower, a police officer directing traffic at a busy intersection, or students and their teacher interacting in a classroom.

Sociologists also turn an investigative eye upon "the big picture" and study social groups and societies. This approach is termed *macrosociology*—macro meaning "large." **Macrosociology** focuses upon large-scale and long-term social processes of organizations, institutions, and broad social patterns, including the state, social class, the family, the economy, culture, and society. At this level, sociologists may direct their attention to the changes in the structure of a religious sect, the impact of population dynamics and computer technologies on the workforce, shifts in the racial and ethnic composition of a city, or the dynamics of intergroup competition and conflict.

The microsociological and macrosociological levels are not independent of one another (Ritzer, 2000; House, 1995). We can most appropriately think of the distinction between "micro" and "macro" as one of degree (Lawler, Ridgeway, and Markovsky, 1993). Macro structures, such as organizations or the hierarchy of social classes, are composed of routine patterns of interaction on the micro level. Macro structures provide the social contexts in which people encounter one another at the micro level. Micro structures, such as friendship relations and work groups, form out of these encounters and provide a link from individuals to macro structures. Micro structures also may cause change and evolution in macro structures. For example, the macro structure of education and an organization embedded in it, your high school, may have provided the social context from which your group of best friends—a micro structure—emerged. Such a group of students, through letter-writing campaigns, sit-ins, formation of clubs, and other means, can cause a high school and education in general—macro structures—to adapt and change. In sum, complex webs of relationship between the micro and macro levels contribute to an ever-changing and diverse social order (Móuzelis, 1992).

The Development of Sociology

Sociology, too, is a product of micro and macro forces. The political revolutions ushered in by the French Revolution in Europe in 1789 and continuing through the 19th century provided a major impetus to sociological work (Ritzer, 2000). At the same time, the Industrial Revolution that swept many Western nations resulted in large numbers of people leaving a predominantly agricultural setting for work in factories. New social and economic arrangements arose to provide the many demands of emergent capitalism. These major changes in the way society was organized led some of the thinkers of the day to turn their attention to the study of social organization and social interactions, resulting in the founding of the science we now call sociology (Ritzer, 2000).

In this section we will consider the contributions of six particularly influential sociologists, the emergence of sociology in the United States, and contemporary sociology.

Auguste Comte: The Founder of Sociology

Auguste Comte (1798–1857) is commonly credited with being the founder of sociology and as having coined the name "sociology" for the new science. He emphasized that the study of society must be scientific, and he urged sociologists to use systematic observation, experimentation, and comparative historical analysis as their methods.

Comte divided the study of society into social statics and social dynamics, a conceptual distinction that is still with us. **Social statics** involves those aspects of social life that have to do with order, stability, and social organization that allow societies and groups to hold together and endure. **Social dynamics** refers to those processes of social life that pattern institutional development and have to do with social change. Although his specific ideas no longer direct contemporary sociology, Comte created the intellectual foundation for a science of social life and exerted enormous influence on the thinking of other sociologists, particularly Herbert Spencer, Harriet Martineau, and Émile Durkheim.

Harriet Martineau: Feminist and Methodologist

While Comte was laying the theoretical foundations for sociology, the English sociologist Harriet Martineau (1802–1876) was paving the way for the new discipline through her observations of social behavior in the United States and England. Like Comte, she insisted that the study of society represents a separate scientific field. Among her contributions was the first book on the methodology of social research, *How to Observe Manners and Morals,* published in 1838. She also undertook the comparative study of the stratification systems of Europe and the United States. Martineau showed how the basic moral values of the young American nation shaped its key institutional arrangements. Throughout her career, Martineau was an ardent defender of women's rights. She showed the similarities between the position of women in Western societies and that of American slaves, and called for freedom and justice for all in an age in which they were granted only to white males (Rossi, 1973; Deegan, 1991).

Though Harriet Martineau was a popular and influential intellectual and author during her lifetime, her contributions to sociology were marginalized by the men who dominated the discipline during its early years and kept women like Martineau out of powerful academic positions (Ritzer, 2000). Consequently, Martineau's significance in the early development of sociology has only recently been fully recognized (Deegan, 2003; Hoecker-Drysdale, 1994; Lengermann and Niebrugge-Brantley, 2000a).

Herbert Spencer and Social Darwinism

Herbert Spencer (1820–1903), an English sociologist, shared Comte's concern with social statics and social dynamics. He compared society to a biological organism and depicted it as a system, a whole made up of interrelated parts. Just as the human body is made up of organs, so society is made up of institutions (e.g., the family, religion, education, the state, and the economy). In his description of society as an organism, Spencer focused on its structures and the functional contributions these structures make to its survival. This image of society is in line with what sociologists now call structural-functional theory.

Spencer viewed static social institutions as the organs of society, but he had an even greater interest in social dynamics. He proposed an evolutionary theory of historical development, one that depicted the world as growing progressively better. Intrigued by the Darwinian view of natural selection, Spencer applied the concept of survival of the fittest to the social world, an approach termed **Social Darwinism.** He sought to demonstrate that government should not interfere with the natural processes going on in a society. In this manner, he argued, people and social patterns that were "fit" would survive and those that were "unfit" would die out. If this principle were allowed to operate freely, human beings and their institutions would progressively adapt themselves to their environment and reach higher and higher levels of historical development (Ritzer, 2000).

Spencer's Social Darwinist ideas were used extensively within England and the United States to justify unrestrained capitalism. John D. Rockefeller, the American oil tycoon, would echo Spencer and observe: "The growth of a large business is merely a survival of the fittest . . . This is not an evil tendency in business. It is merely the working out of a law of nature" (quoted by Lewontin, Rose, and Kamin, 1984:26).

Karl Marx: The Role of Class Conflict

Although Karl Marx (1818–1883) considered himself a political activist and not a sociologist, in truth he was both—and a philosopher, historian, economist, and political scientist as well. He viewed science not only as a vehicle for understanding society but also as a tool for transforming it. Marx was especially eager to change the structure of capitalist institutions and to establish new institutions in the service of humanity. Although born in Germany, authorities there viewed Marx as politically dangerous, and he was compelled to spend much of his adult life as a political exile in London.

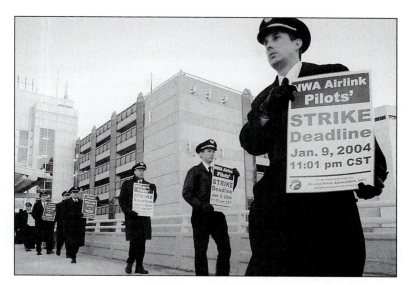

The conflict perspective argues that the structure of our society is powerfully affected by conflicts such as that between airline pilots and Mesaba Airlines in 2004.

Marx tried to discover the basic principles of history. He focused his search on the economic environments in which societies develop, particularly the current state of their technology and their method of organizing production, such as hunting and gathering, agriculture, or industry. At each stage of history, these factors dictate the group that will dominate society and the groups that will be subjugated. He believed that society is divided into those who own the means of producing wealth and those who do not, which gives rise to **class conflict.** All history, he said, is composed of struggles between classes. In contemporary Western societies, class antagonisms revolve about the struggle between the oppressing capitalist class, or bourgeoisie, and the oppressed working class, or proletariat. The former derive their income through their ownership of the means of production, primarily factories, which allows them to exploit the labor of workers. The latter own nothing except their labor power and, because they are dependent for a living on the jobs provided by capitalists, must sell their labor power in order to exist.

Marx's perspective is called **dialectical materialism,** the notion that development depends on the clash of contradictions and the subsequent creation of new, more advanced structures. The approach depicts the world as made up not of static structures but of dynamic processes, a world of becoming rather than of being. In the Marxian view of history, every economic order grows to a state of maximum efficiency; at the same time, it develops internal contradictions or weaknesses that contribute to its decay. The roots of a new order begin to take hold in the old order. In time, the new order displaces the old order while absorbing its most useful features. Marx depicted slavery as being displaced by feudalism, feudalism by capitalism, capitalism by socialism, and ultimately socialism by communism, the highest stage of society.

In Marx's theory, political ideologies, religion, family organization, education, and government make up what he called the *superstructure* of society. This superstructure is strongly influenced by the economic base of society—its mode of producing goods and its class structure. When one class controls the critical means whereby people derive their livelihood, its members gain the leverage necessary to fashion other aspects of institutional life—the superstructure—in ways that favor their class interests. In Marx's view, economic factors—whether one owns and controls the means of production—are primary. For this reason, he is viewed by many as an **economic determinist.**

For most sociologists as for most historians and economists, Marx's work is too outdated to follow in its particulars, but it remains theoretically important and animates much contemporary research and theory (e.g., Wright, 2000).

Émile Durkheim: Social Integration and Social Facts

While Marx saw society as a stage upon which classes with conflicting interests contested with one another, the French sociologist Émile Durkheim (1858–1916) focused his sociological eye on the question of how societies hold together and endure. Central to Durkheim's (1897/1951) sociology is the concept of *social integration*. Social integration refers to the density of social relationships, literally the number of relationships that exist among a collection of people. The more people are connected to one another, the stronger and more meaningful are the sentiments that emerge out of these relationships (Pope, 1976).

Durkheim argued that social integration is necessary for the maintenance of the social order and for the happiness of individuals. In particular, he suggested that happiness depends on individuals finding a sense of meaning outside themselves that occurs within the context of group involvement. Durkheim sought to demonstrate that the destruction of social bonds (e.g., divorce) has negative consequences and under some circumstances can increase the chance that people will commit suicide. Other sociologists picked up on this central idea and showed how the breakdown of group bonds can contribute to deviant behavior (Merton, 1968) and participation in social movements (Kornhauser, 1959).

In *The Division of Labor in Society* (1893/1964), Durkheim examined social solidarity, the tendency of people to maintain social relationships. He distinguished between the types of solidarity found in early and modern societies. In early societies such as hunting and gathering or agrarian societies, the social structure was relatively simple, with little division of labor. People were knit together by their engagement in similar tasks. They derived a sense of oneness from being so much alike, what Durkheim termed *mechanical solidarity*.

Modern societies, in contrast, are characterized by complex social structures and a sophisticated division of labor. People perform specialized tasks in factories, offices, and schools. No one person is self-sufficient, and all must depend upon others to survive. Under these circumstances, society is held together by the interdependence fostered by the differences among people, what Durkheim labeled *organic solidarity*.

In examining social solidarity and other sociological questions, Durkheim believed that we should focus on the group, not the individual. He contended that the distinctive subject matter of sociology should be the study of social facts. **Social facts** are aspects of social life that cannot be explained in terms of the biological or mental characteristics of the individual. People experience social facts as external to themselves in the sense that facts have an independent reality and form a part of people's objective environment. As such, social facts serve to constrain their behavior, and include not only legal and moral rules in society, but also relationships and behavior patterns of others that affect our day-to-day lives.

Durkheim insisted that the explanation of social life must be sought in society itself. Society, he said, is more than the sum of its parts; it is a system formed by the association of individuals that comes to constitute a reality with its own distinctive characteristics.

Durkheim convincingly demonstrated the critical part social facts play in human behavior in his book *Suicide* (1897/1951), a landmark study in the history of sociology. He found that suicide rates were higher among Protestants than Catholics, higher among the unmarried than the married, and higher among soldiers than civilians. Moreover, suicide rates were higher in times of peace than in times of war and revolution, and higher in times of economic prosperity and recession than in times of economic stability. He concluded that different suicide *rates* are the consequence of variations in social solidarity. Individuals enmeshed in a web of social bonds are less inclined to suicide than individuals who are weakly integrated into group life.

Durkheim challenged the idea that suicide was the result of purely individual factors. As an alternative, he proposed that suicide is a social fact: a product of the meanings, expectations, and structural arrangements that evolve as people interact with one another.

Max Weber: Subjectivity and Social Organization

No sociologist other than Marx has had a greater impact on sociology than the German sociologist Max Weber (1864–1920). Among sociologists, he is known not only for his theoretical contributions but also for a number of specific ideas that have generated considerable interest and research in their own right. Many common but important ideas that we use to understand social life have their origin in the work of Weber, including *bureaucracy, lifestyle,* the *Protestant ethic,* and *charisma*, and his work continues to influence sociological scholarship today (e.g., Wright, 2002).

Weber contended that a critical focus for sociology is the study of human subjectivity: the intentions, values, beliefs, and attitudes that underlie people's behavior. Weber employed the German word **Verstehen**—meaning "understanding" or "insight"—in describing this approach for learning about the subjective meanings people attach to their actions. In using this method, sociologists mentally attempt to place themselves in the shoes of other people and identify what they think and how they feel.

Another notable sociological contribution Weber made is the concept of the ideal type. An *ideal type* is a concept constructed by sociologists to portray the principal characteristics of something they want to study. It is a tool that allows sociologists to generalize and simplify data by ignoring minor differences in order to accentuate major similarities. For example, a police department and a hospital differ in many obvious respects, but they share many attributes under the heading "bureaucracy." In Chapter 3 we will see how Weber employed the notion of the ideal type to devise his model of bureaucracy. The ideal type serves as a measuring rod against which sociologists can evaluate actual cases. For example, if sociologists determine, on the basis of historical and contemporary evidence, that the ideal type of bureaucracy has a specific set of characteristics, they can compare this ideal type with actual bureaucracies and then develop explanations for why some of the characteristics of actual bureaucracies deviate from the ideal type.

In his writings Weber stressed the importance of a **value-free sociology**. He emphasized that sociologists must not allow their personal biases to affect the conduct of their scientific research. Weber recognized that sociologists, like everyone else, have individual biases and moral convictions regarding behavior. But he insisted that sociologists must cultivate a disciplined approach to the phenomena they study so that they may see facts as they are, not as they might wish them to be. By the same token, Weber recognized that objectivity is not neutrality or moral indifference. Though he promoted objectivity as an important goal in social science, he did not take a neutral stance as an intellectual or as a citizen. He was not afraid to express a value judgment or to tackle important issues of the day (Ritzer, 2000).

American Sociology

The sociologists we have considered thus far have been of European origin. As sociology entered the 20th century, Americans assumed a critical role in its development.

Early American sociology was optimistic, forward-looking, and rooted in a belief in progress, the value of individual freedom and welfare, and a confidence that, though there might be some flaws, American society was basically sound. Some early American sociologists, like Lester Ward (1841–1918), believed that sociologists should identify the basic laws that underlie social life and use this knowledge to reform society. Others, like William Graham Sumner (1840–1910), adapted a survival-of-the-fittest approach derived from Spencer, believing that society's problems would work themselves out if left alone.

An exception to such optimism is the work of W. E. B. Du Bois (1868–1963), a leading African-American intellectual and one of the founders of the National Association for the Advancement of Colored People, who analyzed racial inequality and advocated radical changes to eliminate it (Du Bois, 1903/1990; Blau and Brown, 2001). Du Bois also took sociology out of the ivory tower and did investigative fieldwork, gathering material on the African-American community of Philadelphia, which appeared as *The Philadelphia Negro* in 1900. Between 1896 and 1914, Du Bois led the annual Atlanta University Conferences on Negro Problems that produced the first reliable sociological research on the South.

W. E. B. Du Bois conducted pathbreaking research on African American life, developed a theoretical understanding of racial inequality, and advocated radical social change to eliminate racism.

Contributions of considerable significance to sociology also were made by sociologists at the University of Chicago, where the first department of sociology in the United States was established in 1893. Here, in the first 30 years of the 20th century, a number of sociologists carried out work that remains influential in sociology today. The city of Chicago was viewed as a "social laboratory," and it was subjected to intense and systematic study. Included in this research were investigations of juvenile gangs, immigrant ghettos, wealthy Gold Coast and slum life, taxi-dance halls, prostitution, and mental disorders.

During the 1940s and until the mid-1960s, sociologists at Columbia, Harvard, and the University of California at Berkeley took the lead and established the major directions for sociological research and theory, crafting techniques for surveying public attitudes and refining models that portrayed society as a system made up of parts with interrelated functions. At this time, the leaders of American sociology believed sociology should be a science concerned with pursuing knowledge for its own sake, so they insisted that the discipline not be focused directly on solving social problems.

However, the social turmoil of the 1960s and early 1970s brought to sociology many students who were activists for civil rights, student power, and peace. These young "new breed" sociologists contended that the doctrine of sociological neutrality was a cloak concealing moral insensitivity. In their reaction against the neutrality of previous decades, they also broke with established sociological theory and sought new directions in theory and research grounded in the work of Karl Marx and C. Wright Mills (see Lemert, 2002; Agger, 1991; and Maynard and Clayman, 1991).

Contemporary Sociology

The evolution of sociology continues. Among the many theoretical developments that have occurred, three influential and related frameworks stand out: critical theory, feminism, and postmodernism.

Critical Theory.

Critical theory grew out of a dissatisfaction with 20th-century sociology in general and Marxism in particular (Ritzer, 2000). Early critical theorists were German sociologists who fled the Nazi regime in the 1930s and came to the United States, where some remained. These critical theorists and their followers criticized sociology for having a scientific approach that viewed individuals as passive and helpless entities locked in social structures, and for analyzing societies without detecting social problems or envisioning what societies should be. They criticized Marxism because they believed it denied the importance of culture by viewing it as part of the "superstructure," largely determined by economic forces. Critical theorists argue that mass culture (e.g., television, film, popular music), a product of a capitalist media industry, cannot be a true reflection of people's beliefs, tastes, values, ideas, and lifestyles. Instead, mass culture pacifies, represses, and controls people who might otherwise recognize important contradictions and inequalities in their social lives. Critical theorists claim that mass culture makes the political system seem to be a benign entity, supporting the status quo, that benefits all.

Critical theory is both an outgrowth of and a contributor to conflict theory, which we will discuss in the next section. It also has had a major influence on two other contemporary movements in sociology: feminism and postmodern social theory.

Feminism.

Feminism is an intellectual movement in the humanities and social sciences that is currently having a profound impact on the nature and direction of sociology (e.g., Thistle, 2000). Sociological feminism begins with the observation that for most of the history of sociology, women hardly appear in social theory and research. Men's experiences have been viewed as universal and women's activities and experiences have been hidden. When women have been studied and theorized about, it is in marginal and secondary roles such as housewife or workers in other low-status occupations. Feminism explicitly examines women's roles and experiences in society, working to fully uncover women's contributions to social life and the nature of the structures and processes that maintain gender inequality. At the same time, sociological feminism has worked to develop theories grounded in the experiences and situations of women that can be used to criticize oppressive social relations and produce social transformation for the betterment of all humankind (Lengermann and Niebrugge-Brantley, 2000b).

The latest major developments in feminist theory and research grow out of the realization that the social experience of gender is not universal. Women's and men's experiences are strongly influenced by social class, race, ethnicity, nationality, age, and sexual preference and by their social positions in the family, the labor force, and the world economic system (Richardson, Taylor, and Whittier, 1997; Lengermann and Niebrugge-Brantley, 2000b).

Postmodernism.   Like feminism, postmodernism (Ritzer, 2000; Best and Kellner, 1991; Rosenau, 1992) is an intellectual movement that has influenced scholarship

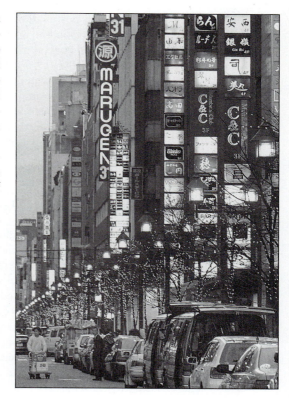

According to postmodernism, we have entered an age in which human society is dominated by images and information disseminated through the mass media.

in literature, art, politics, communications, and other disciplines, as well as sociology. Postmodernists are deeply distrustful of science and the principle of objectivity, arguing that scientific knowledge is as much a product of the socially determined interests and biases of investigators as it is of facts, which themselves are products of social processes. In addition, postmodernists point out that scientific knowledge has failed to solve social problems or to prevent war and genocide.

At the core of postmodern social theory is the assumption that the modern period of history is coming to an end. We are now entering an age dominated not by the goods-producing economy of modernity but by the production and dissemination of images and information through mass media and advanced computer technology. If societies are based on ever-changing signs, codes, and models presented in the media, they have no basic structure, and the grand abstract social theories of Marx, Durkheim, Weber, and others discussed above can be of little use in understanding them.

Postmodernism is a very pessimistic framework (Adam and Allan, 1995; see also Sica, 1996), arguing that there is no foundation for objective, reliable knowledge about social life.

Though postmodernism has no coherent set of theoretical principles, it does point to some of the ways that contemporary societies constrain and control people, particularly through media and advertising (Ritzer, 1995, 1997, 2000), and it suggests ways people can liberate themselves. Postmodernism has also broadened sociology through its emphasis on the multidisciplinary nature of social inquiry, revitalized sociology's debunking function through the method of deconstructing texts to show their hidden assumptions, and encouraged continuous reexamination of basic theoretical assumptions (Ritzer, 2000).

Theoretical Perspectives

As we have seen, sociologists have asked fundamental questions about social life throughout the history of sociology: Why does social inequality exist? How do people learn to interact with each other and be effective participants in society? How and why do societies change? Sociologists have answered these and many more questions by developing social theories. No one social theory has been so successful that it has been able to eliminate its competitors and dominate the field.

There now exist many different social theories to explain many different facets of our social lives. To reduce complexity, we can combine theories with similar approaches into theoretical perspectives. A *theoretical perspective* provides a set of assumptions, interrelated concepts, and statements about how various social phenomena are related to one another.

An important development of 20th-century sociology was the emergence of three general theoretical perspectives. The adherents of each perspective ask somewhat different questions about society and provide different views of social life. We do not need to accept only one model and reject all the others; rather, theoretical perspectives are tools—mental constructs—that allow us to visualize something. Any model necessarily limits our experience and presents just one angle on a concept, but a good model also *increases* what we can see by providing rules of inference through which new relationships can be discovered and suggestions about how the scope of a theory can be expanded.

The three contemporary theoretical perspectives in sociology are *functionalism,* which emphasizes order and stability; *conflict theory,* which focuses on inequality, exploitation, oppression, social turmoil, and social change; and *symbolic interactionism,* which argues that society emerges from and is changed by the process of human beings interacting with one another using symbols based in shared meanings. Together, these three perspectives form the theoretical background of most current sociological work. We will be returning to them throughout the book. For now, let us briefly examine each in turn.

The Functionalist Perspective

The structural-functional—or, more simply, functionalist—perspective draws substantially upon the ideas of Auguste Comte, Herbert Spencer, and Émile Durkheim. Its theorists take a broad view of society and focus on the macro aspects of social life. In the 1950s and early 1960s, the functionalist theories of Talcott Parsons (1949, 1951) and his students occupied center stage in American sociology. Indeed, some proponents such as Kingsley Davis (1959) argued that the approach was essentially synonymous with sociology.

Society as a Social System.

Functionalists take as their starting point the notion that society is a *system,* a set of elements or components that are related to one another in a more or less stable fashion through a period of time. Functionalists focus on the parts of society, particularly its major institutions, such as the family, religion, the economy, the state, and education. They identify the structural characteristics of each part much as biologists describe the principal features of the body's organs. They then determine what the functions of each part are.

One of the features of a system stressed by functionalists is its tendency toward equilibrium, or balance, among its parts and among the forces operating on it. Change in one part has implications for other parts and for the community or society as a whole, with change and adaptation being a continuous process. Some parts also may change more rapidly than others, contributing to social dislocations. For example, as increasing numbers of mothers with preschool children enter the paid labor force, new arrangements are required to take care of their children during the day. Yet licensed day care facilities are currently available for fewer than one-third of the children with mothers in the labor force.

Functions and Dysfunctions.

Within system analysis, functionalists pay particular attention to the **functions** performed by a system's parts, especially organizations, groups, institutions, and cultural patterns. Functionalists say that if a system is to survive, certain essential tasks must be performed; otherwise, the system fails to maintain itself and perishes. If society is to exist, its members must make provision for certain functional requirements. Institutions, to be discussed in more detail in Chapter 2, are the principal structures whereby these critical tasks for social living—functions—are organized, directed, and executed. Each institution, such as education, the economy, and the family, is built around a standardized solution to a set of problems. Functions are the observed consequences of the existence of institutions, groups, and other system parts that permit the adaptation or adjustment of a system (Merton, 1968).

Robert K. Merton (1968) pointed out that just as institutions and the other parts of society can contribute to the maintenance of the social system, they also can have negative consequences. Those observed consequences that lessen the adaptation or adjustment of a system he terms **dysfunctions.** Poverty, for example, has both functional and dysfunctional properties (Gans, 1972). Poverty is functional because it ensures that the nation's "dirty work" is done—those jobs that are physically dirty, dangerous, temporary, dead-end, poorly paid, and menial. However, poverty is dysfunctional because it intensifies a variety of social problems, including those associated with health, education, crime, and drug addiction.

Manifest and Latent Functions.

Merton (1968) also distinguished between manifest functions and latent functions. **Manifest functions** are those consequences that are intended and recognized by the participants in a system; **latent functions** are those consequences that are neither intended nor recognized. Some ceremonials of the Hopi Indians of the Southwest, for example, are designed to produce rain. Though these rituals do not actually produce rain, their latent function is to produce a collective expression by which the Hopi people achieve a sense of social solidarity.

Social Consensus.

Functionalists also assume that most members of a society agree on what is desirable, worthwhile, and moral, and what is undesirable, worthless, and evil. Through a social learning process, they come to share a consensus regarding their core values and beliefs. For example, most Americans accept the values and beliefs inherent in democracy, the doctrine of equal opportunity, and the notion of personal achievement. Functionalists say that this high degree of consensus on basic values provides the foundation for social integration and stability in U.S. society.

Evaluation of the Functionalist Perspective.

The functionalist perspective is a useful tool for describing society and identifying its structural parts and the functions of these parts at a particular point in time. It provides a "big picture" of the whole of social life, particularly as it finds expression in patterned, recurrent behavior and institutions. For some purposes, it is clearly helpful to have a clear description of the parts that make up society and how they fit together.

However, the functionalist approach has difficulty dealing with history and processes of social change. Moreover, the functionalist perspective tends to exaggerate consensus, integration, and stability while disregarding conflict, dissent, and instability. The problems that structural-functional theory has in dealing with change, history, and conflict have led critics to charge that it has a conservative bias and that it tends to support existing social arrangements.

The Conflict Perspective

Conflict theorists, like functionalists, focus their attention on society as a whole, studying its institutions and structural arrangements. Yet the two perspectives are at odds on a good many matters. Where functionalists depict society in relatively static terms, conflict theorists emphasize the processes of change that continually transform social life. Where functionalists stress the order and stability to be found in society, conflict theorists emphasize disorder and instability. Where functionalists see the common interests shared by the members of a society, conflict theorists focus upon the interests that divide. Where functionalists view consensus as the basis of social unity, conflict theorists insist that social unity is an illusion resting on coercion. Finally, where functionalists often view existing social arrangements as necessary and justified by the requirements of group life, conflict theorists see many of the arrangements as neither necessary nor justified.

Diversity of Approaches.

Although conflict theory derives much of its inspiration from the work of Karl Marx, it has many other sources as well, including the work of such sociologists as Georg Simmel (1908/1955, 1950), Lewis Coser (1956), and Randall Collins (1975). Although class conflict was the core of Marx's theory, many contemporary sociologists view conflict as occurring among many groups and interests—religion versus religion, race versus race, consumers versus producers, taxpayers versus welfare recipients, sunbelt versus snowbelt states, central city residents versus suburbanites, the young versus the elderly, and so on.

Sources of Conflict.

The main source of conflict in human societies is scarcity of social and material resources. Wealth, prestige, and power are always in limited supply, so that gains for one individual or group are usually associated with losses for others. **Power**—the ability to control the behavior of others, even against their will—determines who will gain and who will lose (Lasswell, 1936). Power also determines which group will be able to translate its preferences for behavior (its values) into the operating rules for others. Conflict theorists ask how it is that some groups acquire power, dominate other groups, and effect their will in human affairs. In so doing, they look at who benefits and who loses from the way society is organized.

How Society Is Possible.

If social life is fractured and fragmented by confrontations between individuals or groups, how is a society possible? Functionalists say society is held together primarily by a consensus among its members regarding core values and norms, but conflict theorists reject this view. They maintain that society is held together in spite of conflicting interests.

Many divided but overlapping interest groups generate a large number of crosscutting conflicts. People who are opponents in one conflict are allies in another. Society persists because no one conflict can become so great as to tear the society apart (Coser, 1956). For example, an African-American woman at odds with her white neighbor over affirmative action policy may agree with her about increasing funding for their neighborhood schools.

Evaluation of the Conflict Perspective.

The conflict perspective complements functionalist theory. The functionalist approach has difficulty dealing with history and social change; the conflict approach makes these matters its strength. The conflict approach has difficulty dealing with social aspects of consensus, integration, and stability; the functionalist approach affords penetrating insights.

Some sociologists contend that the functionalists and conflict theorists are simply studying two aspects of the same reality. They note that both consensus and conflict are central features of social life. In addition, both approaches have traditionally taken a holistic view of social life, portraying societies as systems of interrelated parts (van den Berghe, 1963).

Other sociologists such as Lewis Coser (1956) suggested that under some circumstances conflict is functional for society. For example, the 1960s conflict over civil rights contributed to the long-term stability of American institutions by bringing African Americans into the "system."

However, it is clear that conflict is often dysfunctional for an existing system. The many destructive conflicts around the world that are preventing societies and nations from fully developing socially and economically, such as those between the Israelis and Palestinians in the Middle East and between Catholics and Protestants in Northern Ireland, serve as examples.

The Interactionist Perspective

The functionalist and conflict perspectives take a big-picture approach to sociology, focusing on the macro, or large-scale, structures of society. In contrast, the interactionist perspective is more concerned with the micro, or small-scale, aspects of social life. Sociologists like Charles Horton Cooley (1902/1964), George Herbert Mead (1934/1962), Manford Kuhn (1964), and Herbert Blumer (1969) turned their attention to the individuals who make up society and asked how social interaction is possible. Answers to this question focus on individuals' subjective experiences and understandings, and especially on how shared understandings of the world emerge from social interaction and form the basis for social life. As with the functionalist and conflict perspectives, a number of themes recur in the various formulations of interactionist thought.

Symbols.   Interactionists emphasize that we are social beings who live a group existence. However, we possess few, if any, innate behaviors for relating to one another. Whatever inborn capacities we have seem to require exposure to others to fully develop; we will discuss this further in Chapter 2. If we are largely lacking in such inborn mechanisms, how is society possible? Interactionists find the answer in the ability of human beings to communicate by means of symbols. A symbol is something that stands for something else. That something else is its *meaning.* Social interaction, and therefore society itself, is possible because people share meanings. The combined emphasis on symbols and interaction gives this perspective its name: *symbolic interactionism.*

Meaning: Constructing Reality.   Symbolic interactionism is based on three core assumptions (Mead, 1934/1962; Blumer, 1969; Fine, 1993). First, we respond to things in our environment on the basis of their meanings—that is, the understandings we have of them. Our responses differ if we see people swinging bats as playing a baseball game or as trying to hit us. Second, meanings are not inherent in things, but emerge from social interaction. Turning 16 years of age is no more meaningful than turning 15, except for the social conventions (e.g., obtaining one's driver's license) that make this a particularly meaningful birthday. Third, because we are continually interacting, shared cultural meanings are continually emerging and changing. The world we live in, therefore, is largely a social reality, manufactured by people as they intervene in the world and interpret what is happening there using the symbols and meanings available to them. Accordingly, symbolic interactionists say that we experience the world as a **constructed reality.**

Symbolic interactionists also emphasize how symbols and meanings emerge to provide a more concrete reality to things that are abstract and elusive, such as societies and nations. Though it is difficult to point to a society the way we can point to a chair or a tree, we give our society a name ("the United States," "Canada," or "India"), we draw borders between our society and others, and we come to treat the United States, Canada, and India as objects. By acting and interacting with others as if the United States is real, we make it real. By treating society and its parts as "things," we give them existence and continuity (Hewitt, 2003).

All this leads symbolic interactionists to say that if sociologists are to understand social life, they must understand what people actually say and do from the viewpoint of the people themselves.

Evaluation of the Interactionist Perspective.   The interactionist perspective has the advantage of bringing "people" into the panorama of sociological investigation. From interactionists we gain an image of human beings as active agents who fashion their behavior, as opposed to an image of individuals who simply respond passively in a manner prescribed by social rules and institutional arrangements. This perspective directs our attention to the activities of individuals as they go about their everyday lives. Through interaction they acquire the symbols and the meanings that allow them to interpret situations, assess the advantages and disadvantages of given actions, and then select one of them.

However, the interactionist perspective has its limitations. First, there is the temptation to conclude that because social reality is constructed, there is no reality independent of social constructions. However, as philosopher John R. Searle (1995) made clear, we can understand social reality as constructed without rejecting the idea that there is a reality totally independent of us that may affect our social constructions. Second, in their everyday lives, people do not enjoy total flexibility in shaping their actions. Although interactionists acknowledge that many of our actions are guided by systems of preestablished meanings, including culture and social order, many interactionists downplay the parts these larger elements play in our lives. And third, research by symbolic interactionists has often focused on narrow aspects of social life, such as nude beaches, the relationships between prostitutes and truck drivers, and the role of odors in social life.

Using the Three Perspectives

The details of and contrasts among the three sociological perspectives will become clearer as we see how they operate in the chapters to come. As we noted, each theoretical approach has its advantages and its disadvantages. (Table 1.1 is a summary of the major theoretical perspectives.) Each portrays a different aspect of reality and directs our attention to some dimension of social life that the other neglects or overlooks.

Conducting Research

The sociologists we have considered have provided us with important theories regarding the nature and workings of social life. A *theory* is a general framework or perspective that provides an explanation for a specific social phenomenon. However, as most sociologists would agree, theory unconfirmed by facts has little solid value. We require both theoretical understanding *and* facts; for this reason, both theory and research are essential components of the sociological enterprise. Theory inspires research that can verify or disprove it. Research provides findings that permit us to accept, reject, or modify our theoretical

Table **1.1**	**Major Theoretical Perspectives in Sociology**		
	Functionalist	**Conflict**	**Interactionist**
Primary level of analysis	Macro	Macro	Micro
Nature of society	A set of interacting parts	A set of competing interest groups	A social reality that is created and recreated in social interaction
Foundations of social interaction	Consensus of shared beliefs and values	Conflict, coercion, and power	Shared meanings
Focus of study	Social order	Social conflict and social change	The dynamic interplay between the individual and society
Advantages	An understanding of social structure and social stability	Uncovers historical processes that lead to social change	An understanding of human beings as active agents in social life
Disadvantages	Ineffective in dealing with social change	A weak understanding of social consensus and social stability	Has difficulty dealing with social structure

formulations, while simultaneously challenging us to craft new and better theories.

Research also provides the information needed to formulate public policy. Many basic human problems are products of social relations and human behavior. For example, about 70 percent of the premature deaths in the United States are caused by individual behaviors and environmental factors (U.S. Department of Health and Human Services, 2000). Sociological research can provide citizens, policy makers, and public officials with basic knowledge to fashion solutions to social problems such as poverty, drug abuse, gender inequality, and racism.

In this section, we will discuss the logic of science, define a number of research methods, list the steps in the scientific method, and consider research ethics.

The Logic and Method of Science

Science makes the assumption that every event or action results from an antecedent cause. Indeed, a primary objective of science is to determine what causes what. The same is true of sociology. Sociologists assume that crime, racism, social inequality, and marriages do not simply happen, but that they have causes. Moreover, they assume that under identical conditions, the same cause will always produce the same effect.

Scientists also assume that truth can be empirically tested; data can be gathered and objectively analyzed by means of careful observation and measurement, and the facts discovered by one scientist can be verified by other scientists. For example, if it is true that people behave differently in the presence of others than when alone, then any social scientist who investigates this using careful observation and measurement will obtain the same results.

However, scientists are subject to a variety of social influences in addition to their core scientific values and principles. These other factors, self-interests, and biases may shape a scientist's research design, collection of data, and interpretation of results. The importance of objectivity is not that it is always realized in science, but that it is a goal toward which all scientists are committed to working.

The *scientific method,* a series of steps that seeks to ensure maximum objectivity in investigating a problem, allows researchers to pursue answers to their questions by gathering evidence in a systematic manner. Although no single method can eliminate uncertainty, the steps embodied in the scientific method maximize the chances for deriving information that is relevant, unbiased, and economical. The scientific method relies on the rigorous and disciplined collection of facts and on the logical explanation of them. Ideally, sociological research follows this step-by-step procedure, although in practice it is not always possible:

1. **Selecting a researchable problem:** Finding a problem that merits study and that can be investigated by the methods of science.

2. **Reviewing the literature:** Surveying the existing theory and research on the subject.

3. **Formulating a hypothesis:** Arriving at a statement that specifies the relationship between the variables and developing an operational definition that states the variables in a form that permits their measurement.

4. **Choosing a research design:** Determining whether to test the hypothesis by designing an experiment, conducting interviews, observing the ways people behave in particular situations, examining existing records and historical evidence, or combining these procedures.

5. **Collecting the data:** Gathering the data and recording it in accordance with the specifications of the research design.

6. **Analyzing the results:** Searching for meaningful links between the facts that emerged in the course of the research.

7. **Stating conclusions:** Indicating the outcome of the study, extracting the broader meaning of the work for other knowledge and research, and suggesting directions for future research.

Basic Concepts in Research.

Scientists look for relationships among variables. A **variable** is a concept that can take on different values. Scientists use this term to refer to something that they think influences (or is influenced by) something else. The variables sociologists typically study have to do with social statuses, conditions, attitudes, and behaviors. In studying political behavior, for example, sociologists might examine variables such as differences in race, gender, age, religion, and socioeconomic standing.

In investigating cause-and-effect relationships, scientists distinguish between the independent and the dependent variable. An **independent variable** is one that *causes* an effect. The **dependent variable** is the variable that *is affected*. The causal variable (the independent variable) precedes in time the phenomenon it causes (the dependent variable). For example, as the education level of women (independent variable) increases, the mortality rate of their infants decreases (dependent variable). In their research, scientists attempt to predict the relationship they will find between the independent and dependent variables. Such a statement—or **hypothesis**—is a proposition that can then be tested to determine its validity.

In testing a hypothesis, scientists try to determine the degree of association that exists between an independent and a dependent variable. If the variables are causally related, then they must be correlated with one another. A **correlation** exists if a change in one variable is associated with a change in the other variable. Because the mortality rate of infants decreases as the education level of women increases, for example, the two variables are said to be *correlated*.

Correlation, however, does not establish causation (Cole, 1972). For example, the amount of damage resulting from a fire is closely associated with the number of fire engines that are on the scene, but we would be wrong to conclude that fire engines cause fire damage. This is an example of **spurious correlation**—the apparent relationship between the two variables is produced by a third variable that influences the original variables. A large, uncontrolled fire is associated with both extensive damage and the mobilization of multiple firefighting units. To reduce the likelihood that their research will be contaminated by third variables, scientists employ *controls,* a matter we will discuss below when we deal with experimentation.

How Do Sociologists Collect Data?

Sociologists must collect facts to support or dispute hypotheses and to answer their questions about social life. They employ four major techniques of data collection: experiments, surveys, observation, and archival research.

Experiments.   The experiment is the ideal design for scientific research because it best provides researchers with data that enable them to accept or reject a hypothesis. To obtain such data, scientists must try to control all the relevant variables to eliminate other explanations for their findings. Though not perfect, the **experiment** best

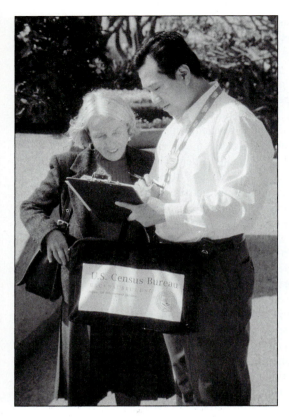

The survey researcher depicted here is gathering data from the respondent through an interview.

meets this requirement. In an experiment, researchers work with two groups that are made to be identical in all relevant respects through a process of random assignment. For example, in an experiment on voter preferences, the two groups studied would need to be of the same size, and their members should reflect a similar socioeconomic, gender, and racial mix. Researchers introduce a change in one group—the **experimental group**—but not in the other group—the **control group.** The two groups are identical except for the factor that the researchers introduce in the experimental group. The control group affords a neutral standard against which the changes in the experimental group can then be measured.

Experiments allow sociologists to test the effects of an independent variable on a dependent variable. In our voter preference example, one group might be asked to watch a series of television commercials on candidates, while the other would spend the same amount of time watching videos unrelated to voting. The effects of television commercials (independent variable) on voter preference (dependent variable) could then be measured.

Surveys.   Some objects of study, such as people's values, beliefs, attitudes, perceptions, motivations, and feelings, are not directly accessible to observation. Others, such as sexual activity, health, religious practices, and drug use, are often sensitive, private matters. Under these circumstances, the **survey** is a valuable tool in the researcher's arsenal.

Survey data are typically gathered in one of two ways. Researchers interview people by reading them questions from a prepared questionnaire, or people can receive a questionnaire in the mail, fill it out, and return it by mail. In either case, *self-reports* are the source of data.

In both interview and questionnaire surveys, sampling procedures are critical. If researchers need information about a large population, they do not need to contact every member of that population. Instead, they can draw on a small but *representative sample,* a sample that accurately reflects the composition of the general public. Public opinion pollsters such as the Gallup and Harris organizations employ a small sample of no more than approximately 1,500 individuals to tap the opinions of more than 290 million Americans. Similarly, physicians need only a small sample of your blood to run tests and draw conclusions about the composition of all your blood and thus about your health.

Sociologists typically employ either a random sample or a stratified random sample in their research. In the **random sample,** researchers select subjects on the basis of chance so that every individual in the population has the same opportunity to be chosen. A **stratified random sample** provides greater precision. Researchers divide the population into relevant categories, such as age, gender, socioeconomic level, and race, and draw a random sample from each of the categories. If African Americans constitute 12 percent of the population and Hispanics 9 percent, African Americans will comprise 12 percent of the sample and Hispanics 9 percent.

Designing good questionnaires is not easy. The wording of the questions, their number, and the format in which they appear are all critical matters (Fowler, 2001). For example, the wording of a question may systematically bias the answers. A *New York Times*/CBS News survey found that only 29 percent of respondents said they favored a constitutional amendment "prohibiting abortions." But in response to a later question in the same survey, 50 percent said they favored an amendment "protecting the life of an unborn child"—which amounts to the same thing (Dionne, 1980).

Probably the major difficulty with self-report information has to do with the issue of its accuracy (Stone et al., 1999). Because individuals are involved in the data they are reporting, they may intentionally or unwittingly supply biased reports. They may withhold or distort information because, even though many surveys are anonymous, telling the truth can cause people to feel threatened or embarrassed.

An increasing problem with survey research is the difficulty in finding respondents (Groves et al., 2002). From 20 to 70 percent of the people who receive a questionnaire in the mail fail to complete or return it, distorting the sample's representativeness. More and more Americans are refusing to answer surveys (Dillman, 2000; Dillman and Carley-Baxter, 2001).

Observation.   As baseball's Yogi Berra once observed, "You can observe a lot just by watching." Observation—watching—is a primary tool of sociological inquiry. Observation becomes a scientific technique when it (1) serves a clear research objective, (2) is undertaken in a systematic rather than haphazard manner, (3) is carefully recorded, (4) is related to a broader body of sociological knowledge and theory, and (5) is subjected to the same checks and controls applied to all types of scientific evidence (Selltiz, Wrightsman, and Cook, 1976).

Sociologists typically observe people in one of two ways. They may observe the activities of people without intruding or participating in the activities, a procedure termed **unobtrusive observation.** Or sociologists may engage in activities with the people that they are studying, a technique called **participant observation.** Elliot Liebow's (1967/2003, see pp. 3–4) study of the African-American streetcorner men, which we discussed earlier in the chapter, involved participant observation. Liebow, a white, began his study by striking up a friendship with an African-American man, Tally Jackson, at the New Deal Carry-out Shop. Over the next several weeks, Liebow often ate at the Carry-out. The streetcorner men were at first suspicious of Liebow, but Tally eased their distrust by, in effect, sponsoring Liebow as his friend.

Within a few months, Liebow was well enough known and accepted by the streetcorner men to go to their rooms or apartments, needing neither an excuse nor an explanation for doing so. Clearly an outsider, Liebow (1967/2003) was accepted by group members who were fully aware that he was observing them.

In many situations, observation is the only way to gather data (Anderson, 2001). At times people are unable or unwilling to tell about their behavior: They may lack sufficient insight to report on it or, because their behavior is illicit, taboo, or deviant, they may be reluctant to do so. But observation has limitations similar to those for field experiments: Researchers have no control over unexpected intrusions, and groups or individuals observed may not be representative of others. Additionally, there is the practical problem of applying observational procedures to phenomena that occur over a long period, such as a certain historical era.

Multiple Methods.   Many methods are used to gather data in sociology, some radically different from others. Some research problems can be studied only with certain methods. The study of sociocultural change over hundreds of years, for example, requires the use of comparative historical analysis of archival data. **Archival research** refers to the use of existing records that have been produced or maintained by persons or organizations other than the researcher. Census data, government statistics, newspaper reports, books, magazines, personal letters, speeches, folklore, court records, works of art, and the research data of other social scientists are all sources for archival research.

On the other hand, if we want to know how employment affects the mental health of U.S. women in the paid labor force today, we would use field observation and survey methods. Using multiple methods, each with its own strengths and weaknesses, can give us a more complete answer to our research question; different methods provide different windows on reality. As Peggy Thoits (1995) showed in her study, what we find with one method may be made understandable by examining data collected using another method. For her study of stresses and psychological symptoms, simply examining the average symptom level associated with each stressor was not enough; she needed to know the context in which stresses had occurred. Divorce, for example, might come as a devastating shock to one person and as a welcome relief to another, depending on each person's particular situation, and only Thoits's qualitative analysis of more extended comments from respondents and interviewers allowed her to interpret her data accurately. Box 1.1 provides a more detailed look at how a researcher selects research methods.

Research Ethics

Though scientific research on human beings is potentially valuable and important, it also can be dangerous and harmful to the people who are studied. Such harm is described in *Darkness in El Dorado: How Scientists and Journalists Devastated the Amazon* (Tierney, 2000), which accuses anthropologists of conducting unethical research among the Yanomami Indians of Venezuela (Holden, 2002). As a result of this and other controversies, sociologists have become increasingly sensitive and committed to ethical considerations in their research.

Yet sociologists confront a dilemma in conducting research. On the one hand, they must not distort or manipulate their findings to serve untruthful, personal, or institutional ends. On the other hand, they are obligated to consider people as ends and not means.

Because of the possible conflicts between these various responsibilities, the American Sociological Association (1989), the major professional organization for the discipline in the United States, has provided a code of ethics to govern the behavior of its members. Among these principles are the following:

- *Sociologists should not misuse their positions as professional social scientists for fraudulent purposes or as a pretext for gathering intelligence for any organization or government. Sociologists should not mislead respondents involved in a research project as to the purpose for which that research is being conducted.*

- *The process of conducting sociological research must not expose respondents to substantial risk of personal harm. Informed consent must be obtained when the risks of research are greater than the risks of everyday life. Where modest risk or harm is anticipated, informed consent must be obtained.*

- *Sociologists must not coerce or deceive students into serving as research subjects.*

Studying Global Inequality Right Here at Home

Go to Google. Type in "nannies." Wait a fraction of a second, and up come the first ten of, according to the search engine, about 123,000 entries: "Nannies of Nebraska"; "Nannies Limited"; "Top Notch Nannies"; "Click here to see 8,900+ Nannies!" The care of babies and children by in-home hired help is a prominent contemporary social phenomenon, one that is fueled by global inequality (Wrigley, 2003). One writer refers to the phenomenon as "transnational motherhood," because immigrant nannies often leave their own children behind when they come to the United States to care for the children of the well-to-do (Hondagneu-Sotelo, 2001).

Sociologist Julia Wrigley (1995) wondered how parents and employees managed their relationships across such a great cultural, economic, and social divide. How does a sociological researcher go about investigating such a question?

Wrigley chose to combine two sociological field methods: *intensive interviewing* and *participant observation*. Working with graduate student research assistants, she conducted 177 tape-recorded interviews, each one usually lasting several hours. Employers—the parents hiring the nannies—were selected from two different neighborhoods in each of two major cities, New York and Los Angeles. She found parents to interview through neighborhood contacts, referrals, and organizations of women lawyers and doctors.

Finding the nannies was tougher. "Many work illegally and are wary of strangers with tape recorders," says Wrigley in *Other People's Children,* the 1995 book that describes her study. She was able to locate employees to interview through employers, immigrant social service agencies, neighborhood contacts, and referrals from one caregiver to the next. Because of her interest in the cultural differences between employer and employee, she selected caregivers from a variety of backgrounds.

Wrigley began learning about the lives of her subjects even before she began interviewing them:

- *No sociologists should discriminate in hiring, firing, promotions, salary, treatment, or any other conditions of employment or career development on the basis of sex, sexual preference, age, race, religion, national origin, handicap, or political orientation.*

In sum, because sociological knowledge can be a form of economic and political power, sociologists must exercise care to protect their discipline, the people they study and teach, and society from abuses that may stem from their professional work.

Key Terms

archival research, 28

class conflict, 9

constructed reality, 21

control group, 26

correlation, 25

dependent variable, 25

dialectical materialism, 9

dysfunctions, 18

economic determinist, 10

The limits on caregivers' freedom became graphically evident during interviewing. Many live-in workers were not allowed to receive phone calls. Even when they said their employers did not mind their taking calls, it was seldom comfortable having the calls go through the employer. With live-in workers, even finding a place to hold the interview was a problem . . . Occasionally employers interrupted the interviews . . . At the end of (one) interview, the caregiver whispered that her employer understood Spanish, so she had not felt able to talk freely.

In contrast, Wrigley commented, "Interviewing employers was much easier. Although busy, they had command of their own schedules and houses."

Because of the difficulties of interviewing the caregivers, Wrigley also relied on participant observation. She explained the benefits of that method:

I also met with caregivers informally when they picked children up from school, when they sat in parks, and when they talked together at children's gymnastics or dance classes . . . These occasions were always valuable, because they allowed a spontaneous quality that could be missing from interviews. Caregivers discussed things I would not have asked about . . . They also advised one another on how to deal with difficult employers and revealed their feelings about particular tasks employers wanted them to do.

Wrigley's findings would not have come to light without the use of her chosen research methods. As she explained, "While nannies are a common sight in the parks of big cities, pushing children on swings and talking to one another, most of their work is performed out of view even of their employers. No government agencies regulate their labor or even count them . . . The nannies themselves . . . are not organized in any formal network."

Questions for Discussion

1. Have you ever had a job in which you believed that your rights and freedom were significantly curtailed?

2. How did Julia Wrigley overcome the difficulties she faced in finding information about nannies?

Review Questions

1. What is the sociological imagination?
2. Define *microsociology* and *macrosociology*.
3. Name four major figures from the history of sociology and briefly describe their contributions to the field.
4. What are the three major sociological perspectives? Give a brief description of each.
5. How do sociologists collect data?

Chapter 2

Culture and Socialization

Components of Culture

Cultural Unity and Diversity

Socialization

In 1789 mutineers led by Fletcher Christian seized control of the ship *Bounty* shortly after it had departed from Tahiti, an island in the South Pacific. They set William Bligh, the ship's captain, and 18 of his men adrift. The mutineers returned to Tahiti, where some of the men decided to remain. Nine men elected to seek another island and induced 6 Tahitian men and 12 Tahitian women to sail with them to Pitcairn Island.

The story of the mutiny on the *Bounty* and the subsequent settlement on Pitcairn Island is a perennial favorite. For sociologists, Pitcairn Island—where descendants of the first settlers still live today—offers a unique social experiment in the founding of a society and the fashioning of a new culture. Imagine the problems that confronted the English and Tahitian colonists when they arrived on this tiny, uninhabited South Pacific island. How would they find food? How would they protect themselves from the elements? How would they maintain order? How would they manage their sexual relationships, a matter of no small concern in a community of 15 men and 12 women? How would they provide for any children born on the island?

In finding solutions to their problems, the English and Tahitian colonists could not fall back on the sorts of genetic adaptations such as those that permit insects to live a group existence. They lacked the built-in behavioral responses and highly specialized appendages that would prepare them for a particular environmental niche. An ability to adapt is not found in human genetic heritage, but in culture and society, the topics of this chapter.

Culture refers to the social heritage of a people—those learned patterns for thinking, feeling, and acting that are transmitted from one generation to the next, including the embodiment of these patterns in material items. It includes both *nonmaterial culture*—abstract creations like values, beliefs, symbols, norms, customs, and institutional arrangements—and *material culture*—physical artifacts or objects such as stone axes, computers, loincloths, tuxedos, automobiles, paintings, electric guitars, hairstyles, and domed stadiums. **Society** refers to a group of people who live within the same territory and share a common culture. Very simply, culture has to do with the customs of a people, and society has to do with the people who are practicing the customs. Culture provides the meanings that enable human beings to interpret their experiences and guide their actions, whereas society represents the networks of social relations that arise among a people.

To participate in society, people must learn a vast array of cultural patterns. In this chapter we will discuss components of culture, consider cultural unity and diversity, and introduce a number of key concepts related to socialization, the process by which culture is internalized.

Components of Culture

Culture provides individuals with a set of common understandings that they use to fashion their actions. It allows us to "know" in rather broad terms what we can expect of others and what they can expect of us. For example, Pitcairn Islanders visiting other Pitcairn Islanders can expect meals in the late morning and early evening (Birkett, 1997); Pitcairn Islanders visiting the United States might be surprised to be served breakfast, lunch, and dinner. Simultaneously, culture affords a kind of map or a set of guideposts for finding our way about life. It provides a configuration of dos and don'ts, a complex of patterned mental stop-and-go signs that tell us about the social landscape: "Notice this," "Ignore that," "Avoid this action," and "Do that" (Kluckhohn, 1960:21). If we know a people's culture—their design for living—we can understand and predict a good deal of their behavior. Why are the Washington beltways crammed with cars early in the morning and again in the late afternoon? Such a pattern of traffic might be mysterious to visitors from another country but an accepted way of life to citizens here.

In providing common understandings, culture binds the separated lives of individuals into a larger whole, making society possible by providing a common framework of meaning. Only by sharing similar perspectives with one another—designs and ways of life—can we weave integrated webs of ongoing interaction. Let us examine more carefully some of the key components of culture that make these shared understandings possible: norms, values, and symbols and language.

Norms

To live with others in a group setting, we must share understandings that tell us which actions are permissible and which are not. For example, unless we have a prior understanding, we cannot take something from a neighbor's yard; the difference between borrowing and stealing is based on shared understandings. These understandings give our daily lives order and allow us to determine which behaviors we can legitimately insist others perform and which they can legitimately insist we perform. When we enter a clothing store, begin a college course, get married, or start a new job, we understand at least some of the expectations that will hold for us and others in these settings. Such expectations are norms. **Norms** are social rules that specify appropriate and inappropriate behavior in given situations. They tell us what we "should," "ought," and "must" do, as well as what we "should not," "ought not," and "must not" do. In all cultures the great body of these social rules deal with matters involving sex, property, and safety.

Though norms are subjective human creations, we experience them as objective and independent features of our social environment (Reno, Cialdini, and Kallgren, 1993). People attach a good deal of importance to some norms, called **mores** (singular *mos*), and they mete out harsh punishment to violators. Other norms, called **folkways**, people deem to be of less importance, and they exact less stringent conformity to them (Sumner, 1906). Some norms are formalized and are enforced by special political organizations. These we refer to as **laws.** Folkways, mores, and laws are discussed below.

Folkways.   Folkways have to do with the customary ways and ordinary conventions by which we carry out our daily activities. We bathe, brush our teeth, groom our hair, wear shoes or sandals, wave greetings to friends, mow our lawns, and sleep in beds. We view people who violate folkways, especially those who violate a good number of them, as somehow "different" and even "strange." However, ordinarily we do not attach moral significance to folkways. For example, we may regard people who wear soiled clothing as crude but not as sinful, and people who are late for appointments as thoughtless but not evil. Gossip and ridicule are important mechanisms for enforcing folkways.

Mores.   Members of a culture or society are more concerned about violations of mores. Murder, theft, rape, treason, and child molestation bring strong disapproval and severe punishment in the United States. Mores are seen as vital to a society's well-being and survival. People usually attach moral significance to mores, and they define people who violate them as sinful and evil. Consequently, the punishment for violators of a society's mores is severe; they may be put to death, imprisoned, cast out, mutilated, or tortured.

Folkways and mores are distinguished from laws by the fact that they are usually enforced by people acting informally in a spontaneous and often collective manner.

Laws.   Some norms are formalized into laws, rules that are enforced by a special political organization composed of individuals who have the right to use force (see Vago, 2003). As anthropologist E. A. Hoebel (1958:470–71) observed: "The essentials of legal coercion are general acceptance of the application of physical power, in threat or in fact, by a privileged party, for a legitimate cause, in a legitimate way, and at a legitimate time." The people who administer laws may make use of physical force with a low probability of retaliation by a third party (Collins, 1975). Laws tend to be the result of conscious thought, deliberate planning, and formal declaration. They can be changed more readily than folkways and mores.

Values

Norms are rules for behavior; **values** are broad ideas regarding what is desirable, correct, and good that most members of a society share. Values are so general and abstract that they do not explicitly specify which behaviors are acceptable and which are not (Rohan, 2000). Instead, values provide us with criteria and conceptions by which we evaluate people, objects, and events as to their relative worth, merit, beauty, or morality. The major value configurations within the dominant American culture include the assignment of high importance to achievement and success, work and activity, efficiency and practicality, material comfort, individuality, progress, rationality, patriotism, and democracy (Williams, 1970). People tend to appeal to values as the ultimate rationales for the choices they make in life.

Symbols and Language

Norms and values are intangible aspects of social life, what sociologists term "nonmaterial culture." But if they lack a physical existence, how can we get a handle on them? How in the course of our daily lives can we talk to one another about rules and standards, mull them over in our minds, and appraise people's behavior in terms of them? The answer has to do with symbols. **Symbols** are acts or objects that have come to be socially accepted as standing for something else. They come to represent other things through the shared understandings people have. Consider the word "computer," a symbol that when spoken or written stands for a physical object. It becomes a vehicle of communication because a community of users (Americans) agree that the symbol and the object are linked. Symbols are a powerful code or shorthand for representing and dealing with aspects of the world about us (Hewitt, 2003).

Symbols assume many different forms. Gestures are one example. Greeting and leave-taking gestures, for instance, are different in different cultures. Even the gestures used to communicate numbers are not universal. Malawians use their thumbs to indicate one, four fingers paired to indicate four, a fist to indicate five, and two shakes of a fist to indicate one hundred, a system very different from that used by most Americans (Selin, 2002). Though gestures are easily understood within a society of persons who share their meaning, they are often the basis for misunderstandings between cultures.

Many of the ordinary features of our everyday lives have important symbolic content. Objects, events, and displays—such as flags, musical performances, paintings, religious icons, badges, ways of wearing hats, parades, and athletic contests—may function as expressive symbols, representing the beliefs of a society or group and implying certain values and norms (Peterson, 1979).

Probably the most important symbols of all are found in **language**—a socially structured system of sound patterns (words and sentences) with specific and arbitrary meanings. Language is the cornerstone of every culture. It is the chief vehicle by which people communicate ideas, information, attitudes, and emotions to one another, and it is the principal means by which human beings create culture and transmit it from generation to generation.

Human beings live their lives primarily within symbolic environments. Other organisms communicate in a variety of generally programmed ways, including the use of gestures, touch, chemical signals, and sounds, but humans stand apart from other species in their use of language. Although great apes can learn sign language, their facility with it is not equivalent to human language use. In fact, the average human fairly effortlessly learns 60,000 words by the time he or she graduates from high school, whereas chimpanzees, given persistent training, can learn only several hundred hand signs (Hauser, Chomsky, and Fitch, 2002). Research on culture in orangutans has shown that, while humans and orangutans share some elements of culture, only human cultures have "unambiguously symbolic elements" (van Schaik

Is Culture Unique to Humans?

In 1960 Jane Goodall sent a message from Zaire to her mentor, anthropologist Louis Leakey, to let him know that she had observed chimpanzees making tools to "fish" for termites. He telegraphed back, "Now we must redefine *tool*, redefine *Man*, or accept chimpanzees as humans" (Goodall, 1990:19).

At that time, scientists believed, and teachers taught, that one of the characteristics dividing humans from all other species was the ability to make and use tools. The sight of a chimpanzee trimming a wide blade of grass and using it to extract termites from a termite mound knocked toolmaking off the list of exclusively human behaviors, and since then many more examples of making and using tools have been found in chimpanzees and other species.

Nearly 50 years later, culture may be suffering the same fate. What makes scientists think animals have culture? Researcher Christophe

Chimpanzee tool-using behaviors appear to be specific to specific groups of chimpanzees, learned from individuals, and passed down to the next generation.

Boesch claims there are three components of culture common to humans and chimpanzees: Culture is learned from group members; culture is a distinctive collective practice; and culture is based on shared meanings between members of the same group (Boesch, 2003:83).

Chimpanzees use tools—evidence of at least 19 different kinds of tool use has been published—and they have complex grooming

et al., 2003). Box 2.1 describes some of the findings on culture in non-human species.

The Linguistic Relativity Hypothesis. The languages found among the world's people are quite diverse. Arabs have some 6,000 words that are connected in some way with the camel, involving camels' colors, camels' breeds, camels for different purposes, states of camel pregnancy, and camel behavior. Inuits (Eskimos) make minute distinctions among different kinds of snow. And Americans have a vast number of words pertaining to automobiles and accessories.

According to the *linguistic relativity hypothesis* (also known as the *Whorfian hypothesis*), proposed by Edward Sapir (1949) and his stu-

and courtship behaviors. These behaviors are specific to specific groups of chimpanzees, and they seem to be learned from individuals and passed down to the next generation. In one of the groups he studied, Boesch observed young chimpanzees learning to crack nuts using hammers (rocks or branches) and anvils (surface roots) (Boesch, 2003). He found that mother chimps stimulate their offspring's attempts by leaving the supplies needed for nut cracking behind while they search for more nuts. They also help their offspring solve technical problems and facilitate their offspring's attempts by providing better hammers and intact nuts.

What about the "shared meanings" component of culture? Some chimpanzees engage in a behavior called "leaf clipping," in which they bite a leaf into pieces without eating any of it. Leaf clipping, it turns out, has a specific meaning—and the meaning is different in different groups of chimps (Boesch, 2003:86):

> All males in the Tai forest regularly leaf-clip before drumming. Among Bossou chimpanzees, leaf clip is performed in the context of playing, as a means to enlist a playmate, while Mahale chimpanzees leaf clip as a way to court estrous females. Tai chimpanzees have never been observed to leaf-clip in the context of playing nor in courtship. Similarly, Mahale chimpanzees have never been seen to leaf-clip in the context of playing nor when drumming.

Primate researchers are careful to define exactly what they mean by *culture*. Recent work with orangutans specified that a behavioral variant be considered cultural only if "it is customary (shown by most or all relevant individuals) or habitual (shown by at least several relevant individuals) in at least one site but is absent in at least one other ecologically similar site" (van Schaik et al., 2003:102). The researchers found many such behaviors and concluded that great ape cultures probably have existed for at least 14 million years.

Studies of primate culture indicate that it is much more complex than the cultures of other species. Likewise, primatologists agree that human cultures are much more complex than those of primates. The use of symbols—language—plays a major role in making human culture more complex, as it introduces a new method for the social transmission of traditions (Boesch, 2003).

Culture has been studied by sociologists and anthropologists for years; now it is of interest to animal behaviorists and evolutionary biologists as well (Perry and Manson, 2003). How genes and culture coevolved, and to what extent our common ancestors had culture, will be topics of research for years to come.

Questions for Discussion

1. What do chimpanzee and orangutan cultures have in common with human culture? Give examples of specific behaviors.

2. How do human cultures differ from those of other primates?

dent Benjamin L. Whorf (1956), people conceptualize the world differently depending on the nature of the concepts available in their language. Language serves as a screen, admitting some things while filtering out others. For example, people living in the Florida Keys, with only a single word for snow, actually fail to distinguish the many types of snow identified by the many Inuit words. Experience as it is perceived through one set of linguistically patterned sensory screens is quite different from experience perceived through another set (Hall, 1966).

The linguistic relativity hypothesis has been somewhat controversial in social science, and some of its major claims have been challenged (Martin, 1983). Most sociologists would not agree that language determines thought. Regardless of their culture, people can make the same

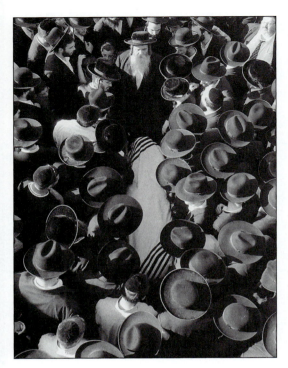

How does this funeral scene differ from a typical funeral in the United States? The funeral rite is a cultural universal, but its specific form is dictated by the culture in which it occurs.

distinctions made by Arabs with regard to camels, Inuits with regard to snow, and Americans with regard to automobiles. Clearly, however, language has a powerful influence on thought by helping or hindering certain kinds of thought. For example, the use of terms such as "broad," "babe," and "chick" to refer to women can promote stereotypical thinking.

Cultural Unity and Diversity

The great merit of culture is that it permits us to circumvent the slow pace of genetic evolution. Behavior patterns that are wired into organisms by their genes do not allow rapid adaptation to changing conditions. In contrast, cultural change can be rapid. Early human cultural evolution probably affected the evolution of the human brain, creating a greater capacity in humans for culture, leading to more cultural evolution, and so on. Indeed, some social scientists contend that cultural evolution is a far more important source of behavioral change for human beings than is biological evolution (Lewontin, Rose, and Kamin, 1984; Wilson, 1988). When cultures change and evolve, cultural unity and cultural diversity are affected, a matter to which we now turn our attention. In this section we will define and discuss cultural universals, cultural integration, ethnocentrism, cultural relativism, and subcultures and countercultures.

Cultural Universals

Although culture provides guideposts for daily living—a blueprint or map for life's activities—these guideposts often differ from one society to another. The "oughts" and "musts" of some societies are the "ought nots" and "must nots" of other societies; the "good" and "desirable" among this people are the "bad" and "undesirable" among that people. Should this fact of cultural variation lead to the conclusion that cultures are different in all respects and hence not comparable? Or, to put the question another way, can we realistically speak of **cultural universals,** the patterned and recurrent aspects of life that appear in all known societies?

There are indeed such common denominators or cultural constants, because all people confront many of the same problems. They must secure a livelihood, socialize children, handle grief, and deal with deviants. Culture represents an accumulation of solutions to the problems posed by human biology and the generalities of the human situation.

George Peter Murdock and his associates at Yale University (1950) developed a classification of cultural components that has universal application. They listed some 88 general categories of behavior that are found among all cultures, including food quest, clothing, settlements, property, travel and transport, fine arts, social stratification, kinship, political behavior, death, religious practices, and infancy and childhood. The 88 categories are subdivided into additional topics. For example, funeral rites always include expressions of grief, means for disposing of the corpse, and rituals to define the relations of the dead with the living. Universal components do not include the specific details of actual behavior. The universals relate to broad, overall categories and not to the content of culture. For example, although marriage is found in all cultures, some societies favor monogamy (one spouse), others polyandry (plural husbands), and still others polygyny (plural wives).

Cultural Integration

The items that form a culture tend to constitute a consistent and integrated whole. For example, societies that value universal education also usually have norms and laws prescribing that children should go to school, organize education into a collective activity, and create expressive symbolism that communicates the values of education, such as degrees, diplomas, graduation ceremonies, and class rings. However, perfect integration is never achieved. The various elements of culture and society are always changing, usually at different rates. This means that there are always inconsistencies, but, as William Graham Sumner (1906:56) observed, the parts are "subject to a strain of consistency with each other." Though human equality and dignity were important values in American culture from the beginning, for the first 86 years of U.S. history, slavery was a legal institution and for another 100 years there were no effective legal guarantees of civil rights for African Americans. This was, as Gunnar Myrdal (1944) pointed out in the title of his landmark study *An American Dilemma,* a contradiction in American culture. The strain of this contradiction was, and is, pushing American society toward a resolution, one that took the form of Supreme Court decisions and civil rights laws in the 1950s and 1960s and continues today in debates about racial equality and affirmative action.

Ethnocentrism

Once we acquire the cultural ways peculiar to our own society, they become so deeply ingrained that they seem second nature to us, and we have difficulty conceiving of alternative ways of life. Just as a fish never "notices" water unless it is out of it, so we tend never to notice our own culture until we are in someone else's. We judge the behavior of other groups by the standards of our own culture, a phenomenon sociologists call **ethnocentrism.** Sumner (1906:13) described this point of view as one "in which one's own group is the center of everything, and all others are scaled and rated with reference to it." A Peace Corps volunteer living in Blantyre, Malawi, several decades ago found a perfect example: the post office had two letter slots, one labeled "Blantyre" and the other labeled "Elsewhere" (Selin, 2002).

All groups are ethnocentric: families, tribes, nations, cliques, colleges, fraternities, businesses, churches, and political parties. The notion that one belongs to the "best people" provides a kind of social glue cementing people together, but it also generates intergroup conflict. When combined with competition for scarce resources and a power imbalance between groups, ethnocentrism can be particularly destructive (Noel, 1968). It plays a part in group conflicts ranging from small skirmishes to world wars. It also can be of more immediate and practical significance. Some analysts blame our surprise at the September 11 attacks partly on ethnocentrism. Although the threat to civilians was not secret, it seemed "too outlandish to be taken seriously . . . In the world of intelligence, this is known as mirror-imaging: the projection of American values and behavior onto America's enemies and rivals" (Goldberg, 2003).

Cultural Relativism

Ethnocentrism can get in the way of the scientific study of culture. We cannot grasp the behavior of other peoples if we interpret it in the context of our values, beliefs, and motives. Rather, we must examine their behavior in the light of their values, beliefs, and motives. This approach, termed **cultural relativism,** views the behavior of a people from the perspective of their own culture.

A perspective characterized by cultural relativism does not ask whether a particular trait is moral or immoral, but what part it plays in the life of a people. For example, early anthropological research found that among some Inuit peoples, the elderly infirm are left behind to perish in the cold. Instead of condemning the practice, social scientists examined the behavior in the context of Inuit culture, where it was defined as a humane measure (Murdock, 1934). The Inuits believe that individuals experience in the next world a standard of health similar to that which they enjoyed in the period preceding death. Consequently, the Inuits see the practice as minimizing the disabilities and infirmities their loved ones would encounter in the hereafter. Social scientists have pointed out that the practice can be adaptive for a people whose subsistence is precarious and who must strictly limit their dependent population. For Americans who are appalled at the traditional Inuit custom, it is worth noting that many Japanese find quite

Media can have a big impact on the content of youth subculture.

abhorrent our practice of placing our elderly infirm in nursing homes rather than caring for them at home.

Subcultures and Countercultures

Cultural diversity also may be found within a society. In many modern nations, the members of some groups participate in the main culture of the society while simultaneously sharing with one another a number of unique values, norms, traditions, and lifestyles. These distinctive cultural patterns are termed a **subculture.** Subcultures abound in American life and find expression in various religious, racial, ethnic, occupational, and age groups.

The Old Order Amish are a case in point. The Amish are a religious sect that originated in Germany and Switzerland during the 16th-century conflicts of the Reformation. Because of religious persecution, many Amish migrated to Pennsylvania in the early 1700s. Most Amish families live on farms, although a minority work in skilled crafts such as carpentry, furniture making, and blacksmithing. They believe in a literal interpretation of the Bible and turn their backs on modern standards of dress, "progressive" morality, "worldly" amusement, automobiles, and higher education. Above all, the Amish value hard physical work and believe that those who do not find joy in work are somehow abnormal. Far from being ashamed of their non-conformity to "worldly standards," the Amish pride themselves on being a "peculiar people" who separate themselves from the world (Hostetler, 1980).

Youth culture is another example of a subculture. Western nations have postponed the entrance of their adolescents into adulthood for economic and educational reasons, segregating them in schools and colleges and effectively relieving them from competing with adults for wealth, power, and status in society's mainstream until they are 21 or older. This has created conditions favorable to the development of a unique culture among youth. Instead of competing with adults along the value dimensions of mainstream culture, adolescents compete with each other along dimensions of youth culture.

Youth culture patterns find expression in fads having to do with popular music, entertainment idols, dance steps, personal adornment and hairstyles, and distinctive jargons. Such patterns change over time, keeping youth always distinctive from generations that have come before. FBI agents posing online as teenage girls to catch pedophiles have discovered that to be effective, they need knowledge of youth culture. Suspects question chatters about trends and pop culture to determine whether they're talking to a teenage girl or a law enforcement officer. For help, the agency turned to eighth-grade girls, three of whom taught a series of classes for the FBI. The classes included tips on instant messaging, celebrity gossip, clothing trends, and popular magazines. Among the lessons: "Never begin a chat with 'hello'; never use proper grammar in instant messages; and 'pos' stands for 'parent over shoulder'" (Ly, 2003).

At times the norms, values, and lifestyles of a subculture are substantially at odds with those of the larger society and constitute a **counterculture**. A counterculture rejects many of the behavioral standards and guideposts that hold in the dominant culture. Delinquent gangs, Satanic cults, and the militia movement are illustrations of counterculture groups.

In many societies, countercultures involve primarily adolescents and young adults (Spates, 1983). In the late 1960s and early 1970s, the dominant youth subculture in the United States included the hippie movement and the anti-Vietnam War movement. It was a counterculture that emphasized political beliefs, sexual standards, and attitudes about drug use that challenged mainstream U.S. culture. In recent years, the Internet has helped to facilitate smaller pockets of countercultural activity within different segments of the population, including right-wing survivalists, skinheads, militia activists, radical environmentalists, and opponents of free trade and globalization. The Internet makes it easier for people with specific grievances to communicate better, organize more effectively, and recruit others to their causes (*The Economist*, 2000a).

Socialization

If there were not a means for people to internalize and then pass on their culture, the renewal of culture could not occur from one generation to the next. We humans are uniquely dependent upon a social heritage—the rich store of adaptations and innovations that countless generations of ancestors have developed over thousands of years. Through culture, each new generation can move on from the achievements of the preceding one.

We are not born as social beings, able to participate in society, but become so only in the course of **socialization**—a process of social interaction by which people acquire the knowledge, attitudes, values, and behaviors essential for effective participation in society. In short, socialization is the process of becoming a social being, a process that continues throughout one's life. The cases of children reared under conditions of extreme isolation illustrate the importance of socialization.

In the remaining part of this chapter, we will examine the process of socialization. We will consider its foundations, its relationship to the development of the self, and its changing nature over the life course.

Foundations for Socialization

What happens when humans are deprived of social interaction? A girl who had been abused by her parents, tied to a potty chair for nearly 12 years, was discovered at age 13. This child, named Genie by those who worked to rehabilitate her, had essentially no language. On attainment and maturity tests, she scored in the range of a one-year-old. She could understand no more than a few words. Specialists designed a program to rehabilitate and educate her, and her vocabulary increased dramatically, but her ability to form sentences and communicate normally never caught up to her age. Her speech remained slow, awkward, and unclear. Born in 1957, Genie is still alive today, living in an adult care home.

Genie's case is not unique. In the 1940s, two girls named Anna and Isabelle were born to single mothers who kept them hidden in secluded rooms, giving them just enough care to be kept alive. When local authorities discovered them, they were about six years old. They were extremely retarded and displayed few human capabilities or responses. Sociologist Kingsley Davis reported on these two cases in a classic 1949 study.

Clearly our biological endowments are not sufficient to produce a normal human personality in the absence of social interaction. A normal human, then, is a product of both hereditary and environmental factors. In this section we will look more closely at how those factors interact. We also will discuss theories and agents of socialization, examine social communication, and consider how socialization provides a socially constructed reality, what sociologists refer to as the "definition of the situation."

Nature and Nurture. Children from severely deprived backgrounds offer a moving illustration of the nurturing that human nature needs to develop, but the relative contributions of nature and nurture are difficult to determine. The issue used to be, nature or nurture? Today the question more likely to be asked is "How do nature and nurture interact to produce behavior?"

Scientists have frequently asked which factor, heredity or environment, is more important in fashioning a particular trait, such as obesity, extroversion, or an individual's intelligence. They have attempted to determine which of the differences they find among people can be attributed to heredity and which to environment. As genetic research continues, evidence accrues that anorexia (Fetissov et al., 2002), alcoholism (Beylotte, 2003), and antisocial behavior (Caspi et al., 2002) all have genetic components. Some studies suggest that heredity is the primary factor in personality and development. For example, in her 1998 book *The Nurture Assumption*, Judith Rich Harris argued that biological parents' genetic influence on their children is far more important than their social influence. Other studies indicate that once we account for siblings' genetic similarity, they are no more alike in personality, abilities, and adjustment than are people selected at random from the population (Turkheimer and Waldron, 2000). However, research also shows that, however important heritable traits are, the expression of those traits depends on a broad range of environmental factors (Collins et al., 2000).

Studies of identical twins (who have exactly the same genes) have provided a unique opportunity for drawing out genetic versus environmental effects. This research found that twins raised apart are as similar as twins raised together on many measures of personality, temperament, interests, and social and political attitudes (Bouchard et al., 1990; Bouchard, 1994; Pinker, 2002), indicating that those characteristics are influenced by genetic factors. At the same time, such studies also suggest that culture and environment may actually play the larger role, accounting for more than half of the variation in personality and behavioral traits (Feldman, Otto, and Christiansen, 2000).

Given the complexities, it is clearly an oversimplification to think of organisms as passive objects either programmed by internal genetic forces or shaped by the external environment. Substantial evidence indicates that hereditary and environmental factors interact with and affect one another (Feldman, Otto, and Christiansen, 2000; Casey, 2002). As children develop, their behavior becomes less directly dependent on nature. Instead, learning becomes more important and the brain itself is affected by interaction with the environment. Not only do nature, nurture, and their interaction affect behavior, but behavior and individual experiences affect neurological development that in turn affects subsequent experience and behavior.

Theories of Socialization.

While social scientists acknowledge that we are biological organisms, biological factors have not been fully integrated into social psychological theory, though there is movement in that direction (Gove, 1987; Rossi and Rossi, 1990; Gove, 1994; Udry, 1995; Udry, 2000; Cacioppo et al., 2000). The theories of socialization emphasized in sociology today continue to emphasize social structure, learning, and social interaction.

Three microlevel theories—social learning theory, cognitive developmental theory, and symbolic interactionism—examine how socialization occurs. We will describe each.

Social Learning Theory. One view of how socialization occurs is that we are socialized through positive and negative reinforcement by our parents, friends, and society and that we observe and imitate socialized behavior around us. The two processes emphasized in social learning theory are conditioning and observational learning (Wiggins, Wiggins, and Vander Zanden, 1994). **Conditioning** is a form of learning in which the consequences of behavior determine the probability of its future occurrence (Skinner, 1953). Consequences of behavior that increase the chance that a behavior will occur are *reinforcements;* consequences that reduce that probability are *punishments.* Socialization occurs when a person's behavior is shaped by the reinforcing and punishing activities of other people and groups.

Psychologist Albert Bandura drew attention to the fact that conditioning, which occurs subsequent to behavior, cannot explain the initial learning of a behavior. Through observation, people may learn both a certain mode of behavior and that the behavior may elicit certain rewards or punishments (Bandura, 1965). **Observational learning** (also referred to as modeling or imitation) occurs when people reproduce the responses they observe in other people, either real or fictional.

Cognitive Developmental Theory. Another view emphasizes that a child's socialization occurs in step with his or her cognitive development. Though learning is a fundamental part of socialization, what and how a person learns depends on his or her ability to understand and interpret the world, something that progresses through several stages. The Swiss psychologist Jean Piaget (1926/1955) hypothesized that every normal child goes through four such stages of cognitive development, each of which is dominated by a different scheme for handling information and understanding how the world works.

In the *sensorimotor stage,* from birth to about 18 months, children learn directly through their senses and their movements. Their initial inability to distinguish between themselves and their environment limits the kind of socialization that can occur. Gradually they realize that they exist independently of the people and things around them. The scheme developed in this stage is essential for moving on to more complex understandings of self, others, and the wider world that develop in subsequent stages.

The *preoperational stage* usually lasts from about 18 months to 6 or 7 years old. A major accomplishment of this stage is *representational thought,* made possible by learning symbols and language. However, children at this stage identify symbols very closely with the objects they represent, making thinking rigid and inflexible and making it difficult to distinguish the real from the make-believe. A critical factor inhibiting socialization at this stage is children's extreme egocentricity—their inability to see things, including themselves, from other people's perspectives. Until this happens, the children's moral sensibility and self-concept remain undeveloped.

From age 6 or 7 until about 11 or 12, children go through the *concrete operational stage* in which they learn to think more abstractly, to do simple arithmetic in their heads, to be able to separate a symbol from the thing it represents, to think less rigidly, and to be able to see things the way others do. Thinking at this stage remains focused on concrete, tangible objects, limiting the abstractions and complexity that can be reached.

Piaget's last stage, from age 11 or 12 to adulthood, is the *formal operations stage,* marked by the further development of abstract and logical abilities, such as the ability to do more complex mathematics and to understand formulas and proofs. Children now begin to be able to develop abstract arguments and to develop a variety of ways of looking at a problem. Identity and moral sensibility become deeper and more complex, influenced by the ability to internalize and critically evaluate the points of view of others.

Symbolic Interactionism.   Social learning theory and cognitive developmental theory are rooted in psychology. A third, more sociological view of socialization comes from the symbolic interactionist perspective. Symbolic interactionism is more than just a theory of socialization. As we pointed out in Chapter 1, it is a broad sociological perspective that helps us understand social processes in many settings. Some symbolic interactionist reasoning is particularly relevant to understanding socialization.

Actions through which people observe, interpret, evaluate, communicate with, and attempt to control themselves—what symbolic interactionists call **reflexive behavior**—are important to socialization (Wiggins, Wiggins, and Vander Zanden, 1994). As we will see, a particularly important kind of reflexive behavior involves people observing their own behavior from the perspective of others. For example, in many cases in which you feel yourself becoming angry, you probably reflect on how your expression of anger will be interpreted by others and then use this reflection to guide your actual expression of anger.

Reflexive behavior is critical in the development of the self—a central part of the socialization process—because it is through reflexive behavior that people learn who they are. And, as with the learning patterns emphasized in cognitive development theory, learning who one is may be influenced both by conditioning and by observational learning. According to the symbolic interactionist view of socialization, however, the individual takes an important and active role in this learning process. Individuals monitor their own behavior, monitor others' responses, make interpretations, try out new ways of behaving, and come to new understandings about themselves.

Agents of Socialization.

The family, peers, schools, and the mass media are important agents of socialization. Traditionally the main social environment for young children, the family has provided the earliest and closest models to guide learning. Sociological research investigates how family structure and parenting styles influence socialization outcomes (Amato and Sobolewski, 2001; Nelson, Clark, and Acs, 2001; Stacey and Biblarz, 2001). However, with day care the norm for so many infants, toddlers, and preschoolers, researchers also have turned their attention to the effects of nonmaternal care on socialization.

As the child's world expands beyond the family, whether the child is of school age or earlier, the *peer group* becomes an important influence on emotional, cognitive, and social development. An increasingly large part of a child's early social life is spent in the peer group, where the reactions of same-age peers serve as powerful reinforcements and punishments that shape behavior. As a child increasingly identifies with his or her peers and uses them as role models, the child's self-definition becomes strongly influenced by the characteristics and standards of his or her peer group—standards that often vary significantly from those of parents and other adults.

Formal socialization occurs in schools through instruction in mathematics, English, and other subjects. But the role of the *school* as agent of socialization goes far beyond teaching the standard subjects. Praise and reprimands in schools are structured to teach and enforce school rules, thus socializing children to adapt to impersonal bureaucratic requirements. Emphasis on grades teaches individualistic values of competition and achievement. The gender, racial, and ethnic composition of teaching staffs teaches lessons about what kinds of people are regarded as knowledgeable and competent to wield authority, and may thus reinforce traditional prejudices against minorities and women. Extracurricular activities from athletics to helping the teacher are differentially distributed across the student body, leading to differences in socialization experiences and thus outcomes.

Although school dominates the lives of most children, television also plays a huge role; the average American child spends between three and six hours with a television every day, watching TV, videotapes, and DVDs and playing video games (American Academy of Pediatrics, 2001). One-third of 2- to 7-year-old American children have a television in their bedrooms; for 8- to 18-year-olds, the number rises to 65 percent. Television and other *media* such as radio, the Internet, popular music, movies, comic books, video games, books, magazines, and newspapers are important in socialization because they provide models for behavior. Laboratory studies, field experiments, survey samples, and longitudinal studies all link television violence to aggression (Anderson and Bushman, 2002; Johnson et al., 2002; Huesmann et al., 2003).

Media also provide images that help form our understandings of the world. For example, a portrayal by the mass media of African Americans as poor, involved with drugs, and in trouble with the law creates negative stereotypes, whereas an accurate portrayal of African Americans in a variety of life pursuits creates positive images and helps dispel negative stereotypes.

Which agents of socialization are most important? The direct impact of mass media on the socialization process can be overestimated. The symbolic interactionist perspective suggests that images from television and other media must be defined and interpreted by viewers before they can influence behavior. If the family, peers, and schools create the meanings people use in interpreting media images, then they are the critical agents in socialization. Media-related aggression, for example, can be lessened by reducing exposure to violent media, but it also can be reduced by changing children's attitudes toward the violence they see on television and in video games (Anderson and Bushman, 2002). The effect of television and other media also may be through the displacement of other activities that might socialize children differently; children who watch television are not reading, visiting interesting places, exercising, or playing (American Academy of Pediatrics, 2001).

Social Communication.   Communication is a fundamental process in socialization. It is also essential in human adaptation. If we are to adapt to the environment, we must be able to communicate with one another. Indeed, all social interaction involves communication. **Communication** refers to the process by which people transmit information, ideas, attitudes, and mental states to one another and is made possible by the human ability to create complex symbol systems including language, as discussed earlier in the chapter. It includes all those verbal and nonverbal processes by which we send and receive messages. Without the ability to communicate, each human being would be locked within a private world such as that experienced by Helen Keller before she acquired language. Communication allows us to establish "commonness" with one another; senders and receivers can come together through a given message. It is this commonness that makes socialization possible. Communication is an indispensable mechanism by which human beings attain social goals. It permits them to coordinate complex group activities, and as such it is the foundation for institutional life.

Verbal Communication.   For years many social scientists asserted that infants come into the world essentially unprogrammed for language use. Then linguists began noticing similarities in languages throughout

Unanticipated consequences of the use of new communication technologies are common.

DILBERT reprinted with permission of United Feature Syndicate, Inc.

the world: all languages have nouns and verbs and allow individuals to ask questions, give commands, and deny statements. Moreover, children acquire language with little difficulty, despite the need to master an incredibly complex, abstract set of rules for transforming strings of sounds into meanings. Even deaf children have a strong bias to communicate in languagelike ways (Goldin-Meadow and Mylander, 1984). And speakers can understand and produce an infinite set of sentences, even sentences they have never before heard or uttered.

In 1957 the eminent linguist Noam Chomsky put these observations together to suggest that human beings possess an inborn language-generating mechanism, which he termed the **language acquisition device.** As viewed by Chomsky (1957, 1980), the basic structure of language is biologically channeled, forming a sort of prefabricated filing system to order the words and phrases that make up human languages. All a child needs to do is learn the peculiarities of his or her society's language.

Chomsky's hypothesis attracted interest, generated controversy, and remains influential (Jackendoff, 2002). Social scientists have pointed out that because a biological predisposition for the development of language exists does not mean that environmental factors play no part in language development. The example of a boy with normal hearing but with deaf parents highlights this point. His parents communicated by American Sign Language, but the boy was exposed daily to television, with the expectation that he would learn to speak English. His social interactions were limited to people who communicated in sign language. By the time he was three, he was fluent in sign language, but he neither understood nor spoke English (Moskowitz, 1978). This case suggests that to learn a language, children must be able to interact with people in that language.

In sum, the acquiring of language cannot be understood by examining genetic factors and learning processes in isolation from one another. Instead, complex and dynamic interactions occur among bio-chemical processes, maturational factors, learning strategies, and the social environment.

Nonverbal Communication.   Verbal symbols are only the tip of the communication iceberg. Nonverbal messages abound, and we "read" a good deal into them without necessarily being aware of doing so. On the basis of his experiments, psychologist Albert Mehrabian (1968) concluded that the total impact of a message is 7 percent verbal, 38 percent vocal, and 55 percent facial. Another specialist has suggested that "no more than 30 to 35 percent of the social meaning of a conversation or an interaction is carried by its words" (Birdwhistell, 1970:197).

Differences in the environment in which nonverbal communication is used affect its meaning. For example, if a man and woman at a singles bar spot each other and become interested, they signal with eye contact. The man might hold the woman's gaze, look away, and then look back quickly once or twice. If the woman responds in kind, the two may maneuver within speaking distance and strike up a conversation. On the other hand, if you establish and hold eye contact with a stranger on an elevator, it is perceived to be a threatening communication. Similarly, in American culture you generally do not look directly at another person unless you are talking (Mazur, 1985).

There are many nonverbal communication systems, including the following:

- **Body language:** Physical motions and gestures provide signals. The way a person stands or sits, for example, can communicate aggression, receptivity, boredom, or hostility.

- **Paralanguage:** Nonverbal vocal cues surrounding speech—voice pitch, volume, pacing of speech, silent pauses, and sighs—provide a rich source of information. Paralanguage has to do with how something is said rather than with what is said.

- **Proxemics:** The way we employ social and personal space also contains messages. Students who sit in the front rows of a classroom communicate that they are interested, while those in the rear communicate that they are alienated and prone to mischievous activities (Sommer, 1969).

- **Touch:** Through physical contact such as touching, stroking, hitting, holding, and greeting (handshakes), we convey our feelings toward one another. However, touch also can constitute an invasion of privacy, and it can become a symbol of power when people want to make power differences visible.

- **Artifacts:** We commonly employ objects, including certain types of clothing, make-up, hairpieces, eyeglasses, beauty aids, perfume, and jewelry, that tell other people our gender, rank, status, and attitude.

Some aspects of nonverbal communication, such as many gestures, are especially susceptible to cultural influence (Ekman, Friesen, and Bear, 1984; see Figure 2.1). The American "OK" gesture made by joining the thumb and forefinger in a circle has quite different meanings, depending on the culture. An American tourist will find that what is taken to be a friendly sign in the United States has an insulting connotation in France and Belgium: "You're worth zero!" In southern Italy it means "You're a jerk," in Greece and Turkey it conveys an insulting or vulgar sexual invitation, and in Germany it is an obscene anatomical reference. However, some facial expressions seem to have universal meanings. Surprise, disgust, fear, anger, sadness, and happiness were identified from photos by people from five different cultures (Ekman, Friesen, and O'Sullivan, 1988). The ways of displaying and interpreting certain feelings may be universal, but each culture provides its own "display rules" regulating how and when given emotions may be exhibited and with what consequences.

Definition of the Situation.

An important part of socialization is learning social definitions of reality—the basic schemes we use to make sense of and to understand the social and physical world. William I. Thomas introduced this through his concept of **definition of the situation**: the interpretation or meaning we give to our immediate circumstances (Thomas and Thomas, 1928; Merton, 1995).

People vary in their perceptions of and reactions to different situations. A man mowing the lawn may be seen as beautifying his yard, avoiding his wife, getting exercise, supporting neighborhood property values, annoying a neighbor who is attempting to sleep, or earning a living by mowing lawns.

Although our definitions of the situation may differ, it is only as we arrive at common understandings that we are able to fit our action to the actions of other people. Whatever we do—play football, chat with a friend on the telephone, rob a store, make love, give a lecture, cross a busy intersection, or purchase a book—we must attribute similar meanings to the situation if we are to achieve joint action with others. Moreover, a definition of the situation arrived at on one occasion may not hold for future occasions. Viewed in this manner, culture may be thought of as the agreed-upon meanings—the shared definitions of situations—that individuals acquire as members of a society. Socialization is the process by which these shared definitions are learned and transmitted from one generation to the next.

Sociologists point out that our definitions influence our construction of reality. William I. Thomas and Dorothy S. Thomas (1928:572; Merton, 1995) captured this insight in what has become known as the **Thomas theorem:** "If [people] define situations as real, they are real in their consequences." The Thomas theorem draws our attention to the fact that people respond not only to the objective features of a situation but also to the meaning the situation has for them. Once the

Kiss on the cheek: How many are appropriate? Zero to one in Britain, two on most of the Continent, three in Belgium and French-speaking Switzerland—and in Paris, four.

The V sign: What Churchill meant was "victory"— but the same signal with the knuckles turned out is England's and Australia's equivalent of the American middle finger.

Tapping the nose: In England, Scotland, and strangely, Sardinia, this means, "You and I are in on the secret." But if a Welshperson does it, he means, "You're really nosy."

Twisting the nose: The French gesture of putting one's fist around the top of the nose and twisting it signifies that a person is drunk, but it is not a gesture used in other cultures.

Tapping the temple: Do this almost anywhere in Europe if you want to say someone or something is crazy—except in Holland, where the gesture means, "How clever!"

Thumbs up: This gesture was employed by Roman emperors to spare the lives of gladiators in the Colosseum. It is now favored by American and Western European airline pilots, truck drivers, and others to mean "All right." But in Sardinia and northern Greece, it is an insulting gesture paralleling the middle-finger gesture of American society.

Thumb-and-index circle: America's "OK" sign means just that in much of Europe—though not in Germany, where it is an obscene anatomical reference.

The chin rub: That's what people in France, French-speaking Switzerland, and Belgium do when they're bored. Don't try it elsewhere: no one will get it.

The wave: Careful with this friendly greeting while in Greece. It could be misinterpreted as "Go to hell." When Greeks wave goodbye, they show the backs of their hands.

Figure 2.1   Symbolic Gestures: Barriers to Cross-Cultural Communication

Source: Text from "In Athens, It's Palms In," *Newsweek,* November 12, 1990 © 1990 Newsweek, Inc. All rights reserved. Reprinted by permission.

meaning has been assigned, it serves to shape not only what people do or fail to do but also some of the consequences of their behavior. In this way, a definition of the situation can become a self-fulfilling prophecy.

For example, one of the reasons that racial prejudices are so damaging is that they are definitions of the situation that can become self-fulfilling prophecies. For many generations whites defined African Americans as racially inferior. By acting upon their racial definitions, whites fashioned social structures—institutional arrangements—in which African Americans have enjoyed fewer advantages than whites. And while most African Americans live well above the poverty line (Proctor and Dalaker, 2003), compared to whites, African Americans are less likely to be well educated and have high incomes and more likely to hold menial jobs, live in poor housing, and have poor health than whites. Thus, by creating and applying definitions of the situation, whites have created a social order characterized by institutional discrimination.

The Self and Socialization

The formation of the **self**—the set of concepts we use in defining who we are—is a central part of the socialization process. It is not a biological given but emerges in the course of interaction with other people. The self represents the ideas we have regarding our attributes, capacities, and behavior. In everyday speech, we note the existence of the self in phrases such as proud of myself, talking to myself, losing control of myself, ashamed of myself, testing myself, hating myself, and loving myself. These conceptions represent the heart of our humanness, our awareness that each of us is a unique being apart from other beings and is the same person across time. This development of the self begins at birth as the process of socialization begins.

Symbolic interactionists point out that we can be objects of our own action. We mentally take a place on the outside and, from this vantage point, become an audience to our own actions and an active agent in our own self-development and change (Kiecolt, 1994). Viewed in this dynamic manner, the self is a process by which we devise our actions in order to fit them to the ongoing actions of other people—a process central to socialization. Sociologists such as Charles Horton Cooley, George Herbert Mead, and Erving Goffman have contributed a good deal to our understanding of these matters. We will consider their insights, and those of researchers who followed them, in this section.

Charles Horton Cooley: The Looking-Glass Self.   At the beginning of the 20th century the notion was prevalent in both scientific and lay circles that human nature is biologically determined. Charles Horton Cooley (1864–1929) vigorously challenged this assertion. He maintained that people transform themselves and their worlds as they engage in social interaction. In particular, Cooley (1902/1964)

contended that our consciousness arises in a social context. This notion is best exemplified by his concept of the **looking-glass self**—a process by which we imaginatively assume the stance of other people and view ourselves as we believe they see us. Our ability to take the perspective of another person is a basic requirement of all social behavior.

Self-Awareness.   Cooley suggested that the looking-glass self is an ongoing mental process characterized by three phases. First, we imagine how we appear to others. For example, we may think of ourselves as putting on weight and becoming "fat." Second, we imagine how others judge our appearance. We are aware, for instance, that people typically think of obese people as unattractive. Third, we have an emotional reaction, such as pride or shame based on what we perceive others' judgments to be. In this case we are likely to experience anxiety or embarrassment regarding our "obese" state. The looking-glass self entails a subjective process and need not accord with objective reality. For example, victims of anorexia nervosa willfully starve themselves, denying that they are actually thin or ill, in the belief that they are too fat.

The notion of the looking-glass self does not imply that our self-conception changes radically every time we encounter a new person or a new situation. Accordingly, it is useful to distinguish between self-images and self-conceptions (Turner, 1968; Marsh, 1986). A **self-image** is a mental conception or picture that we have of ourselves that is relatively temporary; it changes as we move from one context to another. Our **self-conception** is a more overriding view of ourselves, a sense of self through time—"the real me," or "I myself as I really am." Layers of self-images typically build up over time and contribute to a relatively stable self-conception. For the most part, this succession of self-images edits rather than supplants our more crystallized self-conception or identity.

Self-Evaluation.   Self-conception is not only a description of who we are. It also includes our evaluation of ourselves. Two important dimensions of this evaluation are self-esteem and personal efficacy (Cast and Burke, 2002).

Self-esteem is the belief that one is a good and valuable person. Why do some people have high self-esteem and others low? Self-esteem is governed by three principles (Rosenberg, 1981). First, as we interact with others, we monitor their behavior for pieces of information about how they are appraising us. These are **reflected appraisals,** appraisals of ourselves that we see reflected in the behavior of others. If we conclude from our observations that others respect and look up to us, we will probably have good self-esteem, but if we think that they look down upon and disparage us, our self-esteem will probably be low (Rosenberg, 1973).

People also arrive at evaluations of themselves through **social comparisons,** comparing their performance, ability, or characteristics with those of others and rating themselves as superior, equal, or inferior (Pettigrew, 1967). We cannot compare ourselves with everyone else along all dimensions, so we use dimensions that we learn are important through the various agents of socialization (family, peer group, school, and the mass media), and we compare ourselves with relevant others. For example, instead of comparing themselves with middle-aged people with respect to personal income, adolescents compare themselves with others of their own age and in a similar situation.

Even if we feel that others respect us and we are able to compare ourselves favorably with them, we still may not experience high self-esteem if we do not believe that we can take credit for what produces the respect and the favorable comparisons. By the same token, if we do not blame ourselves for how others are evaluating us or for our negative comparisons, we will probably not suffer low self-esteem. This is because of the principle of *self-attribution:* For a characteristic to affect our self-esteem, we must believe we are responsible for it and therefore deserve the credit or blame that results.

Personal efficacy is another aspect of self-evaluation that is influenced by socialization processes. It is the belief that one can overcome obstacles and achieve goals. The primary determinant of personal efficacy is the nature of personal experience. When we experience ourselves as effective actors and then attribute to ourselves the characteristic of being effective, our personal efficacy is increased (Gecas and Schwalbe, 1983). People with higher education, more autonomous jobs, and higher incomes are all in situations that facilitate experiencing oneself as efficacious. People with little education, routine jobs, and low incomes may be locked into situations in which the sense of efficacy necessary for changing one's situation has little chance of developing.

George Herbert Mead: The Generalized Other.

George Herbert Mead (1863–1931), one of the major figures in the symbolic interactionist perspective, elaborated on Cooley's concept of the looking-glass self and contributed many insights of his own to the processes of development of the self and socialization. Mead (1934/1962) contended that we gain a sense of selfhood by acting toward ourselves in much the same fashion that we act toward others. In so doing, we "take the role of the other toward ourselves." We mentally assume a dual perspective: We are simultaneously the subject doing the viewing and the object being viewed. In our imagination, we take the position of another person and look back on ourselves from this standpoint.

Mead designated the subject aspect of the self-process as "I" and the object aspect as "me." Consider what sometimes happens when you contemplate whether to ask your professor a question. You think, "If I ask a question, he'll consider me stupid. I'd better keep quiet." In this example, you imagine the attitude of the professor toward students. In so doing, you mentally take the role of the professor and view yourself as an object or "me." It is you as the subject or "I" who decides that it would be unwise to ask the question. The use of personal pronouns in the statement illustrates the object–subject dimensions.

According to Mead, the key to children's development of the self—a central part of the socialization process—resides in their acquisition of language. Language allows us to carry on an internal conversation. We talk and reply to ourselves in much the same manner that we carry on a conversation with others. In this fashion, we judge how other people will respond to us.

According to Mead, children typically pass through three stages in developing a full sense of selfhood: the "play" stage, the "game" stage, and the "generalized other" stage. In play, children take the role of only one other person at a time and "try on" the person's behavior. The model, usually an important person in the life of the child, such as a parent, is called a **significant other.**

Whereas children in the play stage take the role of only one other person at a time, in the game stage they assume many roles. Individuals must take into account the roles of many people, and children must become familiar with the expectations that hold for a variety of roles if they are to play their own roles successfully.

In Mead's third stage, children recognize that they are immersed within a larger community of people and that this community has very definite attitudes regarding what constitutes appropriate and inappropriate behavior. The social unit that gives individuals their unity of self is called the **generalized other.** The attitude of the generalized other is the attitude of the larger community. Although we gain our conceptions of given rules from particular people (our mother, a teacher, or a peer), these notions are generalized or extended to embrace all people within similar situations. To think about our behavior, then, is to interact mentally with ourselves from the perspective of an abstract community of people. According to Mead, the generalized other is the vehicle by which we are linked to society. By means of the generalized other, we incorporate, or internalize, the organized attitudes of our community within our own personalities so that social control becomes self-control. According to Mead, our ability to participate effectively in society is the end result of passing through the play, game, and generalized other stages.

Erving Goffman: Impression Management.

Erving Goffman (1922–1982) has provided an additional dimension to our understanding of the self and socialization. Cooley and Mead examined how our self-conceptions arise in the course of social interaction and how we fashion our actions based on the feedback we derive about ourselves and our behavior from other people. Goffman (1959) directed our attention to another matter. He pointed out that only by influencing other people's ideas of us can we hope to predict or control who we become. We have a stake in presenting ourselves to others in ways that will lead them to view us in a favorable light, a process Goffman called **impression management.** In doing so, we use both concealment and strategic revelation. You are probably aware of engaging in impression management when deciding what to wear for a particular occasion, such as a party, a physician's appointment, a job interview, or a date (Leary and Kowalski, 1990).

Goffman saw the performances staged in a theater as an analytical analogy and tool for depicting and understanding socialization and the shaping of the self, a perspective called the **dramaturgical approach.** He depicted social life as a stage on which people interact; all human beings are both actors and members of the audience, and the parts are the roles people play in the course of their daily activities. According to Goffman, the self is a product of the ongoing performances that characterize a person's everyday interaction with others and of how these performances are interpreted by others. In this view, the self is not so much something that people possess and then carry unchanged from situation to situation, but is a "dramatic effect" (Goffman, 1959:253) that emerges from social situations in which people attempt to manage others' impressions of them.

Goffman illustrated his approach by describing the changes that occur in waiters' behavior as they move from the kitchen to the dining room. As the nature of the audience changes, so does their behavior. "Frontstage" in the dining room, the waiters display a polite demeanor to the guests. "Backstage" in the kitchen, they openly flaunt and otherwise ridicule the servility they must portray frontstage. Further, they seal off the dirty work of food preparation—the gristle, grease, and foul smells of spoiled food—from the appetizing and enticing frontstage atmosphere. As people move from situation to situation, they drastically alter their self-expression. They undertake to define the situation for others by generating cues that will lead others to act in ways they wish.

Socialization across the Life Course

Socialization is a continuing, lifelong process. The world about us changes and requires that we also change. The self is not carved in granite, somehow finalized for all time during childhood. Life is adaptation—a process of constant renewing and remaking. Three-year-olds are socialized within the patterns of a nursery school, engineering students within their chosen profession, new employees within an office or plant, a husband and wife within a new family, and elderly patients within a nursing home.

In one way or another, all societies have to deal with the **life course** that begins with conception and continues through old age and ultimately death. Societies weave varying social arrangements around chronological age (Nanda and Warms, 2002). A 14-year-old girl may be expected to be a middle school student in one culture and a mother of two in another; a 45-year-old man may be at the peak of a business career, still moving up in a political career, retired from a career as a professional football player, or dead and worshipped as an ancestor in some other society. All cultures divide biological time into socially relevant units. While birth, puberty, maturity, aging, and death are biological facts of life, it is society that gives each its distinctive meaning.

Modern societies are ordered in ways that formally structure people's preparation for new roles through education, rehabilitation, and resocialization. This *role socialization* commonly involves three phases (Mortimer and Simmons, 1978). First, people think about, experiment with, and try on the behaviors associated with a new role, what sociologists term **anticipatory socialization.** Children informally acquaint themselves with such adult roles as spouse and parent by "playing house." Most college-bound high school students go through such a process by learning about and then adopting clothing styles and recreational habits that are common among college students. Second, once individuals assume a new status, they find that they must not only learn the expectations of the associated role, but they may need to shape the role itself in response to new situations and to their individual needs. For example, a couple entering marriage must evolve new interpersonal skills because as children they learned little about the marital role. Third, as individuals move through their lives, they not only enter roles but must disengage or exit from many of them. Such rituals as graduation exercises, marriage, retirement banquets, funerals, and other rites of passage are socially established mechanisms for easing some role transitions.

Key Terms

anticipatory social-
    ization, 60

body language, 52

communication, 50

conditioning, 47

counterculture, 44

cultural relativism,
    42

cultural universals,
    40

culture, 34

definition of the situ-
    ation, 53

dramaturgical
    approach, 59

ethnocentrism, 42

folkways, 35

generalized other,
    58

impression manage-
    ment, 59

language, 37

language acquisition
    device, 51

laws, 35

life course, 59

looking-glass self, 56

mores, 35

norms, 35

observational learn-
    ing, 47

paralanguage, 52

personal efficacy, 57

proxemics, 52

reflected appraisals,
    56

reflexive behavior, 48

self, 55

self-conception, 56

Review Questions

1. What is the difference between norms and values, and what part does each play in society?
2. How do symbols and, more particularly, language, shape the way we see our world?
3. Name six cultural universals.
4. What is cultural integration?
5. Define *ethnocentrism* and describe at least one phenomenon in which it plays a part.
6. What is a subculture? Describe the characteristics of a specific subculture.
7. Describe the interplay of nature and nurture as understood today.
8. Name two macrolevel and three microlevel theories of socialization.
9. What are some of the important agents of socialization in today's society? How might they differ from the past?
10. What are some forms of nonverbal communication?
11. What is the looking-glass self?
12. What is the generalized other?
13. Describe impression management.

Chapter 3

Social Structure, Groups, and Organizations

Social Structure

Groups and Group Processes

Formal Organizations

Anyone who has paid for car insurance as a teenaged driver—or begged their parents to do so for them—knows that the rates are high. And with reason: insurance companies know that accident rates are high for teen drivers. In fact, the leading cause of death for U.S. teenagers is car crashes; more than a third of all deaths of 15- to 19-year-olds result from motor vehicle crashes (Chen et al., 2000).

This death rate is higher when teens travel in groups. In fact, the more teenage passengers per car, the higher the fatal crash rate for teen drivers. The highest death rate is for drivers with three or more passengers in the car, but simply adding a single male teen passenger nearly doubles the probability that the driver will be killed in a wreck. It is just the opposite for older drivers—for 30- to 59-year-olds, fatal crash rates go *down* significantly for drivers with passengers (Chen et al., 2000).

What is going on with this driving phenomenon? It turns out that dangerous driving behaviors—driving while drunk or high, speeding, skidding, swerving, running red lights, and the like—are "strongly associated with the presence of peers" (Chen et al., 2000:1581). In other words, teen drivers are much more likely to show off, goof off, and in general take more risks when their friends are in the car cheering them on. Older drivers, on the other hand, are probably motivated to be more careful than usual when driving with passengers, especially when those passengers are children.

Sociologists would say that a social structure made up of teenagers inside a moving vehicle is different than that made up of older drivers, and that this difference results in dramatic differences in accidental death rates. But the concept social structure is much broader than this and can be used to understand what happens in classrooms, families, workplaces, government, football teams, and even whole societies.

Social Structure

In the previous chapter, we noted that culture has to do with the customs of a people, and society with the people who are practicing the customs. Culture supplies the framework that allows people to interpret events and guide their actions; society consists of the actual web of relationships that people enter into as they go about their daily activities. For the most part, people do not interact in a haphazard or random manner. Rather, their relationships are characterized by social ordering. Sociologists apply the term **social structure** to this social ordering—the interweaving of people's interactions and relationships in more or less recurrent and stable patterns. It finds expression in a matrix of social positions and the distribution of people in them.

Social structure provides an organized and focused quality to our group experiences, and it allows us to achieve our collective purposes. By virtue of social structure, we link certain experiences, terming them, for example, "the family," "the church," "the neighborhood," and "General Motors." A clique, a family, a rock band, a group of teenagers riding around in a car, an army, a business organization, a religious group, and a nation are social structures. Social structure consists of the recurrent and orderly relationships that prevail among the members of a group or society. It gives us the feeling that life is characterized by organization and stability.

Consider the social structure of your college. Each term you enter new classes, yet you have little difficulty attuning yourself to unfamiliar classmates and professors. Courses in sociology, calculus, American history, English composition, and physical education are offered year after year. A new class enters college each fall, and another class graduates each spring. Football games are scheduled for Saturday afternoons in the autumn, and basketball games for evenings during the winter months. New students, professors, coaches, players, and deans pass through the system and in due course make their exits. Yet even though the actual people that comprise a college change over time, the college endures.

Sociologists view social structure as a social fact of the sort described by Émile Durkheim (see Chapter 1). We experience a social fact as external to ourselves—as an independent reality that forms a part of our objective environment. Consequently, social structures constrain our behavior and channel our actions in certain directions. When you entered college for the first time, you felt somewhat awkward because you did not yet fit into your college's way of doing things. The college's way is social structure, the shape or form that a particular organization has taken through the years as students, professors, and administrators have interacted on a regular basis.

As sociologist William H. Sewell Jr. (1992:27) observed: "Structure is dynamic, not static; it is the continually evolving outcome and matrix of a process of social interaction." Thus, a college is not a fixed entity that, once created, continues to operate perpetually in the same manner. All social ordering must be continually created and re-created through the interweaving and stabilizing of social relationships. For this reason, organized social life is always undergoing modification and change. In the next sections, we will discuss the concepts that help us to understand social structure and to describe our social environment: statuses, roles, groups, institutions, and societies.

Statuses

In our daily conversations, we use the word *status* to refer to a person's ranking as determined by wealth, influence, and prestige. However, sociologists employ status somewhat differently: **status** means a position within a group or society. By means of statuses we locate one another in various social structures. Mother, mayor, management trainer, friend, supervisor, female, elementary school principal, child, Cuban American, shopper, professor, convict, and fortune teller are all statuses.

As Theodore Newcomb observed in his classic social psychology textbook (1950), a status is like a ready-made suit of clothes. Within certain limits, the prospective buyer can choose regarding matters of style and fabric. Our choice is limited to a size that will fit, as well as by our pocketbooks. Having made our choice within these limits, we can have certain alterations made. But apart from minor modifications, we tend to be limited to what retailers already have on their racks. Statuses, too, come ready-made, and the range of choice among them is limited. Societies commonly limit competition for statuses with reference to gender, age, and social affiliations. For instance, realistically, not every American can be elected president. Women, African Americans, and members of the lower class suffer severe handicaps from the outset. This observation brings us to a consideration of ascribed and achieved statuses.

Ascribed and Achieved Statuses.

Some statuses are assigned to us by our group or society and termed **ascribed statuses.** Age and gender are common ascribed statuses. For example, age is assigned to us according to the passage of time. Besides staying alive, there is nothing one can do to change one's age. Race, ethnicity, and family background are also common bases for assigning statuses to individuals.

We secure other statuses on the basis of individual choice and competition. We call these **achieved statuses.** All societies recognize some kinds of individual accomplishment and failure, which results in the allocation of some statuses on the basis of individual achievement. Quarterback, choir director, physician, ballet dancer, college student, pastor, nurse practitioner, pickpocket, prostitute, president of Exxon, hair stylist, and teacher are illustrations of achieved statuses.

Master Statuses.

Some of our statuses overshadow our other statuses both in our own minds and in those of other people. A **master status** is a key or core status that carries primary weight in a person's interactions and relationships with others. For children, age is a master status; similarly, gender is a master status in most societies. Additionally, race and occupation are particularly critical statuses in American life. Master statuses tend to lay the framework within which our goals are formulated and our training is carried out (Adler and Adler, 1989).

Roles

A status carries with it a set of culturally defined rights and duties, what sociologists term a **role.** These expectations define the behavior people view as appropriate and inappropriate for the occupant of a status. Quite simply, the difference between a status and a role is that we occupy a status and play a role (Linton, 1936).

Roles allow us to formulate our behavior mentally so that we can shape our actions in appropriate ways. They permit us to assume that in some respects we can ignore personal differences and say that people are interchangeable. For example, every American knows the difference between a physician and a carpenter. Hospitalized for emergency surgery, we probably won't ask many questions about who is handling the emergency, as long as it is a physician and not a carpenter.

Role Performance.

In real life, a gap often exists between what people should do and what they actually do. A role is the *expected* behavior we associate with a status. **Role performance** is the *actual* behavior of the person who occupies a status. People vary in how they

"Ok, you be the doctor, and I'll be the Secretary of Health and Human Services."

implement the rights and duties associated with their roles. You frequently take differences in role performance into account when you select one professor over another for a given course. One professor may have a reputation for coming late to class, lecturing in an informal manner, and assigning difficult term papers. Another professor may be a distinguished authority in the field, monitor class attendance, and assign take-home examinations. Regardless of which professor you select, you will still occupy the status of student and play its associated role. However, you will have to modify your behavior somewhat depending upon your selection.

Role Set.   A single status may have multiple roles attached to it, constituting a **role set.** The status of student may involve one role as pupil, one role as peer of other students, one role as loyal supporter of your school's teams, one role as user of the library, and one role as "good citizen" of the college community.

A role does not exist in isolation. Instead, it is a bundle of activities that are meshed with the activities of other people. Indeed, the definition of one role depends upon the existence of another: there can be no professors without students, no wives without husbands, no police officers without criminals, and no psychiatrists without the mentally ill. Every role has at least one reciprocal role attached to it.

Role relationships tie us to one another because the rights of one end of the relationship are the duties of the other. **Duties** are the actions others can legitimately insist that we perform, and **rights** are the actions we can legitimately insist that others perform (Goffman, 1961a). The rights of one role are the duties of the other role. For example, your rights as a student—to receive authoritative material in lectures, to be administered fair exams, and to be graded objectively—are the duties of your professor.

Individuals are linked together in groups through networks of reciprocal roles. Groups consist of intricate complexes of interlocking roles, which their members sustain in the course of interacting with one another. People experience these stable relationships as social structure—a school, a hospital, a family, a gang, an army, and so on.

Role Conflict.   **Role conflict** results when individuals are confronted with conflicting expectations stemming from their simultaneous occupancy of two or more statuses. A football coach whose son is a member of the team may experience role conflict when deciding whether to make his own son or another more talented player the starting quarterback. One way to handle role conflict is to subdivide or compartmentalize one's life and assume only one of the incompatible roles at a time. For example, college students may attempt to segregate their school and home experiences so they do not have to appear before their parents and peers simultaneously.

Role Strain.   **Role strain** occurs when individuals find the expectations of a single role incompatible, so that they have difficulty performing the role. The relationship physicians have with their patients provides an example (Klass, 1987). Doctors are expected to be gentle healers, humanitarians, and self-sacrificing saviors of the sick. They also are expected to be small-business retailers of knowledge that they have obtained at considerable cost and sacrifice. While aggressive bill collecting is consistent with the small-business-retailer aspects of the role, it is inconsistent with that of the gentle healer.

Groups, Aggregates, and Categories

Statuses and roles are building blocks for more comprehensive social structures, such as groups. Sociologists define a **group** as two or more people who are bound together in relatively stable patterns of social interaction and who share a feeling of unity. We consider groups in detail in the sections below on groups and group processes and on formal organizations.

As previously pointed out, roles link us within social relationships. When these relationships are sustained across time, four things can happen: First, we come to think of the relationships as encompassed by boundaries, so that people are either inside or outside a group. Second, we attribute an "objective" existence to groups and treat them as if they are real and exact things. Third, we view a group as having a distinct subculture or counterculture—a set of unique norms and values. Fourth, we develop a sense of allegiance to a group that leads us to feel we are a unit with a distinct identity.

Sociologists mean something quite specific when they use the word *group*. For example, they distinguish a group from an **aggregate,** which is simply a collection of anonymous individuals who are in one place at the same time such as shoppers in a mall or individuals waiting in line for football tickets. Individuals shift in and out of an aggregate rather easily and frequently. Because the people in aggregates interact with one another only transiently and temporarily, patterns of social ordering in them are short-lived. However, this quality should not lead us to dismiss aggregates as inconsequential. They provide the foundation for many forms of collective behavior (see Chapter 10).

A group also differs from a **category,** a collection of people who share a characteristic—such as a status, a physical characteristic, or a behavior pattern—that is deemed to be of social significance. Common categories include the subdivisions of age, gender, race, occupation, and educational attainment, but being tall, living alone, and having indoor plumbing also qualify one for being in a particular category. Categories differ from groups because they are so broad that social relations and group dynamics linking all members may not occur. However, common experiences of persons in categories, particularly those who share a status, may be the basis for social movements or political activity. For example, some women have banded together in the League of Women Voters and the National Organization for Women (NOW) by virtue of an awareness that they are a social category that shares certain problems.

Institutions

Sociologists use the term **institution** for the principal social structures that organize, direct, and execute the essential tasks of living. Each institution is built about a standardized solution to a set of problems. For example, all human societies face the problem of how to protect and nurture children in their early years. This is one of many problems that the institution of the family deals with. All societies face the problem of how to transfer raw materials into products and how to distribute those products to people. This problem is dealt with by the institution called the economy. All societies face the problem of helping people to understand the inexplicable events in their lives; religion is the institution that deals with the death of loved ones, fatal events, and the like. A wide variety of interconnected institutions serve diverse human needs and desires, including the institutions of sports, entertainment, organized crime, prostitution, medicine, and journalism.

Societies

Societies represent the most comprehensive and complex type of social structure in today's world. As we noted earlier in the chapter, society refers to a group of people who live within the same territory and share a common culture. By virtue of this common culture, the members of a society typically possess similar values and norms and a common language. Its members perpetuate themselves primarily through reproduction and comprise a more or less self-sufficient social unit. A society can be as small as a tribal community of several dozen people or as large as modern nations with hundreds of millions of people.

Although we often use the term *nation-state* interchangeably with *society,* the two are not necessarily the same. A state is a political entity centering on a government. Among many peoples of the world, the state binds together nationality and tribal groups that in their own right constitute societies. For example, Great Britain is made up of Scots, Welsh, and English. Belgium is composed of Flemings and Walloons. Similarly, many African nation-states contain multiple tribal groups: 250 in Nigeria, 200 in Zaire, and 130 in Tanzania.

Sociologists have classified societies in many ways. One popular approach is based on the principal way in which the members of a society derive their livelihood (Nolan and Lenski, 1999). All peoples must provide for such vital needs as food, clothing, and shelter; the manner in which they do so has vast consequences for other aspects of their lives. Each of these types of societies has different institutions and different numbers of institutions, depending on the complexity of the societies and of the problems to be solved in each.

Hunting and gathering societies represent the earliest form of organized social life. Individuals in groups of about 50 survive by hunting animals and gathering edible foods. Kinship—ties by blood and marriage—is the foundation for most relationships and is the principal institution for hunting and gathering societies. There are no specialized and enduring work groups, governments, or standing armies.

Some 10,000 years ago, human beings learned how to cultivate a number of plants on which they depended for food. The more efficient economies of these *horticultural societies* allow for the production of a social surplus—goods and services over and above those necessary for human survival. This surplus becomes the foundation for social stratification; the specialization of some economic, political, and religious roles; a growth in the importance of warfare; and more complex forms of culture and social structure (Lenski, 1966; Kerbo, 2003). Even so, the upper limit for most horticultural communities is about 3,000 persons.

Five to six thousand years ago, the plow heralded an agricultural revolution and the emergence of *agrarian societies* (Childe, 1941), with larger crops, more food, expanding populations, and even more complex forms of social organization. Continuing advances in productive and military technologies contributed to a substantial growth in the power of the state, the size of the territory it controlled, and the emergence of large capital cities. The massive pyramids of Egypt, the roads and aqueducts of Rome, the great cathedrals of medieval Europe, and the far-flung irrigation systems of the Middle East and China are products of agrarian societies.

About 250 years ago, the Industrial Revolution gave birth to *industrial societies* whose productive and economic systems are based on machine technologies. Economic self-sufficiency and local market systems were displaced by complex divisions of labor, exchange relationships, and national and international market systems. The ability to read and write became essential in advanced industrial societies and led to the growth of educational institutions. Many activities that were once the responsibility of families were relinquished to other institutions. Populations grew and people increasingly congregated in cities. Large-scale bureaucracies and formal organizations came to predominate in both the private and public spheres, finding expression in big business, big unions, big universities, big hospitals, and big government.

As we discuss in more detail in Chapter 10, some social analysts contend that the United States is currently moving in the direction of a *postindustrial society*. This is presumably a new historical period, often referred to by journalists as the "information age" or "service society." In a postindustrial society, increasing numbers of workers find employment in the provision of services rather than the extraction of raw materials and the manufacture of goods. Simultaneously, new techniques permit the automation of many processes in the workplace with the use of computers and complex feedback regulation devices. All these changes are accompanied by the knowledge explosion based on the creating, processing, and distribution of information (Lyman and Varian, 2000), and where they will lead us is hard to predict because the changes are so rapid. For example, in 1990 less than half a million computers in the United States had access to the Internet. This number grew to 30 million by 1998 (Brown and Flavin, 1999), and by 2001, 54 million U.S. households had computers with Internet connections (U.S. Department of Commerce, 2002).

Groups and Group Processes

Life places us in a complex web of relationships with other people. When an association continues long enough for two people to become linked together by a relatively stable set of expectations, it is called a

relationship. It is on the basis of such relationships that groups are formed.

People are bound within relationships by two types of bonds: expressive ties and instrumental ties. **Expressive ties** are social links formed when we emotionally invest ourselves in and commit ourselves to other people. Through association with people who are meaningful to us, we achieve a sense of security, love, acceptance, companionship, and personal worth. **Instrumental ties** are social links formed when we cooperate with other people to achieve some goal. Occasionally, this may mean working with our enemies. More often, we simply cooperate with others to reach some end without endowing the relationship with any larger significance.

In this section we will discuss several types of groups: primary groups and secondary groups, in-groups and out-groups, and reference groups.

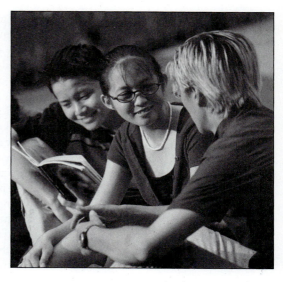

A primary group involves two or more people who enjoy a direct, intimate, cohesive relationship with one another.

Primary Groups and Secondary Groups

Sociologists have built on the distinction between expressive and instrumental ties to distinguish between two types of groups: primary and secondary. A **primary group** is a small group characterized by intimate, informal interaction. Expressive ties predominate in primary groups; we view the people—friends, family members, and lovers—as ends in themselves and valuable in their own right. Primary group relationships are more likely to emerge if the number of people is small enough so that each person can establish rapport with each other person, if there is enough face-to-face contact so that people can exchange ideas and feelings in subtle and personal ways, and if people interact frequently and continuously enough to deepen their ties and develop interlocking habits and interests.

Primary groups are critical to the socialization process. Within them, infants and children are introduced to the ways of their society. Such groups are the breeding grounds in which we acquire the norms and values that equip us for social life. Sociologists view primary groups as bridges between individuals and the larger society because they transmit, mediate, and interpret a society's cultural patterns and provide the sense of oneness so critical for social solidarity.

Primary groups also are fundamental because they provide the settings in which we meet most of our personal needs. Within them we experience companionship, love, security, and an overall sense of well-being. Not surprisingly, sociologists find that the strength of a group's primary ties has implications for its functioning. For example, the stronger the primary group ties of troops fighting together, the better their combat record (Elder and Clipp, 1988; Copp and McAndrew, 1990).

Primary groups serve as powerful instruments for social control. Their members command and dispense many of the rewards that are so vital to us and that make our lives seem worthwhile. Should the use of rewards fail, members can frequently win compliance by rejecting or threatening to ostracize those who deviate from the group's norms. For instance, some religious cults employ "shunning" (i.e., a person can remain in the community, but others are forbidden to interact with him or her) as a device to bring into line individuals whose behavior goes beyond that allowed by the group's teachings. Even more importantly, primary groups define social reality for us by "structuring" our experiences. By providing us with definitions of situations, they elicit from us behavior that conforms to group-devised meanings. Primary groups, then, serve both as carriers of social norms and as enforcers of them.

A **secondary group** entails two or more people who are involved in an impersonal relationship and have come together for a specific, practical purpose. Instrumental ties predominate in secondary groups; we perceive people as means to ends rather than as ends in their own right. Illustrations include our relationships with a clerk in a clothing store and a cashier at a service station. Sometimes primary group relationships evolve out of secondary group relationships. This happens in many work settings. People on the job often develop close relationships with coworkers as they come to share gripes, jokes, gossip, and satisfactions.

In-Groups and Out-Groups

It is not only the groups to which we immediately belong that have a powerful influence upon us. Often the same holds true for groups to which we do not belong. Accordingly, sociologists find it useful to distinguish between in-groups and out-groups. An **in-group** is a group with which we identify and to which we belong. An **out-group** is a group with which we do not identify and to which we do not belong. In daily conversation, we recognize the distinction between in-groups and out-groups in our use of the personal pronouns "we" and "they." We can think of in-groups as "we-groups" and out-groups as "they-groups." In-groups typically provide us with our *social identities*—those aspects of our self-concept that we derive from a sense of belonging to groups and the feelings and emotional significance we attach to this belonging (Crocker and Luhtanen, 1990).

The concepts of in-group and out-group highlight the importance of *boundaries*—social demarcation lines that tell us where interaction begins and ends. They prevent outsiders from entering a group's sphere, and they keep insiders within that sphere.

At times we experience feelings of indifference, disgust, competition, and even outright conflict when we think about or have dealings with out-group members. An experiment undertaken by Muzafer Sherif and his associates (1961) showed how our awareness of in-group boundaries is heightened and antagonism toward out-groups is generated by competitive situations. The subjects were 11- and 12-year-old boys, all of whom were healthy, socially well-adjusted youngsters from stable, middle-class homes. The setting was a summer camp where the boys were divided into two groups.

During the first week at the camp, the boys in each group got to know one another, evolved group norms, and arrived at an internal division of labor and leadership roles. During the second week, the experimenters brought the two groups into competitive contact through a tournament of baseball, touch football, tug-of-war, and treasure hunt games. Although the contest opened in a spirit of good sportsmanship, positive feelings quickly evaporated. During the third week, the "integration phase," Sherif brought the two groups of boys together for various events, including eating in the same mess hall, viewing movies, and shooting off firecrackers. But far from reducing conflict, these settings merely provided new opportunities for the two groups to challenge, berate, and harass one another. The experimenters then created a series of urgent and natural situations in which the two groups would have to work together to achieve their ends, such as the emergency repair of the conduit that delivered the camp's water supply. The pursuit of common goals led to a lessening of out-group hostilities and the lowering of intergroup barriers to cooperation.

This study demonstrates how competition with out-groups can create in-group solidarity and out-group hostility. However, other research shows that feelings of in-group favoritism do not require competition with out-groups, but seem to emerge spontaneously from the belief that one is connected to some category of people (see Box 3.1). In one experiment, subjects were found to be more likely to trust faces resembling their own (DeBruine, 2002), suggesting a biological basis to some in-group behavior.

Reference Groups

More than a century ago, American writer Henry Thoreau observed: "If a man does not keep pace with his companions, perhaps it is because he hears a different drummer." Thoreau's observation contains an important sociological insight. We evaluate ourselves and guide our behavior by group standards. But since Americans are dispersed among many different groups—each with a somewhat unique

What Does Bias Come From?
Sometimes, Almost Nothing

When you crack an egg, do you crack it at the small end or at the large end? Who cares, right? Well, if you have a preference, it would place you in one or the other warring nation in Jonathan Swift's *Gulliver's Travels*. Swift was poking fun at the Catholic–Protestant conflict, but social psychologists Myron Rothbart and Oliver P. John (1993:35) saw more: "This example offers a profound insight into the nature of intergroup conflict . . . In effect, Swift says that differences regarded as profound and intractable may, with a change in perspective, be thought of as trivial." Such an insight applies to conflicts between nations, between groups, and even between individuals today as well as in Swift's day. But is it well founded?

Rothbart and John described a set of experiments done with English schoolboys that suggest that bias against the out-group can develop among people who have almost no differences at all. Here's the evidence: Social psychologist Henri Tajfel asked schoolboys to estimate the number of

dots they saw projected on a screen. Then the boys were told that they would be placed into two categories, underestimators or overestimators of the number of dots. The boys were then told which category they were in, but they were placed into categories randomly—they were not necessarily overestimators if placed in that category, and vice versa.

Once the boys knew which category they were in, each subject was asked to allocate rewards to two other boys, about whom he knew only their category (over- or underestimator). When both boys receiving rewards were in the same category, the subject divided the rewards for them equally. When one boy was an in-group member (the same category as the subject giving the rewards) and one an out-group member (the other category), the rewards were given preferentially to the in-group member.

Others have replicated this study and affirmed the findings that subjects favor in-group over out-

subculture or counterculture—the frames of reference we use in assessing and fashioning our behavior differ. In brief, we have different **reference groups**—social units we use for appraising and shaping attitudes, feelings, and actions (Singer, 1981). For a high school student who aspires to achieve academically, a positive reference group might be the students who get high grades and belong to the National Honor Society, whereas a negative reference group could be students who attend erratically and fail their classes.

A reference group may or may not be our membership group. We may think of a reference group as a base we use for viewing the world, a source of psychological identification. It helps account for seemingly contradictory behavior: the upper-class person who supports a revolution, the Catholic who speaks against the Pope, the union member who supports management, and those who collaborate with the enemy in wartime. These individuals have simply taken as their reference group people other than those from their membership group (Hyman and Singer, 1968). The concept thus helps to illuminate such central sociological concerns as social networks, socialization, and social conformity.

group members. Rothbart and John commented on the results (1993:36):

> The two groups were not competing for a limited resource. There was no . . . competition or cooperation between the two groups. There was no historical enmity. There was no aroused frustration in the subjects. There was no objectively determined difference between the two groups; the groups did not differ in terms of language, culture, or physiognomy . . . As a result of . . . categorization, subjects favored ingroup members with greater resources.

The Tajfel experiments are now referred to as the *minimal group paradigm.* This research showed that bias against an out-group does not depend on a history of enmity between the groups, competition, aggression due to frustration, physical differences, religious differences, or any important value differences at all.

How does the minimal group paradigm relate to group conflict in the real world? Some research suggests that simply the act of categorizing people into groups can lead to significant bias against outgroups: "Categorization generated by the minimal group paradigm implicitly activates the expectation of ingroup superiority ("we" are better than "they"), and . . . subjects will then selectively remember ingroup and outgroup behaviors in accordance with their perceived superiority" (1993:37).

Other recent research shows that it also activates people's assumption that members of their ingroups are more likely than out-group members to reciprocate favoritism. Gaertner and Insko's 2000 study of the minimal group paradigm found that category members favored the in-group only in situations in which they thought other in-group members could, and would, reciprocate.

So what is bias based on? Well, not much. According to these experiments, merely being told that one belongs to some category is enough to generate group feeling—*for* one's own group and *against* another. "Even in the absence of real differences, competition, and aggression," wrote Rothbart and John, "bias against an outgroup can develop."

Questions for Discussion

1. What was the basis for grouping boys in the Tajfel experiment?

2. Do the results of the minimal group experiments indicate that intergroup conflict is inevitable?

3. In view of minimal groups effects, what should we do in our society to reduce intergroup conflict?

When our membership group does not match our reference group, we may experience feelings of **relative deprivation**—discontent associated with the gap between what we have (the circumstances of our membership group) and what we believe we should have (the circumstances of our reference group). Feelings of relative deprivation often contribute to social alienation and provide fertile conditions for collective behavior and revolutionary social movements. The reference group concept, then, contains clues to processes of social change.

Group Dynamics

To understand groups is to understand much about human behavior. Groups are the well-springs of our humanness. Although we think of groups as things—distinct and bound entities—it is not their static but their dynamic qualities that make them such a significant force. We need to examine what happens within groups. In this section we will consider group size, leadership, groupthink, and conformity.

Group Size.   The size of a group is important because it influences the nature of interaction. The smaller the group, the more opportunities we have to get to know other people well and to establish close ties with them. Two-person groups—**dyads**—are the setting for many of our most intense and influential relationships, including that between parent and child and between husband and wife. Indeed, most of our social interactions take place on a one-to-one basis.

The popular adage "two's company, three's a crowd" captures an important difference between two-person and three-person groups. As the German sociologist Georg Simmel (1950) pointed out, forming a **triad** by adding one person to a dyad is far more consequential than adding one person to any other size group. What was a group with one relationship now has three. This change fundamentally alters the social situation. Coalitions become possible, with two members joining forces against a third member. With this arrangement, one person may be placed in the role of an "intruder" or "outsider." Under some circumstances, however, the third person may assume the role of a "mediator" and function as a peacemaker.

Leadership.   Imagine a football team without a quarterback, a class of students without a teacher, or youth gangs without chiefs. Without overall direction, people typically have difficulty coordinating their activities. Consequently, in group settings some members usually exert more influence than others. We call these individuals *leaders.* Small groups may be able to get along without a leader, but in larger groups a lack of leadership leads to chaos.

Two types of leadership roles tend to evolve in small groups (Bales, 1970). One, a **task specialist,** is devoted to appraising the problem at hand and organizing people's activity to deal with it. The other, a **social-emotional specialist,** focuses on overcoming interpersonal problems in the group, defusing tensions, and promoting solidarity. The former type of leadership is *instrumental,* directed toward the achievement of group goals; the latter is *expressive,* oriented toward the creation of harmony and unity. Usually each role is played by a different person, since typically it is the stress created by the task leader that is managed or relieved by the social-emotional leader. Attempting to incorporate both functions in a role played by one person can create role strain.

Leaders differ in their styles for exercising influence. In classic experiments in leadership by Kurt Lewin and his associates (Lewin, Lippitt, and White, 1939; White and Lippitt, 1960), adult leaders working with groups of 11-year-old boys followed one of three leadership styles. In the *authoritarian style,* the leader made unilateral decisions, gave step-by-step directions, assigned work partners, provided subjective praise and criticism, and remained aloof from group participation. In contrast, in the *democratic style*, the leader allowed the boys to help make decisions, outlined only general goals, suggested alternative procedures, permitted the members to work with whomever they wished, evaluated the boys objectively, and participated in group activities. In the *laissez-faire style*, the leader adopted a passive, uninvolved stance; provided materials, suggestions, and help only when requested; and refrained from commenting on the boys' work.

The researchers found that authoritarian leadership produces high levels of frustration and hostile feelings toward the leader. Productivity remains high as long as the leader is present, but it slackens appreciably in the leader's absence. Under democratic leadership, members are as productive as under authoritarian leadership but are happier, feel more group-minded and friendlier, display independence (especially in the leader's absence), and exhibit low levels of interpersonal aggression. Laissez-faire leadership resulted in low group productivity and high levels of interpersonal aggression. While these classic studies suggest that democratic leadership is clearly superior, subsequent research failed to confirm that it always yields better results than authoritarian leadership (Bartol and Martin, 1998; Bass, 1981).

Probably no one leadership style works best in all situations. Different styles may be appropriate in different situations. Important contingencies include the leader's personality; the ability, skill, and willingness of followers: and whether the task is clearly defined or involves considerable uncertainty (Fiedler and Garcia, 1987; Vroom and Jago, 1988; Hersey and Blanchard, 1988). Although gender differences in leadership are small, and both women and men can be effective leaders, recent research indicates that female leaders exhibit more characteristics of effective leadership than male leaders (Eagly, Johannesen-Schmidt, and van Engen, 2003).

Groupthink.   In 1961 the Kennedy administration undertook the ill-fated Bay of Pigs invasion of Cuba. Nothing went right for the 1,400 Central Intelligence Agency (CIA)-trained Cuban invaders, most of whom were killed or captured by Fidel Castro's forces. Not only did the invasion solidify Castro's leadership, it consolidated the Cuban–Soviet alliance and led the Soviet leadership to attempt to place nuclear missiles in Cuba. Later, President John Kennedy was to ask: "How could we have been so stupid?" Not only had the president and his advisers overlooked the size and strength of the Castro army, but in many instances they even had failed to seek relevant information.

Social psychologist Irving Janis (1972, 1982, 1989) suggested that the president and his advisers were victims of **groupthink**—a decision-making process found in highly cohesive groups in which the members become so preoccupied with maintaining consensus that their critical faculties are impaired. In groupthink, members share an illusion of invulnerability that leads to overconfidence, a greater willingness to take risks, and a tendency to ignore contrary evidence. Members of the group demand conformity and apply pressure to those who express doubts about a proposed course of action; they withhold dissent and exercise self-censorship. As a result, decisions are made without the benefit of critical analysis.

Conformity.   Groupthink research testifies to the powerful social pressures that operate in group settings and produce conformity. Although such pressures influence our behavior, we often are unaware of them. In a pioneering study, Muzafer Sherif (1936) demonstrated this point with an optical illusion. If people view a small, fixed spot of light in a darkened room, they perceive it as moving erratically in all directions. However, individuals differ in how far they think the light "moves." Sherif tested subjects alone and found the reference point for each individual. He then brought together in group settings people with quite different perceptions and asked them again to view the light and report aloud on their observations. Under these circumstances, their perceptions converged toward a group standard. Later, in solitary sessions, they did not return to the standard they had at first evolved but adhered to the standard of the group. Significantly, most subjects reported that they arrived at their assessment independently and that the group had had no influence on them.

Sherif presented subjects with an ambiguous situation; Solomon Asch (1952) asked subjects to match lines of the same length from two sets of cards displayed at the front of the room. He instructed the members of nine-person groups to give their answers aloud. However, only one of the individuals was a subject in the experiment; the others were graduate students working with Asch, and they unanimously provided incorrect answers on certain trials. Despite the obviousness of the correct answer, nearly one-third of all the subjects' judgments contained errors identical with or in the direction of the rigged errors of the majority. Some three-fourths of the subjects conformed on at least one of the trials. Thus, Asch demonstrated that some individuals conform to the false consensus of a group even though the consensus is contradicted by the evidence of their own eyes. Asch's findings have been replicated many times and in many nations and cultures, and although people in some countries conform more than in others, the differences are not very great (Sunstein, 2003).

The Sherif (1936) and Asch (1952) studies illustrate two of the main reasons that people conform: the desire to be correct and the desire to be accepted by the group (Aronson, 1994). It is possible that the conforming subjects in Asch's experiment could see that the task had little significance and thus conformed because it was easy and had no serious consequences. But other experiments have shown that humans are likely to obey orders and to go along with the group even when they believe that what they are doing is harming others (Ritch, 2002; Milgram, 1963; Haney, Banks, and Zimbardo, 1973).

Formal Organizations

As modern societies have become increasingly complex, so have the requirements of group life. As we noted earlier in the chapter, the social organization of traditional societies revolves primarily around kin relations. The division of labor is simple, the people are culturally homogeneous, and there is no formal law. But contemporary societies composed of millions of people can no longer rely entirely on primary group arrangements to accomplish the tasks of social life. Food has to be produced, preserved, and transported over considerable distances to support large urban populations. The residents of large, anonymous communities can no longer count on family members and neighbors to enforce group norms and standards. Children can no longer be educated by the same natural processes by which they learn to walk and talk. For these and many other tasks, people require groups they can deliberately create for the achievement of specific objectives. Such groups are **formal organizations.**

In recent decades, the United States has increasingly become a society of large, semiautonomous, and tightly knit formal organizations that appear, disappear, change, merge, and enter into countless relationships with one another. Although formal organizations have existed for thousands of years, dating back to ancient Mesopotamia, Egypt, and China, only in recent times have their scope and centrality become so pronounced.

In this section, we will introduce types of formal organization, define bureaucracy and list its characteristics, discuss problems of bureaucracy, consider various theoretical approaches, and discuss how to humanize bureaucracies.

Types of Formal Organization

People enter formal organizations for a variety of reasons. Sociologist Amitai Etzioni (1975) classified organizations on the basis of these reasons and identified three major types: voluntary, coercive, and utilitarian. **Voluntary organizations** are associations that members enter and leave freely. College campuses abound with examples: hiking and biking groups, service organizations, and intramural sports teams are just a few. Members are not paid for participation; they join voluntary organizations to fill their leisure time, to enjoy the company of like-minded people, to perform some social service, to advance some cause,

These students are participating in a utilitarian organization, a university, for a particular reason: to get a degree.

or to change themselves through self-help organizations (Woodard, 1987).

People also become members of some organizations—**coercive organizations**—against their will. They may be committed to a mental hospital, sentenced to prison, or drafted into the armed forces. Sociologist Erving Goffman (1961b) studied life in what he called **total institutions**—places of residence where individuals are isolated from the rest of society for an appreciable period of time and where behavior is tightly regimented. In these environments, the "inmates" or "recruits" are exposed to **resocialization** experiences that systematically seek to strip away their old roles and identities and fashion new ones. The induction process often includes **mortification.** New members are humiliated by being forced to assume demeaning postures, to engage in self-effacing tasks, and to endure insulting epithets (what sociologists term a *degradation ceremony*). These procedures leave individuals psychologically and emotionally receptive to the roles and identities demanded of them by the total institution.

Individuals also enter formal organizations formed for practical reasons—**utilitarian organizations.** Universities, corporations, farm organizations, labor unions, and government bureaus and agencies are among the organizations people form to accomplish vital everyday tasks. Utilitarian organizations fall between voluntary and coercive organizations: Membership in them is neither entirely voluntary nor entirely compulsory. For example, we may not be compelled to secure employment with a corporation, but if we wish to support ourselves, doing so is an essential element of life.

Bureaucracy: A Functional Approach to Organizations

As we saw in Chapter 1, the functionalist perspective attempts to understand the existence and structure of social patterns by examining the contributions those patterns make to the larger system of which they are a part. In modern societies, large complex organizations perform many tasks that are required for those societies to survive and grow. Organizations that manage sewers, the water supply, electricity, phones, public safety, the administration of government, and the manufacturing and distribution of goods are some of the most important examples of these. The functionalist perspective developed the concept *bureaucracy* to explain the existence and structure of this organizational type.

As long as organizations are relatively small, they can often function reasonably well on the basis of informal face-to-face interaction. But if larger organizations are to attain their goals, they must establish formal operating and administrative procedures. Only as they standardize and routinize many of their operations can they function effectively. This requirement is met by a **bureaucracy**, a social structure made up of a hierarchy of statuses and roles that is prescribed by explicit rules and procedures and based on a division of function and authority. Sociologists use the concept in a way that differs sharply from the negative connotation "bureaucracy" has when we use it in everyday conversation to refer to organizational inefficiency.

By providing for the performance of tasks on a regular and orderly basis, bureaucracies permit the planning and coordination of these activities in an efficient manner. Additionally, they aim to eliminate all unrelated influences on the behavior of their members so that people act primarily in the organization's interests. Although most complex organizations in the United States are organized as bureaucracies, the degree and forms of bureaucratization vary (Perrow, 1986). In addition, globalization, rapid social change, and the introduction of new technologies are producing much innovation in real-world organizations, and this is changing how social scientists think about organizations (Liker, Haddad, and Karlin, 1999; Jaffee, 2001).

Characteristics of Bureaucracies

The German sociologist Max Weber (1946, 1947) was impressed by the ability of bureaucracies to rationalize and control the process by which people collectively pursue their goals. He developed a description of bureaucracy as an *ideal type* of organization. As pointed out in Chapter 1, an ideal type is a concept constructed by sociologists to portray the principal characteristics of a phenomenon. Such an analysis of bureaucracy abstracts common elements from organizations as diverse as a government agency, the Roman Catholic Church, the

How Does Weber's Ideal Bureaucracy Work?

1. Each office or position has clearly defined duties and responsibilities. In this manner, the regular activities of the organization are arranged within a clear-cut division of labor.

2. All offices are organized in a hierarchy of authority that takes the shape of a pyramid. Officials are held accountable to their superiors for subordinates' actions and decisions in addition to their own.

3. All activities are governed by a consistent system of abstract rules and regulations that define the responsibilities of the various offices and the relationships among them. They ensure the coordination of essential tasks and uniformity in performance regardless of changes in personnel.

4. All offices carry with them qualifications and are filled on the basis of technical competence, not personal considerations. Presumably, trained individuals do better work than those who gain an office on the basis of family ties, personal friendship, or political favor. Competence is established by certification (e.g., college degrees) or examination (e.g., civil service tests).

5. Incumbents do not "own" their offices and cannot use offices for personal ends. Positions remain the property of the organization, and officeholders are supplied with the items they require to perform their work.

6. Employment by the organization is defined as a career. Promotion is based on seniority or merit, or both. After a probationary period, individuals gain the security of tenure and are protected against arbitrary dismissal. In principle, this feature makes officials less susceptible to outside pressures.

7. Administrative decisions, rules, procedures, and activities are recorded in written documents preserved in permanent files.

Figure 3.1   Characteristics of Weber's Ideal Bureaucracy

Teamsters' Union, IBM, and Yale University and arrives at a model for describing and analyzing organizational arrangements. Perhaps no actual organization is exactly like the model in all respects, but the model isolates the important elements of organizational structure in contemporary society, which are presented in Figure 3.1.

At first glance, the abstract description presented in Figure 3.1 seems pretty irrelevant to our daily lives. But it does outline the kind of organizational structure most of us would like to be able to take for granted. Though we dislike bureaucracy and can feel alienated by it, most of us expect that the organizations we encounter will work the way Weber described, and we feel mistreated if they do not.

For example, we wish those holding positions in our schools, government, and corporations to gain these offices and exercise power because of their ability and competence, not because of their race, gender, personal connections, or physical attractiveness (characteristic 4). We would not like courthouse clerks, police officers, or the mayor of our town to sell services to the highest bidder; we define this kind of behavior as the crime of bribery (characteristic 5). We expect that rules will be followed and that exceptions will not be made at the whim of officeholders. For example, we expect that government contracts will be awarded to bidders who follow the correct procedures and submit the lowest bids, not simply to family members of the responsible government official; when we suspect that such a thing has taken place, we complain of nepotism (characteristic 3). When things go wrong with what an organization does, we expect some responsible official to react, track down and correct the problem, and discipline those in the organization who may have fallen short (characteristics 2 and 7). If we are employed in a bureaucracy, we expect there to be clear expectations of what we and others are to do and how we are to coordinate our activities. For example, we expect that other officeholders cannot usurp our authority simply because they want to and can get away with it (characteristic 1). And if we obey the rules and perform competently, we expect that we should be able to make a career within the organization and should not be let go without a very good reason (characteristic 6).

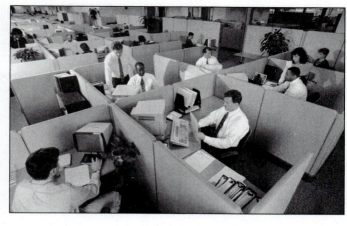

Bureaucracies perform many of the tasks that are required for society to survive and grow. At the same time, as Max Weber and other sociologists have pointed out, they turn people into cogs in organizational machines.

Thus, as much as we sometimes complain about the "red tape" of bureaucracies and although we all might like to be treated as special cases, bureaucracy is with us because we expect it to be there and to function as Weber said that it should. To live otherwise in modern society is almost unthinkable.

Problems of Bureaucracy

Oligarchy.   Critics point out that all too often the needs of organizations take priority over those of individuals (Glassman, Swatos, and Rosen, 1987; Dandeker, 1990). Robert Michels (1911/1966), a sociologist and friend of Weber, argued that bureaucracies contain a fundamental flaw that makes them undemocratic social arrangements: They invariably lead to *oligarchy*—the concentration of power in the hands of a few individuals who use their offices to advance their own fortunes and self-interests. He called this tendency the **iron law of oligarchy:** "Whoever says organization, says oligarchy" (p. 365).

Michels cited a variety of reasons for the oligarchical tendencies found in formal organizations, even those that are presumably democratic, such as political parties, labor unions, and voluntary associations. First, because they have hierarchical leadership structures involved in everyday administration, most voting by the membership becomes a ritualistic confirmation of leaders' decisions. Second, officials have special advantages: access to information unavailable to others, superior political skills and experience, and control of a variety of administrative resources, including communication networks, offices, and a treasury, that can be used to ward off challengers and co-opt dissidents and rivals. Third, ordinary members tend to be uninterested in assuming leadership responsibilities and are apathetic toward the problems of the organization.

Dysfunctions of Bureaucracy.

Bureaucracy may not be as functional as Weber thought. Even when they function as they were designed to, bureaucracies may produce harmful consequences. For example, in many organizations, management specialization—not production or meeting consumer needs—becomes the way to the top. Such outcomes are the typical by-product of a bureaucratic dysfunction that C. Northcote Parkinson (1962) termed **Parkinson's law:** "Work expands so as to fill the time available for its completion." Despite the tongue-in-cheek tone of his writing, Parkinson showed that "the number of the officials and the quantity of the work are not related to each other." He contended that bureaucracy expands not because of an increasing workload but because officials seek to have additional subordinates hired in order to multiply the number of people under them in the hierarchy. These subordinates, in turn, create work for one another, while the coordination of their work requires still more officials.

Another dysfunction of bureaucracy was first noted by social critic Thorstein Veblen (1921), who pointed out that bureaucracies encourage their members to rely on established rules and regulations and to apply them in an unimaginative and mechanical fashion, a pattern he called **trained incapacity.** As a result of the socialization provided by organizations, individuals often develop a tunnel vision that limits their ability to respond in new ways when situations change. Government bureaucracies are especially risk-averse because they are caught up in such complex webs of constraint that any change is likely to rouse the ire of important constituencies (J. Q. Wilson, 1990, 1993). This problem may be particularly significant in very successful organizations that often resist change because of the fear that to do so will prevent repetition of past successes. Such inflexibility can result in self-perpetuating organizational mediocrity.

Bureaucracy Is an Idealized Model.

The bureaucratic model is difficult, if not impossible, to realize in practice. A number of forces undermine its operation (Perrow, 1986; Jaffee, 2001). First, human beings do not exist only for organizations. People track all sorts of mud from the rest of their lives, including their prejudicial attitudes, with them into bureaucratic arrangements, and they have numerous interests independent of the organization. Second, bureaucracies are not immune to social change. When such changes are frequent and rapid, the pat answers supplied by bureaucratic regulations and rules interfere with rational operation. Third, bureaucracies are designed for the "average" person. In real life, however, people differ in intelligence, energy, zeal, and dedication, so they are not interchangeable in the day-to-day functioning of organizations. Fourth, forms of informal organization emerge within real bureaucracies in response to the tensions and contradictions of organizational life and, thus, as a model of what happens within an organization, the bureaucratic model is

"Does this mean I'm out of the loop?"

incomplete. By competing with the formal organization for members' loyalties and by challenging bureaucratic rules and authority, informal organization is a particularly serious threat to organizational goals. As a result, it has been the focus of much attention by sociologists.

Informal organization consists of interpersonal networks and ties that arise in a formal organization but are not defined or prescribed by it. Based on their common interests and relationships, individuals form primary groups. These informal structures provide means by which people bend and break rules, share "common knowledge," engage in secret behaviors, handle problems, and "cut corners." Work relationships are much more than the lifeless abstractions contained on an organizational chart that outlines the official lines of communication and authority.

Factory workers typically evolve their own norms regarding what constitutes a "reasonable" amount of work, and these norms often do not conform with those of management (Roethlisberger and Dickson, 1939; Hamper, 1991). Sociologist Michael Burawoy (1979) studied informal organization among shop workers while working for a year as a machine operator at a large Chicago-area plant. He found that relations on the shop floor were dominated by "making out"—a competitive game the machine operators played by manipulating the rules and regulations governing their work to their benefit.

Conflict and Interactionist Perspectives

The Conflict Perspective.   Conflict theorists contend that organizational goals reflect the priorities of those who occupy the top positions. Viewed in this manner, organizations are not neutral social structures pursuing clear goals but arenas for conflicting interests in which the social issues and power relations of society are played out (Collins, 1975; Jaffee, 2001). Marxist social scientists have followed in the tradition of Karl Marx (1970), who saw bureaucracy as a manifestation of the centralizing tendencies of capitalism and an instrument of class domination. They analyze organizations within the context of the broader inequalities that operate within society and find that the distribution of power and the allocation of rewards within them mirror the larger society's class structure (Edwards, 1979; Jaffee, 2001).

Studies by Marxist social scientists suggest that bureaucratic mechanisms arose as much from the desire of capitalists to control workers as from abstract notions of efficiency and rationality (Friedman, 1977; Edwards, 1978). For example, Katherine Stone (1974) found that early 20th-century steel magnates established top-to-bottom chains of command and job ladders to isolate individual workers, break the power of skilled artisans, and combat growing labor militancy.

The Symbolic Interactionist Perspective.   Symbolic interactionists contend that human beings in organizations are not sponge-like, malleable organisms who passively conform to the bureaucratic requirements. Instead, they portray people as active agents who shape and mold their destinies and continually fashion new joint actions based on their definitions of the situation (Blumer, 1969). Organizational constraints only provide the framework with which people appraise and then decide among alternative courses of organizational behavior on the basis of meanings they share with others in the organization. The model of organizations that results is one that emphasizes dynamism and malleability of organizational forms rather than fixed structures and procedures.

A good example of the application of symbolic interactionism to organizations is the classic study by Anselm Strauss and his colleagues (1964) of organizational behavior in two Chicago-area psychiatric hospitals. They treated a formal organization as a **negotiated order**—the fluid, ongoing understandings and agreements people reach as they go about their daily activities. To outsiders the hospitals appeared to be tightly structured organizations that functioned in accordance with strict bureaucratic rules and regulations. However, the researchers found that in practice the hospitals operated quite differently. The organizations were simply too complex for a single set of rules to hold or for any one person to know all the rules, much less in exactly what situations they applied, to whom, in what degree, and for how long. Given these circumstances, most house rules served more as general under-

Conflict theorists argue that employee-participation programs are designed to function as sophisticated control strategies.

DILBERT reprinted by permission of United Feature Syndicate, Inc.

standings than as commands, and they were stretched, argued, reinterpreted, ignored, or applied as situations dictated. Individuals reached agreements with one another that provided a consensus for a time, but the understandings were subject to periodic modification and revision.

Chaos did not reign in the hospitals because the negotiations followed patterns that permitted some degree of predictability. Even so, Strauss and his colleagues concluded:

> Practically, we maintain, no one knows what the hospital "is" on any given day unless [he or she] has a comprehensive grasp of the combinations of rules, policies, agreements, understandings, pacts, contracts, and other working arrangements that currently obtain. In a pragmatic sense, that combination "is" the hospital at the moment, its social order. (1964:312)

A Synthesis of Alternative Perspectives. Sociologist Charles Perrow (1982) joined threads from the symbolic interactionist and conflict perspectives to argue that the notion of bureaucratic rationality masks the true nature of organizational life. He claimed that our world is more "loosely coupled"—characterized by a substantial measure of redundancy, slack, and waste—than structural theories admit. Perrow said that organizations do not have goals, only constraints. Take the Sanitation Department of New York City:

> To say its goal is to pick up the garbage—even to pick it up frequently, pick it all up, and do it cheaply—does not tell us much. These are not goals of that department but merely loose constraints under which those who use the organization must operate, and these are not really any more important than the following constraints: The cushy top jobs in the department can be used to pay off political debts; some groups can use the Sanitation Department as an assured source of employment and keep others out; upper management can use its positions as political jumping off places or training spots;

equipment manufacturers use it as an easy mark for shoddy goods; and, finally, the workers are entitled to use it as a source of job security and pensions and an easy way of making a living. (p. 687)

Perrow contended that private profit-making organizations are not much different. Aerospace companies can be seen as pension plans that make missiles and planes on the side so that their pension plans can be funded. Steel plants are closed even though they make a respectable profit because they are worth more as tax write-offs. Countless other organizations continue to exist even though they fail to provide decent mail service, prepare students for careers, or offer acceptable medical care. But should the organizations fail to satisfy some special-interest group that lives off them, then the consequences are defined as a major social problem. In short, organizations pursue a variety of courses of action, some of them with more enthusiasm than they pursue their publicly stated goals. Perrow concluded, therefore, that organizations do not have goals in the rational sense suggested by organizational theory. Instead, actions are determined by the interests and desires of executives, employees, and other stakeholders, and formally stated goals are determined after the fact, on the basis of what executives observe themselves doing.

Perrow next linked the conflict perspective to his analysis by arguing that social efforts at stating goals, giving accounts, and attributing rationality to organizations serve elites much more than they serve other people. These efforts create a world in which organizational hierarchy, technological requirements, and profit-making motives become legitimized.

Humanizing Bureaucracies

Since large organizations play such a critical part in our daily lives, it may be well to conclude the chapter by asking, "Can we make bureaucracies more humane instruments for modern living?" If we value freedom and independence—if we are disturbed by the conformity of attitudes, values, and behavior that bureaucracies often induce—then we may wish to set up conditions that foster uniqueness, self-direction, and human dignity. Although affording no panaceas, a number of programs have been proposed that allow individuals greater range for developing their full capacities and potential in the context of organizational life. Let us briefly consider a number of these.

Employee Participation.
About the same time that Japanese manufacturers vigorously entered U.S. markets, American business leaders began trying to breathe new life and competitive fire into their

companies. Many corporations have tried an approach known as "quality circles," "participative management," or "working smarter" to promote employee participation and thereby to increase competitiveness and productivity. A group of up to a dozen workers and one or two managers from the same department meet together on a regular basis to figure out ways of getting along better with each other, making work easier, raising output, and improving the quality of their products. Proponents of the programs say that where management and workers are committed to them, absenteeism, tardiness, grievances, strikes, and labor costs are reduced. Moreover, product quality improves and pilferage lessens.

Although some 6,000 American companies, including General Motors, IBM, and AT&T, adopted employee participation programs, most of these programs failed (Saporito, 1986). A Gallup survey found that only 14 percent of corporate employees who worked for firms with quality-improvement and employee participation programs thought their companies gave them a chance to participate in the important decisions (Bennett, 1990). Conflict theorists argue that because the relationship between management and labor is inherently adversarial, worker participation programs are simply cosmetic efforts that mask corporate attempts to control workers and to avoid collective-bargaining obligations.

Another approach entails "self-managed teams" or "autonomous work groups," an arrangement in which workers largely operate without bosses (Bartol and Martin, 1998). Employees set their own work schedules, prepare their own budgets, and receive group bonuses on the basis of the team's productivity. Managers, termed "coaches," function as advisers (Selz, 1994). The approach appears highly adaptable within the computer industry, where many tasks are not easily routinized and where small groups, given great freedom, can react quickly to abrupt technological change. Small groups can focus their energies on a single goal, foster creativity, and reward employees commensurate with their contributions (Bartol and Martin, 1998). Beyond the small work groups approach is the "no-collar" approach, in which informally dressed employees manage themselves, use the office as a "funhouse" (because play promotes creativity), and are expected to work 70-hour weeks (Ross, 2003).

Overall, new management strategies over the past 30 years have emphasized a lessening of hierarchy and authoritarianism and an increase in worker participation in workplace decision making. But the changes should not be overestimated. When managers must make a tough decision, they often revert to the direct, authoritarian mode.

Alternative Work Schedules.   Some companies have attempted to boost job satisfaction and motivation by allowing some flexibility in how work time is scheduled. Flextime is one example; workers are allowed to decide how to organize their eight-hour workday. Some may wish to come in early and get off early; others may wish to have their early mornings free and work into the evening. These plans can benefit working parents who often need to schedule their work hours so that adequate child care can be arranged. They also benefit companies since they result in lower absentee and turnover rates (Bartol and Martin, 1998).

Another example is the compressed workweek. This plan involves scheduling workers to put in four 10-hour days per week with three days off. Such a plan can work well for construction, for example, where more can be accomplished on-site during each 10-hour day, and workers can enjoy long weekends. For some types of jobs, such as nursing, 12-hour shifts with appropriate time off works well.

Virtual Offices. Some companies find that workers do not need to report to a central office but can work from anywhere and communicate with managers, workers, customers, and others via the Internet (Davidow and Malone, 1993; Jaffee, 2001). These "virtual corporations" with their "virtual offices" provide employees with the ultimate in autonomy and flexibility in organizing their work. Verifone, Inc., a company that designs, manufactures, sells, and services the machines that read credit cards in retail establishments, is a successful example of a virtual corporation (Jaffee, 2001). It has 3,000 employees worldwide, but no corporate office and no identification with a nation-state. Corporate operations never cease, with employees communicating and accessing company information through the Internet.

Though workers may find that working in a virtual office enables them to manage the conflicts between their personal lives and their work lives more effectively, it is unclear what the ultimate impact will be on the structure of organizations. The unintended consequences of such arrangements may include increased alienation, the loss of a sense of community, and a weakening of organizational integration (Snizek, 1995).

Specialized Benefits. In an attempt to reduce employee turnover, some companies offer a variety of new benefits to workers. A number offer child care either on-site or nearby in company-owned buildings, providing parents with opportunities to visit their children during the day and cutting day care costs. Some make contributions to college education funds for employees' offspring. Company-provided transportation to jobs has resulted in reductions in tardiness and absenteeism for some employers. Workers in some states can attend classes on company time to earn their high school graduate equivalency diplomas (GEDs). At least one company offers 24-hour on-call social workers to help employees with their personal problems. These specialized benefits programs reflect both a change in attitudes toward workers and the inability of most companies to offer increased wages (Grimsley, 1997).

Employee Stock Ownership Plans.

By 2002 nearly 10,000 companies in the United States shared some measure of ownership with more than 8 million employees. Workers owned the majority of the stock in some 2,500 companies. Although employee stock ownership plans (ESOPs) grew rapidly from their inception in 1974 until 1990, there has been little overall growth since then. Nonetheless, the number of majority employee– and 100 percent employee–owned companies continues to increase (ESOP Association, 2003).

In many cases, large-scale employee ownership has changed the way companies operate, including their labor–management relationships (Klein, 1987; Blasi, 1988). Greater employee initiative in the workplace has been found to cut costs, but much depends on a firm's profitability. When a company becomes profitable, differences tend to get smoothed over quickly, but a firm that continues to lose money will see dissatisfaction rise and difficulties deepen. For instance, in the early 1990s, the men and women at Weirton Steel found that ownership did not always translate into power. These employee-owners took pay cuts, accepted layoffs, and acquiesced as management spent $550 million to revamp the company's mill. After years of butting heads with management, the workers launched a battle in 1993 to gain actual control of the firm (Baker, 1993). Thus, employee ownership does not guarantee labor peace.

Key Terms

achieved status, 65

aggregate, 68

ascribed status, 65

bureaucracy, 81

category, 68

coercive organization, 80

duties, 67

dyad, 76

expressive ties, 71

formal organization, 79

group, 67

groupthink, 77

in-group, 72

informal organization, 85

institution, 68

instrumental ties, 71

iron law of oligarchy, 83

master status, 65

mortification, 80

negotiated order, 86

out-group, 72

Parkinson's law, 84

primary group, 71

reference group, 74

relationship, 71

relative deprivation, 75

resocialization, 80

rights, 67

role, 65

role conflict, 67

role performance, 65

role set, 66

role strain, 67

secondary group, 72

social-emotional specialist, 76

social structure, 63

Review Questions

1. How do sociologists define status? What is the difference between ascribed and achieved statuses?

2. Give one example of role conflict.

3. Define *group, institution,* and *society.*

4. How do primary groups differ from secondary groups? List three of each from your own life.

5. What are in-groups and out-groups?

6. Define *reference group* and give at least two examples from your own life.

7. What are two major styles of leadership?

8. Describe a social dilemma from your own life.

9. What is groupthink? Have you ever experienced this phenomenon as a member of a decision-making group?

10. Joining a sorority or fraternity is voluntary. Do such organizations have any characteristics of a coercive organization?

11. Define *bureaucracy* and list the characteristics of Weber's ideal bureaucracy.

12. What are some of the problems of bureaucracy?

13. What do conflict theorists have to say about bureaucracy? How does it differ from the view of symbolic interactionists?

four

Chapter 4

Deviance and Crime

The Nature
of Deviance

Theories of Deviance

Crime and the
Criminal Justice
System

T he term *deviance* suggests unusual and strange behavior of
people with twisted minds pursuing twisted things. However,
what we think of as deviant is often an ordinary part of everyday life.
More than a hundred years ago, for example, many students at the
best U.S. colleges cheated most of the time. "Whole classes
cheated on examinations," says historian Helen Lefkowitz Horowitz
(1987:33). "The use of ponies (translations of texts) was almost universal. At Yale in the 1860s, perhaps less than half of the composi-
tions were actually written by the supposed author for the occasion."

Today many campuses have honor systems run by the students
themselves, yet cheating remains a common form of behavior
among college students. In one study, 83 percent of university students admitted to at least one act of academic dishonesty. A quarter
said they had lied to an instructor and falsified material on a term
paper, a third said they had looked at other students' answers during exams, and nearly a fifth said they had plagiarized a term paper
(Cochran et al., 1999; see also Michaels and Miethe, 1989). Other
studies suggest that the percentage of students who cheat in college is at least 90 percent and may be as high as 99 percent (Sperber, 2000).

Is cheating deviant or is it a normal feature of everyday life? If so many people cheat, why are there still rules against it? These questions introduce two important ideas that form the backdrop for our analysis of deviance. First, whether something is deviant depends on who is evaluating it. In 19th-century colleges, for example, faculty believed that cheating was deviant. Students, on the other hand, believed it was deviant *not* to cheat, and being proud of having achieved good grades through "honest" means was clearly deviant (Horowitz, 1987).

Second, when important *norms,* or rules, are violated, norms and social control function to maintain social organization, social relationships, and the meanings that underlie them. Norms against cheating still exist in spite of widespread cheating because without such norms and mechanisms for their enforcement, the nature of the university and its place in society would be very different. When universities react to cheating, they protect the idea that people earn grades honestly and that grades are at least a rough measure of merit. Norms and defending norms in the face of violation are necessary for social order to exist and to be maintained over time.

In this chapter, we will consider the nature and significance of deviance. We will discuss sociological definitions of deviance and see what various sociological perspectives contribute to our understanding of deviance. In addition, we will examine a form of deviance that is particularly prevalent in modern society: crime.

The Nature of Deviance

Deviant behavior is not an anomaly in social life. It is a part of ongoing social processes in all societies and groups and is both cause and consequence of other social processes and outcomes that we discuss in this section.

Social Properties of Deviance

Deviance is behavior that a considerable number of people in a society view as reprehensible and beyond the limits of tolerance. In most cases it both is negatively valued and provokes hostile reactions. Deviance does not exist independently of norms. Without norms, and without the application of norms in interpreting behavior, there is no deviance. That is, deviance is not a property inherent in certain forms of behavior (Erikson, 1962; Becker, 1963; Lemert, 1972); it is a property conferred upon particular behaviors by social definitions. In the course of their daily lives, people use the normative schemes available to them and make judgments regarding the desirability or undesirability of this or that behavior. They then translate their judgments into favorable or unfavorable consequences for those who engage in the behavior. In this sense, then, deviance is what people say it is.

The Relativity of Deviance.

Which acts are defined as deviant vary greatly from time to time, place to place, and group to group. For example, in many cultures homosexual behavior is considered to be deviant, and any sexual behavior involving juveniles is criminal. For the Etoro of New Guinea, homosexual acts between adult males and young boys are not just a part of everyday life, they are an essential part of the culture.

As reported by anthropologist Raymond Kelly in 1976, the Etoro believe that humans have a special life force they call the *hame*. According to Etoro culture, this vital energy in men can be diminished through witchcraft and also through sexual relations, because it is especially concentrated in semen. Depletion of the life force is accompanied by weakness and illness and is characterized by labored breathing, coughing, short-windedness, and chest pains, all referred to as *hame hah hah*. Each act of sexual intercourse a man engages in depletes his *hame* further, and heterosexual relations among the Etoro are completely prohibited for as many as 260 days per year, or more than 70 percent of the time. The Etoro believe that breaking these prohibitions has serious repercussions, including crop failure. Thus, heterosexual intercourse during the exclusionary period, even between marital partners, is seriously deviant and is severely punished.

Why, then, are homosexual relations essential in this culture? Is not the vital life force lost through loss of semen whether that loss is to a female or a male? Yes, but for the male receiving the semen, it is an essential gain. Boys lack semen—the most critical attribute of manhood to the Etoro—and the Etoro believe that semen must be "planted" in them. Young Etoro males are continually inseminated from age 10 until the early to midtwenties, according to Kelly. All the physical and emotional changes that occur during this time are regarded as the direct results of the oral insemination practiced by the Etoro. Because the *hame* of a youth is strengthened by insemination, there are no prohibitions about when or where such insemination can take place.

As norms vary from one society to the next and from one time to another, so too does deviance. A social audience, through the application of norms, decides whether or not some behavior is deviant. To the Etoro of New Guinea, sexual activity involving children is a normal part of everyday life. In the United States, it can cause an adult to be labeled a criminal.

The concepts that the Etoro use to think about sexuality and the moral system that governs sexual behavior are fundamentally different from the cultural principles that shape sexuality and behavior in our own society—so different, in fact, that some readers may find the example to be difficult to think about. Such reactions illustrate the point of the example: that deviance is relative, and such relativity often involves fundamental, even extreme, differences in how deviance is defined in different cultural systems.

Saying that deviance is relative and is a matter of social definition does not mean that "anything goes" or that morality has no importance. On the contrary, the relativity of deviance means simply that there are many moralities across societies and over time and that we cannot understand deviant behavior and the reactions to it without knowing the normative context in which they occur. As the description of homosexual and heterosexual behavior in Etoro society makes clear, using a traditional Western antihomosexual moral scheme to define deviance among the Etoro would reveal nothing about the processes of deviance and reaction that occur there.

The Power to Make Definitions Stick.

In 1776 the British labeled George Washington a traitor; 20 years later he was the first president of the United States and beloved as the father of his country.

This example illustrates the fact that who is defined as deviant and what is defined as deviance depend on who is doing the defining and who has the power to make the definitions stick. Individuals stigmatized and victimized by prevailing social definitions see their circumstances quite differently from those who enjoy power and enforce norms that embody their moral codes. In recent years, some groups, such as gays, lesbians, the disabled, and welfare mothers, have entered the political arena and have had some success in challenging official definitions that portray them as "social problems."

The Functions and Dysfunctions of Deviance.

Not all behavior has a purpose or a use. The same is doubtless true for many instances of deviance. Indeed, most of us think of deviance as "bad"— as behavior that poses a "social problem." Such a view is not surprising given the negative or disruptive consequences of much deviance, or what sociologists call *dysfunctions* (see Chapter 1). But deviance also has positive or integrative consequences for social life, what sociologists call *functions*.

The Dysfunctions of Deviance.   Social organization derives from the coordinated actions of numerous people. Should some individuals fail to perform their actions at the proper time in accordance with accepted expectations, institutional life may be jeopardized. For instance, the desertion of a family by a parent commonly complicates the task of child care and rearing. And when a squad of soldiers fails to obey orders and runs away in the midst of battle, an entire army may be overwhelmed and defeated. Apparently most societies can absorb a good deal of deviance without serious consequences, but persistent and widespread deviance can impair and even undermine organized social life.

Deviance also undermines our willingness to play our roles and contribute to the larger social enterprise. If some individuals get rewards, even disproportionate rewards, without playing by the rules, we develop resentment and bitterness. Morale, self-discipline, and loyalty suffer.

Moreover, our social life requires that we trust social institutions and one another. Trust makes conventional social life, from communities to economic exchange to families, possible. The most mundane, but essential, aspects of life would be impossible without trust. The use of checks and credit cards, for example, requires that we trust our banks to keep our money safe, to honor the checks that we write, and to charge our credit cards only as we have authorized. Normal community life is impossible where people cannot trust that those passing them on the street will not try to harm them. The maintenance of families and family life requires that people can trust others to live up to their obligations. Deviant behavior is dysfunctional because it can undermine this trust, threatening our most important social relationships and institutions.

The Functions of Deviance. Although deviance may undermine social organization, it also may facilitate social functioning in a number of ways. First, as sociologist Edward Sagarin (1975) has pointed out, reacting publicly to deviance can promote conformity. Such reactions create a community of the "good," those who know the cost of deviating and who can now define themselves as an *in-group* in contrast to the *out-group* of deviants.

Second, because norms are not always clear, each time the members of a group censure some act as deviance, they highlight and sharpen the contours of a norm (Stevenson, 1991; Durkheim, 1893/1964). Their negative reactions clarify precisely what behavior is disallowed by the "collective conscience."

Third, by directing attention to the deviant, a group may strengthen itself. A shared enemy arouses common sentiments and cements feelings of solidarity. The emotions surrounding "ain't it awful" deeds quicken passions and solidify "our kind of people" ties. For example, campaigns against witches, traitors, perverts, and criminals reinforce social cohesion among "the good people."

Fourth, deviance is a catalyst for change. Every time a rule is violated, it is being contested. Such challenges serve as a warning that the social system is not functioning properly. Deviance is often a vehicle for placing on a society's agenda the need for social repair and remedies.

Social Control and Deviance

If the work of the world is to get done, people must follow rules. Social order dictates that people have to be kept in line, at least most people, and that the line must be adhered to within allowable limits (Sagarin, 1975; Gibbs, 1989; Tyler, 1990; Liska, 1986). Without social order, interaction would be a real problem and expectations would be meaningless. Societies seek to ensure that their members conform with basic norms by means of **social control,** the methods and strategies that regulate behavior within society.

There are three main types of social control processes operating in social life: (1) those that lead us to internalize our society's normative expectations, (2) those that structure our world of social experience, and (3) those that employ various formal and informal social sanctions. Let us briefly consider each of these processes.

Internalization of Norms.

As we saw in Chapter 2, the members of a society undergo continuous *socialization,* a process by which individuals acquire those ways of thinking, feeling, and acting characteristic of their society's culture. For infants and young children, conformity to the expectations of others is primarily a product of external controls. As they grow older, an increasing proportion of their behavior becomes governed by internal monitors. These internal monitors carry on many of the functions earlier performed by external controls. **Internalization** is the process by which individuals incorporate within their personalities the standards of behavior prevalent within the larger society.

Critical steps to social control through internalization are (1) learning what the norms are and (2) learning to believe that the norms are legitimate. In addition, through the process of internalization, norms become part of people's personalities, as discussed in Chapter 2 with the internalization of the "generalized other." Such standards are often accepted without thought or questioning—indeed, we commonly experience them as "second nature." The group is our group, and its norms are our norms. Social control thus becomes self-control.

The Structure of Social Experience.

Our society's institutions also shape our experiences. In large part, we unconsciously build up our sense of reality by the way our society orders its social agendas and structures social alternatives. If we are locked within the social environment provided by our culture, we inhabit a somewhat restricted world and it may not occur to us that alternative standards exist. A song popular during World War I questioned what might happen if this form of social control failed: "How ya gonna keep 'em down on the farm after they've seen Paree?" That is, how would the American soldiers be able to resume their conformist rural life after experiencing the wild city life available in Paris, France, in 1917 and 1918, with nightclubs, dancing girls, and prostitutes in abundance? Without experiences that take us out of the patterned routines dictated by the institutions that make up our society, we are *culture-bound.* Many

SPEED BUMP   Dave Coverly

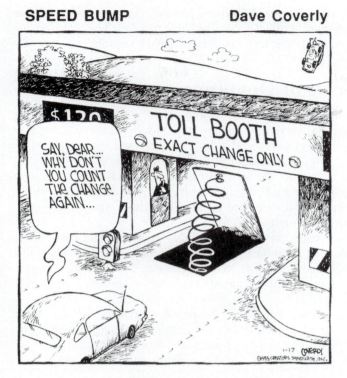

Our adherence to norms often depends on what we perceive the rewards or penalties to be.

By permission of Dave Coverly and Creators Syndicate, Inc.

nonconformist patterns do not occur to us because they are not known to our society.

Formal and Informal Sanctions.

Finally, we conform to the norms of our society because we realize that to do otherwise is to incur punishment. Those who break rules are met with dislike, hostility, gossip, ridicule, and ostracism—even imprisonment and death—while the conformist wins praise, popularity, prestige, and other socially defined good things. Clearly there are disadvantages to nonconformity and advantages to conformity.

Formal sanctions are reactions of official agents of social control, such as the courts, the honor systems that control cheating, and the principal's office in the high school. Students who are caught cheating, for example, may be formally sanctioned by being expelled from school. *Informal sanctions* are reactions to deviance that occur in small communities, in groups of friends, and in the family. Students who report cheating by their friends may be deviant from the point of view of their friendship group, and may be informally sanctioned by being ostracized. Informal sanctions generally are more effective than formal sanctions, particularly if they are part of the interaction in the primary groups to which people are strongly committed.

Theories of Deviance

Deviance may have both positive and negative consequences for the functioning and survival of groups and societies. But why, we may ask, do people violate social rules? Why are some acts defined as deviance? Why are some individuals labeled deviants when they engage in essentially the same behaviors as other individuals who escape retribution? And why does the incidence of deviance vary from group to group and society to society? It is these types of questions that interest sociologists.

In this section, we depart from our usual consideration of the functionalist, interactionist, and conflict perspectives to discuss five specific theories of deviance that have emerged from these perspectives: the anomie, cultural transmission, conflict, labeling, and control theories. As you will see, each theory of deviance has a connection to the basic reasoning in the three theoretical perspectives we use in this book. Anomie and control grew out of *functionalism,* cultural transmission and labeling emerged from *symbolic interactionism,* and conflict theory is the application of the *conflict perspective* to deviance.

Anomie Theory

As we noted earlier in the chapter, Émile Durkheim (1893/1964, 1897/1951) contended that deviance can be functional for a society. But he also realized that deviance is simultaneously dysfunctional and made another contribution to our understanding of deviance with his idea of **anomie**—a social condition in which people find it difficult to guide their behavior by norms that they experience as weak, unclear, or conflicting. As Durkheim pointed out, anomie is a common occurrence when people's expectations about rewards and gratifications are not closely matched by what they actually receive. In a gold rush, for example, many people believe that they can become wealthy overnight. The norms that bind people to their conventional lives become weak, and as a result, some people abandon their families and jobs, travel long distances in search of riches, and set up nontraditional communities that promote crime, violence, prostitution, and general disorder. Similarly, when an economy collapses and few jobs are available, the rewards that people are used to receiving are no longer available, the norms that have governed people's work and family lives weaken, and deviance, including crime and delinquency, increases.

Merton's Theory of Structural Strain.   Robert K. Merton's theory of structural strain is an adaptation of Durkheim's anomie theory

that emerged from the *functionalist* perspective (Liska and Messner, 1999). Merton (1968) built on Durkheim's ideas and linked them to American life. He said that for large numbers of Americans, worldly success—especially as it finds expression in material *wealth*—has become a cultural goal. However, only certain *means*—most commonly securing a good education and acquiring high-paying jobs—are the institutionalized and approved ways to achieve success. There might not be a problem if all Americans had equal access to these institutionalized means for realizing monetary success, but this is not the case. The poor and minorities often find themselves handicapped by little formal education and few economic resources.

Americans who internalize the goal of material success but who do not have access to the institutionalized means are pushed by strong social structural strains toward the use of unconventional means. They cannot achieve the culturally approved goals by using the institutionalized means for attaining them. One solution to this dilemma is to obtain the prestige-laden ends by any means whatsoever, including vice and crime.

Merton emphasized that a "lack of opportunity" and an exaggerated material emphasis are not enough to produce strains toward deviance. A society with a comparatively rigid class or caste structure may lack opportunity and simultaneously extol wealth—the medieval feudal system serves as a case in point. Only when a society extols common symbols of success for the entire population, while structurally restricting the access of large numbers of people to the approved means for acquiring these symbols, is antisocial behavior generated.

Merton identifies five responses to the ends-means dilemma, four of them deviant adaptations to conditions of anomie (see Figure 4.1).

Conformity.   Conformity will be common in a society in which people accept the cultural goal of material success and the institutionalized means to achieve this goal are available. Such behavior is the bedrock of a stable and properly functioning society.

Innovation.   In innovation, individuals hold fast to the culturally emphasized goals of success, but because the institutionalized means to achieve the goals are not available, they pursue their goals in innovative ways. Such people may engage in prostitution, peddle drugs, forge checks, swindle, embezzle, steal, burglarize, rob, or extort to secure money and purchase the symbols of success.

Ritualism.   Ritualism involves losing touch with success goals while abiding compulsively by the institutionalized means. For instance, the ends of the organization become irrelevant for many zealous bureaucrats. Instead, they cultivate the means for their own sake, making a fetish of regulations and red tape (see Chapter 3).

Retreatism.   In retreatism individuals reject both the cultural goals and the institutionalized means without substituting new norms. For

Modes of Adaptation	Cultural Goals	Institutionalized Means
I Conformity	+	+
II Innovation	+	−
III Ritualism	−	+
IV Retreatism	−	−
V Rebellion	±	±

+ = Acceptance

− = Rejection

± = Rejection of prevailing values and substitution of new values

Figure 4.1   Merton's Typology of Modes of Individual Adaptation to Anomie

Source: Adapted with the permission of The Free Press, a Division of Simon & Schuster, from *Social Theory and Social Structure* by Robert K. Merton. Copyright © 1949, 1957 by The Free Press; copyright renewed 1977, 1985 by Robert K. Merton.

example, skid row alcoholics, drug addicts, vagabonds, and derelicts have dropped out of society; they "are in society but not of it."

Rebellion.   Rebels reject both the cultural goals and the institutionalized means and substitute new norms for them. Such individuals withdraw their allegiance from existing social arrangements and transfer their loyalties to new groups with new ideologies. Radical social movements on the right and left, such as the militia movement and radical socialism, are good illustrations of this type of adaptation.

Sociologists have applied structural strain theory to a variety of problems. In a classic study, Albert Cohen (1955) found that lower-class boys often find themselves failing in middle-class school environments that reward verbal skills, neatness, and an ability to defer gratification. The boys respond by banding together in juvenile gangs where they evolve "macho" standards that reward "toughness," "street smarts," and "troublemaking"—standards that allow them to succeed. Sociologists Steven Messner and Richard Rosenfeld (1997a, 1997b) extended Merton's structural strain theory. They argue that the strain toward deviance, particularly crime, is stronger when the economy is the dominant institution in society and when social status is primarily dependent on performance in economic roles. Crime rates are particularly high in societies where people are completely dependent on the labor market for resources necessary for survival; on the other hand, societies that guarantee an acceptable level of income regardless of participation in the labor market have less crime.

Cultural Transmission Theory

A number of sociologists have emphasized the similarities between the way deviant behavior is acquired and the way in which other behavior is acquired (Schwendinger and Schwendinger, 1985). One of the first was French sociologist Gabriel Tarde (1843–1904), who in the late 19th century formulated a theory of imitation to explain deviance. Tarde was impressed by the importance of imitation in human behavior. He argued that criminals, like "good" people, imitate the ways of individuals they have met, known, or heard about. In contrast to law-abiding people, however, they imitate other criminals.

During the 1920s and 1930s, sociologists at the University of Chicago were struck by the concentration of high delinquency rates in some areas of Chicago (Thrasher, 1927; Shaw, 1930; Shaw and McKay, 1942; Sampson and Groves, 1989). In a series of investigations, they found that neighborhood delinquency rates remained much the same over time despite the changing composition of the neighborhoods (Shoemaker, 2000). They concluded that delinquent and criminal behaviors are in part a product of economic conditions, but are also culturally transmitted from one generation of juveniles to the next. As new ethnic groups enter a neighborhood, their children learn the delinquent patterns from the youth already there. Hence, the Chicago sociologists contended that youths become delinquent because they associate and make friends with other juveniles who are already delinquent.

Sutherland's Theory of Differential Association.   A classic statement of the cultural transmission of deviance is Edwin H. Sutherland's **differential association** theory. Sutherland (1939) argued that individuals learn deviance primarily in intimate groups of deviant others, such as small groups of friends. People learn not only how to be deviant—for example, how to mug people, how to smoke marijuana, and how to apply graffiti—but also they learn attitudes favorable to deviance. Of course, people who are involved in deviant groups are also usually involved in more conventional relationships in their families, at school, at work, in church, and in other settings. Sutherland argued that if the definitions favorable to deviance outweigh the definitions unfavorable to deviance learned in other situations, deviance is likely to occur.

The differential association theory provides a sophisticated version of the old adage that "good companions make good children; bad companions make bad children." By the same token, the theory suggests that imprisonment may be counterproductive when juveniles are incarcerated with experienced criminals.

Recent studies of differential association have provided strong support for the theory (Matsueda, 1988; Shoemaker, 2000). Sociologist James Orcutt (1987), for example, found that having marijuana-smoking friends and favorable attitudes about marijuana are strong predictors of marijuana smoking. However, just as Sutherland's theory suggests, favorable attitudes lead to marijuana smoking only when they are stronger than unfavorable attitudes. Haynie's (2001) study showed that the impact of friends' delinquency on one's own delinquency is much greater when one is popular and central to the group and where the density of ties among friends is high.

Conflict Theory

Conflict theorists argue that the most important question about deviance and social control is, "Which group will be able to translate its values into the rules of a society and make these rules stick?"

Although in recent decades the conflict approach has taken many new directions (Hagan, 1989; Messner and Krohn, 1990; Grant and Martinez, 1997), its early roots can be traced to the Marxist tradition and the conflict perspective that grew out of it (see Chapter 1). According to orthodox Marxism, a capitalist ruling class exploits and robs the masses, yet avoids punishment for its crimes. Individuals victimized by capitalist oppression are driven by their struggle to survive to commit acts that the ruling class brands as criminal (Bonger, 1936; Liska and Messner, 1999). Marxists regard other types of deviance—alcoholism, drug abuse, mental illness, family violence, sexual immorality, and prostitution—as products of the moral degeneration and estrangement fostered by the oppression and exploitation of the poor, women, and African Americans or other minorities.

Quinney's Theory of Class, State, and Crime.   Because Marx wrote little about crime, it fell to a 20th-century U.S. sociologist, Richard Quinney (1974, 1980), to write a now-classic statement of the conflict theory of crime. Quinney said that the U.S. legal system reflects the interests and ideologies of the ruling capitalist class. Law makes illegal certain behavior that is offensive to the morality of the powerful and that threatens their privileges and property. Quinney (1980:39) contended that if we are "to understand crime we have to understand the development of the political economy of capitalist society." Since the state serves the interests of the capitalist class, crime is ultimately a class-based political act embedded in capitalist social arrangements.

In striving to maintain itself against the internal contradictions eating away at its foundations, capitalism commits *crimes of domination* (Quinney, 1980:57). Indeed, "one of the contradictions of capitalism is that some of its laws must be violated in order to secure the existing system." These crimes include those committed by corporations and range from price fixing to pollution of the environment. But there are also *crimes of government* committed by the officials of the capitalist state, Watergate being a well-publicized instance. In contrast, much of the criminal behavior of ordinary people, or *predatory crime*—burglary, robbery, drug dealing, and hustling of various sorts— is "pursued out of the need to survive" in a capitalist social order. *Personal crime*—murder, assault, and rape—is "pursued by those who are already brutalized by the conditions of capitalism." And then there are *crimes of resistance* in which workers engage in sloppy work and clandestine acts of sabotage against employers.

Conflict theory has led social scientists to investigate the ways in which the making and administration of law are biased by powerful interests (Jacobs and Helms, 1996, 1997). Numerous sociologists have noted that crime is defined primarily in terms of offenses against property (burglary, robbery, auto theft, and vandalism), whereas corporate crime is deemphasized (Sutherland, 1949; Coleman, 1987). Moreover, the penalty for crimes against property is imprisonment, whereas the most common form of penalty for business-related offenses is a monetary fine. In the most comprehensive study of its kind, Clinard and Yeager (1980) found that over a two-year period, the federal government charged nearly two-thirds of the Fortune 500 corporations (the 500 largest U.S. corporations) with violations of the law. Estimates of the yearly cost of such crimes run as high as $200 billion, compared with $3 to $4 billion a year for conventional street crimes (Clinard and Meier, 1995). This basic problem appears not to have improved over time (Clinard, 1990). In 1994, for example, at the end of a seven-year investigation, the 10 largest defense contractors serving the U.S. government were fined more than $250 million for engaging in fraud, and 54 corporate employees involved were convicted of crimes (Clinard and Meier, 1995). And while the Federal Bureau of Investigation (FBI) keeps track of every murder, rape, assault, and auto theft reported in the United States, no agency keeps a record of crimes committed by corporations themselves.

Labeling Theory

Labeling theorists are interested in the process by which some individuals come to be tagged as "deviants," begin to think of themselves as deviants, and enter deviant careers.

Edwin Lemert, Howard S. Becker, and Kai T. Erikson: The Social Reaction to Deviance Approach.   The three sociologists responsible for making the classic statements of labeling theory— Edwin M. Lemert (1951, 1972), Howard S. Becker (1963), and Kai T. Erikson (1962, 1966)—make a number of points. First, they contend that no act by itself is inherently criminal or noncriminal, deviant or not deviant. The "badness" of an act does not stem from its intrinsic content but from the way other people define and react to it. Deviance

is always a matter of social definition. Similarly, according to labeling theory, a person who engages in deviant behavior is deviant only if he or she has been so labeled.

Second, labeling theorists point out that we all engage in deviant behavior by violating some norms. They reject the popular idea that human beings can be divided into those who are normal and those who are pathological. For example, some of us exceed the speed limit, experiment with cocaine, shoplift, cheat on a homework assignment, sample homosexual publications, underreport our income to income tax authorities, swim in the nude, become intoxicated, commit vandalism in celebration of a football victory, or trespass on private property. Labeling theorists call these actions **primary deviance**—behavior that violates social norms but usually goes unnoticed by the agents of social control.

Third, labeling theorists say that whether people's acts will be seen as deviant depends both on what they do and on what other people do about it. In short, deviance depends on which rules society chooses to enforce, in which situations, and with respect to which people. Not all individuals are arrested for speeding, shoplifting, underreporting income on their tax returns, trespassing, or the like. African Americans may be censured for doing what whites are "allowed" to do, women censured for doing what men are "allowed" to do, certain individuals censured for doing what their friends are also doing, and some may be labeled as deviants even though they have not violated a norm but simply because they are so accused (e.g., they appear "effeminate" and are tagged as "gay"). Of critical importance is the social audience and whether or not it labels the person a deviant.

Fourth, labeling people as deviants has consequences for them. It tends to set up conditions conducive to **secondary deviance**—deviance individuals adopt in response to the reactions of other individuals. In brief, labeling theorists contend that new deviance is manufactured by the hostile reactions of rule makers and rule abiders. An individual is publicly identified, stereotyped, and denounced as a "delinquent," "mental fruitcake," "forger," "rapist," "drug addict," "bum," "pervert," or "criminal." The label serves to lock the individual into an outsider status. Such a master status overrides other statuses in shaping a person's social experiences and results in a self-fulfilling prophecy. Rule breakers come to accept their status as a particular kind of deviant and organize their lives around this master status. Rejection and isolation may push a stigmatized individual toward a deviant group that solidifies a deviant self-image, fosters a deviant lifestyle, and weakens ties to the law-abiding community.

Unlike structural strain and cultural transmission theory, labeling theory does not focus on why some individuals engage in deviant behavior. Rather, labeling theory helps us to understand why the same act may or may not be considered deviant, depending on the situation and the characteristics of the individuals who are involved.

Sociologist William J. Chambliss (1973) employed labeling theory to explain the differing perceptions and definitions that community members had of the behavior of two teenage gangs. At Hanibal High School, Chambliss observed the activities of the Saints, a gang of eight white upper-class boys, and the Roughnecks, a gang of six lower-class white boys. Although the Saints engaged in as many delinquent acts as the Roughnecks, it was the Roughnecks who were in "constant trouble" and universally considered to be "delinquent." The community, the school, and the police related to the Saints as though they were good, upstanding youths with bright futures, but they treated the Roughnecks as young punks headed for trouble.

A number of factors contributed to the differential treatment given the two groups. For one thing, the Saints had access to automobiles and engaged in out-of-town escapades that were less visible to Hanibal citizens than those undertaken by the Roughnecks in the center of town. For another, when the Saints were confronted with an accusing police officer, they were apologetic and penitent, whereas the Roughnecks were hostile and belligerent. Finally, police officers knew that irate and influential upper-middle-class parents would come to the aid of their youngsters, whereas powerless lower-class parents would have to acquiesce in the law's definition of their son's behavior.

Chambliss (1973) concluded that when the community responded to the Roughnecks as boys in trouble, the boys' pattern of deviancy was reinforced. As their self-conception as deviants became more firmly entrenched, they began to try new and more extreme acts of deviance. Their growing alienation led to greater disrespect and hostility, which increased the community's negative attitude toward them.

Control Theory

The theories discussed above are all attempts to explain why people deviate. Control theory turns the question around and asks why people *do not* deviate (Reckless, 1961, 1967; Hirschi, 1969; Shoemaker, 2000). Though we are frequently concerned that there is too much deviance in our society, what is truly remarkable is how much conformity there is. As you walk to and attend class each day, your behavior and that of others around you almost always fits within a narrow and predictable pattern. Most of us conform most of the time; even "deviants" conform most of the time. Such rigid control is particularly remarkable given that the possibilities for human behavior are virtually infinite, limited only by physical laws and people's imaginations.

Control theory's answer to why people conform is an outgrowth of *functionalist* ideas. People conform because they are integrated into mainstream institutions. Societies that have properly functioning institutions will have low deviance.

Travis Hirschi and the Elements of the Social Bond.

Travis Hirschi's study (1969) of juvenile delinquency in Richmond, California, provided a classic statement of control theory. Hirschi's argument is that young people are more likely to conform if their bond to society is strong. This bond has four parts: attachment, involvement, commitment, and belief.

Attachment is the process of being involved in social relationships with others. All social relationships entail some degree of control for all participants. Control is more likely where the psychological and emotional connections among group members are high and members care about one another's opinions (Shoemaker, 2000). Being involved in a family, having friends in the community, and being a member of a club are all examples of attachments that reduce the chance that deviance will occur.

By *involvement*, Hirschi meant involvement in conventional activities. One way to keep people from being deviant is to get them to spend their time conforming. Boy Scouts, Girl Scouts, youth fellowship, band, and athletics are only a few of the myriad activities that parents, schools, religious organizations, and neighborhood associations create to take up the leisure time of children and adolescents. A main purpose of these activities is to provide an alternative to drug and alcohol use, sexual activity, vandalism, and crime.

Commitment refers to the strength of the investment people have made in conventional social ties and relationships. People who have strong commitments in their social lives are not likely to deviate because of the losses they may incur if they are identified as deviant. A student who aspires to become a police officer and who has earned the trust and respect of teachers, school administrators, and local law enforcement officials is unlikely to become a drug dealer; she would risk losing the benefits of the investments she has made in pursuit of her career.

Finally, the bond to society is cemented by *belief* in conventional values and ideas about morality. The less people believe in the conventional values of society, the more likely it is that deviance will occur. If young people do not believe in the conventional idea that having a job or running a legitimate business is the acceptable way to make money, they are more likely to attempt to get money in criminal ways.

Because the essence of control theory is that people will be less likely to deviate if they are integrated into mainstream institutions, much research on control theory has focused on the controlling power of three primary social institutions: religion, the family, and education (Shoemaker, 2000).

Somewhat surprisingly, a number of studies have found that religion seems to have little or no impact on deviant behavior (Jensen and Rojek, 1992; Hirschi and Stark, 1969). The reason is not that religion is ineffective in social control, but that religion is only one of a number of social institutions involved in controlling behavior and therefore it is hard to see its impact. It is easier to see the controlling effect of religion where there is low consensus about the deviant nature of acts; nearly everyone agrees that murder is wrong, but fewer people would argue strongly that smoking marijuana is wrong. Religion does control deviant behavior, and its effect is clearly seen where competing secular controls are weak (Tittle and Welch, 1983; Burkett and White, 1974).

Most studies of the family and deviant behavior have been concerned with young people. These studies have shown that intact families and good family relations decrease the chances of delinquent behavior among youths (Shoemaker, 2000). However, the effect of intact families is relatively weak and has not been found in all studies. The more important factor is not family structure (broken versus intact), but the way parents communicate and get along with their children (Yablonsky and Haskell, 1988; Cernkovich and Giordano, 1987).

Involvement in schooling controls deviant behavior not only because it takes up people's time in conventional pursuits, but also because it promotes conventional attachments, commitment, and beliefs. Hirschi (1969) found that attachment to school and having positive relationships with teachers reduced the chance of delinquency. More recent studies continue to find a positive influence in schools. Cernkovich and Giordano (1992) found that attachment and commitment to school reduced delinquency, although this effect was somewhat less among black males. Zingraff's 1994 study showed that schooling is an important deterrent to delinquency even when family relations are poor or abusive. And Crutchfield and Pitchford (1997) showed that among people 18 years and over, being a student reduces the likelihood of criminal involvement.

Crime and the Criminal Justice System

Within modern societies, law is a crucial element in social control. Unlike informal norms such as folkways and mores, laws are rules enforced by the state. As we defined it at the beginning of the chapter, *deviance* is behavior that a considerable number of people view as reprehensible and beyond the limits of tolerance. **Crime** is an act of deviance that is prohibited by law. As we have seen, not all deviant acts are crimes; they may break rules defined only by folkways and mores. As with other forms of deviance, there is nothing inherent in an act that makes it criminal. For an act to be considered criminal, the state must undertake a political process of illegalizing—or *criminalizing*—it. Because anything can be a crime if a law is established making it illegal, an infinite variety of acts can be crimes.

What crimes have in common is not that they are necessarily acts we regard as immoral or wicked. For example, many Americans consider it no more "evil" to cheat on their income taxes than did their parents or grandparents to purchase and consume illegal alcoholic beverages during Prohibition. Rather, the distinguishing property of crime is that people who violate the law are liable to be arrested, tried, pronounced guilty, and deprived of their lives, liberty, or property. In brief, they are likely to become caught up in the elaborate social machinery of the **criminal justice system**—the reactive agencies of the state that include the police, the courts, and prisons. So common are "scrapes with the law" that U.S. men have nearly a 50 percent chance of being arrested at least once in their lives (Uggen, 2000).

Forms of Crime

In this section we consider a number of forms of crime within the United States.

Violent and Property Crime.

The Federal Bureau of Investigation annually reports on eight types of crime in its Uniform Crime Reports. These offenses are called **index crimes** and consist of four categories of violent crime against people—murder, rape, robbery, and assault—and four categories of crimes against property—burglary, theft, motor vehicle theft, and arson. Index crimes are declining in the United States, with property crimes dropping steadily since 1974 and violent crime since 1994 (Rennison, 2002a) (see Figure 4.2).

In spite of this reduction, there is still a large amount of crime in the United States. In 2000 there were 15,517 murders in the United States. The rate of murder and manslaughter combined was 5.5 per 100,000 people. The total number of criminal victimizations—both property and violent crimes—in 2001 was 24.2 million. Crime victimization rates also show that victims of violent crime are likely to be male, poor, urban, young, and black or Hispanic.

Decreases in violent crime during the 1990s represent a greater decline than at any time since World War II and resulted in many headlines and discussions on television talk shows. While significant, the rates of decline during the 1990s were not as great as the rates of increase experienced during the 1960s and early 1970s (LaFree, 1999). What accounts for the drop in violent and property crime over recent decades? Pinpointing the causes of crime trends ("booms" and "busts") is difficult because the kinds of data necessary to draw such conclusions have not been collected over a long enough time period. But various explanations have been suggested. Some authors believe that changes in drug subcultures are linked to changes in violent crime rates, with the cocaine/crack subculture of the 1980s responsible for more crime than the marijuana subculture of the 1990s. Others associate the crime rate decreases with higher rates of incarceration, more

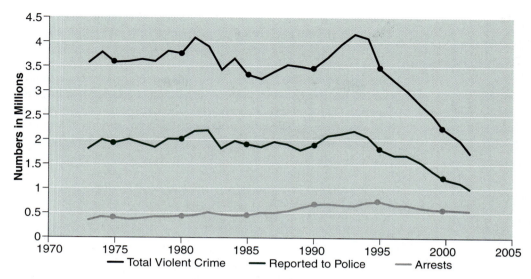

Figure 4.2   Numbers of Violent Crimes, Violent Crimes Reported to Police, and Arrests for Violent Crimes in the U.S., 1973–2001

The crime rate has been declining since the early 1990s and in 2001 was the lowest recorded since 1973.

Source: Bureau of Justice Statistics (http://www.ojp.usdoj.gov/bjs/glance/cv2.htm).

effective gun policies, changes in policing (Bartollas, 2003), a stronger economy, and growing family stability (LaFree, 1999).

Juvenile Crime.   We have seen that young people are more likely to be victims of crime. They also are more likely than older people to commit crime. Though persons 13 to 18 years of age represent only 8.5 percent of the population, they constitute 20.5 percent of those arrested for committing crimes (Pastore and Maguire, 2003). The peak age for property crime is 16 to 18 and for violent crime it is 18 to 19 (Pastore and Maguire, 2003). Juvenile involvement in violent crime has increased over the past several decades (Bartollas, 2003). The percentage of people arrested for committing crimes drops steadily with increasing age. If we could prevent all crimes committed by persons under 25 years of age, much of conventional crime would be eliminated from society, though we would still have many white-collar, corporate, and government crimes and about half the homicides. With an ever-increasing number of young people in the country, however, many of whom are at high risk for delinquent behavior, some analysts predict a violent juvenile crime wave (Bartollas, 2003).

   It is clear that the present system of juvenile justice has encountered substantial failures either in deterring violent crime by the young or in rehabilitating young criminals. Critics point to statistics by some researchers showing that about 7 percent of young offenders are responsible for up to three-quarters of the violent crimes committed by juveniles (Tracy, Wolfgang, and Figlio, 1990).

Organized Crime.

Organized crime refers to large-scale bureaucratic organizations that provide illegal goods and services in public demand. Such crime is likely to arise where the state criminalizes certain activities—prostitution, drugs, pornography, gambling, and loan-sharking—that large numbers of citizens desire and for which they are willing to pay. Drug and arms trafficking by major crime organizations is the largest business in the world, bringing in between $700 billion and $1 trillion a year (Adler, Mueller, and Laufer, 2004).

The most publicized crime organization has been an Italian-American syndicate, variously termed the Mafia or Cosa Nostra, which gained a substantial impetus from Prohibition. The Mafia seems to be a loose network or confederation of regional syndicates coordinated by a "commission" composed of the heads of the most powerful crime "families" (Adler, Mueller, and Laufer, 2004; Tittle and Paternoster, 2000). Organized crime is hardly an Italian monopoly, however. Chinese gangs, Colombian and Cuban drug rings, and groups of southern white moonshiners also fall under the category of organized crime. Although we may associate organized crime with various immigrant groups, it is not the case that immigration is tied to higher crime. For example, Hispanic immigrants are less involved in crime than are U.S. citizens (Hagan and Palloni, 1999).

White-Collar and Corporate Crime.

One type of crime that has been of particular interest to sociologists is **white-collar crime**—crime most commonly committed by relatively affluent persons, often in the course of business activities (Sutherland, 1949). Martha Stewart and the Enron scandal are well-known examples of white-collar crime in the news. Included in white-collar crime are corporate crime, fraud, embezzlement, corruption, bribery, tax fraud or evasion, stock manipulation, insider trading, misrepresentation of advertising, restraint of trade, and infringement of patents. More recent research has focused on workplace misconduct at a different level, including such things as drinking or doing drugs on the job, short-changing customers, damaging or stealing employers' property, and falsifying time records (Wright and Cullen, 2000).

White-collar crime costs society just as other crimes do, and we are more likely to be victims of corporate crime than of street crime (Simon and Eitzen, 1993). In 1999, the U.S. Department of Justice had nearly 9,000 cases of financial institution fraud and failure pending (Pastore and Maguire, 2003). Tax evasion is the most costly white-collar crime in the United States. Fraud, the second-most costly white-collar crime, costs citizens $300 per household in higher insurance premiums (Soupiset, 2003). And *shrinkage,* a term used by retailers to encompass theft by employees, shoplifting, and clerical errors, cost $33.2 billion in 2001 (Pressler, 2003).

Corporations have been implicated in a variety of crimes, including overcharging the government on contracts, polluting the environment, shortchanging consumers, violating employee privacy, price-rigging school milk contracts, disposing of hazardous waste in violation of the law, adulterating fruit juice, and engaging in accounting irregularities (Clinard, 1990; Rothchild, 1993).

The small number of white-collar criminals who are prosecuted and convicted are rarely given sentences comparable to those of other criminals. Street criminals who steal $100 may find their way to prison, while an executive who embezzles $1 million may receive a suspended sentence and a relatively small fine.

Crime Committed by Government.

Conflict theorists have drawn our attention to crime committed by governments (Barak, 1991). Nazi Germany provides an extreme example: More than 6 million Jews were murdered during the Holocaust of the Hitler years (Dawidowicz, 1975). More recently, other governments have participated in "ethnic cleansing" and murdered citizens who were the "wrong" religion or ethnic background. The U.S. government massacred countless Native Americans during the colonization of the country; even as late as 1890, U.S. Army forces armed with machine guns mowed down nearly 300 Sioux at Wounded Knee, South Dakota (Brown, 1971).

But there are other sorts of government crimes. At the federal level, the Iran-contra scandal during President Reagan's term showed that operatives of the nation's security organizations engaged in secret arms shipments to the Nicaraguan contra rebels during the years that Congress barred aid to them. The Oval Office tapes of the Richard Nixon White House revealed a president bent on victimizing his enemies by using his presidential powers illegally. The accusations of perjury against President Clinton with regard to his testimony about a relationship with White House intern Monica Lewinski consumed much of his second term in office. Today's students have grown up with at least one well-publicized scandal for every presidential administration.

As with white-collar and corporate crime, those involved in government crime are less likely than "street criminals" to be caught and punished despite the fact that their crimes may cost us more.

Victimless Crime.

Usually a crime has an identifiable victim who suffers as a result of another person's criminal behavior. A **victimless crime** is an offense in which no one involved is considered a victim (Schur, 1965). These crimes include gambling, the sale and use of illicit drugs, and prohibited sexual activities between consenting adults (e.g., prostitution and, in some states, fornication and homosexuality). In victimless crime, if there is any suffering, it is by the offenders themselves, by "innocent bystanders" (as in the case of experiencing the odors associated with public urination), or by the tax-paying public at large.

The behaviors in question in victimless crime are criminalized because society, or powerful groups within a society, defines them as immoral or in some other way a threat to society.

As we have pointed out, crime is an act of deviance that is prohibited by law. Laws prohibiting victimless offenses, thereby, create crime and cost society money by way of the efforts to arrest and process suspects. When such laws are struck down, the act is decriminalized, as in the 2003 Supreme Court decision overturning Texas's ban on private consensual sex between same-sex adults (Lane, 2003).

Measuring Crime

How do we know how many crimes are committed in the United States? Statistics on crime are among the most unsatisfactory of all social data (Biderman and Lynch, 1991). Official crime records suffer from numerous limitations (Tittle and Paternoster, 2000). First, a large proportion of the crimes that are committed go undetected; others are detected but not reported; and still others are reported but not officially recorded when police officers and politicians manipulate their reports to show low crime rates for political purposes. Second, perceptions of crime vary from community to community; what is viewed as a serious crime by a citizen of a small town may be shrugged off by a big-city resident as an unpleasant bit of everyday life.

Two main data sources are used by researchers who study violent crime trends: the Uniform Crime Reports (UCR), collated by the FBI, and the National Crime Victimization Survey (NCVS), collected by the Bureau of Justice Statistics (LaFree, 1999; Klaus, 2002). The rates of various crimes in the United States are substantially higher according to the NCVS than the UCR, which are based on reports to police. Justice Department studies reveal that less than half of all crimes are reported to the police.

Self-report-based measures of crime, involving anonymous questionnaires that ask people which offenses they have committed, also reveal much higher rates of crime than those found in official crime statistics. For instance, studies of juvenile crimes show that many youngsters of all social classes break some criminal laws, and that the amount of unreported crime is enormous (Regoli and Hewitt, 2000; Tittle and Paternoster, 2000).

The Uniform Crime Reports focus on crimes that are most likely to be committed by young people and individuals from lower socioeconomic backgrounds. Statistics on many categories of crime, such as white-collar, government, and organized crime, are not routinely compiled. Additionally, some cases of criminal offenses, such as income tax evasion and fraud, are unlikely to be reported in victimization studies.

Women and Crime

Women accounted for 22 percent of all arrests in 2000 (Pastore and Maguire, 2003), a proportion that reflects the 1990s trend of an increasing percentage of females in the criminal population (Steffensmeier and Allan, 1996). In the 2000 arrest rate data, women accounted for 17 percent of violent crime arrests and 30 percent of property crime arrests (Pastore and Maguire, 2003). In some crimes, women outnumber men as perpetrators; 59 percent of those arrested as runaways are female, and 62 percent of prostitution arrests are women. Arrest rates are about equal for women and men in embezzlement; other crimes in which women are arrested at high rates are fraud (45 percent), forgery and counterfeiting (39 percent), and larceny and theft (36 percent). Women's participation in violent crime is much lower than men's, and in 2001 only 51 of the 3,581 prisoners on death row were female (Snell and Maruschak, 2002).

The participation of females in juvenile delinquency is higher than the proportion of adult female criminals; one-quarter of the youths arrested in the United States are females. Girls are typically arrested for less serious offenses than boys; half of all girls arrested are charged with either larceny-theft (often shoplifting) or with running away from home (Chesney-Lind and Shelden, 1998). Studies show that females seem to perceive legal sanctions as more threatening than do males (Blackwell, 2000).

Gender also plays a part in crime victimization. Whereas males are more likely to be victims of robbery, total assault, and aggravated assault, females are more likely to be victims of rape and sexual assault (Rennison, 2002a). Female victims account for 89 percent of sexual assaults, 91 percent of attempted rapes, and 94 percent of completed rapes (Rennison, 2002b). However, only about a third of rapes and sexual assaults are reported to the police, and thus there is a very low conviction rate for perpetrators. Although rates of violent victimization have been declining in recent years, they have not been declining for women as fast as for men (Rennison, 2002a).

The Criminal Justice System

On television, the evildoer nearly always gets caught and punished. In real life, however, the picture is quite different. According to statistics from the Justice Department, of every 100 criminal victimizations

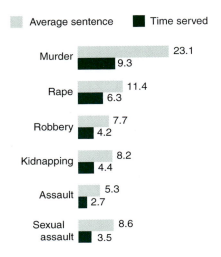

(a) Sentences versus Time Served, 2000

Average years *sentenced* to prison and average years *actually served* by state prison inmates for various convictions

Average sentence   Time served

Murder   23.1 / 9.3

Rape   11.4 / 6.3

Robbery   7.7 / 4.2

Kidnapping   8.2 / 4.4

Assault   5.3 / 2.7

Sexual assault   8.6 / 3.5

(b) Time from Arrest to Sentencing in State Courts, 1998

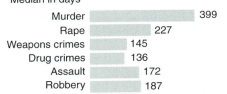

Median in days

Murder	399
Rape	227
Weapons crimes	145
Drug crimes	136
Assault	172
Robbery	187

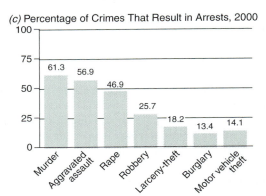

(c) Percentage of Crimes That Result in Arrests, 2000

Murder 61.3, Aggravated assault 56.9, Rape 46.9, Robbery 25.7, Larceny-theft 18.2, Burglary 13.4, Motor vehicle theft 14.1

Figure 4.3   The Operation of the Criminal Justice System in the United States

Sources: (a) Bureau of Justice Statistics (http://www.ojp.usdoj.gov/bjs/prisons.htm; (b) and (c) Pastore and Maguire, 2003.

committed in the United States, only 36 are reported to the police. Of these 36, only 7 or 8 are cleared by arrest, meaning that someone is arrested for the crime. Of these 7 persons arrested, only 5 are prosecuted and convicted. Of these, only 1 is sent to prison; the other cases are rejected or dismissed because of problems with the evidence or witnesses, or the perpetrators are diverted into treatment programs. Of those convicted in state courts, more than half receive a sentence of at least 3.5 years, but the average inmate is released in about 1.5 years (see Figure 4.3a for data on the processing of serious criminals). Perhaps not surprisingly, only 27 percent of survey respondents say they have much confidence in the criminal justice system (Pastore and Maguire, 2003).

In this section we will briefly consider the components of the criminal justice system: the police, the courts, and the prisons. Each of these components operates at local, state, and federal levels.

The Police.   The police are a citizen's first link with the criminal justice system, and in many ways the most important one. When a crime occurs, the police are usually the first agents of the state to become involved. Yet police officers spend only about 15 percent of their time dealing with crime. Competing demands on their time vary from filling out reports and directing traffic to handling complaints about uncollected trash and responding to medical emergency calls.

The Courts.   In the United States the criminal justice system is an adversary system. The person accused of a crime—the *defendant*—is presumed to be innocent until proved guilty in a court of law by the representative of the state—the *prosecutor.* In many nations the questioning of witnesses is handled by judges, and guilt and innocence are decided by a judge or panel of judges. But the U.S. system assumes that justice is best served by pitting opposing lawyers against each other before a neutral judge and jury.

In practice, the fate of most of those accused of crime is determined by prosecutors. Prosecutors typically reject or reduce the severity of 50 to 80 percent of the criminal charges filed by police. The reasons prosecutors cite range from case overload to police inefficiency in producing evidence. Of some 2 million serious criminal cases filed each year in the United States, fewer than one in five goes to trial. The others end in dismissals or guilty pleas.

Prisons.   We have said that the crime rate has been declining over the past decades. The prison population, on the other hand, has been steadily increasing. In 2002, 6.7 million people in the United States were in jail, in prison, on probation, or on parole, comprising a total of 3.1 percent of the adult population (Bureau of Justice Statistics, 2003). There were nearly 1.5 million inmates in state and federal prisons and more than 0.5 million in local jails, more than four times as many as 30 years ago. The United States has the highest incarceration rate in the world, nearly 5 times England's rate and 14 times higher than the incarceration rate in Japan (http://www.sentencingproject .org/policy/9030.htm; Walmsley, 2003).

What purpose is served by locking offenders away? Let's take a look at traditional purposes of imprisonment.

Punishment.   Prior to 1800 it was widely assumed that the punishment of deviants was required if the injured community was to feel morally satisfied. In recent years there has been a renewed interest in punishment. The "moral order" argument runs like this: Certain acts are basically antisocial and heinous (e.g., murder, rape, genocide, and the sexual abuse of children). When grossly immoral behavior goes unpunished, people's commitment to social order and to basic values and norms is weakened; punishment is essential to maintain moral order. This approach draws on the functionalist perspective for support.

Rehabilitation.   Toward the latter part of the 18th and the early part of the 19th centuries, the idea that prisons might rehabilitate criminals came to the forefront. The word *penitentiary* was coined to describe a place where a criminal might repent and then resolve to follow a law-abiding life. Rehabilitation may include educational, vocational, or psychological programs geared at helping inmates overcome drug and alcohol addiction, earn their general equivalency diplomas, and gain job skills.

Critics of rehabilitation cite statistics on the high rate of **recidivism** (relapse into criminal behavior). In a recent study, it was found that 67.5 percent of those released from prisons were rearrested within three years. The prisoners had been charged with an average of 5 offenses each before their release, and another 2.7 in the three years after their release (Langan and Levin, 2002). Recidivism is particularly high for those charged with robbery and property crimes. With over-crowded prisons and budgets stretched to the limit, rehabilitation programs become a low priority.

Deterrence.   The notion of deterrence rests on assumptions about human nature that are difficult to prove. Even so, sociological studies seem to suggest that the certainty of apprehension and punishment does tend to lower crime rates (Waldo and Chiricos, 1972; Wolfgang, Figlio, and Sellin, 1972; Paternoster, 1989). But allegiance to a group and its norms typically operates as an even stronger force than the threat of societal punishment in bringing about conformity (Heckathorn, 1988, 1990). By the same token, informal standards and pressures within delinquent subcultures may counteract the deterrent effects of legal penalties (Tittle and Rowe, 1974; Heckathorn, 1988, 1990).

Incapacitation.   There are those who argue that neither rehabilitation nor deterrence really works, but that imprisonment can be used to reduce crime rates because it keeps criminals off the streets. Peter W. Greenwood (1982) asserts that incarcerating one robber who is among the top 10 percent in offense rates prevents more robberies than incarcerating 18 offenders who are at or below the median. On the other hand, long prison sentences may represent a waste of prison capacity; most crimes are committed by young people, and most "career criminals" retire fairly early from these careers.

Capital Punishment.   **Capital punishment** is the imposition of the death sentence for a capital offense. Since 1622, 18,000 to 20,000 people have lost their lives in America through capital punishment (Adler, Mueller, and Laufer, 2004). Capital offenses vary by state and have included murder, kidnapping, rape, drug trafficking, and treason (Snell and Maruschak, 2002). Legal execution methods also vary by state

Race, Crime, and Punishment

African Americans account for 12 percent of the U.S. population, 30.4 percent of all those arrested for index crimes, and 45 percent of the prison population nationwide (Adler, Mueller, and Laufer, 2004; Pastore and Maguire, 2003). During their lifetimes, 28.5 percent of African-American men will spend time in prison, which makes them 6.5 times more likely to "do time" than white men (Bonczar and Beck, 1997). Race also plays a part in capital punishment, with offenders being more likely to be sentenced to death when the victim is white, and some research shows that the race of the offender also affects outcomes (Radelet and Borg, 2000).

How much of the disproportionate representation of African Americans in the criminal justice system is due to racial discrimination? Research is divided. Studies of traffic stops show that black men are a third more likely than white men to be stopped by the police and twice as likely to have their cars searched once they are stopped (Lundman and Kaufman, 2003). Whites who favor the death penalty are more likely to be racially prejudiced and to prefer convicting the innocent over letting a murderer go free (Young, 2004); since potential jurors who oppose the death penalty are typically dismissed from jury duty on capital cases, death penalty juries are thus more likely to be both prejudiced and in favor of conviction.

But other studies on arrests, processing, and sentencing do not provide consistent evidence of racial bias. Some studies show that black offenders receive harsher sentences, some find that there are no significant racial differences, and some find that race influences sentencing in certain circumstances (Spohn, 2000). A review by the National Institute of Justice of 40 recent studies of race and sentencing severity showed that race plays a role in sentencing but that the primary determinants of sentencing decisions are the seriousness of the offence and the offender's prior criminal record (Spohn, 2000).

Regardless of the causes of the disproportionate representation of African Americans in the criminal justice system, it has serious consequences. The losses to African Americans are not limited to disproportionate imprisonment and execution.

Those imprisoned—approximately 12 percent of all young black men—are unable to support their families or contribute to their communities, and the economic cost of serving time continues beyond one's sentence. Once out of prison, a criminal record is a major barrier to employment, and this problem is substantially greater for blacks than for whites (Pager, 2003). Ex-inmates who find employment earn an average of 10 to 20 percent less than those who have not been in prison, and incarceration reduces the rate of wage growth for workers by 30 percent (Western, 2002). Participation in our political system also is taken away, and this appears to have affected election outcomes; 48 of 50 states bar felons, including those on probation or parole, from voting and 10 states bar ex-felons (Uggen and Manza, 2002). As the prison population has grown, the percentage of the population that is disenfranchised also has grown, and that disenfranchised population is made up primarily of young, poor, black males.

For many people, punishing those who commit crime seems rational and just. But as this analysis shows, pursuing these policies has unintended consequences. The imprisonment of so many young black men reduces their life chances, damages the economic life of the black community, dampens civic involvement, and promotes alienation.

Questions for Discussion

1. Are you aware of a specific instance of a member of a minority group who got involved with the criminal justice system? What was his or her experience?

2. What social interest is furthered by preventing felons from voting? For example, is this a deterrent to crime? Does it serve as a reasonable form of retribution? Does it serve as a symbolic marker that distinguishes morally upright citizens from law violators? Does it prevent incompetent people from voting? How can a society pursue the goals of both reducing crime and promoting the inclusion of everyone in civic engagement and economic growth?

and include lethal injection, electrocution, lethal gas, hanging, or firing squad. In 2001, all executions were carried out by lethal injection.

What purpose does capital punishment serve? One argument in favor of applying the death penalty is *deterrence,* the idea that punishing offenders deters others from committing similar crimes. Research has shown, however, that capital punishment is not superior to long prison sentences in deterring crime (Radelet and Borg, 2000). Another use of capital punishment is *incapacitation;* an executed offender cannot be a repeat offender. Supporters of capital punishment also have argued that it is less costly than long-term imprisonment, although recent analyses show that the cost of trials and lengthy appeals far outruns the cost of imprisonment, changing cost to an argument against capital punishment in contemporary times. Nevertheless, the death penalty has gained in popularity over the years, and the majority of U.S. adults currently support capital punishment (Pastore and Maguire, 2003). Forty years ago, only 38 percent said they believed in the death penalty, but in 2001 that proportion had risen to 67 percent. When asked why they favor it, nearly half of those surveyed respond with retribution—supporters of capital punishment say the punishment fits the crime.

In the past 35 years, 80 people have been released from their death sentences when it was discovered that they were in fact innocent of the crime of which they had been convicted (Radelet and Borg, 2000). Americans know there are problems with the system; although 67 percent of respondents support capital punishment, only 53 percent say they think the death penalty is applied fairly, and that number drops to 18 percent for black respondents (Pastore and Maguire, 2003). Box 4.1 (p. 119) presents data that may help explain why race affects people's attitudes toward capital punishment.

Other Penalties and Approaches.

For all of those who are incarcerated, many more criminal offenders do not serve time in jails and prisons. Probably the most widely used response to criminal behavior is *probation,* the integration of offenders into law-abiding society under the supervision of a trustworthy person (Adler, Mueller, and Laufer, 2004). Probationers are bound by specific conditions but are able to work, care for their families, and pay taxes. Currently, nearly 4 million people are on probation in the United States. *Parole* is somewhat similar to probation, but it involves releasing a prisoner, again under supervision, before the end of his or her sentence. In *home confinement programs,* offenders serve time at home, usually monitored by electronic devices. Offenders also may pay fines, be required to perform community service, or pay restitution to victims. About 40 percent of convicted felons are required to serve time in prison or jail or on probation *and* comply with other penalties, including paying fines, paying victim restitution, receiving treatment, or performing community service (Bureau of Justice Statistics, 2003).

Key Terms

anomie, 100

capital punishment, 118

crime, 109

criminal justice system, 110

deviance, 94

differential associa-
    tion, 103

index crimes, 110

internalization, 98

organized crime, 112

primary deviance, 106

recidivism, 118

secondary deviance, 106

social control, 98

victimless crime, 113

white-collar crime, 112

Review Questions

1. Define deviant behavior and give two examples.
2. What functions does deviant behavior have?
3. What are the three main types of social control?
4. List and briefly describe the five main theories of deviance.
5. Define crime and list at least six types of crime.
6. Why are so many crimes not reported to the police?
7. Why is the prison population increasing in the United States?
8. Do you think capital punishment should be legal in the United States? Support your answer.

Chapter 5

Social Stratification

Patterns of Social
Stratification

The American Class
System

Social Mobility

Explanations of Social
Stratification

A s part of an introductory sociology course, students were asked
to record their observations of inequality on campus. One student contributed the following:

> Our math classroom is on the third floor of a building that overlooks
> the top floor of a parking ramp. At most three or four cars are
> parked up there, although it contains enough space for at least fifty
> cars. The lower levels of the ramp are also fairly empty. The ramp is
> only for the use of faculty. We students have to park some distance
> from campus and even then we have to get to school by 7:30 in the
> morning if we are to find a parking space . . . The faculty enjoy
> many privileges. They have special offices; departmental chairpersons
> have more spacious offices; and deans and the university president
> have even more magnificent offices. The faculty have "faculty rest-
> rooms" which are distinct from those simply labeled "restroom."
> Each dean has his own private restroom.

This student observed something that pervades all aspects of
social life: social stratification. **Social stratification,** the term sociologists apply to the ranking or grading of individuals and groups into

hierarchical layers, represents structured inequality in the allocation of rewards, privileges, and resources. Some individuals, by virtue of their roles or group memberships, are advantaged, while others are disadvantaged.

College life is not exempt from these patterns, despite the fact that college communities might seem to be places in which administrators, faculty, and students work together in the pursuit of knowledge and human betterment. In fact, wherever one turns, social inequality confronts the members of the college community.

The student quoted above was complaining about disparities among students, faculty, and administrators, but it is possible to observe social stratification without leaving the ranks of students. Your status as a university student may differ depending on whether you're an athlete (and within the world of athletics, on whether you're an especially valuable player), an exceptional student, a commuter, a senior, or a fellowship student. Status also may be based on physical attractiveness, accomplishments in intramural sports or other extracurricular activities, or involvement in counterculture movements. The position of your family outside the campus may influence your position on campus: Race, ethnicity, wealth, and prestige all play important roles, often determining group memberships and social connections. In student clubs and organizations, there are presidents, vice presidents, secretaries, and treasurers, all of whom are ranked with respect to one another and have more power and prestige than the other members. Student government has offices of power and prestige, often controlled by members of fraternities and sororities. Greek organizations also typically hold the key to election of the Homecoming Queen and King.

If social stratification affected only such matters as who gets elected Homecoming Queen, we might not devote an entire chapter to its discussion. But social stratification does much more: It results in some members of society benefitting greatly and others suffering. Most societies of the world are organized so that their institutions systematically distribute benefits and burdens unequally among different categories of people. Social arrangements are not neutral, but serve and promote the goals and interests of some people more than those of other people.

In this chapter we will examine patterns of social stratification. We will attempt to answer the questions of who gets what and why. We will use a country with which we are familiar, the United States, to discuss class systems. We will see how social inequality has serious consequences for individuals' lives: It affects income, lifestyle, health, and even the number of years one can be expected to live. We will define and discuss social mobility, and we will see what the conflict and functionalist perspectives have to offer to our understanding of social stratification.

Patterns of Social Stratification

Social stratification depends upon but is not the same thing as **social differentiation**—the process by which a society becomes increasingly specialized over time. Very early in their history, human beings discovered that a division of functions and labor contributed to greater social efficiency. Consequently, in all societies we find that different people typically perform different tasks and as a result they occupy different statuses.

Although the statuses that make up a social structure may be *differentiated*, they need not be *ranked* with respect to one another. For instance, the statuses of farmer and shop owner in a rural community are differentiated, but one is not obviously of higher rank than the other. They are merely different. Social differentiation creates a necessary condition for social ranking, but it does not create the ranking itself. Whenever we find social stratification, we find social differentiation, but not the other way around.

We begin our consideration of social stratification by examining open and closed stratification systems and some of the important dimensions of stratification: economic standing, prestige, and power.

Open and Closed Systems

Stratification systems differ in the ease with which they permit people to move in or out of particular strata (Kerbo, 2003). As we will see later in the discussion of social mobility, people often move vertically up or down in rank or horizontally to another status of roughly similar rank. Where people can change their status with relative ease, we refer to the arrangement as an **open system.** In contrast, where people have great difficulty in changing their status, we call the arrangement a **closed system.** A somewhat similar distinction is conveyed by the concepts *achieved status* and *ascribed status* that we considered in Chapter 3. Achieved statuses are open to people on the basis of individual choice and competition and are common in open stratification systems. Ascribed statuses are assigned to people by their group or society and are typical of closed systems.

Although no societies are entirely open or entirely closed, the United States provides a good example of a relatively open system. The American folk hero is Abe Lincoln, the poor boy who made good, the rail-splitter who through hard work managed to move from log cabin to the White House. The American dream portrays a society in which all people can alter and improve their lot.

The Hindu caste arrangement, particularly as it operated in India prior to 1900, serves as an example of a closed system. Under the traditional Hindu system, life was ordered in terms of castes in which people inherited their social status at birth from their parents and could not change it in the course of their lives. Members of the lower castes in India were considered inferior, scorned, snubbed, and oppressed by higher-caste members regardless of personal merit and behavior. Even today, caste still shapes behavior in some localities, especially in rural areas, setting the rules of courtship, diet, housing, and employment (Nanda and Warms, 2002).

Although the distinction between open and closed systems of stratification is clear in theory, in practice systems of one type typically have some of the characteristics of the other type. In Box 5.1 (p. 126) you will see that the U.S. system of racial inequality has many characteristics of a caste system.

Dimensions of Stratification

Karl Marx and Max Weber have helped us to unravel the nature of social stratification. Marx believed that the key to social stratification in capitalist societies is the division between those who own and control the crucial means of production—the oppressing capitalist class or bourgeoisie—and those who have only their labor to sell—the oppressed working class or proletariat. In Marx's view, these two groups and their conflicting interests provide the foundation for stratification in capitalist nations. For Marx, social stratification consists of a single economic dimension.

Weber (1946) felt that Marx provided an overly simplistic image of stratification. He contended that other divisions exist within society that are at times independent of the class or economic aspect. Consequently, he took a multidimensional view of stratification and identified three components: *class* (economic standing), *status* (prestige), and *party* (power). Each of these dimensions constitutes a distinct aspect of social ranking. Some statuses rank high in wealth, prestige, and power, such as that of most physicians. Yet the rankings of some statuses may be dissimilar. Some prostitutes and professional criminals enjoy economic privilege, although they possess little prestige or power. Members of university faculties and the clergy, while enjoying a good deal of prestige, typically rank comparatively low in wealth and power. And some public officials may wield considerable power but receive low salaries and little prestige. For the most part, however, these three dimensions hang together, feeding into and supporting one another (Kerbo, 2003). Let us examine each of them in turn.

Economic Standing.   The economic dimension of stratification consists of wealth and income. **Wealth** has to do with what people own at a particular point in time. **Income** refers to the amount of new money people receive within a given time interval. Thus, wealth is based on what people have, whereas income consists of what people get. For example, one individual may have a good deal of property—wealth—in the form of rare coins, precious gems, or works of art but

Is Race the Basis for an American Caste System?

Americans often are fascinated by India's traditional caste system. The idea of groups of people having special status and performing only certain jobs seems very undemocratic. The Brahmins, the most pure caste, serve as priests and have special privileges. The Kshatriyas protect society, holding top military and political positions. The Vaisyas fill farming, livestock production, and commerce jobs, and the last caste, the Sudras, serves those above it. The untouchables, not strictly a part of the caste system, do those jobs Hindus consider to be the most polluting: working with body parts, excrement, and dead bodies.

Does the United States have a caste system? We have said that in some ways the United States provides a good example of an open system of stratification. But we will see in Chapter 6 that the United States also has an entrenched system of racial inequality. Is it a racial caste system?

Let's see if the basic characteristics of a caste system apply to American society. In a caste system, caste membership is hereditary, marriage within one's caste is mandatory, moving out of one's caste is nearly impossible, and occupation is strongly related to caste (Hurst, 1998).

Hereditary caste membership obviously applies to race. In India, people are sometimes able to move up in the caste system by "marrying up." In the United States, in contrast, the racial status of biracial children born of black and white parents is governed by what is often referred to as the "one drop rule" (Davis, 1991): In the South during the eras of slavery and Jim Crow laws, a person with "one drop of black blood" was black. This idea translated into the practice of classifying a person as black if he or she had any known black ancestors (Davis, 1991).

Does the "one drop" rule still hold today? Professional U.S. golfer Tiger Woods has a mother from Thailand and a father with African, European, and Native American ancestors (Page, 1997), and he has described himself as "Cablinasian" (for Caucasian, black, Indian, and Asian), yet he is widely regarded as African American in the United

receive little income from it because it does not grow in value or generate any regular income. Another individual may receive a high salary—income—but have little wealth. A salary of $2 million a year does not constitute wealth if the person receiving it spends $2 million a year on travel, food, entertainment, and personal services.

Prestige. **Prestige** involves the social respect, admiration, and recognition associated with a particular social status. It entails a feeling that we are admired and well thought of by others. Prestige is intangible, something that we carry about in our heads. However, in our daily lives we commonly seek to give prestige a tangible existence through titles, special seats of honor, deference rituals, honorary degrees, emblems, and conspicuous displays of leisure and consumption. These activities and objects serve as symbols of prestige to which we attribute social significance and meaning. Much of our interaction with others consists of subtle negotiation over just how much deference, honor, respect, and awe we are to extend and receive.

We show deference—behavior dramatizing and confirming a person's superior ranking—in many ways. In *presentation rituals* we

States (Nolan, 1997; Foster, 1997; Brand-Williams, 1997).

The second basic characteristic, that marriage within one's caste is mandatory, is not true in the legal sense; there are no longer any laws in the United States that forbid interracial marriages. But in the United States in the 1990s, fewer than .68 percent of all marriages involving whites and blacks were marriages between a white and a black person (U.S. Census Bureau, 2003).

The third characteristic of caste, that mobility is virtually impossible, is clearly true of the black–white distinction. There is essentially no mobility from black to white or from white to black for typical white and black people in the United States. Of course, the phenomenon of "passing" can occur; persons with a small amount of African background and substantial, obvious "white" characteristics have been known to "pass for white" (Johnson, 1927/1989; Scales-Trent, 1995). But passing is something that occurs only in a closed system; were there no racial caste system, passing would have no meaning.

The fourth characteristic, that occupation is strongly related to caste, also describes American society to a substantial degree. Occupations that can be held by blacks or whites are not dictated by law. But in the 19th and 20th centuries, African-American physicians, dentists, engineers, and corporate executives were nearly nonexistent, and nearly all agricultural field workers in the South were black. By now, there has been substantial occupational mobility for African Americans, just as there has been for lower-caste persons in India in the late 20th century. But the occupational distribution in the United States retains significant castelike properties. African Americans are substantially overrepresented in low-status service and manufacturing jobs and underrepresented in highly paid, high-status professional jobs—just as the caste model predicts.

The southern United States before the civil rights movement clearly operated under a castelike system based on race. African Americans rode in the back of the bus, drank from "colored" water fountains, and used "colored" restrooms. The racial caste system in the United States today may be less rigid than this, but nonetheless it has yet to completely disappear.

Questions for Discussion

1. We have argued that the four characteristics of a caste system apply to American society with regard to race. Do you agree? Support your position.

2. Is being gay another factor on which an American caste system is based? Why or why not?

engage in symbolic acts, such as revealing regard and awe by bowing, scraping, and displaying a humble demeanor. In *avoidance rituals* we achieve the same end by maintaining a "proper distance" from prestigious figures.

More than a century ago, Thorstein Veblen (1899) highlighted the part that *conspicuous leisure* and *conspicuous consumption* play in revealing social ranking. He noted that it is not enough merely to possess wealth and power to gain and hold prestige. The wealth and power must be put on public view, for prestige is awarded only on evidence. One way we undertake to advertise high status is to lavish expenditure on clothing, because we can size up one another's apparel at a glance. The automobile serves a similar purpose, particularly a very expensive one. Veblen documented how relative success, tested by comparing one's own economic situation with that of others, becomes an established end. Thus, comparisons find symbolic expression, since displaying one's bankbook or stock certificates would be impractical and considered in poor taste.

As our social positions change throughout the life cycle, the sorts of things that serve as symbols of status change. For young people, having the right clothes is often very important. Tattoos and piercing various parts of the body with jewelry can serve as status symbols for youth. Knowing a great deal about sports, movies, or popular music all serve as status symbols, as does being on the cutting edge of any kind of fashion, be it in clothes, music, cars, computers, literature, or another cultural product. These also may be important to adult status, but the core of adult status has to do with income, occupation, and lifestyle (Coleman and Rainwater, 1978) and with the status of the people in one's social networks. Adult status is symbolized primarily by where one lives, the nature of one's occupation, and the roles one plays as well as by the status of those with whom one associates in the community, in voluntary organizations, and in informal social relations.

Family background and wealth count for less than they did early in the 20th century. Simultaneously, an individual's "personality" and "gregariousness" have taken on greater importance. Although people still think that money is the most important thing, the lifestyle individuals project and the values they reflect are a critical part in determining their prestige (Jackman and Jackman, 1983).

Power.   Prestige typically leads others to conform to our wishes through voluntary compliance, deference, and acceptance; power, in contrast, entails conduct by which we compel others to do what they do not wish to do. As we will see in Chapter 8, power determines which individuals and groups will be able to translate their preferences into the reality of social life. **Power** refers to the ability of individuals and groups to realize their will in human affairs even if it involves the resistance of others. It provides answers to the question of whose interests will be served and whose values will reign. Wherever we look, from families to juvenile gangs to nation-states, we find that some parties disproportionately achieve their way. Even in such a simple matter as eye contact, we find the operation of power. Low-power people typically look less at an individual when they are speaking to a high-power person than when they are listening. In contrast, high-power people display nearly equivalent rates of looking while speaking and listening (Ellyson et al., 1980).

Power affects the ability of people to make the world work on their behalf. To gain mastery of critical resources creates dependency and thus allows one to gain mastery of people. To control key resources is to interpose oneself (or one's group) between people and the means whereby people meet their biological, psychological, and social needs. To the extent that some groups command rewards, punishments, and persuasive communications, they are able to dictate the terms by which the game of life is played, making its outcome a foregone conclusion.

The American Class System

We have discussed open and closed systems of stratification and economic standing, prestige, and power. How is stratification actually manifested in society? In this section, we will look first at the question of how much inequality there is in the United States. We will then describe how social classes are identified, discuss the significance of social class, and look at poverty in the United States.

Is There Inequality in American Society?

Traditionally, Americans have thought of theirs as an egalitarian society. As the Declaration of Independence puts it, the United States is a country in which all persons are "created equal." If so, there would be little for a student of stratification to study in the United States. What do the data show on this issue? It is sometimes difficult to reliably measure inequality in power and prestige, so let's look at inequality in terms of something we can easily measure: economic standing in terms of income and wealth.

Figure 5.1 shows the percent of aggregate income received by each fifth (or 20 percent) of households in the United States. In a highly egalitarian society, where we still might expect some inequality, the percentages within each year should be fairly close to each other. Where substantial inequality is present, we expect large differences across the categories, with very small shares going to the poorest fifth and large shares going to the highest fifth. Over the past 45 years, the lowest 20 percent of households in income in the United States never received more than 5.2 percent of aggregate income, while the highest 20 percent has always received 40 percent or more. Since the mid-1960s, income inequality in the United States has been increasing, most rapidly between 1980 and 1992 (Jones and Weinberg, 2000), and is now at its highest level in over 50 years. In 2001, the top 5 percent of families received 22.4 percent of the income, more than four times what it would receive if incomes were equal across families.

Inequality in wealth is even greater. We define income as money people receive within a given time interval, such as wages and salaries, while wealth is what they own at a particular time. Figure 5.2 presents an analysis of data from the Federal Reserve Board's 2001 Survey of Consumer Finances (see Aizcorbe, Kennickell, and Moore [2003] for a description of the data). Wealth can be measured by the net worth of a household, the value of all assets minus debts. The top 20 percent of households in wealth own more than 80 percent of all wealth. If we combine this highest fifth with the next highest category (the "fourth fifth"), we find that nearly 94 percent of wealth is owned by the top 40 percent of households, leaving just over 6 percent of all wealth distributed among the remaining 60 percent of households.

White households are far wealthier than African-American and Hispanic households. For every dollar in wealth owned by a white household, the average African-American household owns 16 cents and the average Hispanic household owns 9 cents.

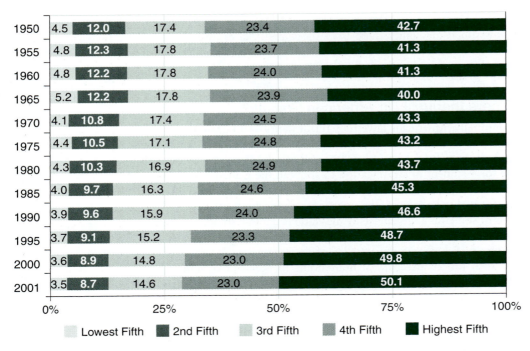

1950	4.5	12.0	17.4	23.4	42.7
1955	4.8	12.3	17.8	23.7	41.3
1960	4.8	12.2	17.8	24.0	41.3
1965	5.2	12.2	17.8	23.9	40.0
1970	4.1	10.8	17.4	24.5	43.3
1975	4.4	10.5	17.1	24.8	43.2
1980	4.3	10.3	16.9	24.9	43.7
1985	4.0	9.7	16.3	24.6	45.3
1990	3.9	9.6	15.9	24.0	46.6
1995	3.7	9.1	15.2	23.3	48.7
2000	3.6	8.9	14.8	23.0	49.8
2001	3.5	8.7	14.6	23.0	50.1

Lowest Fifth   2nd Fifth   3rd Fifth   4th Fifth   Highest Fifth

Figure 5.1   The Rich Get Richer and the Poor Get Poorer: Share of Income Received by Households in the United States, 1950–2001

Income data show that the United States is moving away from income equality, not toward it. Within each bar, the percentages represent the percentage of the total income in the United States that is received by each fifth of households, from the lowest (i.e., poorest) fifth to the highest (i.e., wealthiest) fifth. Looking at 1950, for example, we see that the poorest fifth of households received only 4.5 percent of the income for the whole country, while the wealthiest fifth received 42.7 percent. Since 1950, percentages have fluctuated a bit, but, in general, the percentages received by each of the poorer three-fifths of U.S. households have decreased and the percentage received by the wealthiest fifth has increased.

Source: Figure generated by the authors using data from the U.S. Census Bureau, *Current Population Survey,* Annual Demographic Supplements, 2003. http://www.census.gov/hhes/income/histinc/h02.html.

The very rich in the United States increased their share of the nation's total pool of privately held wealth during the economic boom of the 1980s and 1990s, and this trend continued into the early 2000s (Keister and Moller, 2000; Kennickell, 2003; Johnston, 2003). The 1998 Survey of Consumer Finances shows that the wealthiest 1 percent of U.S. households own 34 percent of all private wealth, up from 31 percent in 1983. The latter half of the 1990s was a time of sharp acceleration in the growth of wealth for the 400 richest people in the United States. Between 1995 and 1999, the number of U.S. billionaires doubled, and the total amount of wealth owned by the richest 400 people grew by more than 95 percent (Kennickell, 2000). Wealth is

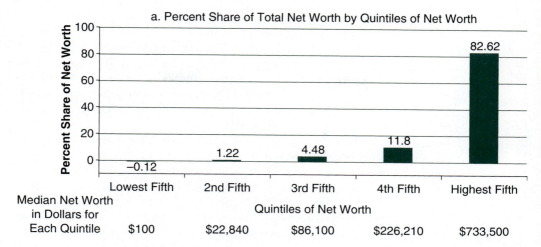

a. If we measure wealth by net worth (assets minus debts), inequality in wealth is extremely high in the United States. More than 80 percent of the wealth is owned by the wealthiest 20 percent of families. The poorest 20 percent of families owe more than they own. The bottom three-fifths of familes (60 percent) own less than 6 percent of all wealth.

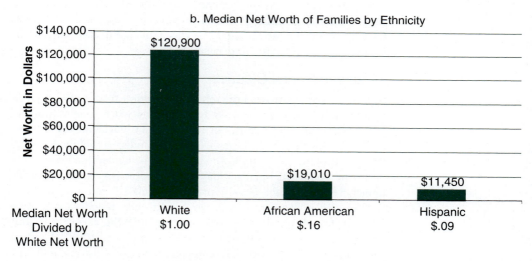

b. White families are, on average, much wealthier than African-American and Hispanic families. Differences in median net worth across the three categories show that for every dollar of net worth owned by a typical white family, the typical African-American family owns 16 cents and the typical Hispanic family owns 9 cents.

Figure 5.2   The Concentration of Wealth in the United States, 2001

Source: Analysis by the authors of data from the 2001 Survey of Consumer Finances, Board of Governors of the Federal Reserve System.

distributed so unequally that the top 1 percent of households are worth more than the bottom 90 percent.

The surge in wealth at the top has been accompanied by a sharp increase in the percentage of full-time workers who earn less than $12,195 annually ($6.10 an hour for someone working 40 hours a week, 50 weeks a year) from 12.1 percent of all full-time employees in 1979 to 18 percent in 1990 (DeParle, 1992) and 20 percent in 1997 (Bureau of Labor Statistics, 1997).

Clearly, there is much inequality in the United States to explain. Further, there is substantial inequality in every region of the world (Deininger and Squire, 1996). Sociologists agree that social inequality is a structured aspect of contemporary life. In saying this, they mean more than that individuals and groups differ in the privileges they enjoy, the prestige they receive, and the power they wield. Structuring means that inequality is hardened or institutionalized, so that there is a system for determining who gets what. Inequality does not occur in a random fashion but follows relatively consistent and stable patterns that persist. One reason for this persistence is that inequalities are typically passed on from one generation to the next. Individuals and groups that are advantaged commonly find ways to ensure that their offspring also will be advantaged; for those that are disadvantaged, the disadvantage may persist for generations.

Identifying Social Classes

Sociologists have borrowed the term *stratification* from geology. Geologists usually find it rather easy to determine where one stratum of rock ends and another begins. But social strata often shade off into one another so that their boundaries are dim and indistinct. How do we go about identifying social strata, or classes, in the United States?

In the course of our everyday conversations, we talk about the "upper class," "middle class," and "lower class," referring to these social classes as distinct groups. Do such groups actually exist? Two views are found among sociologists concerning the accuracy of this popular conception (Lucal, 1994; see also Sørensen, 2000). The first view holds that classes are real, bounded strata that exist in conflicting relations with one another (the *relational model*). Although this position has been a central element in Marxist formulations (Marx and Engels, 1848/1955; Wright, 1985), it also emerges in the work of other sociologists who have identified a blue-collar/white-collar division in American life (Blau and Duncan, 1972; Sobel, 1989). The second view portrays U.S. society as essentially classless, one in which class divisions are blurred by virtue of their continuous and uninterrupted nature (the *distributional model*). Seen in this manner, social classes are culturally quite alike and simply reflect gradations in rank rather than hard-and-fast social groups (Hodge and Treiman, 1968; Eichar, 1989).

The differing conceptions derive in large measure from different approaches to identifying social classes: (1) the objective method, (2) the self-placement method, and (3) the reputational method. Although all the approaches produce some overlap in classes, there are appreciable differences in the results afforded by each (Kerbo, 2003). Moreover, each approach has certain advantages and disadvantages. Let's consider each method more carefully.

The Objective Method.

The **objective method** views social class as a statistical category. The categories are formed by sociologists and/or statisticians. Most commonly, people are assigned to social classes on the basis of income, occupation, or education (or some combination of these characteristics). The label *objective* can be misleading, for it is not meant to imply that the approach is more "specific" or "unbiased" than either of the others. Rather, it is objective in that it uses numerically measurable criteria to categorize individuals.

The objective method provides a statistical measure for investigating various correlates of class, such as life expectancy, mental illness, divorce, political attitudes, crime rates, and leisure activities. It is usually the simplest and least expensive approach to research social classes because statistical data can be obtained from government agencies and the Census Bureau. However, there is more to class than simply raw statistical data. In the course of their daily lives, people size up one another on many standards of excellence. It is not only the actual income, education, or occupational categories that matter, but also the meanings and definitions others assign to these qualities.

For example, one part of the cultural definition of an occupation is its prestige, the respect and admiration people accord it. Sociologists wishing to assign an "objective" ranking to occupations that reflects the subjective meanings people attach to occupations use occupational prestige scores. To determine the prestige of occupations, researchers do large surveys and ask respondents to estimate the social standing of each of a large number of occupations. The results have been used to assign prestige scores to occupations, with physician, lawyer, and college teacher at the top of the ranking and occupations such as janitor, parking lot attendant, and car washer at the bottom of the ranking (Nakao, Hodge, and Treas, 1990). Many electricians, funeral directors, and farm owners run very successful businesses and have high incomes. But because of the meanings people attach to these occupations, their prestige rankings fall in the middle of the range.

The Self-Placement Method.

The **self-placement method** (also known as the subjective method) has people identify the social class to which they think they belong. Class is viewed as a social category, one in which people group themselves with others they perceive as sharing certain attributes in common. The class lines may or may not conform to what social scientists think are logical lines of cleavage in the objective sense. Researchers typically ask respondents to identify their social class.

Within American life, a family's class position historically derived from the husband's position in the labor market. But long-term social and economic changes, particularly the movement of many women into the workplace and declining family size, seem to be altering the way many women assess their class identity (Baxter, 1994). Most employed women used to appraise their class position primarily in terms of the class position of their husbands. Now both men and women look at husband's and wife's combined income in identifying class but only at the husband's occupational prestige (Yamaguchi and Wang, 2002). Men and women disagree about the contribution of education to class identity. And single men and women look increasingly to their own characteristics rather than those of their parents in assessing their class identities (Davis and Robinson, 1988).

The major advantage of the self-placement approach is that it can be applied to a large population. However, the approach has its limitations. The class with which people identify may represent their aspirations rather than their current associations or the appraisals of other people. Further, when placing themselves in a national class structure, people commonly use fewer categories than they do when interacting with actual people and sizing them up in terms of subtle distinctions.

The Reputational Method.

In the *self-placement* method, people are asked to rank themselves. In the **reputational method,** they are asked how they classify other individuals. This approach views class as a social group, one in which people share a feeling of oneness and are bound together in relatively stable patterns of interaction. Therefore, class rests on the knowledge of who associates with whom. The approach gained prominence in the 1930s when W. Lloyd Warner and his associates studied the class structure of three communities: "Yankee City" (Newburyport, Massachusetts), a New England town of some 17,000 people (Warner and Lunt, 1941, 1942); "Old City" (Natchez, Mississippi), a southern community of about 10,000 (Davis, Gardner, and Gardner, 1941); and "Jonesville" (Morris, Illinois), a midwestern town of about 6,000 (Warner, 1949). In Yankee City and Old City, Warner identified six classes: the upper upper, the lower upper, the upper middle, the lower middle, the upper lower, and the lower lower. Warner's sociological conception of the U.S. class system was popularized by the media and gained considerable public appeal. Even today his formulations carry considerable weight in how the American public has come to view and think about social class in American life.

The reputational method is a valuable tool for investigating social distinctions in small groups and small communities. It is particularly useful in predicting associational patterns among people, but it is difficult to use in large samples where people have little or no knowledge of one another.

The Significance of Social Classes

Few aspects of social life affect so strongly the way people behave and think as does social class. For one thing, it largely determines their **life chances**—the likelihood that individuals and groups will enjoy desired goods and services, fulfilling experiences, and opportunities for living healthy and long lives. Broadly considered, life chances have to do with people's level of living and their options for choice. For example, social class affects education. The higher the social class of parents, the further their children go in school and the better they perform (Mickelson, 1990). Long-term poverty experienced during childhood affects cognitive ability, and poverty experienced during adolescence affects cognitive achievement (Guo, 1998). By five years of age, youngsters who have always lived in poverty have IQs on average nine points lower than those who were never poor; this gap cannot be explained by differences in mothers' education, divorce rates, or race (Elias, 1994).

Class also affects health and life expectancy. As a doctor expressed in the *Journal of the American Medical Association*, "Lower socioeconomic status (SES) is probably the most powerful single contributor to premature morbidity and mortality, not only in the United States but worldwide" (Williams, 1998:1745). Health is affected by income, education, and social class in all industrialized societies (Dunn and Hayes, 2000). As with education, childhood poverty continues to affect health into adulthood (Reynolds and Ross, 1998). Although health risk factors including obesity, smoking, and lack of exercise are more common among people of low socioeconomic classes, researchers also point to differences in exposure to occupational and environmental health hazards in explaining class differences in morbidity and mortality (Lantz et al., 1998).

Social class affects life chances in other ways. During the Vietnam War, some 80 percent of the 2.5 million men who served in Southeast Asia—of 27 million men who reached draft age during the war—came from working-class and impoverished backgrounds (Appy, 1993). When the *Titanic* sank in 1912, passengers traveling in first class were more than twice as likely to survive as those traveling third class (Dawson, 1995).

Social class also affects people's **style of life**—the magnitude and manner of their consumption of goods and services. Convenience foods—TV dinners, potato chips, frozen pizza, and Hamburger Helper—are more frequently on the menus of lower-income than higher-income households. Lower-class families drink less vodka, scotch, bourbon, and imported wine but consume more beer and

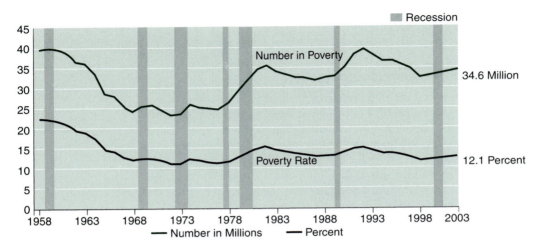

Figure 5.3   People in Poverty in the United States, 1959–2002

In 2002 the government classified a family of four as poor if it had cash income of less than $18,244.

Source: Figure generated by the authors using data from Proctor and Delaker, 2003; U.S. Census Bureau, March Current Population Survey, http://www.census.gov/hhes/income/histinc/h17.html.

Note: The data points represent the midpoints of the respective years.

blended whiskey. Social class even affects such things as the styles of furniture people buy and the programs they watch on television.

Social class is associated with various patterns of behavior. For instance, voting increases with socioeconomic status in most Western nations (Gaither and Newberger, 2000). And people in the lower classes begin sexual activities at a younger age, but people in the upper classes are more tolerant of sexual variations and engage in a wider variety of sexual activities (Laumann et al., 1994). In sum, one's social class leaves few areas of life untouched.

Poverty in the United States

More than 30 years after President Lyndon Johnson announced that his Great Society program would end poverty in the United States, poverty remains a significant feature of American life. Census Bureau statistics reveal that the percentage of Americans below the poverty line dropped from 22.4 percent in 1959 to a low of 11.1 percent in 1973. The poverty rate has fluctuated since then, with a recent upturn (see Figure 5.3). In 2002, the official poverty rate was 12.1 percent, with 34.6 million people living in poverty (Proctor and Dalaker, 2003).

What exactly is poverty? Who are the poor in the United States? Does the United States have an "underclass"? What causes poverty?

And how does the United States approach the problems of poverty? We will discuss these issues in this section.

Defining Poverty.   The definition of poverty is a matter of debate. In 1795, a group of English magistrates decided that a minimum income should be "the cost of a gallon loaf of bread, multiplied by three, plus an allowance for each dependent" (Schorr, 1984). Today the Census Bureau defines the threshold of poverty in the United States as the minimum amount of money families need to purchase a nutritionally adequate diet, assuming they use one-third of their income for food. Traditionally, liberals have contended the line is too low because it fails to take into account changes in the standard of living (Ruggles, 1992). Conservatives have said it is too high because the poor receive in-kind income in the form of public assistance, including food stamps, public housing subsidies, and health care (Rector, 1990). In 2002, the poverty threshold for a family of four was $18,244 (Proctor and Dalaker, 2003). For a single person under 65 to be defined as poor, he or she must earn less than $9,359 per year.

Who Are the Poor?   About 62 percent of the nation's poor live in large cities, but between 2001 and 2002 the poverty rate increased not among city dwellers but among those who live in suburbs (Proctor and Dalaker, 2003). High-poverty counties are found in Appalachia, the Mississippi delta, and Texas along the Mexican border. The poverty rate is highest in the South, with Mississippi, Louisiana, and New Mexico leading the states with the highest poverty rates. Overall, poverty has become increasingly the lot of single and divorced parents and their children. For example, in 2002 the poverty rate for married-couple families was 5.4 percent, while that for families headed by a female with no spouse present was five times higher (Proctor and Dalaker, 2003). This feminization and juvenilization of poverty has changed course as women have made gains in both employment and wage equality (Bianchi, 1999). Nevertheless, women still have a significantly higher risk of poverty than men (Haynie and Gorman, 1999). In 1999, fatherless families represented 18 percent of the nation's families, but 53 percent of the households living in poverty. Further, in 2002, 16.7 percent of all American children—12.1 million children—were living in poverty (Proctor and Dalaker, 2003). Poverty rates vary greatly by race, with non-Hispanic whites (8 percent) and Asians (10.0 to 10.3 percent) having the lowest rates and Hispanics (21.8 percent) and African Americans (23.9 to 24.1 percent) the highest rates of poverty (Proctor and Dalaker, 2003).

The poverty rate for the elderly dropped from 35.2 percent in 1959 to 10.4 percent in 2002. Even so, 20 percent of widowed and 24 percent of divorced older women remain impoverished. Farmers are more likely to be poor than their city cousins, and there are thousands of American farmworkers who are poor, many of whom lack access to toilets and clean water at their work sites. Handicapped individuals are more than twice as likely as other workers to be poor. About 23 percent of working-age people who receive food stamps and 37 percent of Medicaid recipients are disabled.

Not everyone who is poor receives welfare. And contrary to popular stereotype, whites use government safety-net programs more than African Americans and Hispanics. Although the poverty *rate* is lower for whites, there were 15.6 million non-Hispanic whites living in poverty in 2002, compared to 8.6 million African Americans and the same number of Hispanics (Proctor and Dalaker, 2003).

An "Underclass"?   The term *underclass* has been applied by some social scientists to a population of people, concentrated in an inner city, who are *persistently* poor, unemployed, and dependent on welfare (Coughlin, 1988). Initially, sociologist William Julius Wilson (1987) championed the concept to describe the plight of "the truly disadvantaged." Some argue that the term *underclass* has come to reflect the stereotype that the poor have created their own plight and that the inhabitants of inner-city neighborhoods are both fundamentally different from other Americans and violently dangerous. The term is used by sociologists, however, to describe the phenomenon of persistent poverty. As historian Jacqueline Jones (1992) showed, the kind of poverty associated with contemporary urban ghettos has a long history dating back at least to the Civil War and has included white sharecroppers, Appalachian white migrants, and marginal white factory workers of the North.

Simply being poor does not make a person a part of the underclass. Indeed, the underclass constitutes a minority of the poor. Research indicates that over a four-year period in the 1990s, about 34 percent of the population lived in poverty for at least two months, but only 2 percent were continuously in poverty over the entire period (Proctor and Dalaker, 2003). The underclass is a core of inner-city poor, those individuals and families who are trapped in an unending cycle of joblessness and dependence on welfare or criminal earnings. Their communities are often plagued by drug abuse, lawlessness, crime, violence, and poor schools (Wilson, 1996). Many underclass women were teenage mothers and high school dropouts who subsequently found themselves sidetracked without the resources or skills to escape a life of poverty. The rise of female-headed families is associated with the inability of underclass men to find steady jobs (Wilson, 1987, 1991; Massey, 1990; Jencks, 1992).

In the next section, we consider the three major theories of poverty.

Theories of Poverty.   Various theories have been advanced through the years to explain poverty.

One approach looks to the characteristics of the poor to explain their difficulties. According to the **culture of poverty** thesis, the poor in class-stratified capitalist societies lack effective participation and integration within the larger society (Lewis, 1966). Clustered in large ghettos in cities such as New York, Mexico City, and San Juan, the poor develop feelings of marginality, helplessness, dependence, and inferiority, which allegedly breed weak ego structures, lack of impulse control, a present-time orientation characterized by little ability to defer gratification, and a sense of resignation and fatalism. The resulting lifeways are both an adaptation and a reaction of the poor to their disadvantaged positions. They become self-perpetuating patterns as the ethos associated with the culture of poverty is transmitted to successive generations (Murray, 1994). Political scientist Lawrence M. Mead (1992) offered a modified version of the theory, arguing that the sources of contemporary poverty are essentially psychological and not cultural. He argued that the dependent poor share the values of the larger society but lack the confidence to try to live by them.

Many sociologists argue that the culture of poverty thesis has serious shortcomings (Valentine, 1968; Duncan, Hill, and Hoffman, 1988; Jaynes and Williams, 1989; Demos, 1990). For instance, as we pointed out in Chapter 1, Elliot Liebow depicted the economically poor street-corner men of Washington, D.C., as very much immersed in American life and not as carriers of an independent culture of poverty. They, too, want what other American men want, but they are blocked from achieving their goals by a racist social order.

Another view sees poverty as largely *situational*. This view is supported by a study that showed that a majority of the U.S. population uses the welfare system at some point (Rank and Hirschl, 2002). Two-thirds of Americans between the ages of 20 and 65 will use a welfare program, and 90 percent of those who do will use it more than once. Similarly, a long-term study done in the 1970s and 1980s found that only 2.6 percent of 5,000 families could be classed as persistently poor over a 10-year period, whereas 25 percent of the families received welfare at some time, often for very short periods (Duncan, Hill, and Hoffman, 1988). Many people who slip into poverty do so for a limited time after major adverse events, such as divorce or illness. For many families, welfare serves as a type of insurance protection, something they use for a brief period but dispose of as quickly as they can. The study, undertaken by the University of Michigan's Institute for Social Research (Duncan, 1984, 1987; Duncan, Hill, and Hoffman, 1988), casts doubt on the culture of poverty thesis. Instead it portrays the poverty population as a pool, with people flowing in and out. The researchers found "little evidence that individual attitudes and behavior patterns affect individual economic progress." To a far greater extent, individuals "are the victims of their past, their environment, luck, and chance."

Still another view portrays poverty as a *structural feature* of capitalist societies. The cyclical movements between economic expansion and contraction—boom and bust—contribute to sharp fluctuations in employment. More than a century ago, Marx contended that an industrial reserve army is essential for capitalist economies. The industrial reserve army consists of individuals at the bottom of the class structure who are laid off in the interests of corporate profits during times of economic stagnation and then rehired when needed for producing profits during times of economic prosperity. It is disproportionately composed of minorities, who traditionally have been the last hired and the first fired. Contemporary structuralists say that a "new industrial order," characterized by a significant shift from manufacturing to service-sector employment, has produced massive vulnerability among all blue-collar workers. This structuralist view sees poverty as deriving from a lack of income-producing employment (Moller et al., 2003). Problems in the economic organization of society also result in high inner-city rates of family disintegration, welfare dependency, drug abuse, and crime (Marks, 1991; Jones, 1992).

Poverty Programs.   The United States is the only industrialized nation that has no guaranteed income program for families in poverty and no national health program to meet the medical needs of its citizens (Kerbo, 2003).

A government poverty program established in the 1930s, Aid to Families with Dependent Children (AFDC), was replaced in 1996 by the Temporary Assistance for Needy Families (TANF) program as part of former President Bill Clinton's welfare reform. The welfare reform program focuses primarily on encouraging work, eliminating long-term use of welfare, and handing welfare over to the states. Its key elements are

1. Welfare recipients must work after two years of assistance.

2. Recipients are limited to five years' total assistance, including cycling on and off.

3. The guarantee of assistance that was built into AFDC has been replaced with a system of block grants to the states, money that can be used largely as each state wishes. Under this new system, states may limit assistance to less than five years and may use the money from the federal government for things other than welfare assistance (Bane, 1997; Super et al., 1996).

The promotion of marriage also was a key element of TANF, with "encouraging the formation and maintenance of two-parent families" a stated means to ending dependence on government benefits (Lichter, Graefe, and Brown, 2003). The welfare reform program was reauthorized under President George W. Bush's administration in 2003.

What are the consequences of welfare reform? Judging its success is a matter of perspective. The number of people receiving government assistance definitely decreased. Between 1996 and 2000, the number of

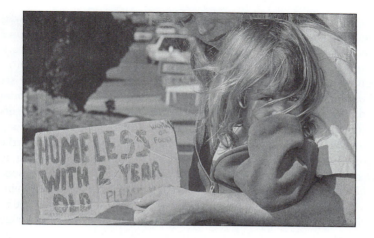

More than 23 million white people were living in poverty in 2002. Although African Americans are more likely than whites to be poor, 68 percent of the poor in the United States in 2002 were white (Proctor and Dalaker, 2003).

people receiving government handouts dropped by 6.5 million, and by 2001 the welfare caseload was lower than it had been since 1969 (Lichter and Jayakody, 2002). The proportion of people on welfare—less than 3 percent—was the lowest on record. Further, welfare reform seems to have been accompanied by a drop in out-of-wedlock child-bearing and a rise in family stability. The majority of people leaving the welfare rolls found employment, most full time (Corcoran et al., 2000).

The decline in welfare recipients, however, did not translate into a decrease in the poverty rate (Lichter and Jayakody, 2002). Although poverty rates did fall in the first years after welfare reform, the size of the decline did not match the numbers of people off welfare. And in both 2001 and 2002, poverty rates increased (Proctor and Dalaker, 2003). According to some analysts, welfare reform served primarily to transform welfare recipients into the working poor (O'Connor, 2000).

Why are people who work full time unable to rise above the poverty line? One reason is that the cost of living—and especially the cost of housing—has increased much more quickly than the level of wages. A report released in 2002 by the National Low Income Housing Coalition indicated that the average household needs an income of $14.66 per hour in a full-time job to be able to afford a two-bedroom rental, close to three times the federal minimum wage of $5.15 (Kennedy, 2002). That number was based on a national average; in some areas, the income required is much higher. Despite the variability in housing costs, there is no state in which an extremely low-income family can afford to rent a decent two-bedroom house at market value (MCCD, 2003). And surveys show that one clear result of pushing people off welfare has been to *decrease* wages for low-skilled workers (Kerbo, 2003).

How might poverty be handled differently? Based on the assumption that poverty is caused by low income and a lack of well-paying jobs (Jencks, 1992), Bane and Ellwood (1994) suggested replacing welfare with a system of income-support policies designed to reinforce principles of family, work, and independence. First, people who work should not be poor; minimum wages should be set high enough to keep people in low-paying jobs out of poverty. Eleven states have set minimum wages higher than the federal level (Armas, 2003), and more than 50 cities have livable wage ordinances that require government-hired contractors to pay wages in line with local costs of living (Krasikov, 2001). Second, families should not be forced to rely on the income of only one parent. The government needs to better enforce laws requiring absent parents to pay child support and should provide child-support payments when support from parents is not forthcoming. Third, jobs must be made available to those who are willing to work. The government should be the employer of last resort to provide jobs when the economy falters and in areas where jobs are scarce.

Social Mobility

In many societies individuals or groups can move from one level (stratum) to another in the stratification system, a process called *social mobility*. Social inequality has to do with differences in the distribution of benefits and burdens; social stratification is a structured system of inequality; and **social mobility** refers to the shift of individuals or groups from one social status to another.

Social mobility can occur in at least two ways. First, societies change, altering the division of labor, introducing new positions, undermining old ones, and shifting the allocation of resources. Sometimes such social change occurs because members of the lower strata resent their exclusion from higher ranks and work to change the established social order. Second, social mobility can take place when shifts occur in the availability of different types of talent. Although those in the higher strata may monopolize the opportunities for training and education, they do not control the natural distribution of talent and ability. People often must be recruited from the lower ranks to perform roles in society that increase their status.

In this section, we will describe the forms social mobility can take and discuss social mobility and status attainment processes.

Forms of Social Mobility

Social mobility can take a number of forms. For example, mobility may be vertical or horizontal. **Vertical mobility** involves movement from one social status to another of higher or lower rank. Americans differ in the prestige ratings they give to various occupations. If an auto mechanic (prestige score 40) became a lawyer (score 75), this shift constitutes upward mobility. On the other hand, if the auto mechanic became a garbage collector (score 28), this change involves downward mobility. If the auto mechanic took a job as a restaurant manager (score 39), this shift represents horizontal mobility. **Horizontal mobility** entails movement from one social status to another of approximately equivalent rank.

Mobility also may be intergenerational or intragenerational. **Intergenerational mobility** involves a comparison of the social status of parents and their children at some point in their respective careers (e.g., as assessed by the rankings of their occupations at roughly the same age). Research shows that a large minority, perhaps even a majority, of the U.S. population moves up or down at least a little in the class hierarchy in every generation. **Intragenerational mobility** entails a comparison of the social status of a person over an extended time period. There are limits to the variety of most people's mobility experience. Small moves tend to be the rule, and large moves the exception.

Social Mobility and Status Attainment

When sociologists talk about social mobility, they usually have intergenerational occupational mobility in mind. Over the history of the United States, social mobility has occurred as a result of changes in occupational structure and the economy (Beeghley, 2000). For example, early in the country's history, the sons of farmers became farmers, but as industrialization and urbanization occurred, the offspring of farmers became less and less likely to grow up to be farmers themselves. In general, more Americans are upwardly mobile than downwardly mobile across generations.

What accounts for the higher rate of upward than downward intergenerational mobility in the United States? First, changes in occupational structure over time: With technological advances, more jobs are created toward the top of the occupational structure than toward the bottom. Second, fertility differences associated with social class: White-collar fathers generate fewer children than blue-collar fathers, making more room toward the top of the class hierarchy. Over time, more than twice as many men have moved into white-collar jobs as have moved out of them (Davis, 1982).

The Classic Studies.

We can learn more about social mobility by looking at status attainment studies, which identify the processes by which individuals enter occupations and attain status in society. Two classic sociological studies of status transmission and attainment have pinpointed some key factors. The first involved the development of a technique for studying the course of an individual's occupational status over the life cycle (Blau and Duncan, 1972). Called the **socioeconomic life cycle**, it involves a sequence of stages that begins with birth into a family with a specific social status and proceeds through childhood, socialization, schooling, job seeking, occupational achievement, marriage, and the formation and functioning of a new family unit. The second study, conducted by William Sewell and his associates (Sewell, Haller, and Ohlendorf, 1970; Sewell and Hauser, 1975), was based on a survey of high school seniors and follow-up work over the decade following their graduation from high school.

Both these studies found that education—the years of schooling completed—has the greatest influence on occupational attainment. Blau and Duncan concluded that the social status of one's parents has little *direct* impact on occupational attainment; rather, it plays an *indirect* role on status attainment through its effect on schooling. Sewell and his associates found that another important factor linking family background to adult status was the level of achievement aspirations one learned in the family. A recent study that followed the participants of Sewell and colleagues' original study from the 1950s to the 1990s found that the impact of family background on occupational attainment operates entirely through educational achievement and cognitive ability (Warren, Hauser, and Sheridan, 2002).

The Critics.

Critics of status attainment research contend that it has a functionalist bias (Knottnerus, 1991). They argue that it is not the case that the job market is fully open to individuals who acquire positions based on education and ability. Although some of the most important factors affecting status attainment among white males have been identified, it turns out that for women and African Americans the processes of status attainment are different.

Race.

Let's look first at African Americans. A nationwide sample of boys revealed a number of differences between blacks and whites in terms of educational attainment (Portes and Wilson, 1976). Using a model similar to that developed by Sewell and others, based on parents' education, offspring's education and aspirations, and other factors, these researchers found that the model predicted attainment for whites better than it did for blacks. This suggested that the factors that are most important for educational attainment among blacks were not included in the model. Socioeconomic background, mental ability, and academic performance were found to be more important for white attainment, while self-esteem and educational aspirations were significant variables for blacks.

Gender.

Research in Great Britain has shown that social mobility findings for white men also cannot be generalized to women (Abbott and Wallace, 1997). While the proportion of jobs done by women and the proportion of women working for pay both have increased, women typically come in as routine workers and at the bottom of job categories. Similarly, in the United States, women are more likely than

"Actually, Lou, I think it was more than just my being in the right place at the right time. I think it was my being the right race, the right religion, the right sex, the right socioeconomic group, having the right accent, the right clothes, going to the right schools. . . ."

men to be and remain at the bottom of any scale of salaries and wages and less likely than men to be or remain at the top (Gittleman and Joyce, 1995). Daughters are less likely than sons to "inherit" their fathers' occupations and are more likely to be influenced by their mothers' occupations (Hurst, 1998). For males, education is one of a number of variables affecting status attainment; for females, education is clearly *the most significant* factor related to status attainment (Hurst, 1998). Women also are more likely than men to be affected by family and home-life factors; Waddoups and Assane (1993) found that having a child dampens the upward mobility of women but not of men.

Dual Labor Market.   The structural model of Blau and Duncan and the social/psychological model of Sewell and his colleagues do not explain all that we need to know about status attainment for a diverse population in the United States. Another factor operating to channel individuals into various occupations is the **dual labor market,** with the primary, or *core,* sector of the economy offering "good jobs" and the secondary, or *periphery,* sector offering "bad jobs" that provide poor pay, poor working conditions, and little room for advancement. Recruitment to these two sectors varies, with African Americans, Hispanics, Native Americans, and women found more often in the periphery sector (Beck, Horan, and Tolbert, 1980; Sakamoto and Chen, 1991). If we want to gain a better understanding of how status attainment functions not just for white men but for both women and men of a variety of races and ethnicities, we need to look beyond education and fathers' occupations and look instead at how race, class, and gender affect the status attainment process.

Explanations of Social Stratification

As sociology developed, the question of why social inequality and division should characterize the human condition provided a central focus of the new science. Through the years, two strikingly divergent answers have emerged. The first—the *conservative* thesis that is rooted in functionalism—has supported existing social arrangements, contending that an unequal distribution of social rewards is a necessary instrument for getting the essential tasks of society performed. In sharp contrast, the second view—the *radical* thesis that is rooted in conflict theory—has been highly critical of existing social arrangements, viewing social inequality as an exploitative mechanism arising out of a struggle for valued goods and services in short supply.

The Functionalist Theory of Stratification

The functionalist theory of social inequality holds that stratification exists because it is beneficial for society. All societies require a system of stratification if they are to fill all the statuses comprising the social structure and to motivate individuals to perform the duties associated with these positions. Consequently, society must motivate people at two different levels: (1) It must instill in certain individuals the desire to fill various positions, and (2) once the individuals are in these positions, it must instill in them the desire to carry out the appropriate roles. This theory was most clearly set forth in 1945 by Kingsley Davis and Wilbert Moore, although it has been subsequently modified and refined by other sociologists. Davis and Moore argued that social stratification is both universal and necessary, and hence no society is ever totally unstratified or classless.

Society must concern itself with human motivation because the duties associated with the various statuses are not all equally pleasant to the human organism, are not all equally important to social survival, and are not all equally in need of the same abilities and talents. Moreover, the duties associated with a good many positions are viewed by their occupants as onerous. Hence, in the absence of motivation, many individuals would fail to act out their roles. For example, imagine being a dentist. How likely is it that talented and intelligent people would train to become dentists—pulling teeth, working to correct extensive (and bad-smelling) decay; bending near to people's faces even when they have runny noses, coughs, and bad breath, causing people pain, anxiety, and distress—if the pay and status were not fairly high? Maintaining the dental health of our population is important to society, and so we need to motivate people to become dentists.

On the basis of these social realities, functionalists contend that a society must have (1) some kind of rewards that it can use as inducements for its members and (2) some way of distributing these rewards among the various statuses. Inequality is the motivational incentive that society has evolved to meet the problems of filling all the statuses and getting the occupants to enact the associated roles to the best of their abilities. Since these rewards are built into the social system, social stratification is a structural feature of all societies.

Employing the economists' model of supply and demand, functionalists say that the positions most highly rewarded are those (1) that are occupied by the most talented or qualified incumbents (supply) and (2) that are functionally most important (demand). For example, to ensure sufficient physicians, a society needs to offer them high salaries and great prestige. If it did not offer these rewards, functionalists suggest that we could not expect people to undertake the "burdensome" and "expensive" process of medical education. People at the top must receive the rewards they do; if they do not, the positions would remain unfilled and society would disintegrate.

Evaluation of the Functionalist Perspective. This structure-function approach to stratification has been the subject of much criticism. For one thing, the labor market does not operate freely, rewarding only those of high ability. Often jobs and positions are allocated on the basis of social connections and power. In addition, many people are born into family positions of privilege or lack of privilege, and as we saw in our discussion of social mobility, this may have a strong influence on where people end up in the stratification system (Kim, 1987).

A 1980s study showed that nearly two-thirds of the chief executives in 243 large U.S. corporations grew up in upper-middle- or upper-class families. Such findings lead conflict theorists to contend that society is structured so that individuals *maintain* a ranking that is determined by birth and that is *irrespective* of their abilities, and thus that stratification is *dysfunctional* rather than functional. Melvin Tumin (1953), in his classic critique of the functional theory of stratification, argued that because access to important, highly paid occupations is not entirely determined by ability, many talented people are discouraged from moving into such positions and as a result our society functions less effectively and is less productive than it could be. Recent research by Kim A. Weeden (2002) shows that social and legal barriers around occupations such as licensing restrictions, educational requirements, associational representation, and unionization restrict the labor supply, increase demand, and thus increase salaries and wages in higher-status occupations. These income-enhancing processes are independent of functional occupational characteristics such as the complexity of an occupation's knowledge base.

Critics also point out that many of the positions of highest responsibility in the United States—in government, science, technology, and education—are not financially well rewarded (Bok, 1993). The officers of the largest U.S. corporations, for example, earn about 100 times more than the president of the United States and about 200 times more than Supreme Court justices. Critics also ask whether garbage collectors, with their lower pay and prestige, are more important to the survival of the United States than top athletes who receive incomes in seven and even eight figures. Entertainers also receive disproportionately high incomes. In 2002, Ozzy Osbourne, the heavy metal rock star who starred in a reality TV program in which he used bad language and seemed seriously befuddled, earned $30 million (Brenner, 2003). "Judge Judy," a TV judge, earns $25 million a year, while Supreme Court justice Ruth Bader Ginsburg earns $190,100 annually (Brenner, 2004). In sum, the notion that many low-paying positions are functionally less important to society than high-paying positions is often difficult to support.

The Conflict Theory of Stratification

The conflict theory of social equality holds that stratification exists because it benefits individuals and groups who have the power to dominate and exploit others. Whereas functionalists stress the common interests that members of society share, conflict theorists focus on the interests that divide people. Viewed from the conflict perspective, society is an arena in which people struggle for privilege, prestige, and power, and advantaged groups enforce their advantage through coercion (Grimes, 1991).

The conflict theory draws heavily on the ideas of Karl Marx. As discussed in Chapter 1, Marx believed that a historical perspective is essential for understanding any society. To grasp how a particular economic system works, he said that we must keep in mind the predecessor from which it evolved and the process by which it grows. For instance, under feudalism, the medieval lords were in control of the economy and dominated the serfs. Under the capitalist system, the manor lord has been replaced by the modern capitalist and the serf by the "free" laborer—in reality a propertyless worker who "has nothing to sell but his hands."

Marx contended that the capitalist drive to realize surplus value is the foundation of modern class struggle—an irreconcilable clash of interests between workers and capitalists. *Surplus value* is the difference between the value that workers create (as determined by the labor-time embodied in a commodity that they produce) and the value that they receive (as determined by the subsistence level of their wages). Capitalists do not create surplus value; they appropriate it through their exploitation of workers. Consequently, as portrayed by Marx, capitalists are thieves who steal the fruits of the laborer's toil. The capitalist accumulation of capital (wealth) derives from surplus value and is the key to—indeed, the incentive for—the development of contemporary capitalism. Marx believed that the class struggle will eventually be resolved when the working class overthrows the capitalist class and establishes a new and equitable social order.

Workers may remain exploited and oppressed for a protracted period, blinded by a *false consciousness*—an incorrect assessment of how the system works and of their subjugation and exploitation by capitalists. But through a struggle with capitalists, the workers' "objective" class interests become translated into a subjective recognition of their "true" circumstances and they formulate goals for organized action—in brief, they acquire *class consciousness*. For Marx, it is not enough for the working class to be a "class in itself"; it must become a "class for itself."

Marxists have long argued that investigating stratification that uses dimensions such as income, education, and occupational prestige overlooks the key underlying issue in stratification: one's relations to the means of production. In an influential series of studies designed to rectify this problem, Erik Olin Wright (1985, 1993; Steinmetz and Wright, 1989) investigated class relations in the United States, using Marx's idea that class must be defined in terms of people's relation to the means of production. He identified four classes: capitalists (people who own large businesses), managers (those who manage large businesses), workers (nonmanagers employed by others), and the petite bourgeoisie (small entrepreneurs such as shop owners, restaurateurs, and real estate and insurance agents). Using samples of people in the labor force, Wright found that these categories are about as good in explaining differences in income among people as occupation and education. Even allowing for the effects on income of occupation, education, age, and job tenure, capitalists have higher incomes than the other classes. Thus, Wright concluded that being a capitalist makes a difference (Kamolnick, 1988).

Evaluation of the Conflict Perspective.

The emphasis on economic relations in Marx's conflict theory results in a limited view of both conflict and power. Conflict is a pervasive feature of human life and is not restricted to economic relations. Ralf Dahrendorf (1959) held that group conflict is an inevitable aspect of society that would not be eliminated by revolution as Marx had argued. The Marxist dichotomy between the capitalist class and the working class directs our attention away from other important conflicts that animate social life in modern societies. Debtor and creditor have stood against each other throughout history, as have consumers and sellers. And divisions between racial and ethnic groups, skilled workers and unskilled laborers, and union organizations have been recurrent features of the American landscape.

Ownership of the means of production constitutes only one source of power. Control over human beings—the possession of the means of administration—provides another (Giddens, 1985), as illustrated by the communist regimes in the former Soviet Union and the nations of Eastern Europe prior to 1991. Power also flows from knowledge. For example, within contemporary American life, engineers, systems analysts, and software design specialists derive organizational and social power by virtue of their expertise. In large corporations, a good deal of power derives from office rather than ownership. But in all these examples, influence lasts only as long as officeholders stay in their positions. Their hold on power is often tenuous and they are easily replaceable. Much the same picture emerges from government. The people who actually hold and exercise power are not the owners of the means of production, and they are powerful only as long as they hold office. Marx's response to this point would be his contention that in a capitalist society, the government is an administrative unit that runs the society in the service of those who own the means of production. As we will see in Chapter 8, there are a variety of positions in social science about this issue.

A Synthesis of Perspectives

Many sociologists have noted that both the functionalist and conflict theories have merit, but that each is better than the other in answering different questions (Sorokin, 1959; van den Berghe, 1963; Milner, 1987). For example, as the functionalists have proposed, some of the distribution of rewards within the occupational structure is explained by the supply and demand factors in the labor and job markets (Kerbo, 2003). But, as conflict theorists have pointed out, the markets for labor and jobs are not free and unrestricted, and some of the inequality in outcomes can be explained by differences in power and influence across social classes.

Some sociologists have tried to synthesize the functionalist and conflict perspectives. Harold R. Kerbo (2000), for example, has argued that stratification systems are institutions that have evolved in order to reduce conflict. Without systems of stratification, there would be continuing conflict and aggression over the distribution of scarce resources. Institutionalized inequality provides at least a temporary answer to the question "who gets what and why." Kerbo bases much of his reasoning on the work of sociologist Gerhard Lenski (1966), who tried to formally integrate the functionalist and conflict perspectives. Lenski agreed with functionalists that the chief resources of society are allocated as rewards to people who occupy vital positions and that stratification fosters a rough match between scarce talents and rewards. But as a society advances in technology, it becomes capable of producing a considerable surplus of goods and services. This surplus gives rise to conflicts over who should control it. Power provides the answer to the question of control and determines the distribution of the surplus. Consequently, with technological advance, an increasing proportion of the goods and services available to a society are distributed on the basis of power. In short, Lenski held that the functionalist and conflict positions provide part of the answer, but that neither contains the whole truth.

Key Terms

closed system, 124

culture of poverty, 139

dual labor market, 145

horizontal mobility, 143

income, 125

intergenerational mobility, 143

intragenerational mobility, 143

life chances, 135

objective method, 133

open system, 124

power, 128

prestige, 126

reputational method, 134

self-placement method, 133

social differentiation, 124

social mobility, 142

social stratification, 122

socioeconomic life cycle, 143

style of life, 135

vertical mobility, 142

wealth, 125

Review Questions

1. What is social stratification? What are three components of it?
2. Describe the differences between open and closed systems.
3. Discuss inequality in U.S. society with regard to wealth and income.
4. How do sociologists identify social classes?
5. How many people in the United States are living in poverty? How do sociologists account for the existence of poverty?
6. What is social mobility and how does it occur?
7. How do the processes of status attainment differ for different groups of people?
8. How do the functionalist and conflict theories of stratification differ?

Chapter 6

Inequalities of Race, Ethnicity, and Gender

Racial and Ethnic
Stratification

Prejudice and
Discrimination

Patterns of Intergroup
Relations: Assimilation
and Pluralism

Racial and Ethnic
Groups in the United
States

Sociological
Perspectives
on Inequalities
of Race and Ethnicity

Gender Stratification

Sources of Gender
Differences

Sociological
Perspectives on Gender
Stratification

R ace and gender dramatically affect people's opportunities and
outcomes in life. The discrimination faced by African Americans
in the U.S. labor market provides an example. In a recent study,
researchers (Bertrand and Mullainathan, 2003) sent 5,000 fake
résumés to 1,300 employers. Half of the résumés contained names

selected from a list of 20 "stereotypically black names" (Tanisha, Jamal, Lakisa), and the other half had names from a list of "stereotypically white names" (Emily, Brad, Kristen).

The results? Applicants with white names averaged 1 callback for every 10 résumés, while African-American names on résumés resulted in 1 callback for every 15 résumés sent out. A white name, the researchers found, was the equivalent of an additional eight years of job experience in terms of producing callbacks. As you might expect, a "glittering" résumé (one showing that the applicant had lots of job experience and excellent qualifications) generated many more calls—but only for white names. Identical résumés with African-American names were hardly more likely to get callbacks than the average résumés. "Racial discrimination," the researchers concluded, "is still a prominent feature of the labor market." Obviously this pattern of discrimination contributes to racial differentials in unemployment and earnings.

Because of both subtle and blatant discrimination, race and ethnicity are significant factors of life in the United States—factors that affect health, employment, income, residence, and happiness. Gender also is associated with inequality. As we will see in this chapter, women are more likely than men to be sexually victimized in courtship, to be disadvantaged in the labor market, and to be overburdened by household labor regardless of their status in the paid labor market.

Sociologists are interested in race, ethnicity, and gender and the stratification that results from them. Where do these categories come from? Why and how are they associated with the distribution of society's rewards? This chapter tries to answer these questions by examining the processes of racial, ethnic, and gender stratification.

Racial and Ethnic Stratification

In the previous chapter, we discussed the class system of stratification. Stratification represents institutionalized inequality in the distribution of social rewards and burdens. In this chapter, we turn our attention to a related system of stratification, that of race and/or ethnicity.

Races

When the U.S. Census Bureau collected data in 2000, every U.S. resident was asked to indicate his or her race. Respondents could select as many races as were appropriate from a list of 15 choices (Ogunwole, 2002), reflecting an increasingly diverse U.S. population and an increase in the number of multiracial citizens. But what is race?

Scientists have considerable difficulty identifying races and cate-gorizing people in terms of them (Molnar, 1997; Begley, 2003; Cooper, Kaufman, and Ward, 2003; Burchard et al., 2003). For the most part, races are not characterized by fixed, clear-cut differences, but by fluid, continuous differences, and these differences also change considerably with time (American Anthropological Associa-tion, 1997).

Human beings do not lend themselves readily to cut-and-dried "racial" classifications, and the number of features that humans every-where share are substantially larger and of considerably greater impor-tance than their differences. Recent research shows that the characteristics typically used to classify people into racial categories (skin color, hair texture, and facial features) vary more across races than do genes in general (Feldman, Lewontin, and King, 2003). When researchers examine the full range of genetic data, there are fewer dif-ferences, overall, between races than within races; about 94 percent of genetic variation is within races, and less than 5 percent is between them (Rosenberg et al., 2002).

How, then, is the concept "race" useful? For sociologists race is a social construct (Davis, 1991). A **race** is a group of people who see themselves, and are seen by others, as having hereditary traits that set them apart. What interests sociologists is the social significance people attach to various traits. By virtue of individuals' social definitions, skin color or some other trait becomes a sign or mark of a social status (Denton and Massey, 1989).

Race, Ability, and Culture.

It has been common throughout his-tory for people to believe that race is associated with personality, moral character, competency, intelligence, and other characteristics. Prominent among recent claims of this kind is the widely publicized study *The Bell Curve* (Herrnstein and Murray, 1994) that included the argument that racial groups differ in intelligence. The consensus in the scientific community today, however, is that the biological factors that presumably underlie race do not cause race differences in intelligence (Fischer et al., 1996; Jencks and Phillips, 1998; Arrow, Bowles, and Durlauf, 2000), and that claims such as those of Herrnstein and Mur-ray ignore the important impact that environmental conditions have on the measurement of intelligence.

Research in Western societies over the past 50 years shows sub-stantial increases in scores on intelligence tests that are much larger than can be explained by genetic change. This finding indicates that environmental factors, particularly culture, can exercise a strong influ-ence on group differences in measured intelligence (Flynn, 2000).

Racism.

An important concept based on race is **racism.** Racism exists at two levels: individual and institutional. At the *individual level,* racism is the belief that some racial groups are naturally superior and others are inferior. Individual racism depends on two ideas that have been discredited in contemporary scholarship: (1) that people may be reliably classified into biologically meaningful racial groups (Rosenberg et al., 2002; Feldman, Lewontin, and King, 2003) and (2) that these groups are inherently different in regard to ability, character, intelligence, social behavior, and culture (Block and Dworkin, 1976; Fischer et al., 1996; Nisbett, 1998). Generally, this form of racism gives rise to attitudes of aversion and hostility toward others based on their race. We discuss this below in the section on prejudice.

At the *institutional level*, racism involves discriminatory policies and practices that result in unequal outcomes for members of different racial groups. We discuss this below in the section on discrimination. While individual racism exists in people's beliefs and attitudes, institutional racism is imbedded in the social structure and may operate independently of individual racism.

Ethnic Groups

Groups that we identify chiefly on cultural grounds—language, folk practices, dress, gestures, mannerisms, or religion—are called **ethnic groups**. Within the United States, Jewish Americans, Italian Americans, and Hispanics are examples of ethnic groups. The ethnicity choices for the Census 2000 were "Hispanic or Latino" and "Not Hispanic or Latino," along with Mexican, Chicano, Puerto Rican, Cuban, and others, which respondents were to select in addition to their race(s) selections.

Ethnic groups often have a sense of peoplehood, and to some degree many of them deem themselves to be a nation (Marger, 2003; Stack, 1986). In addition, ethnic groups have a sense of shared history and shared fate that can draw people together into a powerful social unit.

Ethnic identities often are "constructed" by their bearers. For instance, an Asian-American consciousness has arisen among many disparate Asian nationality groups in the United States (Espiritu, 1992). The new identity arose in part as a response to political expediency. Political mobilization also has contributed to a supratribal identity among many Native Americans (Nagel, 1994).

Minority Groups

Throughout much of U.S. history, African Americans, Hispanics, Native Americans, Asian Americans, and Jews have been the victims of prejudice and discrimination and have been unjustifiably confined to subordinate statuses. Sociologists refer to such groups as minority groups.

Minority groups have five main characteristics (Wagley and Harris, 1964; Vander Zanden, 1983):

1. A minority is a social group whose members experience discrimination, segregation, oppression, or persecution at the hands of another social group, the *dominant group*, and lack access to the power necessary to change their situation.

2. A minority is characterized by physical or cultural traits that distinguish it from the dominant group.

3. A minority is a self-conscious social group characterized by a consciousness of oneness. Its members possess a social and psychological affinity with others like themselves, providing a sense of *identity*.

4. Membership in a minority group is generally not voluntary. It is often an ascribed position because an individual is commonly born into the status.

5. The members of a minority, by choice or necessity, often marry within their own group (endogamy).

We may define a **minority group** as a racially or culturally self-conscious population, with hereditary membership and a high degree of in-group marriage, that suffers oppression at the hands of a dominant group (Williams, 1964). The critical characteristic that distinguishes minority groups from other groups is that they have less power than the dominant group.

Prejudice and Discrimination

Prejudice and discrimination are so prevalent in contemporary life, so much a part of the racial and ethnic stratification that exists in the United States, that we often assume they are merely "part of human nature." Yet this view ignores the enormous variation among individuals and societies in levels of prejudice and discrimination. Even in Hitler's Germany, where large numbers of Germans supported and participated in the Nazi Holocaust (Goldhagen, 1996), some non-Jews opposed anti-Semitism and helped Jews escape. And during the civil rights movement in the United States, some southern whites had progressive racial attitudes and supported the African-American struggle for equality (e.g., Durr, 1985).

In this section we will define and discuss prejudice and discrimination and consider institutional discrimination.

Prejudice

Prejudice refers to attitudes of aversion and hostility toward the members of a group simply because they belong to it and hence are presumed to have the objectionable qualities ascribed to it (Allport, 1954;

Devine, 1989). As such, prejudice is a subjective phenomenon—a state of mind.

Why are people prejudiced toward members of other groups? Social scientists in the United States have been studying this issue for more than 75 years and have come up with two kinds of explanations, one emphasizing social psychological processes and the other emphasizing social structure.

Social Psychology.

Most social psychological theories of prejudice argue that prejudices are learned as part of ordinary socialization processes. In frustration-aggression theory, prejudice is a form of scapegoating that results from displaced aggression. For example, members of the dominant group may blame immigrants or minority groups when the economy is in decline. Authoritarian personality theory argues that the tendency to be prejudiced emerges out of overly strict child-rearing practices that result in people valuing obedience to authority and desiring to dominate others. There is some value in these theories, but neither provides a satisfactory explanation of the prejudice we observe in society. Frustration-aggression theory cannot explain why ethnic minority groups are chosen as targets of prejudice (Marger, 2003). And prejudice is often so widespread and pervasive that it could not be entirely due to the existence of persons who have authoritarian personalities.

Such socialization theories view prejudiced attitudes as part of the culture that people internalize during socialization by parents, friends, and associates in the community, whose messages are reinforced by educational experiences and stereotypes presented in media.

For sociologists, race is a social construct, not a set of biological traits. Gregory Howard Williams, whose father was half black, grew up thinking he was white and being treated by others as if he were white. In his book *Life on the Color Line* (1995), he describes what happend when he, his schoolmates, and others in the community learned of his father's background: overnight, he became black.

Social Structure.

Social structural theories, in contrast, argue that prejudice is a cultural mechanism emerging out of competition and conflict between groups, and that it can be an important factor enabling a single group to achieve and maintain dominance. In the view of realistic group-conflict theory (Campbell, 1965; Bobo, 1983; Sears, Sidanius, and Bobo, 2000), when the interests of groups coincide, intergroup attitudes will be relatively positive. However, if the interests of groups diverge, as is the case when groups compete for scarce resources such as land, jobs, or power, negative prejudicial attitudes will result.

Symbolic Racism.

Traditional prejudice in the United States has declined over the past 50 years (Schuman et al., 1997; Firebaugh and Davis, 1988). At the same time, new forms of prejudice emerged. This new complex of attitudes is termed **symbolic racism** (Kinder and Sears, 1981), modern racism (McConahay, 1986), or racial resentment (Kinder and Sanders, 1996) by various researchers. It stereotypes African Americans as people who do not share the American work ethic, who would rather be on welfare than work, who would be as well off as whites if they would "try harder," and who have recently been "getting more than they deserve." Evidence shows that even as whites' support for the *principle* of racial equality has increased, support for policies that would effectively reduce racial inequality has not changed appreciably (Schuman et al., 1997). Symbolic racism and similar attitudes are now the prime determinants of whites' racial policy attitudes (Kinder and Sanders, 1996; Tuch and Hughes, 1996; Hughes, 1997).

Discrimination

We have said that prejudice is an attitude or a state of mind. **Discrimination** is action. Discrimination is a process in which members of one or more groups or categories in society are denied the privileges, prestige, power, legal rights, equal protection of the law, and other societal benefits that are available to members of other groups. Discrimination is a form of racism when those discriminated against are a racial minority.

Institutional Discrimination

The institutions of society may function in such a way that they produce unequal outcomes for different groups. This is called **institutional discrimination,** or *institutional racism* if the disadvantaged group is a racial minority. Businesses, schools, hospitals, and other key institutions need not be staffed by prejudiced individuals in order for discrimination to occur (Carmichael and Hamilton, 1967). For example, when banks provide mortgage loans to those buying homes in middle-class neighborhoods, this appears nondiscriminatory because it applies to all individuals regardless of race, creed, or color. But applying this "color-blind" standard results in large numbers of blacks, who are more likely to live in working-class neighborhoods than whites are, being denied the opportunity to own their own homes.

Environmental racism—the practice of locating incinerators and other types of hazardous waste facilities in or next to minority communities—is another form of institutional discrimination. One researcher found that 21 of Houston's 25 legally operating incinerators, mini-incinerators, and landfills were in predominantly African-American neighborhoods (Horowitz, 1994).

Patterns of Intergroup Relations: Assimilation and Pluralism

In multiethnic societies, ethnic groups may either lose their distinctiveness through a process of *assimilation* or retain their identity and integrity through *pluralism*. In this section, we will examine these two patterns of intergroup relations.

Assimilation

Assimilation refers to those processes whereby groups with distinctive identities become culturally and socially fused (Marger, 2003). Assimilation is a complex process in which cultural changes precede widespread structural change. Members of different groups within a single society must share some cultural elements in order to communicate and carry on ordinary interaction. When cultural elements of one group change in the direction of another group, we call this cultural assimilation, or *acculturation*.

Cultural assimilation makes more extensive social relations among groups possible. When members of different ethnic groups participate with one another in the major institutional structures of society, this is structural assimilation, commonly referred to as *integration*. Typically, structural assimilation occurs first in secondary groups—at work and at school, for example—and then later at the primary group level—clubs, cliques, neighborhood relations, and close friendships (Gordon, 1964). Once structural assimilation occurs, routine marriage across ethnic group boundaries (marital assimilation) and the sharing of a single ethnic identity (identificational assimilation) are natural consequences. Eventually social participation, cultural sharing, and intermarriage may occur to such an extent that it is impossible to distinguish the ethnic groups that were formerly distinct within a society. This is the final stage of assimilation, *amalgamation*.

Pluralism

Ethnic groups do not always completely assimilate into the dominant society or into one another. Examples abound in the contemporary world of separatist movements, including the French Canadians in Canada, the Palestinians in Israel, the Irish Catholics of Northern Ireland, the various Muslim and Christian factions in Lebanon, and the Sikhs in India's Punjab.

However, this is not the path taken by mainstream ethnic movements in the United States. American Jews, African Americans, Chinese Americans, and numerous other groups have retained their identities and distinctiveness for many years without separating from U.S. society. This is an example of **pluralism,** a situation in which diverse groups coexist and boundaries between them are maintained.

Pluralism may be perpetuated because minority groups do not wish to be assimilated, valuing their separate identities and customs. Such groups generally favor what Marger (2003) called *equalitarian pluralism;* cultural identity and group boundaries are maintained, but ethnic group members participate freely and equally in political and economic institutions.

Pluralism also may be promoted by dominant groups who wish to maintain their power and privilege by controlling the participation of minority groups in society. This is *inequalitarian pluralism;* ethnic group distinctiveness is maintained, but economic and political participation of minority groups is severely limited by the dominant group. The caste system of racial segregation in the southern United States before the 1960s is a good example of inequalitarian pluralism.

Inequalitarian policies are at their most extreme when they entail the expulsion or extermination of minorities. History abounds with examples of **genocide**—the deliberate and systematic extermination of a racial or ethnic group.

Racial and Ethnic Groups in the United States

We have defined races and ethnic groups and considered the nature of minority groups and the potential for conflict and separation. We have discussed prejudice, discrimination, and institutional discrimination. Here we will take a closer look at the circumstances of a number of groups within the United States to see the effects of racial and ethnic stratification.

The United States is in transition from a predominately white society rooted in Western European culture to a global society composed of diverse racial and ethnic groups. While 69 percent of the U.S. population was non-Hispanic white in 2002 (McKinnon, 2003), by the year 2050, according to Census Bureau projections, today's minorities will comprise nearly 50 percent of the U.S. population. In some regions of the country, the nonwhite population exceeds the white population today. Los Angeles, for example, is 42 percent white, and El Paso and San Antonio are 74 and 53 percent Hispanic (U.S. Census Bureau, 1999). Hispanic Americans are expected to grow to 24 percent of the population in 2050. The Asian-American population is expected to grow to 8 percent of the total population by midcentury. The African-American population is projected to grow to nearly 14 percent in 2050. Native Americans will remain below 1 percent but are expected to increase from 0.7 to 0.9 percent (U.S. Census Bureau, 1999).

In this section we will look more closely at the circumstances of Hispanics/Latinos, African Americans, Native Americans, Asian Americans, and white ethnics.

Hispanics/Latinos

In 2002, those who were born in or whose ancestors were born in Latin American nations or in Spain became the largest ethnic minority group in the United States; more than one-eighth of the U.S. population is now Hispanic, or as some prefer, Latino (Ramirez and de la Cruz, 2002).

While there has been some blurring of differences among some Hispanic origin groups, making many Hispanic Americans more conscious of themselves as a homogeneous group, the U.S. Census Bureau recognizes four distinct categories: Mexicans, Puerto Ricans, Cubans, and Central and South Americans.

The 37.4 million Hispanics living in the United States in 2002 represent a substantial increase from the 14.6 million recorded in 1980 and 22.4 million in 1990 (U.S. Census Bureau, 1996, 1999). Between 2000 and 2002, Latinos accounted for half of the population increase for the entire country, with more than 50 percent of the Latino increase attributed to international migration (Ramirez and de la Cruz, 2002). Just over 40 percent of the Hispanic population in 2002 was foreign born.

Latinos now account for slightly more than half of the foreign-born population in the United States, up from only 9 percent in 1960; Mexico alone accounts for more than a quarter of the foreign-born population (U.S. Census Bureau, 2000).

As might be expected for recent immigrants in any country, Latinos lag behind the rest of the country in terms of education, employment, and income. Fewer than half of foreign-born Latinos in the United States have a high school education or higher (U.S. Census Bureau, 2000), compared with 57 percent of the combined native and foreign-born population (Ramirez and de la Cruz, 2002). The education disadvantage extends to employment and income, as well. In 2001, 21.4 percent of Hispanic families were living in poverty, compared with a 7.8 percent rate of poverty for non-Hispanic whites (Ramirez and de la Cruz, 2002).

African Americans

In spite of serious obstacles caused by past and present racism and discrimination, the African-American population in the United States has been remarkably successful. In 2002, African Americans comprised 13 percent of the U.S. population (McKinnon, 2003). The South was home to 55 percent of the nation's blacks, and more than half of all African Americans were living in central cities.

Until 2001, poverty rates had been declining for African Americans. More than half of all black married-couple families were earning $50,000 or more per year in 2002, with 27 percent earning incomes greater than $75,000. Similar proportions of white and black men are employed in technical, sales, and administrative support jobs, but black men and women are disproportionately represented in service jobs and as operators, fabricators, and laborers. The unemployment rate was twice as high for blacks as for whites in 2002, and although blacks accounted for only about a fourth of the country's citizens living in poverty, the African-American poverty rate (23 percent) was almost three times higher than that of non-Hispanic whites (McKinnon, 2003). The poverty associated with female-headed households takes its toll: 43 percent of black families are headed by females, with no spouse present, and 35 percent of those families live in poverty (McKinnon, 2003). Female-headed white families account for only 13 percent of all white families. African-American students, then, are more likely than white students to suffer from the range of problems associated with poverty.

African Americans have made significant advances in education in recent years. In 2002, similar percentages of blacks and whites had finished high school and gone on to college. But fewer blacks (16.4 percent of males, 17.5 percent of females) than whites (31.7 percent of males, 27.3 percent of females) finish college (McKinnon, 2003). Blacks remain less likely to be employed in managerial and professional specialty jobs and more likely to be employed in service and labor occupations.

Native Americans

In 2000, 2.5 million Native Americans (Indians, Eskimos, and Aleuts) lived within the United States (Ogunwole, 2002). In addition, another 1.6 million people reported that they were American Indian or Alaskan Native as well as one or more other races (primarily white). Although there are some 500 tribes, ranging in size from under 100 to more than 250,000 tribal members, Native Americans make up less than 1 percent of the total U.S. population. Including those who are reported to be both American Indian and another race brings the population up to 1.5 percent (Ogunwole, 2002). If these figures reflected a natural increase, they would represent a population increase of 26 to 110 percent over 10 years, compared to a 13 percent increase for the United States as a whole, but it is more likely that they also reflect changes in the way American Indians are counted (Paisano, 2003).

Native Americans vary substantially in their history, lifestyles, kin systems, language, political arrangements, religion, economy, current circumstances, and identities. As with Hispanics/Latinos, this group has many names, including Indian, indigenous peoples, First People, and Native American. Native Americans are the most severely disadvantaged of any population within the United States (Snipp, 1989; Visgaitis, 1994).

Today about one-quarter of Native Americans live on Indian reservations, which cover 52.4 million acres in 27 states. Forty-one percent of those on reservations live below the poverty level; almost 70 percent of Navajos, the largest nation, are still without electricity. Overall, unemployment among males 20 to 64 years old is about 60 percent (Valente, 1991; Kilborn, 1992). Life expectancy in some tribes is 45 years. Other problems include alcoholism, suicide, obesity, adult-onset diabetes, and other health problems. Tribes across the United States also are grappling with some of the nation's worst pollution problems—uranium tailings, land and water contamination, chemical lagoons, and illegal dumps (Satchell, 1993).

Despite the myriad problems faced by Native Americans, they have both survived and increased in population since the low of 100 years ago. The three-quarters of Indian people who live off reservations live primarily in cities; the largest Indian populations are in Los Angeles, Tulsa, New York, Oklahoma City, San Francisco, and Phoenix (Page, 2003).

Asian Americans

There is a great diversity of Asian Americans in the United States. According to the 2000 census, the ancestry of this group breaks down into 2.3 million Chinese, 1.8 million Filipinos, 1.7 million Asian Indians, 1.1 million Koreans, 1.1 million Vietnamese, and 797,000 Japanese (Barnes and Bennett, 2002). In addition, there are smaller numbers of Hawaiians, Laotians, Cambodians, Thais, Hmong, Pakistanis, Samoans, and Guamanians. All told, 12.5 million persons in the Asian and Pacific Islander population (defined by the Census Bureau as persons with origins in the Far East, Southeast Asia, the Indian Subcontinent, or the Pacific Islands) lived in the United States in 2002 (Reeves and Bennett, 2003). More than half of all Asian Americans live in California, New York, and Hawaii (Barnes and Bennett, 2002). Asian Americans are twice as likely as non-Hispanic whites to live in central cities, and the populations of some cities in California are now between a quarter and a half Asian American (Barnes and Bennett, 2002).

Asian Americans now enjoy the highest median family income of the nation's ethnic groups: $60,158 in 2001 (U.S. Census Bureau, 2001). They are known for their educational and occupational successes; of those 25 years or older, half the men and 44 percent of the women have finished at least four years of college, compared to 32 percent (males) and 27 percent (females) of non-Hispanic whites (Reeves and Bennett, 2003). See Box 6.1 for more on the "model minority."

Although many Asian-American youths enjoy remarkable academic success, evidence suggests that they have sometimes encountered discrimination when they applied to the nation's most prestigious universities (Lindsey, 1987; Bunzel, 1988). On the job, too, Asian-American workers face widespread discrimination and are often the

Model Minorities—Does Class or Do Values Spell Success?

Why do some minorities suffer from poverty, unemployment, and discrimination while others do not? The nation's media have heralded Asian Americans as "the model minority" and "a superminority." Among white ethnic groups, Jewish immigrants and American-born Jews have long been recognized for their quick rise in U.S. society. And while Hispanic Americans as a whole are socioeconomically disadvantaged, Cubans in particular have had quite rapid economic success. What accounts for the successes of these model minorities? Is it their values or is it their class background?

One explanation for successful ethnic groups is that their values contribute to their upward mobility. This argument contends that thrift, strong family ties, and hard work are the keys to Asian-American success and that their emphasis on education and excellence places them at an advantage in U.S. society. For example, a much higher proportion of Asian-American adults than of whites have completed college. Asian-American students are more likely than other students to enroll in college preparatory programs; they take more math and science courses and also spend more time on

homework than other students (Zigli, 1984; Butterfield, 1986; O'Hare and Felt, 1991).

The "values" explanation for Jewish success is similar. Jews have encouraged independence and achievement more than other white ethnic groups, and their emphasis on education extends back for centuries (Marger, 2003). More than half of all Jewish adults have a college degree, compared with 21 percent of U.S. adults in general (Goldstein, 1992). As a result Jewish males are concentrated far more in the professional occupations (39 percent of Jewish males versus 16 percent of all white males) and far less in the working class (20 percent versus 52 percent of all U.S. white males).

But there's another explanation for the success of ethnic groups in the United States, and this explanation takes us back to the immigrants' roots, to their countries of origin. Sociologist Stephen Steinberg (1989) argued that Jewish immigrants had a significant advantage over other immigrants when they first came to the United States. Italians and other groups of European immigrants were primarily of peasant stock; Jews were frequently urban merchants or manufacturers, and they arrived in the

victims of racially motivated harassment and violence (Dugger, 1992; Mura, 1992).

Sociological Perspectives on Inequalities of Race and Ethnicity

Functionalist, conflict, and interactionist theorists have different explanations for racial and ethnic stratification. In this section, we will consider the contributions of each of these three major sociological perspectives to our understanding of the inequalities of race and ethnicity.

The Functionalist Perspective

According to the functionalist perspective, ethnic differentiation and conflict may serve some important functions in a society. First, conflict promotes group formation, and groups are the building blocks of a

United States at a time when its industrial economy was expanding rapidly and their skills could be put to immediate (and remunerative) use. In other words, class, not values, was the determining factor.

Likewise, some Asian immigrant groups have included a high proportion of doctors and engineers and others with advanced education, and their success in the United States reflects their upper-class, professional backgrounds in their home countries. Much of the potential for success was brought with these immigrants when they entered the United States. The income of lower-class Asian immigrants who come from rural areas and who possess few marketable skills is quite low (Dunn, 1994; Marger, 2003). Much of the success of Asians also may be due to other structural factors, such as the development of ethnic enclave economies that formed as a result of discrimination (Hirschman and Wong, 1986; Bonacich and Modell, 1980).

The experiences of Cuban immigrants also supports the class explanation for the success of ethnic groups in the United States. While other Hispanic groups came to the United States in hopes of economic betterment, many Cuban immigrants in the early 1960s were middle-, upper-middle-, and upper-class citizens. These advantaged immigrants used their material, educational, and social resources (networks and relationships from pre-Castro Cuba) to create an ethnic enclave economy that benefited them and subsequent Cuban immigrants (Portes and Bach, 1985; Marger, 2003). Without a doubt, strong family values and a willingness to sacrifice and work hard were critical factors in the success of Cuban Americans. However, the material and social advantages they brought with them assured success for a substantial number of Cuban Americans in considerably less than one generation.

Jewish, Asian, and Cuban Americans are good models of how some ethnic groups in the United States have achieved success. What their stories tell us, however, may be less about the importance of values, beliefs, and good habits and more about the strong influence of material and social advantages in the success of immigrants in a new land.

Questions for Discussion

1. Pundits, radio talk show hosts, and other social commentators sometimes argue that disadvantaged minority groups in the United States such as Hispanics and African Americans would not be disadvantaged if they followed the examples set by "model minorities." How reasonable is this advice?

2. In your experience as a student, have you observed variability in academic success across various ethnic categories either in high school or college? If so, what factors do you think account for these differences? If not, do you think minority status or ethnicity is in any way responsible for students' academic performances in the schools you have attended? Why or why not?

society. It facilitates a consciousness of kind—an awareness of shared or similar values. Groups bind people together within a set of social relationships.

Conflict also promotes group cohesion. It makes group members more conscious of their group bonds and may increase their social participation, providing them with a means of identification in an uncertain, alienated world.

Third, ethnic and racial conflict may function as a safety valve for the society as a whole (Hepworth and West, 1988; Berkowitz, 1989). Prejudice provides for the release of hostile and aggressive impulses that are culturally taboo within other social contexts. This is known as the *scapegoating* mechanism.

Fourth, functionalists point out that a multiplicity of conflicts between large numbers of differing groups within a society may be conducive to a democratic as opposed to a totalitarian order. The multiple group affiliations of individuals contribute to a variety of conflicts crisscrossing society. If people are opponents in one conflict but allies in another, deep cleavages along one axis can be prevented. The different groups thus created operate as a check against one another and ensure input to the government from a variety of diverse points of view. In contrast, totalitarian societies have a maximum concentration of power in one institution—the monolithic state.

The Conflict Perspective

Conflict theorists contend that prejudice and discrimination can best be understood in terms of tension or conflict among competing groups. They point out that three ingredients commonly come into play in the emergence and initial stabilization of racism (Noel, 1972; Vander Zanden, 1983): ethnocentrism, competition, and unequal power.

When individuals are strongly ethnocentric, they find it easy to perceive the out-group as an object of loathing—as a symbol of strangeness, evil, and even danger. Competition intensifies ethnocentric sentiments and may lead to intergroup strife (Olzak, 1992).

Power determines which group will subordinate the other (Noel, 1972). Without power, prejudices cannot be translated into discrimination, and groups cannot turn their claims on scarce resources into institutional discrimination. In brief, power is the mechanism by which domination and subjugation are achieved.

The Interactionist Perspective

Interactionists argue that the way we act is dependent on the meanings we attach to people, objects, and events. In this view, ethnic groups are rooted in neither physical characteristics of people nor their primordial attachments. According to Shibutani and Kwan (1965), "Ethnic groups . . . generally do not share a common genetic strain; they are products of social interaction."

Ethnicity arises when communication channels between groups are limited and the different groups develop different systems of meanings (Shibutani and Kwan, 1965). Ethnic distinctions tend to diminish when people in different groups experience the world in similar ways, are treated alike by others, and are able to communicate freely and easily with members of other groups.

When ethnic groups are stratified and the advantages enjoyed by the dominant group are fixed by custom and law, the prejudices of dominant group members, developed in cultural isolation from minority groups, will reflect a "sense of group position" (Blumer, 1958)—that is, a belief that the dominant group is superior and has a proprietary claim to privileges and resources and that the minority groups are not only alien, but are a threat to the dominant group's advantageous position.

Although interactionists such as Shibutani and Kwan see ethnic stratification and the discrimination that accompanies it as the end result of competition and conflict among groups over scarce resources (as do the proponents of the conflict perspective), it is important to remember that groups can be conflictual only if they see themselves as distinct and different; otherwise people cooperate as part of the same group or society. As Shibutani and Kwan put it, "ethnic stratification persists as long as people on both sides of the color line approach one another with common expectations of how each is to act in the presence of the other."

Gender Stratification

Just as our society structures inequalities based on race and ethnic membership, so it institutionalizes inequalities based on the social distinction people make between men and women—in brief, on gender. Indeed, throughout the world, human activities, practices, and institutional structures are organized by gender. For the most part, the state, the law, politics, religion, higher education, and the economy are institutions that have been historically developed by men, are currently dominated by men, and are symbolically interpreted from the standpoint of men. As such they are "gendered institutions." The only major institution in which women have had a central, defining role, although a subordinate one, has been the family (Acker, 1992).

Before we continue our discussion of gender stratification, we need to define some basic terms. **Sex** refers to whether one is genetically male or female and determines the biological role that one will play in reproduction. **Gender,** on the other hand, is a form of social differentiation; it refers to the sociocultural distinction between males and females. While sex is given in nature, gender is a socially constructed framework that human beings have created to make sense of and deal with the sex difference.

Gender identities are the conceptions we have of ourselves as being male or female. One's gender identity is part of one's self-concept and consequently is a product of social interaction (see Chapter 2). Our gender identity emerges as we enact gender roles and are reacted to by others as being either male or female.

Gender roles are sets of cultural expectations that define the ways in which the members of each sex should behave. Gender roles influence a wide range of human behaviors, including how people speak, dress, walk, engage in courtship, get angry, play sports, deal with distress, and choose a career. Gender roles constitute master statuses that carry primary weight in people's interactions and relationships with others (see Chapter 3). In doing so they place men and women in the social structure, establishing where and what they are in social terms. Thus, gender roles establish the framework within which men and women gain their identities, formulate their goals, and become educated. Gender roles are a major source of social inequality.

In this section, we will consider sexism and patriarchy. We will then take a closer look at women's roles and gender inequality in society both around the world and in the United States.

Sexism and Patriarchy

Gender inequality is perpetuated by a set of complex processes referred to as **sexism.** Like racism, sexism operates at two levels. At the *individual level,* sexism is the belief that one sex is superior to the other. This form of sexism involves two basic ideas: (1) that because of inherent biological differences, men and women are naturally suited to different roles and (2) that this is the primary cause of the differential distribution of status, power, and income by gender. At the *institutional level,* sexism involves policies, procedures, and practices that produce unequal outcomes for men and women. In principle, sexism refers to disadvantages that may be experienced by either sex. In reality, the patterns of gender inequality in history and throughout the world today generally involve disadvantages for women and advantages for men. What we usually mean by sexism, then, is a set of cultural and social processes that justify and promote disadvantage for women.

Sexism also has a wide-ranging impact on how we think about our lives and the places of women and men in them. As sociologist Jessie Bernard put it in a discussion of the impact of sexism on women:

> [Sexism is] the unconscious, taken-for-granted, assumed, unquestioned, unexamined, unchallenged acceptance of the belief that the world as it looks to men is the only world, that the way of dealing with it which men have created is the only way, that the values which men have evolved are the only ones, that the way sex looks to men is the only way it can look to anyone, that what men think about what women are like is the only way to think about what women are like. (Quoted in Gornick and Moran, 1971:xxv)

The most pervasive form of institutional sexism is **patriarchy,** a system of social organization in which men have a disproportionate share of power. Patriarchy is rooted in cultural and legal systems that historically gave fathers authority in family and clan matters, made wives and children dependent on husbands and fathers, and organized descent and inheritance through the male line. Most sociologists believe that patriarchal systems serve the interests of men at the expense of women, and nearly all societies around the world today are patriarchal.

Gender Inequality in the United States

How disadvantaged are women in U.S. society? That varies from state to state. In this section, we look at the division of labor in the family, gender stratification in the workplace, the "glass ceiling," disparities in pay, and sexual harassment and rape.

Dividing Labor in the Family. Sexual inequality has historically been sustained by assigning the economic-provider role to men and the child-rearing role to women. Labor in the public sphere has been rewarded by money, prestige, and power, whereas labor in the domestic sphere typically has been isolated and undervalued (Crittenden, 2001; Daniels, 1987; Ferree, 1990; Kessler-Harris, 1990). Gender stereotypes arise in response to a gender division of labor and then

serve to rationalize it by attributing to the sexes substantially different personality characteristics and traits (Hoffman and Hurst, 1990).

Gender inequality exists in every society around the world, but recent changes have moved many women who traditionally did only unpaid domestic labor into the paid labor force.

Across the years, the gender division of labor has operated to bind women to their reproductive function. Women were viewed as providing a man with sexual and domestic services in exchange for his financial support. Women lost their legal identity when they married and, in the eyes of the law, became "incorporated and consolidated" with their husbands. A wife could not own property in her own right or sign a contract. And a husband could require his wife to live wherever he chose and to submit to sexual intercourse against her will—a practice we now call rape.

Over the last four decades, marriage and family have become less of an organizing force in the lives of contemporary American women. Work outside the home is no longer limited by obligations that traditionally bound women to husbands and children. Although they still place a high value on marriage and the family, younger women are now more likely to delay marriage and childbearing (see Chapter 7). Women in the younger generation are taking greater control of their lives and are integrating labor-force participation and family responsibilities more independently than their older counterparts (McLaughlin et al., 1988).

Gender Stratification in the Workplace.

In 2002, the labor-force participation rate for U.S. women 16 and older was 59.6 percent. In other words, nearly 60 percent of women age 16 or over were working or looking for work (U.S. Department of Labor, 2003). Almost half—47 percent—of all U.S. workers are women.

In the United States, 68 percent of single and 62 percent of married women 16 and older are now in the paid labor force, compared with 73 percent of single and 77 percent of married men (U.S. Census Bureau,

2003). Since 1950 the number of American mothers employed outside the home has tripled. In 72.1 percent of the families with children under age 18, the mother is employed. Even women with very young children are increasingly part of the labor force; 64.3 percent of women with children under age six and more than 60 percent with children under age one are employed (U.S. Department of Labor, 2003).

In 2002, for the first time, women caught up with and passed men in one educational arena: the number of women aged 25 and over with a high school diploma exceeded that of men (Bergman, 2003). Women also have gained ground by entering college in higher numbers than men (U.S. Census Bureau, 2003) and by moving into higher-paying fields traditionally dominated by men. For example, between 1980 and 2000, the percentage of women lawyers rose from 14 percent to 29 percent and the proportion of female doctors increased from 13 percent to 27 percent (U.S. Census Bureau, 2003). Half the entering medical students for the 2003–2004 school year were women (Association of American Medical Colleges, 2003). Additionally, the Department of Education reports that more than 4 in 10 Ph.D. degrees are now earned by women (Gerald and Hussar, 2002).

Despite these changes, many of the current figures on the employment of women bear a striking resemblance to those of previous decades. There was little substantial change in the gender segregation of occupations between 1900 and 1970. Levels of segregation did decline in the 1980s and 1990s, but the decline slowed between 1990 and 1997 (Wells, 1999). Men and women sort into occupational categories in some general ways: 59 percent of men work in precision production, craft, and repair jobs; executive, administrative, and managerial positions; professional specialty; and sales, while 73 percent of women work in administrative support; professional specialty; and service work and hold executive, administrative, and managerial positions (Spraggins, 2003). The increase in female employment has come largely through the displacement of men by women in some low-paying categories and through the rapid expansion of "pink-collar" occupations such as secretary, bookkeeper, and receptionist.

The Glass Ceiling.

The number of women top executives and board directors has increased over the years, but positions at the top still elude women executives. Women in business crash into what has been labeled the "glass ceiling," a set of invisible barriers that prevent women from advancing.

In 2001, 45 percent of the jobs classified as executive, administrative, and managerial were held by women (U.S. Census Bureau, 2003). But only a very few of these women were at the very top. Yet change has occurred; in 2003, 50 of the Fortune 500 companies had women filling at least a quarter of their corporate officer positions, up from only 25 in 1995 (Catalyst, 2003).

Corporate boards of directors in general are still made up primarily of men; only 13.6 percent of Fortune 500 board seats were held by women in 2003 (Guida, 2003). But gains have been made. All of the top 100 companies have at least one woman on their board, and the number of companies with no women directors continues to decrease (Catalyst, 2003).

Disparities in Pay.

Women earn less than men. On average, women employed full-time earn only 76.6 cents for each dollar earned by males, up from 60.7 cents per dollar in 1960 (Hartmann and Lovell, 2003). More women than men have low incomes, with 4.4 percent of women but only 2.8 percent of men reporting incomes of less than $10,000 and 12.9 percent of females but only 10.4 percent of males living below the poverty level. At the other end of the income level, 15.8 percent of men but only 5.5 percent of women reported annual earnings of $75,000 and over in 2001 (Spraggins, 2003). Although the wage gap has closed over the past several decades, the rate of decrease has slowed recently (Hartmann and Lovell, 2003) and significant disparities remain overall (see Figure 6.1). Though the education gap between men and women has closed, there is a sharp disparity in earnings between men and women at all levels of education (see Figure 6.2).

The pay gap is affected by many factors. Sociologist Paula England (1993) suggested three major explanations. First, discrimination in hiring and placement reduces women's chances for high-paying jobs in occupations dominated by men such as management, craft occupations, and some professions. Second, jobs that are occupied mostly by women provide lower wages than jobs that are dominated by men. In one analysis, it was found that nurses were paid less than fire truck mechanics, and librarians were paid less than custodians. Third, women often have less job experience than men because they interrupt their careers to care for children.

Other related factors also contribute to the pay gap. For example, women are less likely than men to work full-time. Although women comprise 47 percent of the workforce, only 41 percent of the full-time, year-round workers in the United States were women in 2001 (Spraggins, 2003). The wage ratio also is affected by age, with the youngest female employees earning wages the most similar to young men and the oldest women having the greatest disparity in pay (Hartmann and Lovell, 2003). These differences reflect differences in education and experience.

Sexual Harassment and Rape.

Sexual harassment remains a common workplace hazard for women (Fitzgerald, 1993).

**Median Yearly Earnings of Full-Time, Year-Round
Workers in the U.S. by Gender, in Constant 2001 Dollars, 1960–2001**

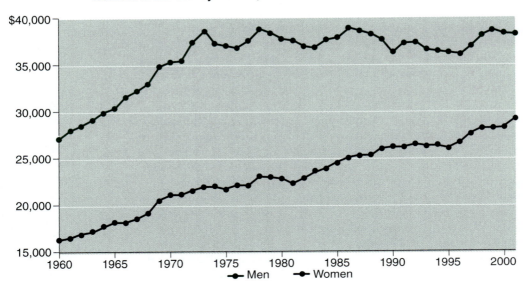

Figure 6.1   Disparities in Earnings Remain Significant

Median yearly earnings of full-time, year-round workers in the United States by gender, in constant 2001 dollars, 1960–2001. Recent gains by women in terms of the ratio of their earnings to those of men is due both to a decrease in earnings of men and to an increase in earnings of women.

Source: U.S. Census Bureau, March Current Population Surveys, available at http://www.census.gov/hhes/income/histinc/p38.html.

The Equal Employment Opportunity Commission defines sexual harassment as "unwelcome" sexual attention, whether verbal or physical, that affects an employee's job conditions or creates a "hostile" working environment (Adler, 1991). Examples of sexual harassment include unsolicited and unwelcome flirtations, advances, or propositions; graphic or degrading comments about an employee's appearance, dress, or anatomy; the display of sexually suggestive objects or pictures; ill-received sexual jokes and offensive gestures; sexual or intrusive questions about an employee's personal life; explicit descriptions of a male's own sexual experiences; abuse of familiarities such as "honey," "baby," and "dear"; unnecessary, unwanted physical contact such as touching, hugging, pinching, patting, or kissing; whistling and catcalls; and leering. One poll found that 4 of 10 women had encountered some form of sexual harassment at work, and 5 of 10 men said that they had said or done something that could be construed as harassment (Kolbert, 1991).

Sexual harassment is not limited to the workplace. Half of all female college students who participated in a nationwide survey

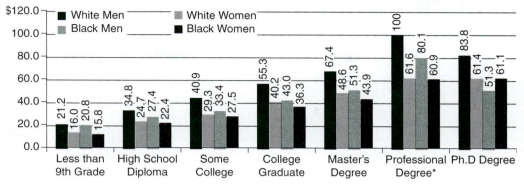

Disparities in Earnings by Race, Gender, and Education in the U.S. 2001

Figure 6.2   Education Is Important, But It Doesn't Eliminate Inequality

Yearly earnings in thousands of dollars of persons 25 years and older, by gender, race, and education, 2001. Black and white women earn less in every educational category than black and white men.

*Professional school degree (e.g., law, medicine).

Source: Bureau of Labor Statistics Current Population Survey, Annual Demographic Supplement (2002), available at http://ferret.bls.census.gov/macro/032002/perinc/new03_000.htm.

reported having been subjected to sexist remarks, catcalls, and whistles. In addition, 15.5 percent reported sexual victimizations other than rape, 13.1 percent reported having been stalked, 20 percent reported getting obscene phone calls, and 10 percent had had false rumors spread about their sex lives (Fisher, Cullen, and Turner, 2000).

Rape is the most violent form of sexual victimization, and it is a form of sexual violence that victimizes women much more than it does men (Kessler et al., 1995). The legal definition of forcible rape varies across states in the United States, but it is generally defined as forcing persons to engage in sexual intercourse against their will. It also can include forcing a person to engage in oral sex and other sex acts. Defined in this way, rape of men by women is extremely rare (Thio, 1998). But rape of women by men is anything but rare: Reasonable estimates of the percentage of women in the United States who have been raped by men sometime in their lifetimes range from 10 to 25 percent (see Box 6.2).

Why do men rape women? Most rapists are *not* psychologically disturbed, sexually inadequate, or unable to relate to women in a normal way. Because psychological explanations at the individual level leave so much unexplained, sociologists have turned to explanations that emphasize culture, socialization, and social structure.

Culture can create a context in which rapes are more likely to occur. It does this through the creation and dissemination of norms,

How Many People Get Raped?

Researcher Mary Koss made headlines—and drew heavy criticism—when she published her findings that more than a quarter of all college women have experienced an act that met the legal definition of rape (Koss, Gidycz, and Wisniewski, 1987). Her estimate was 10 to 15 times higher than comparable rates reported by the Bureau of Justice in statistics from their National Crime Victimization Survey (NCVS). Why are the numbers so different?

Rape may be the crime for which it is most difficult to get reliable numbers, and it seems that how the data are gathered is critical. The Uniform Crime Reports (UCR) data, measured by the FBI Index of Crime, are based on police reports of crime. Before a rape appears in the UCR, it must be reported to the police, and the police must be satisfied that "a man must have had (1) carnal knowledge of a woman, (2) forcibly, and (3) against her will" (Gove, Hughes, and Geerken, 1985).

While the NCVS typically uncovers higher rates of rape than appear in the UCR, the questions used to determine these rates do not actually ask a woman if she has ever been raped. A woman must tell the interviewer that she has been raped in response to general questions about whether she has ever been attacked or threatened. Rape itself is never mentioned; it is up to the person being questioned to volunteer the information (Gove, Hughes, and Geerken, 1985).

An obvious way to get more information is to ask people directly whether they have been raped. A national survey that asked this question of both men and women found that 9.2 percent of women and less than 1.0 percent of men had ever been raped in their lifetimes (Kessler et al., 1995). Both numbers are significantly higher than those that appear in either the National Crime Survey or the UCR.

Even higher rates are obtained when the question is asked in a different way. When respondents were asked if anyone had ever forced them to do something sexual, 22 percent of women and 4 percent of men responded yes (Laumann et al., 1994; Michael et al., 1994). A study of nearly 5,000 women attending U.S. colleges and universities also found that what is asked makes a big difference (Fisher, Cullen, and Turner, 2000). This study included a comparison component that used methods similar to those used in the NCVS. The main study, which used extremely detailed questions about "unwanted sexual experiences," found rates of rape and attempted rape that were 11 and 6 times higher than the rates found by the comparison study.

The rates reported by Bonnie Fisher and her colleagues (2000) are in line with those reported by Mary Koss (1987) for college women and by others for the general population. Fisher's survey responses showed that 1.7 percent of the college women had experienced

values, and ways of thinking that encourage and justify rape. Examples are music videos, movies, television shows, magazine displays, and pornography that portray women as sex objects, always being ready for sex, and being coerced or forced into sexual activity, perhaps even "enjoying it." Masculine culture among young men often involves patterns of discussion, joking, and banter that treat women primarily as objects of sexual desire and as legitimate targets in sexual pursuits (Fields, 1993; Thio, 1998). This may not directly cause rape, but it creates a normative environment that makes the world safer for rape and rapists (Martin and Hummer, 1995). Studies show that campus athletes, perhaps the most heavily influenced by the culture of mas-

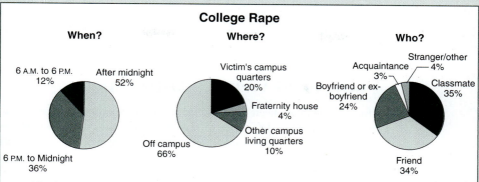

College Rape

When?

6 A.M. to 6 P.M. 12%
After midnight 52%
6 P.M. to Midnight 36%

Where?

Victim's campus quarters 20%
Fraternity house 4%
Other campus living quarters 10%
Off campus 66%

Who?

Acquaintance 3%
Stranger/other 4%
Classmate 35%
Boyfriend or ex-boyfriend 24%
Friend 34%

It would appear that rape is not primarily a problem of public life. These data for college women apply to the general population. Rapists are not likely to be lurking in dark alleys; they are likely to be sitting in your living room or next to you in a car. Rape is primarily a problem of private life, and rapists are most likely to be people with whom the rape victim has a close personal relationship.

Source: Figure generated by the authors using data from Fisher, Cullen, and Turner, 2000.

a rape and 1.1 percent an attempted rape during an average period of about seven months. What does such a rate mean? For a school with 10,000 female students, more than 350 of them experience rape or attempted rape in a single academic year. Projected over the five years that most students now spend getting an undergraduate degree, one-fifth to one-quarter of all college women would experience a rape or attempted rape.

How many rapes we believe occur seems to depend primarily on how victims are asked about their experiences. Fisher and her colleagues concluded, "The use of graphically worded screen questions . . . likely prompted more women who had experienced a sexual victimization to report this fact to the interviewer" (Fisher, Cullen, and Turner, 2000:14).

Questions for Discussion

1. If you were researching rape, what problems would you face in determining the number of rapes that occur in a given time period?

2. The data on college rape show that rapists are most likely to be someone the victim knows, perhaps intimately. Why do rapes occur in such situations? What strategies would help prevent such rapes?

culinity, are more likely to exhibit sexual aggression than other college men (Koss and Gaines, 1993; Nelson, 1994; Crosset et al., 1996).

Culture and gender inequality combine to powerfully influence the prevalence of rape and sexual aggression. Sanday's (1981) study of small societies showed that societies with high rates of rape were those where males were heavily dominant and in which sexual aggression was a symbol of masculinity and of men's control and mastery of women, while those with little rape were those that discouraged sexual aggression. Sanday (1996) and other researchers (Schwartz and DeKeseredy, 1997; Martin and Hummer, 1995; Schwartz, 1995) have found that college campuses with low rates of rape are those in which the culture of masculinity is not strong and where sexual assault and rape are taken seriously and severely punished. Those with high rates of rape are those where the student culture values heavy drinking, male dominance, and traditional masculine values.

Sources of Gender Differences

Thus far, we have been focusing on gender inequality with respect to the macro-structural features of society. What about more micro- or individual-level explanations for gender differences? In this section, we will look at gender differences and biology, culture, and identity.

Gender and Biology

The biological aspects of gender consist of the physical differences between men and women: Women have the capacity to ovulate, carry a fetus until delivery, and provide it with milk after birth; men have the ability to produce and transmit sperm.

The role biology plays in producing behavioral differences between men and women is far less clear than the role it plays in physical differences. For example, testosterone has been linked to competitive drive, but both women and men produce the hormone. Further, the kinds of factors that cause changes in testosterone levels (e.g., the anticipation of competition) cause those changes in both men and women. On average, men produce more testosterone than women, and women produce some hormones in greater quantities than men, but all humans produce estrogen, prolactin, oxytocin, cortisol, and a number of other hormones as well (Blum, 1997).

Are There Real Gender Differences Based on Biology?

On the basis of a survey of over 2,000 books and articles on sex differences, psychologists Eleanor E. Maccoby and Carol N. Jacklin (1974) concluded that there are four fairly "well-established" differences between boys and girls:

1. Beginning about age 11, girls show greater verbal ability than boys.
2. Boys are superior to girls on visual-spatial tasks in adolescence and adulthood, although not during childhood.
3. At about 12 or 13 years of age, boys move ahead of girls in mathematical ability.
4. Males are more aggressive than females.

Rather than settling controversies about the "essential" or "basic" nature of men and women, the Maccoby-Jacklin findings intensified them. Other psychologists promptly launched new surveys of the literature of gender differences and came to quite different conclusions (Halpern, 1992). For example, Janet Shibley Hyde (1991) looked at the evidence for the alleged cognitive differences (verbal ability, visual-spatial ability, and mathematical ability). She concluded that the magnitude of the differences is at best quite small.

In the years that have intervened since the original Maccoby-Jacklin survey, the gap between male and female performance on standardized tests has disappeared on verbal tests and narrowed on mathematics tests; only among highly precocious math students does the disparity between males and females remain large (Hyde, Fennema, and Lamon, 1990). And a Department of Education study of eighth graders in 41 countries found that the United States was one of only 11 nations that did *not* show a substantial gender gap in either mathematics or science (Sanchez, 1996).

One explanation for the narrowing of the gender gap in mathematics is that contemporary girls and young women are more confident about their mathematical talents and capabilities than previous generations of females. But even more important, a close connection exists between the future educational and economic opportunities for women and their performance as youngsters in school: Equality in opportunities for adults yields parity among males and females in earlier preparatory and mathematical performances (Baker and Jones, 1993).

Gender and Culture

Anthropological evidence suggests that gender roles probably represent the earliest division of labor among human beings. Consequently, we are all born into societies with well-established traditions of cultural guidelines for the behavior of men and women. However, anthropological research shows that, across societies, gender roles vary substantially and do not always conform to stereotypes. In New Guinea, the Arapesh assigned women the task of carrying heavy loads because their heads were believed to be harder and stronger than those of men. Among the Tasmanians of the South Pacific, the most dangerous type of hunting—swimming out to remote rocks in the sea to stalk and club sea otters—was assigned to women. Both the Maori of New Zealand and the Trobriand Islanders (near New Guinea) give the prerogative of initiating sexual activity to women (Murdock, 1935; Ford and Beach, 1951).

The great variation in the gender roles of men and women from one society to another and changes over time in sex-linked behavior suggest that gender roles are primarily determined by social definitions and socially constructed meanings (Bernard, 1987; South and Trent, 1988; Intons-Peterson, 1988).

Gender Identities

Gender identities are the conceptions we have of ourselves as being male or female. Most people have a good fit between their anatomy and their gender identity. Boys generally come to behave in ways their culture labels "masculine," and girls learn to be "feminine."

How do individuals develop gender identities? In this section, we examine three explanations.

Cultural Transmission Theory.

Cultural transmission theorists contend that the acquisition of gender identities and behaviors is a gradual process of learning that begins in infancy (Bandura, 1971, 1973; Fagot, Leinbach, and O'Boyle, 1992). They suggest that parents, teachers, and other adults shape a child's behavior by reinforcing responses that are deemed appropriate to the child's gender role and discouraging inappropriate ones. Moreover, children are motivated to attend to, learn from, and imitate same-sex models because they think of same-sex models as more like themselves (Mischel, 1970). Children are given cues to their gender roles in a great variety of ways, from the way their rooms are decorated to the toys they are given to play with and the clothes they are given to wear.

Cognitive-Development Theory.

Cultural transmission theory portrays children as passive individuals who are programmed for behavior by adults. *Cognitive-development theory* calls our attention to the fact that children actively seek to acquire gender identities and roles.

According to cognitive-development theory as discussed in Chapter 2 (Kohlberg, 1966, 1969; Kohlberg and Ullian, 1974), children come to label themselves as "boys" or "girls" when they are between 18 months and three years of age. Once they have identified themselves as males or females, they want to adopt behaviors consistent with their newly discovered status. This process is called *self-socialization*. According to Kohlberg, children form a stereotyped conception of maleness and femaleness—an oversimplified, exaggerated, cartoonlike image. Then they use this stereotyped image to organize behavior and cultivate the attitudes and actions associated with being a boy or a girl.

Both the cultural transmission and cognitive-development theories of gender-role learning have received research support (Maccoby and Jacklin, 1974; Bem, 1981; Serbin and Sprafkin, 1986; Martin and Little, 1990). Social and behavioral scientists increasingly see gender-role acquisition to be explained by elements from both theoretical approaches.

Self-Construals and Gender.

In Chapter 2 we discussed self-conception and identity. Psychologists Susan Cross and Laura Madson used differences in self-construal, which is essentially synonymous to our term self-conception, to explain gender differences in the United States (Cross and Madson, 1997). Individuals in some societies develop a sense of self that is based primarily on relationships and group memberships. Such a definition of self is referred to by psychologists as an *interdependent self-construal*. In contrast, other societies are individualistic, and self-definition is based on one's unique attributes and the importance of an individual distinguishing him- or herself from others as key to developing a sense of self. This definition of self has been called an *independent self-construal*.

Cross and Madson pointed out that the independent self-construal model describes men better than it does women in the United States and that most U.S. women can probably be best described by the interdependent self-construal model. This major difference in self-construal between men and women in the United States, Cross and Madson argued, has important consequences in terms of gender differences, including those in cognition, motivation, emotion, and social behavior. For example, they found that women are more willing to express most emotions, while men are more willing to express anger. Women are also more likely to be sensitive to the emotions of others and base their own emotions on those.

Sociological Perspectives on Gender Stratification

The Functionalist Perspective

Functionalists suggest that a division of labor originally arose between men and women because of the woman's role in reproduction. Because women were often pregnant or nursing, preindustrial societies assigned domestic and child-rearing tasks to them. In contrast, men were assigned hunting and defense tasks because of their larger size and greater muscular strength. Functionalists contend that a gender division of labor promoted the survival of the species and therefore was retained.

An early attempt to formulate a systematic understanding of the differentiation of gender roles was Parsons and Bales' (1955) study of the family from the functionalist perspective. They suggested that families are organized along instrumental-expressive lines. Men specialize in instrumental tasks, particularly roles associated with having a job and making money, and women in expressive tasks, supporting their husbands, doing household labor, and caring for children. Essentially, Parsons and Bales were arguing that it was functional and beneficial for the society, for families, and for individuals if males play instrumental, goal-oriented roles and females play expressive roles, supporting husbands and nurturing children.

Since the 1960s, sociology has been heavily influenced by feminist thinking, and this position has been criticized as taking an idealized family form from the United States in the 1950s and claiming that it was the uniquely superior model for gender and family relations in industrial societies.

The Conflict Perspective

Much of the critique of functionalism from the 1960s to the 1980s came from conflict theorists who rejected functionalist arguments as simply offering a rationale for male dominance. They contended that a sexual division of labor is a social vehicle devised by men to ensure for themselves privilege, prestige, and power in their relationships with women. Gender inequality exists because it benefits men, who use the power it gives them to ensure its perpetuation. By relegating women to the home, men have been able to d   women those resources they need to succeed in the larger world.

Sociologist Joan Acker (1992) suggested that in industrial capitalist societies, production is privileged over reproduction. Whereas business, commerce, and industry are viewed as an essential source of well-being and wealth, childrearing, child care, and elder care are seen as secondary and wealth-consuming. Although "the family" is enshrined and idealized, reproduction (the domain of women) is shrouded in societal shadows and devalued.

The Interactionist Perspective

Interactionism has had a very important impact on the thinking of sociologists about gender inequality. If meanings form the basis of social life, then as meanings change, patterns of social interaction can change, thus changing the nature of social structure. Sociologists also have made use of the interactionist idea that we experience the world as a constructed reality. They developed the idea that while sex is given in nature, gender is socially constructed; it is a product of sociocultural processes involving symbols and meanings. Interactionists argue that cultural meanings, including those that give rise to gender inequality, are continuously emerging and changing through social interaction. If so, then people can intentionally change the structure of gender differentiation and inequality by changing the meanings that underlie them. For example, when men define themselves in traditional masculinist terms, value male dominance, and view women primarily as objects of sexual pleasure, rape and sexual harassment are more likely to occur. When we replace these meanings with those that value gender equality and view women as complete human beings, the rates of rape and sexual harassment decline.

The Feminist Perspective

A number of feminist perspectives on gender inequality have emerged in recent decades. For example, Miriam Johnson (1993) argued that serving the expressive function in family and society need not lead to disadvantage for women, but that it has led to disadvantage because it exists in the context of a patriarchal culture that values men's instrumentality over women's expressiveness. Changing the patriarchal normative order instead of changing patterns of role differentiation, then, is a more effective way to reduce gender inequality.

On the other hand, Myra Marx Ferree and Elaine J. Hall (2000) argue that organizing society on the basis of gender is socially costly because it represses individual variation and potential. They also argue that inequality does not arise from individual differences between people. Rather, their gender-relations model of inequality posits, social institutions produce inequality and gender differences follow from them.

Sociologists Cecilia Ridgeway and Lynn Smith-Lovin (1999) point out that gender is significantly different from other forms of social inequality. Unlike racial and ethnic inequality or class stratification, the key players in gender inequality—men and women—interact extensively at home, at work, at church, and in a variety of role relationships. These everyday interactions, they contend, recreate the gender system. Such interactions would act to undermine the gender system only in two cases: (1) if the interactions feature women with status or power advantages over men or (2) if they are peer interactions not driven by cultural beliefs about the competence of males and females.

Feminist research has added substantially to our knowledge of women's experiential, subjective, and emotional lives. Though a variety of perspectives make up the "feminist perspective," they are unified in the effort to develop understandings of gender inequality that can be used to transform society and women's lives.

Key Terms

assimilation, 159	gender roles, 167	prejudice, 156
discrimination, 158	genocide, 160	race, 154
environmental racism, 158	institutional discrimination, 158	racism, 154
ethnic groups, 155	minority group, 156	sex, 167
gender, 167	patriarchy, 168	sexism, 168
gender identities, 167	pluralism, 159	symbolic racism, 157

Review Questions

1. What is race? How do sociologists define it?
2. What is an ethnic group?
3. List the five characteristics of minority groups.
4. What is the difference between prejudice and discrimination?

5. How does institutional discrimination work?

6. Define and contrast assimilation and pluralism.

7. Briefly describe the major racial and ethnic groups in the United States.

8. How do the functionalist, conflict, and interactionist perspectives explain racial and ethnic stratification?

9. Define sex and gender.

10. How do the terms *gender role* and *gender identity* differ?

11. What is patriarchy?

12. How do U.S. women compare with U.S. men in terms of occupations, employment, and earnings?

13. Compare and contrast biological and cultural bases for gender differences.

14. Briefly describe the theories of gender identity acquisition.

15. How do the functionalist, conflict, interactionist, and feminist perspectives explain gender inequalities?

Chapter 7

The Family

Structure of the Family

Marriage
and the Family
in the United States

Challenges
for American Families
and American Society

Sociological
Perspectives
on the Family

S ome believe that the family has undergone a grave loss over the past 40 years. They cite gay marriage, easy divorce, the postponement of marriage, a rise in the proportion of the never-married, and the ready availability of contraception as forces that have eroded the family and compromised its "ultimate function"—the licensing of reproduction.

Others believe the family is not disintegrating but merely changing, revealing its flexibility and resilience. They say that traditional family forms are no longer appropriate for contemporary times, adding that the structures were flawed as conformity-ridden, male-dominated, and oppressive. They admit that the meaning of marriage has been changing and with it the family institution but claim that pronouncements concerning the death of the family are greatly

Table **7.1**	A Comparison of the State of U.S. Children, 1960 and 2002	
	1960	**2002**
Children born to unmarried mothers	5%	31%
Mothers returning to work within 1 year of a child's birth	17%	55%
Children under 18 living in a one-parent family (approx.)	10%	28%
Infant mortality (deaths before first birthday	28/1,000	6.5/1,000
Children under 18 living below the poverty line	27%	17%
Married women with children under 6 years old in labor force	18.6%	64.3%

Source: U.S. Census Bureau, 2003.

exaggerated. No matter what we think family is, most of us think it's tremendously important. "Protecting family" was ranked at the top of 57 personal values by a majority of survey respondents in the United States, Canada, and many other countries (Roper Starch Worldwide, 2000).

Whether the American family has been disintegrating or merely changing over the last half of the 20th century, widespread behavioral changes have occurred in the United States and throughout Western societies. Table 7.1 compares the circumstances of American children in the late 1990s with those in 1960; Figure 7.1 reveals substantial shifts in American family arrangements. The "family question," despite its many guises, is not new. Concerns about the family have a long history (Coontz, 1992), and it is safe to assume that debate will continue. In this chapter we will look first at the structure of the family from a global perspective, including forms of marriage and family and patterns of courtship around the world. We will then focus on marriage and family in the United States, both the traditional nuclear family and other forms of family life. We will look at special challenges American families and American society face, including divorce, family violence and abuse, child care, and care for the elderly. Finally, we will see what the three major sociological perspectives have to offer to our understanding of the family.

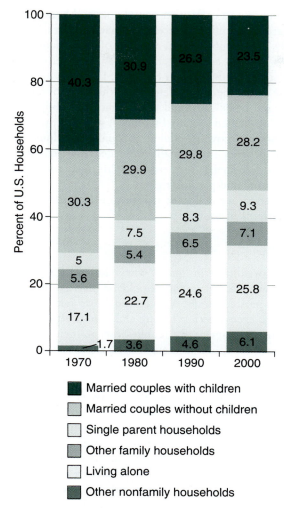

Figure 7.1   Today's Families Differ from Those of an Earlier Generation

Source: Figure generated by the authors using data from Fields and Casper (2001), available at http://www.census.gov/prod/2001/pubs/c2kbr01-2.pdf.

Structure of the Family

What is the family? Sociologists have traditionally viewed the **family** as a social group whose members are related by ancestry, marriage, or adoption and live together, cooperate economically, and care for the young (Murdock, 1949). However, some are unhappy with this definition, arguing that psychological bonds and intimacy are what families are all about; they see the family as a close-knit group of people who care about and respect each other (e.g., Lauer and Lauer, 2000). Many Americans are now willing to accept alternatives to traditional notions of the family. The family, then, is a matter of social definition. Because the family is a social construct, family ties are often independent of legal or kin status (Gubrium and Holstein, 1990).

How we define the family determines the kinds of families we will consider normal or deviant, and what rights and obligations we will recognize as legally and socially binding. A growing number of judges and legislators are now extending to qualifying domestic partners some of the benefits traditionally accorded married heterosexuals, including health benefits, property and life insurance, bereavement leave, and annuity and pension rights.

In this section, we will look at forms of the family, forms of marriage, and patterns of courtship.

Forms of the Family

Families are organized in many ways. Individuals differ in their thoughts about whether parents should be married, how many children make a perfect family, whether male or female offspring are preferable, and even whether having children at all is important (see Box 7.1). More fundamentally, families vary in their composition and in their descent, residence, and authority patterns—characteristics we examine here.

Composition.   Social relationships between adult males and females can be organized within families by emphasizing either spouse or kin relationships. In the **nuclear family** arrangement, spouses and their offspring constitute the core relationship; blood relatives are functionally marginal and peripheral. In contrast, in the **extended family** arrangement, kin—individuals related by common ancestry— provide the core relationship; spouses are functionally marginal and peripheral. Americans typically find themselves members of two nuclear families. First, an individual belongs to a nuclear family that consists of oneself and one's father, mother, and siblings, what sociologists call the **family of orientation.** Second, since over 90 percent of Americans marry at least once, most are members of a nuclear family that consists of oneself and one's spouse and children, the **family of procreation.**

Extended families are found in numerous forms throughout the world. In the Nayara soldiering caste of southwestern India during the pre-British period, spouse ties were virtually absent (Fuller, 1976). When a woman was about to enter puberty, she was ritually married to a man chosen for her by a neighborhood assembly. After three ceremonial days, she was ritually separated from him and was then free to take on a series of visiting husbands or lovers. Although a woman's

A Wide Variety in Family Values

The family is among the most important institutions in every society, but exactly how people value the family varies from one society to the next. A 1997 Gallup survey in 16 countries on four continents found wide variety in attitudes about the importance of parents being married, the ideal number of children to have, whether a boy or a girl was preferable, and even in the degree to which people desire to have children at all (Gallup, 1997).

The ideal number of children for a family varies among countries, from India, where 87 percent of the survey respondents indicated that up to two children was the perfect number, to Iceland, where 69 percent indicated that three or more was the perfect number. Other countries favoring small families (with up to two children as ideal) included Spain, Germany, Colombia, Hungary, Thailand, and Great Britain. Countries favoring three or more children included Guatemala and Taiwan. The United States is divided on the issue of the perfect number of children, with 50 percent favoring up to two children and 41 percent favoring three or more children.

Survey respondents also were asked whether, if they could have only one child, they would prefer to have a girl or a boy. Although more than half the respondents replied "no opinion" in many countries (e.g., Tawian, Hungary, Guatemala, Canada, Singapore, Germany, Iceland, and Spain), when respondents did have an opinion, they tended to prefer boys. In only a few countries did a preference for girls beat a preference for boys, and only by a slim margin.

Finally, whether children are important to one's sense of fulfillment also varied by country, but in almost every country surveyed, most respondents agreed that they were. In Hungary, 94 percent of the respondents said it was necessary to have a child to feel fulfilled. The United States was at the opposite extreme, with only 46 percent of respondents indicating that having a child was important and 51 percent indicating that it was not. In 2000, 19 percent of 40- to 44-year-old U.S. women had not had children, a rate double that from 1980 (U.S. Census Bureau, 2003). Other countries whose respondents felt having a child was important were India, Taiwan, Iceland, Thailand, Lithuania, and Singapore.

Men and women within each country generally agreed on the questions discussed above. The only question on which men and women had clear differences of opinion was gender preference. Women had either no gender preference or a slight preference for boys; men had a strong preference for boys, around the world but especially in the United States and in several less industrialized countries.

Valuing the family may be universal, but family values are not. These findings strongly suggest that, like other cultural traits, family values vary because of differing social, economic, and other factors, such as religion. They also suggest that as our society, economy, and culture change, we are likely to observe more changes in our American family values.

Questions for Discussion

1. How do you account for the small proportion of Americans who believe having a child is important?

2. Why do you think people who express a gender preference for their offspring primarily prefer boys?

---

lovers gave her regular gifts on prescribed occasions, they did not provide support. When a woman had a child, one of the men—not necessarily the biological father—paid a fee to the midwife and thus established the child's legitimacy. However, the man assumed no economic, social, legal, or ritual rights or obligations toward the child. It was the mother's kin who took responsibility.

For some time, sociologists assumed that industrialization undercut extended family patterns while fostering nuclear family arrangements. A closer look shows a different pattern. By virtue of high mortality rates, the nuclear family had come to prevail in England before the Industrial Revolution got under way (Laslett, 1974, 1976; Stearns, 1977; Quadagno, 1982). When Tamara K. Hareven (1982) examined family life in a textile community in 19th-century New Hampshire, she discovered that industrialism promoted kin ties. Not only did different generations often reside together in the same household, but they provided a good deal of assistance to one another. Indeed, economic dislocations and the increased availability of nonnuclear kin may actually have encouraged the formation of extended family households in the early industrialization of England and the United States (Ruggles, 1987). Overall, a growing body of research suggests that a large number of factors—in addition to the nature of the political economy—interact with one another to produce a diversity of family life patterns (Hutter, 1998; Cherlin, 2002; Kertzer, 1991).

Descent.   Societies trace descent and pass on property from one generation to the next in one of three ways. Under a **patrilineal** arrangement, a people reckon descent and transmit property through the line of the father. Under a **matrilineal** arrangement, descent and inheritance take place through the mother's side of the family. Under the **bilineal** arrangement, both sides of an individual's family are equally important. Americans are typically bilineal, reckoning descent through both the father and the mother; however, the surname is transmitted in a patrilineal manner.

Residence.   Societies also differ in where a couple take up residence after marriage. In the case of **patrilocal residence,** the bride and groom live in the household or community of the husband's family. The opposite pattern prevails in **matrilocal residence.** For example, among the Hopi of the Southwest, the husband moves upon marriage into the dwelling of his wife's family, where he eats and sleeps. In the United States, newlyweds tend to follow **neolocal residence** patterns, in which they set up a new place of residence independent of either of their parents or other relatives.

Authority.   Although the authority a man or woman enjoys in family decision making is influenced by their personalities, societies nonetheless dictate who is expected to be the dominant figure. Under **patriarchal authority,** the eldest male or the husband fills this role. The ancient Hebrews, Greeks, and Romans and the 19th-century Chinese and Japanese provide a few examples. Logically, the construction of a **matriarchal authority** family type is very simple and would involve the vesting of power in women. Yet true matriarchies are rare (Hutter, 1998), and considerable controversy exists about whether the balance of power actually rests with the wife in any known society (Stephens, 1963). Matriarchies can arise through default upon the death of or desertion by the husband. In a third type of family, the **egalitarian authority** arrangement, power and authority are equally distributed between husband and wife. This pattern has been on the increase in the United States.

Forms of Marriage

Marriage refers to a socially approved sexual union between two or more individuals that is undertaken with some idea of permanence. The parties to a marriage must be members of two different kin groups, which has crucial implications for the structuring of the family. Indeed, the continuity and therefore the long-term welfare of any kin group depends on

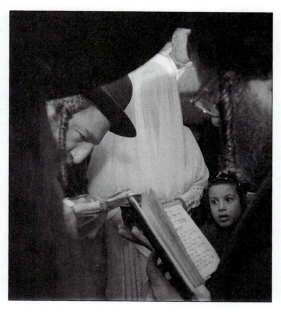

Norms that govern marriage in many ethnic groups, including those among Orthodox Jews, specify *endogamy,* the requirement that marriage occur within the group.

obtaining spouses for the unmarried members of the group from other groups. In this section we will define and discuss exogamy, endogamy, incest taboos, monogamy, polygyny, polyandry, and group marriage.

Exogamy and Endogamy.
All societies regulate the pool of eligibles from which individuals are expected to select a mate. A child's kin generally have more in mind than simply getting a child married. They want the child married to the right spouse, especially where marriage has consequences for the larger kin group. Two types of marital regulations define the "right" spouse: endogamy and exogamy. **Endogamy** is the requirement that marriage occur within a group. Under these circumstances people must marry within their class, race, ethnic group, or religion. **Exogamy** is the requirement that marriage occur outside a group. Under these circumstances, people must marry outside their kin group, be it their immediate nuclear family, clan, or tribe.

Regulations relating to exogamy are based primarily on kinship and usually entail **incest taboos,** rules that prohibit sexual intercourse with close blood relatives and exist today in virtually every society (Olson and DeFrain, 1997).

Types of Marriage.
The relationships between a husband and wife may be structured in one of four ways: **monogamy,** one husband and one wife; **polygyny,** one husband and two or more wives; **polyandry,** two or more husbands and one wife; and **group marriage,** two or more husbands and two or more wives. Monogamy appears in all societies, although other forms may not only be permitted but

preferred. Monogamy was the preferred or ideal type of marriage in fewer than 20 percent of 862 societies included in one cross-cultural sample (Murdock, 1967).

Polygyny has enjoyed a wide distribution throughout the world. The Old Testament, for example, records polygynous practices among the Hebrews. In China, India, and the Islamic countries, polygyny usually has been the privilege of the wealthy few. In the United States, it is not legal, but it does exist. A man in Utah with five wives and 29 children recently was charged with bigamy and rape. An additional 30,000 polygynists are thought to be practicing "underground" (Arrillaga, 2000). The arrangement tends to be favored where large families are advantageous and women make substantial contributions to subsistence.

Although polygyny has a wide distribution, polyandry is exceedingly rare. Polyandry usually does not represent freedom of sexual choice for women; often, it involves the right or the opportunity of younger brothers to have sexual access to the wife of an older brother. If a family cannot afford wives or marriages for each of its sons, it may find a wife for the eldest son only.

Patterns of Courtship

Marriage brings a new member into the inner circle of a family, and relatives have a stake in who is to be the spouse. Random mating might jeopardize these interests: If sons and daughters were permitted to "fall in love" with anybody, they might choose the wrong mate. Instead, courtship in many societies follows specific and traditional patterns, the topic of discussion of this section. We will consider the nature of love and examine some of the factors important to mate selection.

The Social Regulation of Love.

Although love has many meanings, we usually think of the strong physical and emotional attraction between a man and a woman as **romantic love**. The ancient Greeks saw such love as a "diseased hysteria," an overwhelming force that irresistibly draws two people together and leads them to become passionately preoccupied with one another.

Sociologist William J. Goode (1959) found that some societies give romantic love more emphasis than others. At one extreme, societies view marriage without love as mildly shameful; at the other, they define strong romantic attachment as a laughable or tragic aberration. The American middle class falls toward the pole of positive approval; the 19th-century Japanese and Chinese fell toward the pole of disapproval; and the Greeks after Alexander and the Romans of the empire took a middle course.

Factors in Mate Selection.

Given a field of eligible mates, why do we fall in love with and marry one person and not another? A variety of factors are at work. One is **homogamy,** the tendency of like to marry like. People of similar age, race, religion, nationality, education, intelligence, health, stature, attitudes, and countless other traits tend to marry one another to a degree greater than would be found by chance. Although homogamy seems to operate with respect to social characteristics, the evidence is less clear for psychological factors such as personality and temperament.

Physical attractiveness also plays a part in mate selection. We prefer the companionship and friendship of attractive people to that of unattractive people (Feingold, 1990). However, since the supply of unusually beautiful or handsome partners is limited, we tend in real life to select partners who have a degree of physical attractiveness similar to our own (Murstein, 1972, 1976; Feingold, 1988). According to the **matching hypothesis,** we typically experience the greatest payoff and the least cost when we follow this course; individuals of equal attractiveness are those most likely to reciprocate our advances.

The **complementary needs** theory (Winch, 1958) refers to two different personality traits that are the counterparts of each other and that provide a sense of completeness when they are joined. Dominant people find a complementary relationship with passive people, and talkative people find themselves attracted to good listeners. Interpersonal attraction depends on how well each partner fulfills the role expectations of the other and how mutually gratifying they find their "role fit" (Bluhm, Widiger, and Miele, 1990; Collins and Read, 1990).

Exchange theory links these three factors. It is based on the notion that we like those who reward us and dislike those who punish us (Molm, 1991; Lawler and Yoon, 1993). Many of our acts derive from our confidence that from them will flow some benefit—perhaps a desired expression of love, gratitude, recognition, security, or material reward. In the course of interacting, we reinforce the relationship by rewarding each other. Thus, people with similar social traits, attitudes, and values mutually reward one another. In selecting partners of comparable physical attractiveness, we minimize the risk of rejection while maximizing the profit from such a conquest. And the parties in complementary relationships offer each other high rewards at low cost to themselves. In sum, exchange theory proposes that people involved in a mutually satisfying relationship will exchange behaviors that have low cost and high reward.

Marriage and the Family in the United States

The American family has become such a debated subject that sociologists sometimes appear to be at war with one another. Some argue that marriage and family have positive effects on children and marriage partners (Glenn, 1997; Popenoe, 1993). Others—perhaps the majority—say that there are both negative and positive effects and that those who extol the virtues of "family" are traditionalists and conservatives (Scanzoni, 1997; Skolnick, 1997; Cherlin, 1997). This section focuses on the issues that underlie this debate.

We will examine life within marriage and parenthood and will discuss some of the many types of lifestyles in the United States beyond the traditional nuclear family: stepfamilies, singlehood, single parenthood, cohabitation, and gay and lesbian couples.

Life within Marriage

Most adult Americans hope to establish an intimate relationship with another person and make the relationship work. This finding underlies a study of American couples undertaken by sociologists Philip Blumstein and Pepper Schwartz (1983). Though the study is more than 20 years old, it is still the best study of its kind and has much to tell us about American marriages.

More Conventional Than Expected.
American couples are more conventional than Blumstein and Schwartz expected them to be. For example, although 60 percent of the wives were employed outside the home, only 30 percent of the men and 39 percent of the women believed that both spouses should work. As we discussed in Chapter 6, when the wives had full-time jobs, they still did the greater part of the housework. Men do more housework than they used to, but women still do most of the housework and child care, even when both husband and wife have full-time jobs (Bittman et al., 2003).

Emotional and Sexual Relations.
Most of the married couples had sexual relations at least once a week. People who had sex infrequently were just as likely to have a long-lasting relationship as those who had sex often. While couples were happier when the opportunity to initiate and refuse sex was shared equally by the partners, in more than half of the cases the husbands were still the primary initiators. Women tended to link sex and love; men often did not. Less than a third of the couples engaged in extramarital activities. Husbands were more often repeatedly unfaithful than wives, but their transgressions did not necessarily represent dissatisfaction with either their partner or the relationship as a whole. Women, in contrast, often strayed just once, mostly out of curiosity; but for them, infidelity was more likely to blossom into a full-fledged love affair.

Marriage in Middletown.
Like Blumstein and Schwartz, Theodore Caplow and his colleagues (1982) expected to find the American nuclear family in trouble when they undertook a restudy of Robert S. and Helen Merrill Lynd's sociological classic of the 1920s, "Middle-

town" (1929, 1937). The Lynds had made Middletown, a pseudonym for Muncie, Indiana, into a leading sociological laboratory. Caplow and his associates concluded that the doomsayers were wrong and that the family had not lost its attractiveness. Comparing Middletown in the 1970s to Middletown in the 1920s, they found "increased family solidarity, a smaller generation gap, closer marital communication, more religion, and less mobility" (1982:323). They say their findings were as surprising to them "as they may be to our readers." Other researchers have come to essentially the same conclusions (Whyte, 1990).

Are We Giving Up on Marriage?

That depends on who answers the question. Sociologist Judith Stacey would be likely to answer that we ought to give up on marriage. "The Family," she says, "is a concept derived from faulty theoretical premises and an imperialist logic, which even at its height never served the best interests of women, their children, or even of many men" (Stacey, 1996:50). Linda Waite and Maggie Gallagher (2000), on the other hand, recently published *The Case for Marriage*, a book aimed at demonstrating that married people and their children are better off financially, emotionally, and physically. One of the most consistent findings in health research, for example, is that married people typically have better mental and physical health than the nonmarried (Gove, Style, and Hughes, 1990; Gove, Hughes, and Style, 1983). Never married and divorced or separated people are also four times more likely than married people to be victims of crimes (Rennison, 2002a).

What if you probe the general public—or people who are married? Public opinion surveys indicate that Americans depend very heavily on marriage for their psychological well-being (Waite and Gallagher, 2000; Gove, Style, and Hughes 1990; Glenn and Weaver, 1981). Although divorce rates increased dramatically earlier in the century, they have declined gradually since the early 1980s. And almost everyone tries marriage; only about 5 percent of Americans never marry. Most people who get divorced also get remarried.

However, American men and women are marrying at a later age than they have in recent history (U.S. Census Bureau, 2003). The median age at first marriage for U.S. men rose to 26.9 in 2001 from a low of 22.6 in the mid-1950s. For U.S. women, the figure rose to 25.3 years, up from a low of 20.2 years, also in the mid-1950s. In 1890 half of all women were married by the age of 22. Although people are postponing marriage, by their early 40s, 84 percent of men and 88 percent of women have been married at least once. Marriage is no longer seen as a prerequisite for childbearing; 31 percent of U.S. children are born to unmarried parents (U.S. Census Bureau, 2003).

Increasing numbers of Americans no longer view marriage as a permanent institution but as something that can be ended and reentered. The goal of "having a happy marriage" currently ranks well above "being married to the same person for life" and even farther above merely "being married" (Glenn, 1992). And people seem to be reaching that goal: almost two-thirds of married Americans rate their own marriages as "very happy."

Parenthood

Married couples who decide to have children find their lives transformed by parenthood. Among other changes, costs go up when children are added to a family: Total annual expenditures per child are approximately $6,750 for a low-income family and $13,500 for a high-income family (U.S. Census Bureau, 2003). In this section we will discuss the family life course, the adjustments husbands and wives make to their new roles as parents, and the "empty-nest syndrome."

The Family Life Course.

Nuclear families that are not disrupted by divorce, desertion, or death typically pass through a series of changes and realignments across time, what sociologists call the **family life course.** These changes and realignments are related to the altered expectations and requirements imposed on a husband and wife as children are born and grow up.

The family begins with the husband–wife pair and becomes increasingly complex as members are added, creating new roles and multiplying the number of relationships. The family then stabilizes for a time, after which it begins shrinking as each of the adult children is launched. Finally, it returns once more to the husband–wife pair, and eventually terminates with the death of a spouse. Of course, many individual and family behaviors do not occur at the usual ages or in the typical sequence assumed by the family life course model. At times decisive economic, social, political, or military events intervene to alter the normal course of events (Elder, 1983.)

Adjusting to New Roles.

Each change in the role of one family member can affect all the other members. The arrival of the first child compels the reorganization of a couple's life. Parents have to juggle their work roles, alter their time schedules, change their communication patterns, and relinquish some privacy. Parenthood competes with the husband or wife role.

After the birth of a first child, husbands and wives who could once focus unlimited attention on their spouses now have to split their attention between spouse and child. The result is that young parents may feel that their spouses are not paying enough attention to them.

Not surprisingly, marital adjustment ratings, an indicator of marital satisfaction, typically fall after the birth of a first child (Belsky and Rovine, 1990). The addition of a second child changes the family again, reducing the mother's participation in the paid labor force, increasing her responsibilities in housework, and making fathers feel more a part of the family (Boodman, 2000).

A consistent finding is that the psychological well-being of parents is a little worse than that of childless couples, and it remains lower until children grow up and move out of the household (McLanahan and Adams, 1987). And despite the changes a child brings to their lives, most couples report enormous satisfaction with parenthood, ranking their families as more important than work, recreation, friendships, or status.

The Empty Nest. Clinical psychologists and psychiatrists have stressed the problem parents face when their children leave home. But most couples do not experience difficulty with the "empty-nest" period; the majority view this stage as a time of "new freedoms." Indeed, national surveys show that middle-aged women whose children have left home experience greater general happiness and enjoyment of life, in addition to greater marital happiness, than middle-aged women with children still living at home (White and Edwards, 1990; Vander Zanden, 1993). With changes in the family life course, the "empty nest" has become an ill-defined stage; young adults are establishing their own households later and often return to reside for varying lengths of time in their parents' home (Hill and Young, 1999).

Beyond the Traditional Nuclear Family

Much of the public debate over the family in the United States may be misguided because it uses the stereotypical white, middle-class family of the 1950s as a point of departure for either praise or criticism of subsequent changes. Further, the image most of us hold of the 1950s family is less informed by reality than by old television series like *Leave It to Beaver, Ozzie and Harriet,* and *The Donna Reed Show* (Kain, 1990; Skolnick, 1991).

In fact, family relationships are becoming more varied. Transracial adoption results in families whose diversity reflects that of U.S. society. Increasing numbers of children grow up with several sets of parents and an assortment of half brothers and half sisters and stepbrothers and stepsisters. Americans now may have any of a number of **lifestyles,** the overall patterns of living people evolve to meet their biological, social, and emotional needs. In this section, we examine a number of lifestyle options: stepfamilies, singlehood, single parenthood, unmarried cohabitation, and gay and lesbian couples.

Stepfamilies. Remarriage frequently results in stepfamilies, also termed "reconstituted" and "blended" families. Because more than half of remarried persons are parents, their new partners become stepparents. One in six American families are stepfamilies; 35 million Americans live in a stepfamily, including 20 percent of the nation's children under age 18. About 40 percent of remarriages unite two divorced persons; half of them are a first marriage for one member of the couple.

Andrew Cherlin (1978, 2002) has called remarriage an "incomplete institution." Because the situation created by such marriages is ambiguous, most stepparents attempt to recreate a traditional family, which is the only model they have. But a stepfamily functions differently than the traditional nuclear family (Pill, 1990; Larson, 1992). For one thing, the stepparent role does not necessarily approximate that of a biological parent, particularly in authority, legitimacy, and respect. For another, the family tree of a stepfamily can be very complex and convoluted, populated not only by children of both spouses but by six sets of grandparents, relatives of former spouses, relatives of new spouses, and the people former spouses marry. Matters are further complicated because stepparents and stepchildren have no mutual history and often have had no previous opportunity to bond.

Singlehood.   In 2000, 52 percent of men and nearly 40 percent of women age 25 to 29 had never been married. This is more than double the 1970 rate. More liberal sex standards, the high divorce rate, money woes, and the pursuit of education and careers have spurred young adults to marry later than at any time since the Census Bureau started keeping track in 1890. Even so, the population remaining single today is smaller than it was in 1900, when fully 42 percent of all American adult men and 33 percent of adult women never married (Kain, 1984).

Changes in patterns of reported happiness by marital status were uncovered in the 1980s. For many years research had shown that married people reported greater happiness than unmarried, including the never-married. However, in the late 1970s the difference in happiness reported between the never-married and the married began to shift. By the mid-1980s the differences between the never-married and the married had almost disappeared for men and had narrowed considerably for women (Glenn and Weaver, 1988). This pattern remains essentially the same today (Adams, 1998).

Single Parenthood.   More than one American youngster in four lives with just one parent. Of all such children, 82 percent live with their mothers. However, the number of men raising children on their own has risen; in 2002, 5 percent of the nation's children were living with their fathers only, or 18 percent of the children living in single-parent households (Fields, 2003). About two-thirds of single fathers are divorced; roughly 25 percent are among the never-married; and only 7.5 percent are widowers. The largest share of youngsters in single-parent homes—38.6 percent—are living with a divorced parent, and 30.6 percent are living with a parent who has never married; oth-

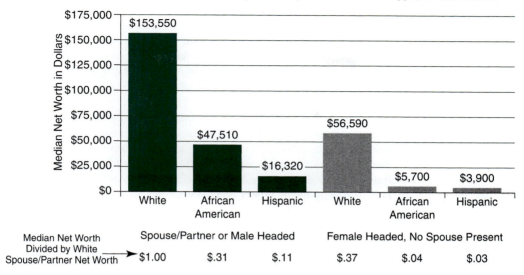

Median Net Worth by Ethnicity and Household Type, United States

Figure 7.2 The Financial Status of Female-Headed Households

Net worth, or wealth, of a household is all the assets of that household minus all debts. Female-headed households have far less net worth than other households. The situation of African-American and Hispanic female-headed households is particularly grave; they have on average 4 and 3 cents, respectively, for every dollar of net worth owned by a white male-headed or spouse/partner household.

Source: Figure generated by the authors using data from the 2001 Survey of Consumer Finances, Board of Governors of the Federal Reserve System.

ers reside with a parent who is married but separated or are offspring of a widowed parent (U.S. Census Bureau, 2003). In 2002, 53 percent of African American children under the age of 18 were living with a single parent. A quarter of Hispanic children, 20 percent of white children, and 15 percent of Asian-American children also were in single-parent families (Fields, 2003).

As we pointed out in Chapter 5, female-headed households are likely to be low-income households. In 2002, 30 percent of all children lived in families with incomes less than $30,000, compared with 65 percent of children living only with their mothers and 45 percent of children living only with their fathers (Fields, 2003). In the case of divorce, marital separation frequently produces a precipitous and sustained decline in household income for the mother and child. The overall financial situation of female-headed households in terms of their net worth can be seen in Figure 7.2.

Unwed motherhood is also on the increase. According to the Census Bureau, one in five of the nation's never-married women 15 to 44 years old have become mothers (Bachu, 1997). Thirty-one percent of all births in the United States were to unwed mothers in 2001 (U.S.

Census Bureau, 2003). Though unwed motherhood is more likely to occur among women in the lower class and those in disadvantaged racial minority groups, recent increases in unwed motherhood have been much greater among whites, and rates for teenagers actually fell 11 percent between 1994 and 1998 and has continued dropping. Such births do not necessarily result in single-parent families; two-fifths of recent nonmarital births were to cohabiting couples (Ventura and Bachrach, 2000).

Women heading a single-parent family typically experience greater stress than women in two-parent families (Fassinger, 1989; Simons, Beaman, et al., 1993). For one thing, lack of job training, loss of skills during the childbearing years, and discriminatory hiring and promotion patterns often mean that single mothers work for low wages. Female family heads report much lower self-esteem, a lower sense of effectiveness, and less optimism about the future than their counterparts in two-parent settings. But research shows that women who head households on their own may choose not to marry depending on a variety of factors, including mistrust of men, fear of domestic violence, household decision making, respectability, and whether the potential marriage partner has a stable job with decent earnings (Edin, 2000).

Single fathers encounter many of the same problems as single mothers. Indeed, research shows that being single and having children to raise is worse on the mental health of men than on that of women (Simon 1998; Hughes, 1989). Juggling work and child care poses considerable difficulties, especially for fathers with preschool youngsters. Because men are not much involved in child care when they are married, they have little to fall back on when they become single fathers.

Many families headed by single parents survive their hardships with few ill effects; some even blossom as a result of the spirit of cooperation brought out by their difficulties. However, a disturbing number of children and their parents are saddled with problems. Some studies show that juvenile delinquency is twice as likely to occur in a single-parent home as in a two-parent home. Children of single parents are more likely to drop out of school, be unemployed when they reach adulthood, have out-of-wedlock children, become sexually active at an earlier age, and cohabit (Musick and Bumpass, 1999). Lack of parental supervision and persistent social and psychological strains are usually complicated by the problems of poverty (Mann, 1983; Bank et al., 1993). The effects of social class on children's experiences are discussed in Box 7.2.

Cohabitation.

Marriage is differentiated from other types of intimate relationships by its institutionalized status. The number of unmarried adults who share living quarters with an unrelated adult of the opposite sex—a type of intimate relationship termed *cohabitation* —has increased in recent decades; 4.2 million American households

Family Backgrounds and Unequal Childhoods

Sociologists have long known that social class has a powerful impact on children's life chances. In a classic study, sociologist James Coleman and his colleagues (Coleman et al., 1966) found that family background was the most important determinant of educational inequality. But what specific family processes are responsible for the link between parents' social class and children's outcomes? This question was addressed in a recent study by Annette Lareau (2002). Lareau systematically observed the daily lives of poor, working-class, middle-class, and upper-middle-class families with 9- and 10-year-old children, spending hours at a time with each family. She found that organized activities dominate the lives of middle-class children; their parents engage in what she calls "concerted cultivation"—they manage their children's lives to optimize the cultivation of their talents and abilities. In poor and working-class families, leisure activities are left to the children themselves; their parents facilitate "the accomplishment of natural growth," and the provision of organized leisure activities is not seen as an essential part of good parenting.

Middle- and upper-middle-class children benefit directly from their parents' attempts to cultivate their talents; further, they gain a sense of entitlement and the skills for getting what they want or need from others, Lareau says. The poorer children she followed, on the other hand, learned to "keep their distance from people in positions of authority, to be distrustful of institutions, and . . . to resist officials' authority" (2002:773).

Data from the Census 2000's "A Child's Day" report (Lugaila, 2003) confirm Lareau's observations and bring into sharp focus the disadvantages faced by many American children. Five percent of all kids under 12, for example, had not been taken on an "outing" during the month before parents filled out their census surveys; an outing includes a trip to a park, a church, a playground, a grocery store, or a visit with friends or relatives. That's 2.4 *million* children who apparently did nothing but go to school and come back home, for an entire month. Eight percent of the nation's 1- to 5-year-olds—1.6 million kids—had not been read to at all

in the week before the survey, and only half were read to every day. As Lareau found in her observational study, many children engage in a variety of organized activities such as soccer, baseball, gymnastics, dance, Girl Scouts, Boy Scouts, violin lessons, choir, and the like, but many children do not.

For many of the factors in the "Child's Day" report, family background, especially the income and education of the parents, is the critical element. For example, family characteristics that are associated with lower levels of reading to children include living in poverty, having parents with a high school education or less, and having never-married parents. Children who live in poverty do not "go on outings," as the Census Bureau puts it, and they are much less likely to be involved in organized sports, clubs, or lessons. The level of education of the parents plays a major role in a child's participation in extracurricular activities, with about half of the children of parents with advanced degrees participating in sports, clubs, and lessons, compared to 20 to 30 percent of the children whose parents have a high school education or less. School opportunities are sorted by social class, too; half of the children whose parents have advanced degrees are enrolled in "gifted classes," compared to only 14 percent of the children whose parents have a high school education or less.

In other words, the children who might benefit greatly from extra attention, special activities, and more caring from adults in their lives—children from low-income families, children whose parents have little education, children from broken homes—are the least likely to get it. As Lareau (2003) says in the book that elaborates her research, America is a land both of opportunity and of inequality.

Questions for Discussion

1. Based on the findings presented here, what sorts of enrichment programs would you recommend for children living in poverty?

2. Are there benefits to a childhood that is not dominated by organized activities?

were made up of unmarried couples in 1998 (U.S. Census Bureau, 1999). A little over 10 percent of all unmarried persons, and 15 percent of the unmarried under 25 years old, currently cohabit. In 2002, 11 percent of the children living with a single mother were living in a household that included the mother's unmarried partner, and 33 percent of the children that lived with a single father were living with his unmarried partner (Fields, 2003). Forty percent of all out-of-wedlock births were to cohabiting parents (Bumpass and Lu, 2000), and cohabitation was the subject of much sociological research (Smock, 2000). For white and Hispanic teens, living in cohabiting families is worse than living with single mothers; those living with cohabitors are more likely to have school troubles and emotional and behavioral problems (Nelson, Clark, and Acs, 2001). Cohabiting also seems to be less effective than remarriage at providing economic stability for the children of divorce (Morrison and Ritualo, 2000).

Only 2 percent of American women born between 1928 and 1932 cohabited before marrying or attaining age 30; 40 percent of those born between 1958 and 1962 did so (Schoen and Weinick, 1993). Cohabiting before marriage has become quite prevalent, with a majority of first marriages preceded by cohabitation (Cherlin, 2002). It is even more common before remarriage. Changes in the economy, including the increase in the labor-force participation of women and the decline in the relative importance of the family in the transmission of power and wealth, have contributed to the growing social acceptance of cohabitation (Parker, 1990).

The high proportion of married couples who live together prior to marriage suggests that premarital cohabitation may become institutionalized as a new step between dating and marriage. Half of cohabiting survey respondents said they had definite plans to marry their partners and 31 percent said they thought they would (Bumpass, Sweet, and Cherlin, 1991). Cohabitation also may serve as a substitute for marriage (Cherlin, 2002). The proportion of couples who marry after cohabiting has decreased and the percentage of cohabiting couples who have children and do not marry has increased. Young people who cohabit become less eager to have children and more tolerant of divorce than those who do not cohabit (Axinn and Barber, 1997). Persons who cohabit prior to marriage are more likely to eventually divorce (DeMaris and Rao, 1992), but this tendency is limited to serial cohabiters (those who cohabit at different times with different partners) and to those with multiple premarital sexual partners. Teachman (2003) finds that persons whose premarital sex and/or cohabitation is limited to the person they eventually marry do not have an elevated risk of marital disruption. Teachman concludes that "premarital sex and cohabitation limited to one's future spouse has become part of the normal courtship process for marriage" (Teachman, 2003:444). Young women with high earnings now are more likely to cohabit than marry, while the opposite is true for young men with high earnings (Cherlin, 2002).

Couples living together but not married are far less liberated about money, sex, and housework than their nontraditional living arrangement might suggest. Like married men, cohabiting men are more likely to initiate sexual activity, make most of the spending decisions, and do far less of the housework than their working women partners (Blumstein and Schwartz, 1983; South and Spitze, 1994). Unmarried couples see themselves as less securely anchored than married couples and accordingly feel more tentative about their ability to endure difficult periods. Half of cohabiting relationships last a year or less and only 10 percent last five years (Bumpass and Lu, 2000).

Gay and Lesbian Couples.

Homosexuality also serves as the basis for family life, though with some differences from heterosexual couples. In terms of love and relationship satisfaction, heterosexual couples, gay couples, and lesbian couples do not differ (Savin-Williams and Esterberg, 2000). Gay and lesbian couples are more likely than heterosexual couples to be well-educated. Their average incomes are similar, but homosexual couples are less likely to own their own homes (Associated Press, 2003). Compared with married couples, gay and lesbian couples are more likely to split up household tasks so that each partner performs an equal number of different tasks. However, lesbian couples tend to share more tasks, whereas gay couples are more likely to have one or the other partner perform the tasks (Kurdek, 1993).

Until recently, cohabitation was the only option for homosexual "family life" in the United States. Unlike Belgium, Denmark, and the Netherlands, where same-sex marriage is legal, the United States has provided little legal protection for homosexual couples. In 2000, the state of Vermont passed the nation's first civil-union law, giving gay and lesbian couples the same rights as heterosexual married couples, and in 2003, Massachusetts followed suit (von Drehle, 2003). Some cities and counties also have provisions for unmarried couples to register as domestic partners, with rights conferred ranging from being allowed to visit hospitalized partners to sharing health insurance benefits (Cherlin, 2002). Canada proposed in 2003 to define marriage as the "lawful union of two persons," a move that would make it the fourth nation to legalize same-sex marriage (*Washington Post,* 2003); Ontario had already granted full and equal family rights to same-sex couples (Stacey and Biblarz, 2001).

Population Size of Homosexuals. Most estimates of the homosexual population range from 1 to 3 percent (Barringer, 1993; Crispell, 1993). One study found that 1.4 percent of women and 2.8 percent of men identified themselves as gay, lesbian, or bisexual (Laumann et al., 1994). The percent of persons who have engaged at some time in homosexual activity may be substantially higher: at least 20 percent of males, according to a Kinsey Institute study (Fay et al., 1989). However, another study puts the figure lower, at 7 percent for men and nearly 4 percent for women (Laumann et al., 1994). The major problem with all these estimates is that they rely on self-reports and therefore almost certainly underestimate rates of homosexual involvement. Many people may be afraid to admit to homosexual activity out of fear of discrimination or ostracism.

What Is Homosexuality?   Is homosexuality a condition or characteristic of people, or is it simply a way we have of describing an activity that some people engage in? Kinsey's study (Kinsey, Pomeroy, and Martin, 1948) revealed the interesting fact that homosexuality/heterosexuality was not a simple dichotomy. Kinsey found people all along the continuum from exclusively homosexual to exclusively heterosexual, combining homosexuality and heterosexuality in a variety of ways. Though he did find the majority to be exclusively heterosexual, he also found people who engaged in homosexual activity in certain periods in the life course and not in others. On the basis of findings like these, many sociologists and psychologists have concluded that it is more reasonable to think about heterosexual and homosexual *practices,* not homosexual *individuals* (Bell, Weinberg, and Hammersmith, 1981; Kirkpatrick, 2000). In this "constructionist" view, homosexuality and heterosexuality are social constructions that describe behaviors, roles that people may play, and identities, not inherent characteristics of persons.

The alternative "essentialist" view argues that homosexual orientation either is inborn or is fixed very early in one's development and thus is an inherent part of what an individual is (LeVay, 1996, 1991). LeVay's 1991 study presented evidence that there are differences in the brain structures of homosexual and heterosexual men. Other studies show that identical twins, who share 100 percent of their genes, are more likely to have the same sexual orientation than fraternal twins, who are as genetically alike as any siblings (Burr, 1996). However, it is still not clear whether findings such as these reflect the fact that homosexual preferences are caused or sustained by biological factors. In 1975 the American Psychological Association urged medical practitioners to stop thinking of homosexuality as a mental illness, and in 1997 it passed a resolution to limit therapy aimed at converting homosexuals to heterosexuals (Weiss, 1997).

What is not controversial is that, for the most part, gay and lesbian people, except for their sexual orientations and practices, are a cross section of the U.S. population, differing little from their heterosexual counterparts (Bell and Weinberg, 1978; Blumstein and Schwartz, 1983). They are found in all occupational fields, political persuasions, religious faiths, and racial and ethnic groups. Some are

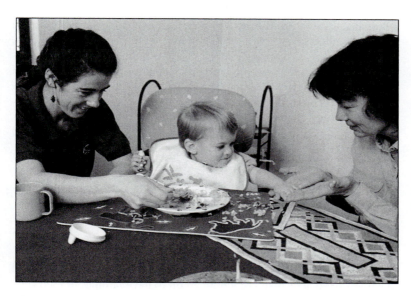

Except for their sexual preferences and practices, gays and lesbians differ little from their heterosexual counterparts. Some are or have been married, have children, and lead lives that in most respects are indistinguishable from those of the larger population.

married, have children, and lead lives that in most respects are indistinguishable from those of the larger population.

Attitudes toward Gay Marriage. Two years after the Netherlands legalized gay marriage, nearly 8 percent of weddings were same-sex couples and the relationships were increasingly seen as commonplace and even "old-fashioned" (Richburg, 2003). What about in the United States? Jeni Loftus (2001) used national survey data from 1973 to 1998 to look at attitudes toward homosexuality. She found that Americans' attitudes toward the morality of homosexuality have fluctuated over that time period, with increasingly liberal attitudes since 1990, and they have become steadily less willing to restrict the civil liberties of homosexuals over that same period. Most Americans think homosexuals should have equal rights in terms of job opportunities (Saad, 1996), and despite the Catholic church's rejection of homosexual activity, U.S. Catholic bishops have urged parents of homosexuals to accept and love them (Murphy, 1997). The percentage of Americans who think gay sex is wrong has dropped, and gay characters star on both sitcoms and reality TV shows (Bumiller, 2003). On the other hand, in 2003 a second-grader was scolded for saying a bad word—the word was *gay*,—in reference to the child's lesbian parents (Stepp, 2003). And most Americans still say that homosexual behavior is "always wrong" (Loftus, 2001).

When it comes to marriage and family, Americans are not quite ready to give their full approval to same-sex unions. In 2003, the Supreme Court struck down a Texas law against sodomy, and social conservatives began warning that traditional marriage was endangered

(Bumiller, 2003). When the Episcopal church gave its bishops the option to allow priests to bless committed homosexual relationships, polls showed that "a strong majority" of the public disapproved, especially frequent churchgoers (Morin and Cooperman, 2003). At the end of 2003, a *New York Times/CBS News* poll found that 55 percent of Americans favored a constitutional amendment that would ban homosexual marriage (Seelye and Elder, 2003). In 2004 four states had constitutional amendments prohibiting same-sex marriage, and 34 had enacted restrictions (*Washington Post,* 2004).

Challenges for American Families and American Society

Some family problems stay in the family; others spill over into society. For example, family violence, child abuse, and incest produce scarred members of society, many of whom go on to have families of their own in which the same terrible acts are repeated. The challenges posed by abuse and neglect, child care, divorce, and an increasing population of elderly are complicated by the public debate over the family we discussed in the chapter introduction. As sociologist and U.S. Senator Daniel Patrick Moynihan (1985) observed, conservatives—fearing government interference—prefer to talk about family values but not new governmental initiatives. Liberals, fearing a "blaming-the-victim" mentality, like to talk about public policy initiatives but not family values. Taking a more centralist position, Dennis A. Ahlburg and Carol J. De Vita (1992:39) observed:

> Valuing the family should not be confused with valuing a particular family form . . . Social legislation (or "pro-family" policies) narrowly designed to reinforce only one model of the American family is likely to be shortsighted and have the unintended consequence of weakening, rather than strengthening, family ties. Recognizing the diversity of American families and addressing the complexity of their needs must lie at the heart of the policy debates on family issues.

Family Violence, Child Abuse, and Incest

Mounting evidence suggests that family violence, child abuse, and incest are much more common than most Americans had suspected. The expression "coming out of the closet" is an apt one when applied to battered women and victims of child abuse and sexual molestation. They have been as reluctant to reveal their plight as gay persons have been to reveal their sexual orientations. In this section we will present and discuss some of the data available about family violence, child abuse, and incest.

Family Violence. Estimates of family violence vary widely. Nearly a quarter of women report having been physically assaulted by an intimate partner, and 8 percent report rape by an intimate partner (Cherlin, 2002). The World Health Organization (WHO) maintains a database on violence against women, and the rates they report for physical assault by an intimate partner range from 13 percent in Switzerland and 22 percent in the United States to 47 percent in Bangladesh and 58 percent in Turkey (WHO, 2000). The Centers for Disease Control and Prevention has estimated that at least 6 percent of pregnant women are battered by their spouses or partners (Hilts, 1994). At least 1 in 10 married women have experienced marital rape (Straus and Gelles, 1986, 1990).

Although both men and women engage in violence, men typically do more damage than their female partners and many more women than men report victimization (Cherlin, 2002). Many of the people who abuse domestic partners also use violence against others (Moffitt et al., 2000).

Women put up with battering for a variety of reasons (Simons, Johnson, et al., 1993). The fewer the resources a wife has in the way of education or job skills, the more vulnerable she is in the marriage. Americans place the burden of family harmony on women, with the implication that they have failed if the marriage disintegrates. A survey of popular women's magazines showed that domestic violence is portrayed as a private problem, with the victim held responsible for solving it (Berns, 1999).

Child Abuse. One need spend only an hour or so in a supermarket or a shopping mall to observe instances of children being physically or verbally abused. Such public behavior is but the tip of the iceberg. A 1994 *USA Today*/CNN/Gallup Poll found that 67 percent of American adults agree that "a good, hard spanking" is sometimes necessary in disciplining a child, despite accumulating evidence that children who get spanked regularly are more likely to cheat or lie, to be disobedient at school, to bully others, and to have less remorse for what they do wrong (Straus, Sugarman, and Giles-Sims, 1997). Child abuse goes far beyond unnecessary spanking; abuse cases may involve burning, scalding, beating, and smothering. Neglect of children is a closely related problem. In 2001, there were 903,000 confirmed cases of child maltreatment; more than half were neglect victims (U.S. Department of Health and Human Services, 2003). Approximately 1,300 children died in 2001 of abuse or neglect.

Child abuse that results in homicide is unfortunately not rare. In fact, the age at which females are most at risk of homicide is from birth to age one, and the perpetrators are nearly always parents, family friends, or guardians (Tucker, 2000). Although the chances of males being murdered during infancy are even greater than for females, it is not the most dangerous time of life for them; the male homicide rate is more than four times higher at age 21 (Tucker, 2000). Child welfare workers say that risk to infants is related to whether parents and caregivers have any parenting skills and to situational factors including stress and social isolation.

Incest and Sexual Abuse.   The status of incest as a taboo has not kept it from taking place but merely from being talked about. Probably the best available figures on sexual abuse come from a national survey of more than 2,000 adults undertaken in 1985 for the *Los Angeles Times* by psychologist David Finkelhor and his colleagues. They found that 27 percent of the women and 16 percent of the men disclosed a history of some sort of sexual abuse during their childhood (Darnton, 1991). A study of first intercourse experiences found that girls who had sex at ages 11 or 12 were much more likely to have partners much older than themselves, and both older partners and early first intercourse were associated with a greater number of problem behaviors (Leitenberg and Saltzman, 2000).

The perpetrator in sexual abuse is commonly the father, uncle, or other male authority figure in the household, "family tyrants" who employ physical force and intimidation to control their families (Finkelhor, 1979; Herman and Hirschman, 1981). The mothers in incestuous families are commonly passive, have a poor self-image, and are overly dependent on their husbands, much the same traits found among battered wives. The victims of molestation are usually shamed or terrified into treating the experience as a dirty secret.

The sexual abuse of children often leads to behavior problems, learning difficulties, sexual promiscuity, runaway behavior, drug and alcohol abuse, gastrointestinal and genitourinary complaints, compulsive rituals, clinical depression, low self-esteem, and suicidal behavior. Victimized women tend to show lifetime patterns of psychological shame and stigmatization (Kendall-Tackett, Williams, and Finkelhor, 1993; Malinosky-Rummell and Hansen, 1993).

Looking to the Future.   The problems of family violence, child abuse, and incest have emerged as major public issues. Some, but not all, researchers find that the arrest of offenders is the most effective means for preventing new incidents of wife battery (Berk and Newton, 1985; Sherman et al., 1992). The adoption of no-fault divorce laws is associated with a drop in suicides among women, murder of women by their partners, and domestic violence against both men and women (Stevenson and Wolfers, 2003). A cultural revolution of attitudes and values is required to eradicate the abuse of women and children (Gelles, Strauss, and Harrop, 1988; Buzawa and Buzawa, 1990).

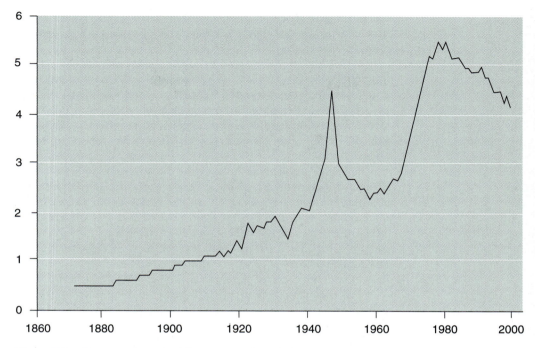

Figure 7.3   Divorces per 1,000 Persons in the U.S. Population
1867–2001

Divorce rates in the United States increased dramatically in the 20th century. The social disruptions caused by World War II produced a very sharp spike in the immediate post-war years. Rates have been declining since the early 1980s. Divorce rates in this chart from the 19th century and very early 20th century are based on limited data.

Source: Figure generated by the authors using data from the U.S. Department of Health, Education, and Welfare (1973), U.S. Department of Health and Human Services (1996), and U.S. Census Bureau (2003).

Divorce

Although divorce rates increased sharply from the 1960s to the early 1980s, they stabilized and have declined since then (see Figure 7.3). Yet divorce could still be said to be running ahead of marriage: For every 1,000 married women, more than 19 got divorced every year from 1975 to 1996, compared with a marriage rate of fewer than 14 weddings per 1,000 Americans age 15 to 64 (U.S. Census Bureau, 1999, 2003). Miami even has a "Divorce Bus," a portable courtroom in which uncontested divorces are granted in 90 seconds for "$500 a pop" (Roig-Franzia, 2003).

When today's elderly were establishing families, divorce was relatively infrequent. With the number of divorced people increasing over the past 30 years and young people delaying the formation of new unions, the number of divorced people per 1,000 married people has more than tripled in the past three decades. There are now 165 divorced people for every 1,000 married people (U.S. Census Bureau, 2003).

The Effects of Divorce on the Family.

More than half of the couples who divorce have children. Researchers find that children of divorced or single parents have higher levels of anxiety, depression, stress, aggression, and school problems and are more likely to drop out of school and become parents themselves at a young age (Lugaila, 2003).

Financial problems complicate the difficulties of both women and men. Only half of divorced mothers receive any money at all from their children's fathers, and this is seldom much. Most men also experience an economic decline following divorce (McManus and DiPrete, 2001). Moreover, divorce is not the end of family changes but often the beginning. Most divorced parents remarry, and because the rate of divorce among remarriages is greater than among first marriages, many children experience complex family lives (Furstenberg and Cherlin, 1991).

The notion that divorce has adverse consequences for children influences many couples to remain unhappily married until their youngsters reach adulthood. However, some evidence suggests that staying together for the sake of the children is not necessarily helpful if the marriage is marred by conflict, tension, and discord. Many of the emotional, behavioral, and academic problems children exhibit after their parents divorce are apparent before the time of the actual breakup of the family. Marital discord has a negative effect on children's emotional bonds with both parents (Amato and Sobolewski, 2001). On the other hand, clinical psychologist Mary Pipher argues that children may not be affected if their parents are unhappy but that divorce "shatters many children" (Pipher, 1994:133). Family sociologist Linda Waite says research supports that view: "As long as Mom and Dad don't fight too much, [children] thrive under the love, attention, and resources two married parents provide" (Waite and Gallagher, 2000:144).

Long-Term Effects.

Although divorce may be more commonplace today, it is no more a routine experience for adults than it is for children. In many cases, divorce exacts a greater emotional and physical toll than almost any other type of stress, including death of a spouse (Kitson and Holmes, 1992). Separated and divorced people are overrepresented in mental institutions; more likely to die from cardiovascular disease, cancer, pneumonia, and cirrhosis of the liver; and more prone to die from accidents, homicides, and suicides.

Middle-aged and elderly women are especially devastated by divorce. These women—called *displaced homemakers*—often have dedicated themselves to managing a home and raising children and then find themselves jettisoned after years of marriage. Within the United States, some 100,000 people over the age of 55 divorce each year.

Grown children of divorce have lower levels of psychological well-being (Amato and Sobolewski, 2001) and die, on average, four years sooner than adults who were raised by parents who did not divorce (Tucker et al., 1997). Children of divorce are more likely to marry as teens but less likely to marry at all once they get past age 20 (Wolfinger, 2003). On the other hand, adult children of divorced parents are now significantly less likely to divorce than children of a generation or two ago; between 1974 and 1993 the propensity to divorce if one's parents had divorced declined by about 50 percent (Wolfinger, 1999).

After Divorce.   Most divorced people remarry. About five of every six divorced men and three of every four divorced women marry again. Divorced men are more likely to remarry than women. Because men usually marry younger women, divorced men have a larger pool of potential partners from which to choose. Divorced men also are more likely to marry someone not previously married. About 61 percent of men and 54 percent of women in their thirties who remarry will undergo a second divorce. It seems that individuals drag into the new marriage many of the insecurities and personality problems that disrupted the previous one. With one divorce under their belt, they are less hesitant about securing a second one should trouble appear.

Sociological Perspectives on the Family

We have been following three major sociological perspectives—the functionalist, conflict, and interactionist—as we move through our introduction to sociology. What do these major theoretical frameworks have to tell us about the family?

The Functionalist Perspective

As we have noted in other chapters, functionalist theorists stress that if a society is to survive and operate with some measure of effectiveness, it must guarantee that certain essential tasks are performed. The performance of these tasks—or *functions*—cannot be left to chance (see Chapter 1). To do so would be to run the risk that some activities would not be carried out, and the society would disintegrate. Although acknowledging that families show a good deal of variation throughout the world, functionalists seek to identify a number of recurrent functions families typically perform (Davis, 1949).

Reproduction.   If a society is to perpetuate itself, new members have to be created; families perform that function by providing social and cultural supports and motivations for having children.

Socialization.

The family functions as an intermediary in the socialization process between the larger community and the individual. At birth, children are uninitiated in the ways of culture, and thus each new generation subjects society to a recurrent "barbarian invasion" (see Chapter 2). Through the process of socialization, children become inducted into their society's ways, and the family usually serves as the chief culture-transmitting agency.

Care, Protection, and Emotional Support.

Human children must be fed, clothed, and provided with shelter well into puberty. Throughout the world, the family has been assigned the responsibility for shielding, protecting, sustaining, and otherwise maintaining not just children, but also the infirm and other dependent members of the community (Rossi and Rossi, 1990). The family also provides an important source for entering into intimate, constant, face-to-face contact with other people. Healthy family relationships afford companionship, love, security, a sense of worth, and a general feeling of well-being.

Assignment of Status.

Infants must be placed within the social structure. The family confers ascribed statuses (see Chapter 2) that orient a person (1) to a variety of interpersonal relationships, including those involving parents, siblings, and other kin, and (2) to basic group memberships, including racial, ethnic, religious, class, national, and community relationships.

Regulation of Sexual Behavior.

A society's norms regulate sexual behavior by specifying who may engage in sexual behavior with whom and under what circumstances. In no known society are people given total freedom for sexual expression. Although some 70 percent of the world's societies permit some form of sexual license, even those societies typically do not approve of childbirth out of wedlock—this is the **norm of legitimacy;** like other norms, this one is occasionally violated, and those who violate it are usually punished.

Critics of the functionalist perspective point out that these tasks can be performed in other ways. Indeed, by virtue of social change, many of the economic, child care, and educational functions once performed by the family have been taken over by other institutions. Even so, the family tends to be the social unit most commonly responsible for reproduction, socialization, and the other functions we considered.

The Conflict Perspective

Functionalists spotlight the tasks carried out by the family that serve the interests of society as a whole. Many conflict theorists, in contrast, have seen the family as a social arrangement benefiting some people more than others. Friedrich Engels (1884/1902), Karl Marx's close associate, viewed the family as a class society in miniature, with one class (men) oppressing another class (women). He contended that marriage was the first form of class antagonism in which the well-being of one group derived from the misery and repression of another. The motivation for sexual domination was the economic exploitation of a woman's labor.

Women as Sexual Property.

Sociologist Randall Collins (1975, 1988a) has said that historically men have been the "sexual aggressors" and women the "sexual prizes for men." Women have been victimized by their smaller size and vulnerability as childbearers. Across an entire spectrum of societies women have been seen as sexual property, taken as booty in war, used by their fathers in economic bargaining, and considered as owned by their husbands.

According to Collins, marriage is a socially enforced contract of sexual property. Within Western tradition, a marriage was not legal until sexually consummated, sexual assault within marriage was not legally rape, and the principal ground for divorce was sexual infidelity. A woman's virginity was seen as the property of her father, and her sexuality as the property of her husband. Thus, rape has often traditionally been seen less as a crime perpetrated by a man against a woman than as a crime perpetrated by one man against another man.

In recent years, however, economic and political changes have improved women's bargaining position. The sexual bargains women strike can focus less on marriage and more on immediate pleasure, companionship, and sexual gratification.

Conflict as Natural and Necessary.

Other social scientists have approached the issue of conflict somewhat differently. At the turn of the century, psychoanalyst Sigmund Freud (1930/1961) and sociologist Georg Simmel (1908/1955, 1908/1959) also advanced a conflict approach to the family. They contended that intimate relationships inevitably involve antagonism as well as love. Sociologists like Jetse Sprey (1979) developed these ideas and suggested that conflict is a part of all systems and interactions, including the family and marital interactions. Viewed in this fashion, the family is a social arrangement that structures close interpersonal relationships through ongoing processes of negotiation, problem solving, and conflict management. This view is compatible with the interactionist perspective.

The Interactionist Perspective

As we saw in Chapter 2, symbolic interactionists emphasize that human beings create, use, and communicate with symbols. One way in which families reinforce and rejuvenate their bonds is through the symbolic mechanism of *rituals*. Social scientists find that household rituals such as gathering for meals are a hidden source of family strength.

It seems that when families preserve their rituals, their children fare better emotionally, even when the family faces other disruptive problems (e.g., alcoholism). Some therapists help families establish rituals as a means to heal family stresses and tensions (Goleman, 1992; Pipher, 1997).

The symbolic interactionist perspective is a useful tool for examining the complexities of a relationship. When the roles of one family member change, there are consequences for other family members. For example, we have seen that parenthood alters the husband–wife relationship by creating new roles and increasing the complexity of the family unit. Likewise, family life is different in homes where a mother is in the paid labor force or where an economic provider is unemployed. And the loss of critical family roles caused by divorce has vast implications for family functioning (Gubrium and Holstein, 1990).

Key Terms

bilineal, 188

complementary needs, 191

egalitarian authority, 189

endogamy, 189

exchange theory, 191

exogamy, 189

extended family, 186

family, 185

family life course, 194

family of orientation, 186

family of procreation, 186

group marriage, 189

homogamy, 191

homosexuality, 201

incest taboos, 189

lifestyle, 195

marriage, 189

matching hypothesis, 191

matriarchal authority, 188

matrilineal, 188

matrilocal residence, 188

monogamy, 189

neolocal residence, 188

norm of legitimacy, 210

nuclear family, 186

patriarchal authority, 188

patrilineal, 188

patrilocal residence, 188

polyandry, 189

polygyny, 189

romantic love, 190

Review Questions

1. Differentiate between nuclear and extended families and between family of orientation and family of procreation.

2. Describe the various forms of marriage found around the world.

3. How do courtship patterns regulate love?

4. What is the family life course?
5. What sorts of lifestyles do Americans adopt besides the traditional nuclear family?
6. Name and describe some of the challenges facing American families today.
7. How do the functionalist, conflict, and interactionist perspectives on the family differ?

Chapter 8

Social Institutions

The Polity

The Economy

Religion

Education

Medicine

I n North Korea's capital city, strict rationing of electricity results in total darkness by 10 p.m. Factories and hotels stand empty and idle. Parts of the city are without water for days on end. When Keith Richburg, a foreign correspondent for the *Washington Post,* visited North Korea in the late 1990s, he found people starving in the countryside. He visited a hospital that had no lights, heat, stretchers, food, antibiotics, or intravenous drips, and a shortage of anesthesia. He went to an orphanage where 20 percent of the children were expected to die because they were beyond help and where 70 percent of the children were there because their parents had died from malnutrition or disease (Richburg, 1997). Recent reports indicate that these problems continue, with public executions of starving people caught stealing food (Amnesty International, 2004). According to refugees and aid groups, government assistance was going to the politically loyal and economically active.

North Korea is a vivid illustration not only of the intimate connections between politics and economics but of the enormous significance of social institutions. In Chapter 2 we noted that institutions are the principal social structures that organize, direct, and execute the essential tasks of living, and that each institution is built around a standardized solution to a set of problems. In the previous chapter, we discussed the institution of the family. In the present chapter, we review the basic elements of five other institutions: the polity, the economy, religion, education, and medicine.

The Polity

Individuals and groups who control critical resources—rewards, punishments, and persuasive communications—are able to dictate

Police officers help citizens with many everyday problems, but the firearms they carry are a constant reminder that they are agents of the state, which has a monopoly on the legitimate use of deadly force.

the way social life is ordered. To command key organizations is to command people and to influence the direction and the outcomes in their lives. Thus, power is the bedrock of social organization (Bierstedt, 1950). Changes in how power is organized and distributed in a society lead to changes in how institutions and groups are created and perpetuated, and thus to fundamental changes in a society's way of life.

Power is the ability of individuals and groups to realize their will in human affairs even if it involves the resistance of others. But when we say that some people have more power and other people have less, we are doing more than describing people's characteristics. We are describing their social relations with others.

As sociologist Richard Emerson (1962) argued, power is an attribute of a social relationship. If we have two people, A and B, the power of person A over B is determined by B's dependence on A. Thus, if A is in control of resources needed or desired by B, A will have some degree of power over B. A's power will be at its maximum when B has no alternative sources of the resource outside the A–B relationship. A and B need not be people. They can be groups, organizations, ethnic groups, or nations—any person or social unit that can be in a social relationship with another.

The **state**—the political institution—is an arrangement that consists of people who exercise an effective monopoly in the use of physical coercion within a given territory. The state rests on **force**—power whose basis is the threat or application of punishment. Clearly the ability to take life and inflict suffering affords a critical advantage in human affairs. In effect, force constitutes a final court of appeals; there is usually no appeal to force except the exercise of superior force. Sovereign nations restrict, and even prohibit, the independent exercise of force by their subjects; otherwise, governments could not suppress forceful challenges to their authority (Lenski, 1966; Lehman, 1988). But even though force is ultimately the basis of the state, it is only in unusual situations that societal power actually takes this form.

Sociological Perspectives on the State

The Functionalist Perspective on the State.

Functionalists contend that there is a good reason why the state arose and why it has assumed a dominant position in contemporary life: society must maintain order and provide for the common good. More particularly, they point to four primary functions performed by the state.

Planning and Direction. The complexity and scope of many activities in contemporary society require overall coordination and integration; personal and informal arrangements no longer suffice. Often, new norms are needed. Such norms—*laws*—result from conscious thought, deliberate planning, and formal declaration. In addition, in times of war, financial panic, or natural disaster, "central direction" is required, performed by only one or at most a few individuals who have the power and authority to implement their plans (Davis, 1949).

Enforcement of Norms. In modern, complex societies characterized by a preponderance of secondary relationships, informal relationships are not adequate to ensure social order. Once laws are created, a special body or organization—the state—is required to ensure law and order by enforcing legal norms.

Arbitration of Conflicting Interests. Because many resources are scarce and divisible—particularly privilege, prestige, and power—people find themselves in conflict as they pursue their goals. If no bonds other than the pursuit of immediate self-interest were to unite people, society would quickly degenerate into a Hobbesian nightmare in which "war against all" prevails. Some agency is required that is sufficiently strong to contain conflict within tolerable limits—and that agency is the state (Goode, 1972).

Protection against Other Societies. Sociologist Charles Tilly (1990) surveyed European history and concluded that states are shaped primarily by the need to prepare for and wage war. Both war and diplomacy call for centralized control and mobilization if a people are to maximize their position relative to their adversaries. The state meets this requirement.

The Conflict Perspective on the State.

Conflict theorists do not see the state as a benign institution. They contend that the state is a vehicle by which one or more groups impose their values and stratification system upon other groups. As they view the matter, the state has its origin in the desire of ruling elites to give permanence to social arrangements that benefit themselves. More fundamentally, they depict the state as an instrument of violence and oppression.

Conflict theorists see the state arising in history along with the production of a social surplus—the goods and services over and above what is necessary for survival. In hunting and gathering societies, land is communally owned, and the members of the community share the food derived from it. The intensive agriculture technologies in agricultural societies produce food surpluses, so it is no longer essential that every human be employed in subsistence activities. Some members of society, those who can engineer more power for themselves, can live off the surplus produced by others. A new institution, the state with its police power, is required to enforce the unequal distribution of social and material rewards in order to preserve the position of this privileged elite.

Legitimacy and Authority

Although force may be an effective means for seizing power, and though it remains the ultimate foundation for the state, it is not the most effective means for political rule (Lenski, 1966). Force is both inefficient and costly. For example, a person who hijacks an airliner by threatening to shoot passengers has considerable power, but it is not likely to last long.

This highlights the importance of the distinction that sociologists make between power that is legitimate and power that is illegitimate. Legitimate power is **authority**. When individuals possess authority, they have a recognized and established right to give orders, determine policies, pronounce judgments, settle controversies, and, more broadly, act as leaders. Legitimacy—the social justification of power—takes a number of forms (Lipset, 1994; Stryker, 1994). Sociologist Max Weber (1921/1968) suggested a threefold classification of authority based on the manner in which the power is socially legitimated: traditional, legal-rational, and charismatic.

Traditional Authority.
In **traditional authority,** power is legitimated by the sanctity of age-old customs. Often the claim to such authority rests on birthright; it is generally inherited, since royal blood is thought to be somehow superior to the blood of commoners. Additionally, a ruler's power may be perceived as eternal, inviolable, and sacred. For example, medieval kings and queens in Europe ruled in the name of "a divine right" ordained by God. A good deal of moral force stands behind traditional authority.

Legal-Rational Authority.
In **legal-rational authority,** power is legitimated by explicit rules and rational procedures that define the rights and duties of the occupants of given positions. Weber depicted

this type of authority as prevailing in his ideal-type bureaucracy (see Chapter 3). Under this arrangement, officials claim obedience on the grounds that their commands fall within the impersonal, formally defined scope of their office. Obedience is owed not to the person but to a set of impersonal principles that have been devised in a rational manner. Presumably, these principles are derived from a set of abstract goals that people agree with. For example, we obey the police officer directing traffic because we agree that traffic must flow smoothly and that for this to occur, people must conform to a set of rational principles and rules devised to ensure this.

Charismatic Authority.

In **charismatic authority,** power is legitimated by the extraordinary superhuman or supernatural attributes people attribute to a leader. Founders of world religions, prophets, military victors, and political heroes commonly derive their authority from charisma (meaning "gift of grace"). Followers are devoted to the person of the leader, not to tradition or to abstract rational rules and principles. Jesus, Napoléon Bonaparte, Fidel Castro, Julius Caesar, Adolf Hitler, Joan of Arc, and Ayatollah Ruhollah Khomeini all are examples.

Political Power

Politics refers to the processes by which people and groups acquire and exercise power. We commonly think of politics as a feature of governments. But there is also politics in religious groups, educational groups, and scientific groups—even in friendship groups and families. When power is organized and wielded by the state, we speak of it as **political power.** In the modern state, power is wielded through democratic, authoritarian, or totalitarian means, depending on how much participation states allow from citizens and how much control is exercised over the everyday lives of citizens.

Types of Government.

Government entails those political processes that have to do with the authoritative formulating of rules and policies that are binding and pervasive throughout a society. In dealing with these matters, three quite different types of government have competed in recent generations for people's allegiance: totalitarianism, authoritarianism, and democracy. Each can be considered an ideal type because in practice many nations have regimes with mixtures of totalitarian, authoritarian, and democratic elements.

Totalitarianism.

Totalitarianism is a "total state," one in which the government undertakes to control all parts of the society and all aspects of social life. Those individuals and groups (elites) who domi-

What Oppression Teaches—The Long Reach of Disenfranchisement

Why don't people long oppressed by authoritarian regimes create effective democracies as soon as authoritarianism is lifted? Why, for example, has it not been easy to establish democracy in Afghanistan and Iraq after the demise of authoritarian regimes in the two countries in 2002 and 2003? Social structures teach people patterns of behavior that are not quickly and easily changed when the rules and laws governing political participation are changed. Though not as drastic as a change in regime, American women gaining the right to vote provides a focused example of this effect in action.

In 1920, the Nineteenth Amendment to the Constitution extended to women the right to vote: "The right of citizens of the United States to vote shall not be denied or abridged by the United States or by any State on account of sex." Women had worked long and hard to gain this right. Yet not nearly as many women as men voted in the first elections after the passage of the voting rights amendment. In fact, it was not until many years afterward that men and women voted at equal rates. Women born after 1925, who grew up after the Nineteenth Amendment was passed and voting for women had become an "inalienable right," were the first group to go out and vote in equal numbers.

Sociologists Glenn Firebaugh and Kevin Chen (1995) showed that the oppression people experience during their early years can continue to affect their behavior long after the oppression itself is lifted. Using postelection survey data gathered from 1952 to 1988, Firebaugh and Chen found that the odds of women born in 1896 voting in any election were less than half as great as the odds of men voting. This disenfranchisement effect—women failing to vote despite having gained the right to do so—was only slightly less in a second group of women, those born between 1896 and 1905. The effect was again smaller for women born between 1906 and 1915, although women in this cohort still did not vote at the same rates as men, and women born between 1916 and 1925 also were somewhat less likely to vote than men.

This study illustrates the long-lasting effects of historical conditions experienced during one's formative years. The data these researchers used were based on elections beginning *30 years* after women gained the right to vote in the United States, yet women born and socialized during and immediately after the period when women could *not* vote continued to vote at lower rates than men. Voting rates for men and women have now converged; women socialized in an era during which women have the right to vote are just as likely to vote as men are. As Firebaugh and Chen put it (1995:978): "After passage of the Nineteenth Amendment, historical conditions no longer 'taught' young women the impropriety of voting."

Questions for Discussion

1. In the U.S., members of racial minority groups are less likely to vote than whites are. Does research presented here help us understand these racial differences in voting? Why or why not?

2. This box suggests people learn not to be involved in voting if they are denied the right to vote. Can you think of other features of democracies in civil society that may be slow to develop after the demise of authoritarian regimes?

nate the state apparatus seek to control all subordinate governmental units, all institutions, and even individual families and cliques.

A totalitarian society typically has three characteristics: a monolithic political party, a compelling ideology, and pervasive social control. One political party is permitted, and it brooks no opposition. Only a small proportion of the population are party members, although party membership is a requisite for all important social positions. A totalitarian ideology is utopian in nature. It stipulates grandiose schemes for social reconstruction and societal betterment. To enforce its power and propagate its ideologies, a totalitarian regime employs every available means of social control. It uses educational and communications networks as well as exercising terror by a secret police.

Authoritarianism. **Authoritarianism** is a political system in which the government tolerates little or no opposition to its rule but permits nongovernmental centers of influence and allows debate on some issues of public policy. Sometimes totalitarian states slowly evolve into authoritarian ones, as happened in China and the Soviet Union from the 1960s through the 1980s. When totalitarian and authoritarian systems fail, democratic ones do not automatically rise in their place.

Democracy. **Democracy** is a political system in which the powers of government derive from the consent of the governed and in which regular constitutional avenues exist for changing government officials. It is an arrangement that (1) permits the population a significant voice in decision making through the people's right to choose among contenders for political office, (2) allows for a broad, relatively equal citizenship among the populace, and (3) affords the citizenry protection from arbitrary state action. Clearly, democratic governments are not distinguished from totalitarian or authoritarian regimes by the absence of powerful officials, and for the most part democracy is not characterized by the rule of the people themselves (direct democracy) but by elected officials (representative democracy).

What factors promote democracy? A number of sociologists have undertaken a search for those factors that promote a social climate favorable to a stable democracy (Kornhauser, 1959; Lindblom, 1990; Patterson, 1991; Lipset, 1994). One factor they identify is the existence of conflict and cleavage associated with a competitive struggle over positions of power, challenges to incumbents, and shifts in the parties holding office. Many well-organized but countervailing interest groups serve as a check against one another. **Interest groups** are organizations of people who share common concerns or points of view. Each group is limited in influence because, in the process of governing, officials also must take into account the **interests,** or points of view, of other groups.

A strong **civil society**—a social realm of mediating groups, networks, and institutions that sustains the public life outside the worlds of the state and the economy—is conducive to democratic life (Cohen and Arato, 1992). Citizens of all political and moral persuasions can link to organizations that are pursuing their goals. Having a large number of such competing groups provides many links to government and ensures that no single group or institution can attain a monopoly of power.

Relatively stable economic and social conditions also seem to favor a democratic order (Neuhouser, 1992). Significant institutional failure confronts people with stressful circumstances that can make them vulnerable to extremist social movements.

Finally, a stable democracy benefits from an underlying consensus among the populace that a democratic government is desirable and valid. Citizens believe they can realize their goals within the existing organizational framework because they enjoy "fair play" access to the seats of power.

The Economy

The economy is a social institution organized around the problem of adaptation to the environment. The earth is a hostile and unforgiving place. Without resources and the ability to use them, organized social life, and indeed human beings themselves, would not survive long. Modern societies and the people in them adapt to their environment through the processes of production, distribution, and consumption of goods and services. The means of such adaptation, including the social organization of the economy, have varied throughout human history.

Comparative Economic Systems

All societies confront three basic economic problems. *What* goods and services should they produce and in what quantities? *How* should they employ their limited resources—land, water, minerals, fuel, and labor—to produce the desired goods and services? And for *whom* should they produce the goods and services? The manner in which they answer these questions has profound consequences for the nature and the structure of the societies. For instance, if they decide to produce guns and weaponry in large quantities, the standard of living of their citizens will be lower than if they emphasize the satisfaction of consumer needs. How they go about producing the desired goods and services shapes the world of work, how it is organized, the satisfactions it provides, and the status it accords. And decisions regarding the "for whom" question influence the distribution of wealth, income, and prestige.

In recent decades two fundamentally different types of economic systems have competed for people's allegiance. In a **socialist economy,** the government directly controls the economy, in many cases setting prices and wages and deciding what will be produced. In a **capitalist economy,** the government oversees and sets parameters for the economy, but in many ways leaves the economy alone, allowing the market to decide what the economy will do. Each has taken a quite different approach to economic organization. And each has had substantially different social and political implications.

The Big Differences.

Modern economic systems differ from one another in their answers to two important questions: How is economic activity organized—by the market or by the plan? And who owns the means of production—individuals or the state? These questions do not demand an "either-or" answer. No contemporary nation falls totally at one or the other pole, although the United States and the pre-1991 Soviet Union typically supplied opposite answers to both questions.

Market and Command Economies.

A *market economy* is one in which decisions about what will be produced, how much will be produced, and what products cost are made in economic transactions between consumers and producers. Products that consumers do not want, or that are overproduced, fall in price. Items that are in short supply and that people want rise in price. Price movements act as signals to profit-making individuals and firms. They cut back on goods with falling prices and increase the production of goods with rising prices. Economists call this mechanism *consumer sovereignty.*

Underlying this approach is a capitalist ideological notion that if each economic unit is allowed to make free choices in pursuit of its own best interests, the interests of all will be best served. However, because markets have little in the way of traditional morality built into them, they are not without problems. A truly free market can supply products many people would rather not exist, including prostitution, child pornography, drugs of all kinds, and the services of hired killers, to name only a few.

A *command economy* is one in which the state or central planning authority determines the items that will be produced and their quantities. A command economy is often very good in moving a peasant society toward industrialization by mobilizing the masses to build miles of railroad and large dams. But a command economy finds it difficult to produce a complex array of consumer goods in the absence of market signals.

Free-market and command economies also differ in how they go about allocating resources to various productive activities. In free-market economies, competition among suppliers of goods and labor services is thought to ensure the most efficient and productive use of resources. Command economies, in contrast, are based on the assumption that rational decision making affords better results than the haphazard operation of market forces.

An Economy for Whom?

Market and command economies differ in how they handle the issue of how income is distributed. Historically, one of the major criticisms of the market system has been that it fails to distribute income equitably. Market economies rely on the same price system that determines wages, interest rates, and profits for the distribution of income among people in the society. Income payments go in substantial amounts to private owners of physical capital—capitalists—or those who manage capitalist enterprises. Critics contend that some social problems like the environmental crisis (see Chapter 9) and the absence of jobs for young inner-city African Americans (see Chapter 5) are not easily solved through the free market because such solutions do not produce a profit for capitalists. Accordingly, they say that different standards are called for in mature industrial societies like the United States where free markets and social welfare must be balanced (Heilbroner, 1993).

Mixed Economies.

When we look at the contemporary world, we are hard-pressed to find a pure form of a capitalist market economy. Even the United States in the early 19th century, which many economic historians deem to be as close to an example of pure capitalism as one can find, had government subsidies for railroads and canals. And socialist countries have had black markets and other "underground" market mechanisms. Most nations are characterized by mixed economies that include elements of both command and market economies.

Some capitalist societies have such mixed economies that their systems are described as "democratic socialism." In such societies, most production is privately owned, but, as under socialism, there is a large public sector with publicly owned enterprises involved in public transportation, health care, air travel, mining, oil production, education, utilities, and more. Some of these societies, such as Sweden, Finland, Denmark, and the Netherlands, have high taxes, particularly on the wealthy, and use the money to redistribute some of the wealth and to fund extensive social welfare and family support programs. In addition to having much lower economic inequality than the United States, societies with mixed economies usually score better than the United States on some important quality-of-life indicators such as rates of crime, divorce, infant mortality, and life expectancy—though the United States does have lower rates of both suicide and births to unmarried women than Sweden, Denmark, Finland, or the Netherlands (U.S. Census Bureau, 1999).

Capitalism around the Globe.

With the ascendancy of capitalism in the 1990s, more and more analysts are noticing that capitalism is not a monolith any more than communism was. With their communist adversaries consigned to history, capitalist nations are jockeying to sell their particular mode of capitalism to the emerging economies of Russia, eastern Europe, Latin America, and Asia (Neff, 1994).

The dynamic Asian nations do not view U.S.-style laissez-faire capitalism as an economic model. In Japan, Singapore, Hong Kong,

South Korea, and Taiwan, government has intervened massively in economic life and fostered a "government-business symbiosis" quite different from the situation in Europe and North America (Scott, 1991). These nations forged strong business–government links, subsidized capital investment, fostered large conglomerates, and resisted imports as part of an economic system some refer to as "state capitalism." Sociologist Peter L. Berger (1986), who stressed the importance of group solidarity and respect for tradition rather than individual achievement in East Asian versions of capitalism, prefers the term *communal capitalism.* Berger concluded that a high degree of state intervention in an economy is quite compatible with successful capitalism development. In brief, laissez-faire capitalism—"let the state leave business alone"—may be only one version of capitalism that works.

The Power of Multinational Corporations in the Global Economy

The rise of multinational corporations and the growing internationalization of the world economy have given a new dimension to economic power (Szymanski, 1981; Fennema, 1982; Biersteker, 1987; Barnet and Cavanagh, 1994). **Multinational corporations** are firms that have their central office in one country and subsidiaries in other countries. With the use of computer communications technology, companies no longer even need a geographical center. Managers and members of work teams can communicate as easily from country to country as they can from office to office. Today the annual income from sales of the largest multinational corporations exceeds the gross national product of most countries in which they do business. About half of the largest economic units in the world are not nations at all but multinational corporations.

Division of Labor.   Multinational corporations are playing a growing role in the structuring of the division of labor within the world economy. The economic integration of less developed nations into the structures of a world economy can be traced to European exploration and colonization beginning in the 15th century. The arrangement has been characterized by the differentiation of core and periphery regions (Wallerstein, 1974, 1980, 1989). **Core regions** consist of geographical areas that dominate the world economy and exploit the rest of the system; **periphery regions** consist of areas that provide raw materials to the core and are exploited by it. At first the peripheral areas exported spices, coffee, tea, and tobacco to Europe. Later, they became suppliers of agricultural and mineral raw materials, while their advantaged classes provided markets for industrial goods from Europe (Boswell, 1989; Chase-Dunn, 1989). Today companies go abroad to develop a source of cheap raw materials and in search of lower wages. This

caused huge losses in textile, clothing, and shoe manufacturing jobs in industrialized countries and huge gains in developing countries in the 1990s, and these trends are continuing.

Private Governments. Multinational firms not only rival nations in wealth, but also frequently operate as "private governments," pursuing their worldwide interests by well-developed "foreign policies." In some instances, multinational corporations have posed a threat to the sovereignty of the nations in which they operate. The governments of host countries find it more difficult to deal with a multinational corporation than with a domestic firm because the multinational corporation can exercise the option of leaving a nation to carry out business elsewhere, which can cause a loss of jobs and tax payments.

Made in America? U.S. multinationals now have a major stake in keeping much of their production overseas. They manufacture and sell nearly three times as much abroad as they make in and export from the United States. The globalization of economic activity is fostering a trend toward a form of "stateless" corporation (Sklair, 1991). In the emerging global economy, it is becoming increasingly difficult to say what is an "American," "Japanese," or "Swedish" product. In some cases, for instance, vehicles sold in the United States are built in 12 countries, with parts coming from all over the world. Indeed, it is now impossible to purchase a completely American-made vehicle.

Impact on Third World Nations.

There is considerable controversy about what impact multinational corporations in general have had on less-developed or peripheral nations. One view, associated with mainstream Marxism, claims that international capitalism has made capitalist countries from precapitalist ones and established the foundation for worker-led socialist revolutions. The contrasting view argues that foreign investments in a country create dependencies that have less positive impact than domestic investment does (Dixon and Boswell, 1996; Firebaugh, 1996). The economies of developing nations have often become tied to a single industry, increasing dependence on foreign investors, distorting patterns of national economic development, and rendering the nations especially vulnerable to bust-and-boom economic cycles (Noble, 1989; Stokes and Anderson, 1990).

What About the Internet?

The Internet has dramatically changed the way companies, including multinational corporations, do business. There are literally millions of Web sites (Wiseman, 2000). Although some see the Internet as likely to increase productivity and benefit consumers, the International Competition Policy Advisory Committee issued a report warning that expansion of e-commerce could result in threats to open competition, primarily through price signaling and cartel creation.

Work is becoming increasingly independent of location, and analysts predict that this will change the quality of work, management practices, and the way work is contracted out (International Labor Organization, 2001). While use of the new information and communication technologies results in job loss, new employment opportunities also are created (International Labor Organization, 2001). The use of new information and communication technologies has the potential for increasing employment in developing countries (International Labor Organization, 2001). Some analysts estimate that up to 5 percent of the service-sector jobs in industrialized nations—approximately 12 million jobs—could be relocated to developing nations. But the "digital divide" is a significant barrier. Despite the Internet's phenomenal growth and increasing availability in nearly every country in the world (International Telecommunication Union, 2003), the fact remains that most Internet users worldwide are in wealthier countries, where Internet costs are only half of what they are in poor countries.

Economic Transitions and the Internet Revolution.

The U.S. economy has long been in flux. Every year thousands of manufacturing jobs are created and thousands more are destroyed as firms go out of business or change operations and other firms start new production lines. The source of much of this change is the rise of the service sector of the economy—comprising industries such as insurance, Internet service, accounting, information processing, and financial services—that provide services rather than manufactured products. As some manufacturing jobs are exported to countries with cheaper labor costs, new jobs are created in this country in service industries. As people lose high-paying manufacturing jobs, they are forced to retrain to make themselves valuable on the job market.

The information and communications technology revolution of the last decade of the 20th century has the potential to cause yet more dramatic changes. In the early 2000s, only about 1 percent of retail trade sales and 8 percent of wholesale trade sales were in e-commerce. But half of all recent investments in plants and equipment were in computer and telecommunications technology, and e-commerce was estimated to add between $100 billion and $200 billion annually (Litan and Rivlin, 2001).

The Internet could increase productivity growth in the following ways (Litan and Rivlin, 2000):

- Significantly reduce the cost of producing and distributing goods and services.

- Increase management efficiency.
- Increase competition.
- Increase the effectiveness of marketing and pricing.
- Increase consumer choice, convenience, and satisfaction.

Changes are inevitable, but analysts disagree about which direction they will take. Skeptics say that large gains in productivity or consumer welfare should not be expected anytime soon. But others expect that use of the Internet will spread from large- and medium-sized companies to small companies rapidly and that its use creates a significant potential for creating a large number of jobs for technically sophisticated workers and raising the standard of living (Litan and Rivlin, 2000).

Religion

As a social institution, religion is organized around the problems of social cohesion and social control as well as providing answers to questions about the meaning and purpose of life. In this section we will review the varieties of religious behavior found among people around the world and take a look at religious organizations. We also will see what the sociological perspectives have to offer to our understanding of religion.

What Is Religion?

Religion has to do with those socially shared and organized ways of thinking, feeling, and acting that concern ultimate meanings about the existence of the supernatural or "beyond" (Stark and Bainbridge, 1987). As Émile Durkheim (1912/1965) pointed out, religion is centered in beliefs and practices that are related to sacred as opposed to profane things. The **sacred** involves those aspects of social reality that are set apart and forbidden. The **profane** has to do with those aspects of social reality that are everyday and commonplace. The sacred, then, is extraordinary, mysterious, awe-inspiring, and even potentially dangerous—it "sticks out" from normal, routine life (Berger, 1967). Because the sacred is caught up with strong feelings of reverence and awe, it can usually be approached only through **rituals**—social acts prescribed by rules that dictate how human beings should behave in the presence of the sacred. In their religious behavior, human beings fashion a social world of meanings and rules that govern how and what they think, feel, and act.

A Global View: Varieties of Religious Behavior

Research shows that religion plays a role in most people's lives, but its importance varies significantly across the globe. Only 15 percent of the world's population is nonreligious or atheist (having no belief in God) (U.S. Census Bureau, 1999). The rest of the world can be categorized by their adherence to various religions, including Hindus (12.8 percent) and Muslims (19.6 percent), Buddhists (6.0 percent) and Roman Catholics (17.3 percent), Protestants (5.3 percent) and Jews (0.1 percent), Sikhs, Baha'is, and New-Religionists. However, data from the World Values Survey (Inglehart et al., 2000) show that the percentage of people reporting that religion is "very important" in their lives ranges from between 80 and 90 percent in Nigeria, Ghana, Bangladesh, and Pakistan to less than 10 percent in Sweden, the Czech Republic, Japan, and China (see Figure 8.1), with an average of about 33 percent across the 71 surveys conducted worldwide.

Religious behavior is so varied that we have difficulty thinking about it unless we devise some means for sorting it into relevant categories. Sociologist Reece McGee (1975) provided us with a scheme with four categories: simple supernaturalism, animism, theism, and a system of abstract ideals.

Simple Supernaturalism.
A belief in the supernatural entails the notion of **mana,** a diffuse, impersonal, supernatural force that exists in nature for good or evil. Mana is usually employed to reach "here-and-now" goals—control of the weather, assurance of a good crop, cure of an illness, good performance on a test, success in love, or victory in battle. With mana people do not entreat spirits or gods to intervene on their behalf. Rather, they *compel* a superhuman power to behave as they wish by manipulating it mechanically. For instance, the act of carrying a rabbit's foot is thought to bring the bearer good luck, while evil is associated with such things as the number 13.

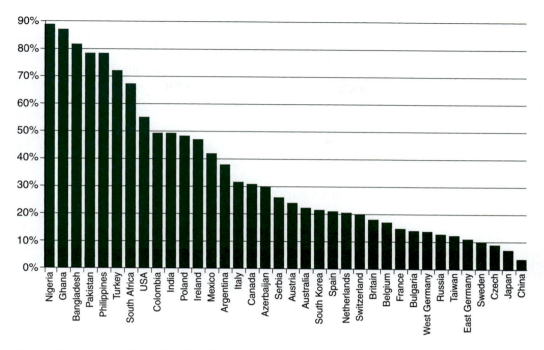

Figure 8.1   Percent Reporting that Religion Is "Very Important" in Their Lives, World Values Surveys, 1980s and 1990s

Source: Figure generated by the authors using data from selected countries surveyed in the World Values Survey, 1981–1984, 1990–1993, and 1995–1997 (Inglehart et al., 2000).

Animism.   **Animism** is a pattern of religious behavior that involves a belief in spirits or otherworldly beings. People have seen spirits throughout nature—in animals, plants, rocks, stars, rivers, and at times in other individuals. Love, punishment, reverence, and gifts have all been used to deal with superhuman spirits, as have cajolery, bribery, and false pretenses. Additionally, in animism, as with mana, supernatural power is often harnessed through rituals that compel a spirit to act in a desired way.

Theism.   In **theism** religion is centered in a belief in gods who are thought to be powerful, to have an interest in human affairs, and to merit worship. Judaism, Christianity, and Islam are forms of **monotheism,** or belief in one god. They have established religious organizations, religious leaders or priests, traditional rituals, and sacred writings. Ancient Greek religion and Hinduism (practiced primarily in India) are forms of **polytheism,** or belief in many gods with equal or relatively similar power. Hindu gods are often tribal, village, or caste deities associated with a particular place—a building, field, or mountain—or a certain object such as an animal or a tree.

Abstract Ideals.

Finally, some religions focus on a set of abstract ideals. Rather than centering on the worship of a god, they are dedicated to achieving moral and spiritual excellence. Many of the religions of Asia are of this type, including Taoism, Confucianism, and Buddhism. Buddhism is directed toward reaching an elevated state of consciousness, a method of purification that provides a release from suffering, ignorance, and selfishness. In the Western world, humanism is based on ethical principles. Its adherents discard all theological beliefs about God, heaven, hell, and immortality, and substitute for God the pursuit of good in the here and now.

Religious Organizations

Norms, beliefs, and rituals provide the cultural fabric of religion, but there is more to the religious institution than its cultural heritage. As with other institutions, there is also the structural mosaic of social organization whereby people are bound together within networks of relatively stable relationships.

Church.

Sociologists use the familiar term "church" to refer to a form of religious organization that has never existed in the United States but has been common in history and still exists in parts of the world. **Church** is a religious organization that considers itself uniquely legitimate and typically enjoys a positive relationship with mainstream society. It usually operates with a bureaucratic structure and claims to include most members of a society. Religions organized along church lines are either integrated into a society's government or operate with explicit government sanction and support. Its members are born into the church if their parents are affiliated with it; they do not have to join the church. The aim of the church is professedly universal. Its response to competing groups is to suppress, ignore, or co-opt them. It strives to dominate all aspects of social life—to teach and guide the members of society and dispense saving grace. The church type is best exemplified by the Roman Catholic Church of 13th-century Europe and the Church of England.

The Denomination.

The **denomination** accepts the legitimacy claims of other religions and enjoys a positive relationship with the dominant society. In many cases, it is a sect in an advanced stage of development and adjustment to the secular world. The membership of the denomination comes largely from the middle class. It usually has an established clergy who have undergone specialized training at a theological seminary to prepare for their positions.

The denomination is content to be one organization among many, all of which are deemed acceptable in the sight of God. Examples of denominations include most of the major religious groups in the United States: Presbyterians, Baptists, Congregationalists, Methodists,

Unitarians, Lutherans, Episcopalians, Roman Catholics, and Reform and Conservative Jews.

The Sect.

The **sect** is a religious organization that stands apart from mainstream society but is rooted in established religious traditions. Sects are often founded by individuals who break away from another religious body and claim that they represent the true, cleansed version of the faith from which they split (Stark and Bainbridge, 1979; Wilson, 1990). The sect considers itself uniquely legitimate but is at odds with the dominant society. The sect does not attempt to win the world over to its doctrines but instead practices exclusiveness. Members who entertain heretical opinions or engage in immoral behavior are subject to expulsion. Examples of sects are the Anabaptists of the 16th- and 17th-century Reformation and the Mormons, Shakers, and Quakers of the 18th and 19th centuries. Most sects are small, and many of them fail to grow larger. Should they survive, gain adherents, and become dominant, they have a natural tendency to become churchlike. If they become widely popular in a religiously diverse and competitive environment like the United States, they become more like denominations.

The Cult.

While a sect is formed out of an existing religion, a **cult** is a religious movement that represents a new and independent religious tradition (Stark and Bainbridge, 1979, 1987). The cult is alienated and viewed as deviant by the dominant society, but it tends to accept the legitimacy of other religious groups. Having no religious tradition, it is difficult for a cult to claim sole legitimacy. In addition, knowing that others view them with suspicion, cults have a sense of vulnerability and thus an interest in publicly supporting norms of tolerance.

Cults usually do not require their new members to pass strict doctrinal tests, but instead invite all to join their ranks. However, many cults are authoritarian and attempt to control the entire lives of their members.

Figure 8.2 depicts these types of religious organizations.

Religion and Social Change: The Protestant Ethic

People's religious beliefs and practices can promote socioeconomic change. Max Weber (1904/1958, 1916/1964, 1917/1958) studied several world religions in order to discern how a religious **ethic**—the perspective and values engendered by a religious way of thinking—can affect people's behavior.

In *The Protestant Ethic and the Spirit of Capitalism* (1904/1958), Weber sought a link between the rise of the Protestant view of life and the emergence of capitalist social arrangements in Western society. He maintained that the development of capitalism depended upon the creation of a pool of individuals who had the attitudes and values necessary to function as entrepreneurs. Once capitalism is established, it carries on in a self-perpetuating fashion.

	Positive Relationship with Society	Negative Relationship with Society
Claims Lone Legitimacy	CHURCH	SECT
Accepts Pluralistic Legitimacy	DENOMI-NATION	CULT

Figure 8.2   Types of Religious Organizations

Source: Adapted from Roy Wallis, *Sectarianism: Analyses of Religious and Non-Religious Sects.* New York: Wiley, 1975, p. 41. Reprinted by permission of Peter Owen Ltd.

The critical problem, Weber said, is to uncover the origin of the motivating spirit of capitalism in precapitalist society. He believed that Protestantism, particularly in the form of Calvinism, was crucial to, but not the only factor in, the rise of this spirit. Calvinism is based on the teachings of the French Protestant theologian and reformer John Calvin (1509–1564) and found expression in a variety of religious movements including Puritanism, Pietism, and Anabaptism.

Weber noted that Protestantism and modern capitalism appeared on the historical scene at roughly the same time, that capitalism initially attained its highest development in Protestant countries and regions, and that it was mostly Protestants, not Catholics, who became the early capitalist entrepreneurs. Based on these observations, Weber (1904/1958:64) concluded that the **Protestant ethic,** particularly as it was embodied in Calvinist doctrine, instilled an "attitude which seeks profit rationally and systematically."

The Calvinist ethos had other elements that fed capitalist motivation, particularly its *doctrine of predestination.* Calvin taught that at birth every soul is predestined for heaven or hell. Because people did not know whether they were among the saved or the damned, they came to accept certain earthly signs of **asceticism** as proof of their salvation and genuine faith: hard work, sobriety, thrift, restraint, and the avoidance of fleshly pleasures. Self-discipline and a willingness to delay gratification are qualities that lead people to amass capital and achieve economic success. Capitalist entrepreneurs could pursue profit and fulfill their Christian obligation; the Calvinist ethos took the spirit of capitalism out of the realm of individual ambition and translated it into an ethical duty.

Many scholars since Weber have raised serious questions regarding his hypothesis (Samuelsson, 1961; Cohen, 1980). They have looked to other factors in explaining the origins of capitalism, including a surge in commerce during the 15th and 16th centuries, technological innovations, the influx of capital resources from New World colonies, unrestrained markets, and the availability of a free labor force. Even so, Weber's early work, although not necessarily accurate in all its particulars, remains a sociological landmark. It demonstrates the impact religion can have on human affairs in producing outcomes that are not necessarily intended or foreseen by its adherents.

According to functionalism, religious rituals create among people a shared consciousness that contributes to a social bonding.

The Functionalist Perspective

Functionalist theorists look to the contributions religion makes to society's survival. They reason that if every known society seems to have something called religion, its presence cannot be dismissed as a social accident (Davis, 1951). Accordingly, they ask what functions are performed by religion in social life. For functionalists, the primary societal functions of religion are the creation, reinforcement, and maintenance of social solidarity and social control.

Religious activity and rituals promote social solidarity, and thus social control, in two ways: First, they provide vehicles by which we *reveal* to one another that we share a common mental state; second, they *create* among us a shared consciousness that contributes to a social bonding.

Religion also performs functions for individuals by providing a sense of life meaning and ways of dealing with uncertainty and change. Although science can tell us much, it cannot inform us about the purpose of the universe and our place in it. It cannot answer questions about the meaning of our lives or how we should understand critical life transitions, such as birth, marriage, death, and so on. Religion provides answers to such questions that stress the supernatural and often link the individual to the supernatural through an intense emotional experience.

The Conflict Perspective

From the writings of functionalist theorists we gain a view of religion as a valuable and positive source promoting social integration and solidarity. We derive a quite different image from conflict theorists, who primarily depict religion as a weapon in the service of ruling elites who use it to hold in check the explosive tensions produced by social inequality and injustice.

The stimulus for many of the contributions made by conflict theorists comes from the work of Karl Marx. Marx (1844/1960:43–44) portrayed religion as a painkiller for the frustration, deprivation, and subjugation experienced by oppressed peoples: "the opium of the people." He said it soothes their distress but that any relief it may provide is illusory.

Marx saw religion as producing an otherworldly focus that diverts the oppressed from seeking social change in this world. More particularly, religion engenders a false consciousness among the working class that interferes with its attainment of true class consciousness. The focus on the supernatural and the afterlife also alienates people from themselves by directing their attention away from the material conditions of their own existence and their potential for controlling their own lives.

Conflict theorists see an inherently conservative aspect to religion. Practices handed down from previous generations, including institutional inequalities and inequities, are often defined as God-approved ways and highly resistant to change.

For example, American slavery was justified as part of God's "natural order." In 1863 the Presbyterian Church of the South met in General Synod and passed a resolution declaring slavery to be a divine institution ordained by God. Imperialism has often been supported by religious or quasi-religious motivations and beliefs. In the 1890s, President William McKinley justified his decision to wage the expansionist war against Spain and seize Cuba and the Philippines as a way of "Christianizing" and civilizing these people (McGuire, 1981:188).

Religious organizations themselves are frequently motivated to legitimate the status quo because they also have vested interests to protect, including power, land, and wealth (Collins, 1981).

Education

Social scientists view **learning** as a relatively permanent change in behavior or capability that results from experience. Because learning is so vital to social life, societies seldom leave it to chance. Most societies undertake to transmit particular attitudes, knowledge, and skills to their members through formal, systematic training—what sociologists call the institution of **education.**

Education is one aspect of the many-sided process of socialization by which people acquire behaviors essential for effective participation in society (see Chapter 2). It entails an explicit process in which some individuals assume the status of teacher and others the status of student and carry out their associated roles.

Schools initially came into existence several thousand years ago to prepare a select few for a limited number of leadership and professional positions. Only in the past century or so have public schools become the primary vehicles by which the members of a society are taught the three Rs, affording them the literacy skills required by large-scale industrial and bureaucratic organizations. The curricula of schools—such "core" subjects as mathematics, natural science, and social science—are remarkably similar throughout the world. Exactly how government interacts with education, however, differs cross-culturally. For example, most nations have a national curriculum in science and mathematics, but the United States does not (Sanchez, 1996).

In this section we will examine the bureaucratic structure of schools, alternatives to traditional public education, and the availability of higher education. We will then take a look at the functionalist and conflict perspectives on education.

The Bureaucratic Structure of Schools

Until a few generations ago, schooling in the United States usually took place in a one-room schoolhouse. One teacher taught all eight grades, with the more advanced and older students helping the less capable and younger students with their lessons. As long as the schools remained relatively small, they could operate on the basis of face-to-face interaction.

Like hospitals, factories, and businesses, however, schools grew larger and more complex. To attain their goals, they had to standardize and routinize many of their operations and establish formal operating and administrative procedures. In brief, they turned to a bureaucratic arrangement, a social structure made up of a hierarchy of statuses and roles prescribed by explicit rules and procedures and based on a division of function and authority (see Chapter 3).

At the very top of this organizational arrangement is the federal government, which through a variety of agencies, including the Department of Education and the federal court system, profoundly influences educational life. State educational authorities set the number of days in a school year and allocate state money for specified programs.

The formal organization of American schools and colleges typically consists of four levels: (1) the board of education or trustees, (2) administrators, (3) teachers or professors, and (4) students. The control of most schools and colleges is vested in an elected or appointed *board* of laypeople. The board generally appoints and assigns administrators and teachers, decides on the nature of educational programs, determines building construction, and approves operational budgets. The *administrators*—superintendents, principals, presidents, chancellors, and deans—are responsible for executing the policies of the board. Although in theory the board determines policy, in practice many policy questions are settled by administrators. *Teachers* are the immediate day-to-day link between the larger system and individual *students,* the latter occupying the lowest position in the school bureaucracy. In sum, the school system is characterized by a chain of command, a network of positions functionally interrelated for the purpose of accomplishing educational objectives.

By virtue of bureaucratic arrangements, most school environments are remarkably standardized in both their physical and social characteristics. These patterns are most apparent at the elementary and secondary school levels. For example, time is usually highly formalized. The Pledge of Allegiance is followed by math at 8:35, which is followed by reading at 9:10, which is followed by recess, and so on over the course of the day.

Individual behavior is governed by sets of rules—no loud talking during desk work, raise your hand to talk during discussions, keep your eyes on your paper during tests, and no running in the halls. The physical layout of the school and the omnipresent symbols of adult authority emphasize and reinforce the subordinate status of the pupils.

Alternatives to Traditional Public Schools

In a movement some predict will transform education in the United States, parents are increasingly choosing to educate their children in ways other than enrolling them in traditional public schools. The number of students attending charter schools and private schools or being educated at home has increased significantly in the past several years.

The number of charter schools, which receive taxpayer money but make their own decisions about how to teach, grew from none to 2,400 in about a decade (Maranto, 2003). Except for those on Indian reservations, there was only one charter school in the United States in 1992; in 2002, charter schools were serving 2.2 percent of the public school students in California; 4 percent of those in Delaware, Michigan, and Colorado; 7.4 percent in Arizona; and 14.5 percent of the students in Washington, D.C. (Palmer and Gau, 2003). Charter schools vary widely in their instructional approach and in the degree to which they are used in each state; in some states, "cyber" charter schools are being tested, with students "attending school" over the computer (Fletcher, 2002).

Private schools educate even more students: 14 percent of all kindergarten through 12th graders were enrolled in private schools in 2000 (U.S. Census Bureau, 2003).

Enrollment in private Christian academies doubled in 10 years. Catholic schools, which had had a long period of declining enrollment, now have increasing enrollment and increasing numbers of non-Catholic students (Sanchez, 1997). The provision of vouchers for low-income children to attend private schools has increased private-school enrollments.

The number of students taught at home is thought to have tripled over a 10-year period to between 700,000 and 1.2 million in 1999 (Rudner, 1999); the number of home-schooled students reported by parents in 1999 was 850,000 (U.S. Census Bureau, 2003), although not all home-schooling families officially register their children as home schooled, making the actual numbers hard to estimate. Home schooling is legal in every state. Although it is difficult to compare achievement among home-schooled and other students, research indicates that home-schooled children do well on standardized tests (Byfield, 2001). Studies also show that home-schooled children do not suffer disadvantages in self-esteem, leadership, or other dimensions of personal development (Medlin, 2000).

The Availability of Higher Education

Despite our cherished picture of the United States as a place where education is available to all, college and university student populations are highly skewed in terms of race, ethnicity, and family income. Although we tend to picture college students as "youngsters" fresh out of high school, only 20 percent of the nation's undergraduates are young people between 18 and 22 years of age who are pursuing a parent-financed education. Two-fifths of all students are part-timers; and more than one-third of all undergraduates are over age 25.

A report by the American College Testing Program concluded that inadequate financial aid, poor academic preparation, and low college retention rates are responsible for the continuing gaps in college-completion rates between wealthier and poorer students and between white and minority students (Mortenson and Wu, 1991). According to data from the U.S. Department of Education and the College Board, there is a sharp disparity between rich and poor in college attendance. Research shows that a much higher percentage of students whose family incomes are $67,000 and above finish college than do students from poor backgrounds (Sanchez and Chandler, 1997).

The likelihood that African Americans and Hispanics receive a college education has improved over the past 40 years, but sharp disparities with whites and now Asian Americans remain (U.S. Census Bureau, 2003). Many factors make it difficult for minority youth to gain entrance to and then remain in college. First, many of the students have weaker academic preparation in elementary and secondary schools than white students. Second, most campuses lack a "critical mass" of minority students and faculty who can serve as role models and make new students feel at home. Third, many minority students are first-generation collegians, and they do not secure the emotional or financial support from home that second- and third-generation collegians receive (Johnson, 1988). The cost of a college education plays an important role in selecting who will receive a degree. In recent years,

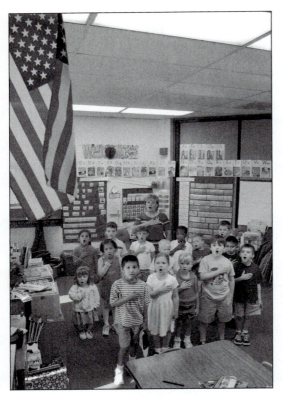

the cost of higher education has outpaced the growth in family income and is nearly triple the rate of inflation.

The Functionalist Perspective

Viewed from the functionalist perspective, schools make a number of vital contributions to the survival and perpetuation of modern societies. Functionalists see schools as serving to complete socialization, socially integrate a diverse population, screen and select individuals, and develop new knowledge. In this section we will look at each of these functions in more detail.

Completing Socialization.

Many pre-literate and peasant societies lack schools. They socialize their youngsters in the same "natural" way that parents teach their children to walk or talk. According to functionalists, the knowledge and skills required by contemporary living cannot be satisfied in a more or less automatic and "natural" way. Instead, a specialized edu-

Functionalists say that one of the functions of public education is social integration. In performing this function, schools promote dominant values and try to shape a common national consciousness.

cational agency is needed to transmit to young people the ways of thinking, feeling, and acting mandated by a rapidly changing urban and technologically based society.

Social Integration.

Functionalists say that the education system functions to inculcate the dominant values of a society and shape a common national mind. Within the United States, students learn what it means to be an American, become literate in the English language, gain a common heritage, and acquire mainstream standards and rules. Youngsters from diverse ethnic, religious, and racial backgrounds are immersed within the same Anglo-American culture and prepared for responsible citizenship (see Chapter 6). Historically, the nation's schools played a prominent part in Americanizing the children of immigrants (Dunn, 1993), and in the contemporary United States, the schools are geared to integrating the poor and disadvantaged within the fabric of dominant, mainstream institutions.

Screening and Selecting.

We noted in Chapter 2 that some statuses in society are achieved through choice and competition. Modern societies in particular must select certain of their youth for positions that require special talents. The educational institution commonly per-forms this function, serving as an agency for screening and selecting individuals for different types of jobs. By conferring degrees, diplomas, and credentials that are prerequisites for many technical, managerial, and professional positions, it determines which young people will have access to scarce positions and offices of power, privilege, and status.

Research and Development.
Schools, particularly universities, may not only transmit culture; they also add to the cultural heritage. Modern society places a good deal of emphasis on the development of new knowledge, especially in the physical and biological sciences, medicine, and engineering. In recent decades, the nation's leading uni-versities have increasingly become research centers. This emphasis on research has led universities to judge professors not primarily in terms of their competence as teachers but as researchers with a primary func-tion of the university being viewed as research.

Functionalism sees the university combining the functions of research and education. Even when students are not themselves involved in research projects, they benefit from the intellectual stimula-tion a research orientation brings to university life.

The Conflict Perspective

Conflict theorists see schools as agencies that reproduce and legitimate the current social order through the functions they perform. By repro-ducing and legitimating the existing social order, the educational insti-tution is seen as benefiting some individuals and groups at the expense of others (Collins, 1977, 1979, 1988b). Let's take a closer look at how conflict theorists think this occurs.

Reproducing the Social Relations of Production.
Some con-flict theorists depict U.S. schools as reflecting the needs of capitalist production (Apple, 1982). The **correspondence principle** states that the social relations of work find expression in the social relations of the school (Bowles and Gintis, 1976). Schools mirror the workplace and hence on a day-to-day basis prepare children for adult roles in the job market. The authoritarian structure of many schools reproduces the bureaucratic hierarchy of the corporation, rewarding diligence, sub-missiveness, and compliance. The system of grades employed to moti-vate students parallels the wage system for motivating workers. In short, the schools are seen as socializing a compliant labor force for the capitalist economy.

Control Devices.
Conflict theorists agree with functionalist theo-rists that schools are agencies for drawing minorities and the disadvan-taged into the dominant culture. But they do not see the function in

benign terms. Sociologist Randall Collins (1976) contended that the educational system serves the interests of the dominant group by defusing the threat posed by minority ethnic groups. Compulsory education erodes ethnic differences and loyalties and transmits to minorities and those at the bottom of the social hierarchy the values and lifeways of the dominant group. Schools, then, are viewed by conflict theorists as control devices employed by established elites.

Productive Capital.

Conflict theorists see the research and development function of the universities quite differently than functionalist theorists do. For example, Michael W. Apple (1982) provided a Marxist twist to the functionalist argument by contending that the educational institution produces the technical and administrative knowledge necessary for running a capitalist order. Viewed in this manner, education is part of the system of production. It not only reproduces existing social arrangements but also develops the know-how needed by capitalists to fuel the economy and gain competitive advantage in world markets (Barrow, 1990).

Credentialism.

Collins (1979) also downplayed the functionalist argument that schools serve as mobility escalators. He cited evidence that students acquire little technical knowledge in school and that most technical skills are learned on the job. Although more education is needed to obtain most jobs, Collins said that this development is not explained by the technical requirements of the job. The level of skills required by typists, receptionists, salesclerks, teachers, assembly-line workers, and many others is not much different than it was a generation or so ago. Collins called these tendencies **credentialism**—the requirement that a worker have a degree for its own sake, not because it certifies skills needed for the performance of a job.

Conflict theorists are also interested in what they call the **hidden curriculum,** which consists of a complex of unarticulated values, attitudes, and behaviors that subtly mold children in the image preferred by the dominant institutions. Teachers model and reinforce traits that embody middle-class standards—industry, responsibility, conscientiousness, reliability, thoroughness, self-control, and efficiency. Even when teachers are originally from another social class, they still view their role as one of encouraging the development of a middle-class outlook on such matters as thrift, cleanliness, punctuality, neatness, ambition, sexual morality, and respect for property and established authority. Children learn to be quiet, to be on time, to line up, to wait their turn, to please their teachers, and to conform to group pressures. In some cases middle-class teachers, without necessarily being aware of their bias, find inner-city and minority children unacceptable. Their students tend to respond by taking the attitude, "If you don't like me, I won't cooperate with you." The net result is that the youngsters fail to acquire basic reading, writing, and math skills.

Medicine

Like the educational institution, the functions now carried out by the medical institution were once embedded in the activities of the family and religious institutions. Only in relatively recent times has **medicine** emerged as a distinct institution, providing an enduring set of cultural patterns and social relationships responsible for problems of health and disease. The World Health Organization defines **health** as "a state of complete physical, mental, and social well-being and not merely the absence of disease or infirmity." We usually assess people's health by how well they are able to function in their daily lives and adapt to a changing environment. Health, then, has a somewhat different meaning for a soldier, a nursing home resident, an airline pilot, a steelworker, a high school football player, a presidential candidate, and a computer programmer. In contrast to health, most of us think of disease as an undesirable, serious, and limiting circumstance. **Disease** is a condition in which an organism does not function properly because of biological causes. The problems may result from microbial infection, dietary deficiency, heredity, or a harmful environmental agent.

In this section we will look at the American health care delivery system and at what the sociological perspectives contribute to our thinking about medicine.

The U.S. Health Care Delivery System

How does the United States deal with sickness? In this section we will examine the health care system in the United States, including a discussion of hospitals, physicians, and nurses.

A Disease-Cure System.   In some senses, the United States does not have a "health care system" but a "disease-cure system" instead (Konner, 1993; Spiegel, 1994). The public believes, and a good many physicians behave as if, most illnesses are curable.

The expectation of cure in the U.S. health care system has generated an explosion of invasive, expensive, and often risky medical interventions. The emphasis falls on disease, not on the people who have the diseases. For example, most clinicians and researchers in the field of coronary artery disease concentrate on ways to clear out fatty plaque buildups in arteries or to replace clogged arteries surgically. These techniques do not cure the disease, work less often than we wish, are performed at great risk to patients, and cost a colossal amount of money.

Much evidence suggests that behaviors such as eating a diet low in saturated fat and cholesterol, avoiding smoking, and getting moderate exercise can both prevent and reverse much heart disease. Yet 21 percent of U.S. adults meet the medical definition of obesity, with another 56 percent of the population overweight. Although some have a genetic predisposition for weight gain, our lifestyle choices play a major role. In 2003, the U.S. Surgeon General, Richard Carmona, said he would devote his term to disease prevention, commenting, "We can no longer tolerate treating people who make poor choices" (Carmona, 2003). But rather than focusing on disease prevention and promoting health, most Americans still look to the "disease-cure system" to solve their problems. Social pathologies such as drug and alcohol abuse and poor health practices such as lack of exercise and unhealthy diet show up in medical costs for all of us (Kuttner, 1994; U.S. Department of Health and Human Services, 2000a).

Health economists say that a medical system should have about 50 percent of its doctors practicing primary care—the initial care a patient receives before being referred, if necessary, to a specialist. Primary care includes family practice, internal medicine, and pediatrics. Nonetheless, in 1992 only a third of the nation's physicians were in primary care and less than 15 percent of medical students had decided to go into general medicine, an all-time low (Rosenthal, 1993). Medical care tends to be high-tech and highly specialized.

Hospitals.   Separate facilities for the ill came into existence among the ancient Greeks. But not until the Middle Ages in western Europe did the hospital movement begin in earnest. By 1450 there were some 600 hospitals in England alone. Most hospitals were run by Catholic religious orders because healing and health care were deemed to be the province of religion. The hospitals also cared for the poor, the disabled, and the itinerant. Toward the end of the 17th century and during the 18th century, financial abuses and the mismanagement of funds by some religious orders led local governments to take on greater responsibility for the management of hospitals (Rosen, 1963).

By the late 19th century, hospital services were improving. Advances in medical research, especially bacteriology, provided a stronger scientific basis for treatment and the control of infection. New diagnostic tools such as X rays and advances in surgical procedures made many diseases, injuries, and deformities more amenable to medical operations. At the same time, hospitals became businesses governed by commercial incentives. As insurance developed first for hospital bills and later for physicians' bills, the hospital industry and the medical profession flourished. By 1965 Congress had established Medicare to pay some of the health care costs of the elderly, and Medicaid for those of the "deserving" poor. By the mid-1960s, then, hospitals, physicians, private insurers, and the government had devised a system for financing health care that was ripe for big business and the emergence of for-profit hospital chains (Gray, 1991; Lindorff, 1992).

Physicians.   Sociologist Paul Starr (1982) traced the transformation of health care from a household service to a market commodity and the rise of the private medical practice. He showed that well into the 19th century most U.S. doctors eked out scant incomes. Following the Civil War, however, a contracting household economy, a growing urban population, and more efficient transportation and communication expanded the market for medical services. By the turn of the 20th century, doctors were well on the road to endowing their profession with a "cultural authority" sufficient to justify claims to self-regulation, state protection, client deference, and control of the means of work. In turn, doctors capitalized on these gains to develop medical specialties and mutual networks that decreased competition and increased their economic and political power. By the 1930s private practitioners had acquired sufficient influence and prestige to establish themselves as virtually the sole arbiters of medicine in the United States. They dominated hospitals, medical technology, and other health practitioners, including nurses and pharmacists. Additionally, doctors institutionalized their authority through a system of medical education and standardized educational licensing.

Nurses.   The nursing profession grew out of the religious and charitable activities of early hospitals. Religious orders of nuns took on the care of the sick and the poor. By the latter half of the 19th century, however, increasing numbers of nonreligious personnel were employed to perform various custodial functions in hospitals. Since the jobs required no formal training and were deemed to be menial labor, many poor and uneducated women entered the field. This heritage has contributed to the undeservedly low prestige that the profession of nursing has long endured (Baer, 1991). Additionally, wages in nursing, like those in other fields with a large concentration of women, remain low even today, despite the fact that most nurses now earn a bachelor of science degree in nursing in a four-year college degree program, and many go on to secure master's degrees in specialized areas.

Through the years, the profession of nursing has remained almost exclusively female—in 2002, 91.9 percent of America's nurses were women. About 60 percent of all registered nurses work in hospitals, where they serve simultaneously as managers of hospital wards and assistants to physicians. These dual functions often place nurses in situations of role conflict because they are responsible to both administrative and medical authorities. Nurses have been steadily acquiring more autonomy in health care. At the same time, their workloads have increased so greatly that many say they cannot give patients the quality of care they need (Gordon, 1997; Trafford, 2001).

The Functionalist Perspective

Functionalists argue that the medical institution evolved across time to deal with problems of health and disease. More specifically, they see the medical institution performing a number of key functions in modern societies. First, it treats and seeks to cure disease. Second, the medical institution attempts to prevent disease through health maintenance programs (HMOs), including vaccination, health education, periodic checkups, and public health and safety standards. Third, it undertakes research in the prevention, treatment, and cure of health problems. Fourth, it serves as an agency of social control by defining some behaviors as "normal" and "healthy" and others as "deviant" and "unhealthy."

Sociologist Talcott Parsons (1951) expanded upon the functionalist position in his analysis of the **sick role**—a set of cultural expectations that define what is appropriate and inappropriate behavior for people with a disease or health problem (see also Turner, 1987). He said one way societies contain the negative effects of health problems is through institutionalizing illness in a special role, one having the following characteristics:

- Sick people are exempt from their usual social roles and responsibilities. They need not attend school or go to work, and other people will not censure them for doing so.
- Sick people are not thought to be at fault for their condition. Being sick is a physical matter, not a moral one.
- Sick people have the duty to get well and "not enjoy themselves too much." Because being sick is an undesirable state, sick people are obligated to seek competent help from medical practitioners.
- Sick people should cooperate with medical practitioners and follow their instructions.

Like other functionalists, Parsons assumes illness must be socially controlled lest it impair societal functioning.

The Conflict Perspective

Implicit in the functionalist image of the sick role is the assumption that health care services are impartially and equally available to all members of a society. This image is challenged by conflict theorists (Waitzkin, 1983). They say that people of all societies prefer health to illness. Yet some people achieve better health than others because they have access to those resources that contribute to good health and to recovery should they become ill.

Conflict theorists point out that the higher our social class, the more likely we are to enjoy good health, receive good medical care, and live a long life. Poor people experience more disability and lower levels of health than affluent people. Even though access to health care among the poor has improved in recent years, low socioeconomic status is still the strongest predictor of illness and death in the United States and the world (Williams, 1998). It has been argued that educational differences are most responsible for this disparity, with well-educated people more likely to live a healthy lifestyle and to be able to avoid economic hardship (Mirowsky and Ross, 2003). There is also a racial divide. Much research indicates that racial and ethnic minorities receive lower quality health services than whites, even when their incomes and insurance coverage are the same (Smedley, Stith, and Nelson, 2003).

In practice, U.S. medical care has traditionally operated as a dual system in which the poor have utilized public sources—hospital outpatient departments, emergency rooms, and public clinics—while middle- and upper-income Americans use private sources such as physicians in private or group practice. Patients using public sources often must maneuver between multiple clinics to obtain their services, and the services are usually disease-oriented rather than preventive.

Key Terms

animism, 229

asceticism, 232

authoritarianism, 220

authority, 217

capitalist economy, 221

charismatic authority, 218

church, 230

civil society, 220

core regions, 224

correspondence principle, 239

credentialism, 240

cult, 231

democracy, 220

denomination, 230

disease, 241

education, 234

ethic, 231

force, 215

government, 218

health, 241

hidden curriculum, 240

interest groups, 220

interests, 220

learning, 234

legal-rational authority, 217

mana, 228

medicine, 241

monotheism, 229

multinational corporations, 224

periphery regions, 224

political power, 218

politics, 218

polytheism, 229

profane, 228

Protestant ethic, 232

religion, 227

rituals, 228

sacred, 228

sect, 231

sick role, 244

socialist economy, 221

state, 215

theism, 229

totalitarianism, 218

traditional authority, 217

Review Questions

1. Define *the state* as sociologists use the term.
2. How do the functionalist and conflict perspectives on the state differ?

3. What do sociologists mean by legitimacy and authority? What are the three types of authority and how do they differ?

4. Define politics and political power.

5. How do totalitarianism, authoritarianism, and democracy differ?

6. How do multinational corporations function?

7. What is religion? Discuss the differences among supernaturalism, animism, theism, and abstract ideals.

8. How do churches, denominations, sects, and cults differ?

9. What is the Protestant ethic?

10. Compare the functionalist and conflict perspectives on religion.

11. How does learning differ from education?

12. Describe school bureaucracy.

13. Describe higher education in the United States today.

14. Discuss the functionalist and conflict perspectives on education.

15. Define medicine and describe the U.S. health care system.

16. How do the functionalist and conflict perpectives on medicine differ?

Population and Environment

Population

The Urban
Environment

The Ecological
Environment

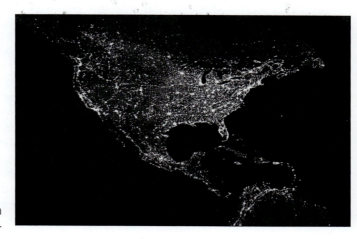

W orld   population reached 6 billion before the end of the 20th century and stood at 6.3 billion, with a 1.3 percent growth rate, in 2003 (McFalls, 2003). The effects of a world so populated with humans are evident everywhere: global warming, depleted water supplies, mass extinctions, the destruction of the world's rain forests, the spread of deserts, air and water pollution, famine. By the year 2025 more than 60 percent of the world's population will be concentrated in cities (Gottdiener and Hutchison, 2000), where many of our most serious pollution problems already are to be found.

In the coming decades, population increases will occur almost entirely in developing countries. Industrialized countries, including the United States, will be affected more by migration than by internal population increases, with many countries actually experiencing population declines. But industrialized nations consume the vast majority of the world's resources, so even without substantial population increases they play a major role in resource consumption, pollution, and habitat destruction—and a major role in providing direction and assistance to developing countries.

In this chapter we provide the basics for an understanding of population, the environment, and life in cities. First, some definitions:

The **environment** consists of all the surrounding conditions and influences that affect an organism or a group of organisms—a *population*. Among the chief adaptive mechanisms of human populations are social organization and technology; sociologists are interested in how these two mechanisms will be employed to deal with the population and environment problems we face. **Ecology** is the study of the interrelations between the living and nonliving components of an ecosystem. In 1921 two Chicago sociologists, Robert Park and Ernest Burgess, originated the term *human ecology*. They applied theories of plant and animal ecology to the study of human communities (Palen, 1997). In examining the relationship between humans and their environment, sociologists look not at individuals but at populations of humans.

Ecologists typically study smaller ecosystems, but the earth itself also can be considered an ecosystem. An **ecosystem** is a relatively stable community of organisms that have interlocking relationships and exchanges with one another and their environment. While biologists focus on plant and animal species, sociologists find ecosystem analysis a useful way to view the environments humans inhabit. How important are other species and the environment to humans? Beyond aesthetics, nature provides many services to humans: the raw materials for foods, medicines, building materials, and energy; the production of oxygen, without which people cannot live; the filtering and detoxifying of pollutants; the provision of fresh water; and much more (Wilson, 2002). Humankind cannot afford not to take care of it.

Population

Demography is the science dealing with population size, distribution, composition, and change. Demographic data show that population growth is at once both awesome and sobering. The world's population has reached 6 billion; during the last century, major improvements in nutrition, health care, and education resulted in people living longer lives and being more likely to live to reproduce. Both these contributed to very large increases in population growth rates: Many more humans were born than died. More than half the people in the world live in six nations: China, India, the United States, Indonesia, Brazil, and Russia.

It is estimated that some 40,000 years ago the world population stood at about 3 million. At 8000 BC, the dawn of agriculture, it was 5 million. At the time of Christ, it was 200 million. By 1650 it had climbed to 500 million, and by 1830 to 1 billion. At the end of World War II and the advent of the nuclear age, world population stood at 2.3 billion. It took nearly 200,000 years (White et al., 2003) for humankind to reach 1 billion in number, but within a century it had

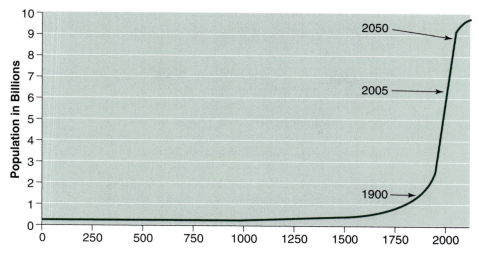

Figure 9.1   World Population Growth Data (from the United Nations) with Projections to 2150

For most of human history, population growth was very slow. During the 20th century, however, rates of growth were extraordinarily high. World population reached 6 billion in 1999, growing from 1 billion to 6 billion in less than 200 years. Demographers predict that rapid growth in world population will continue during most of the 21st century, will begin to taper off slightly by 2050, and may slow considerably in the 22nd century, with total world population size leveling off somewhere between 8.5 and 12 billion people (McFalls, 2003).

Sources: Figure generated by the authors using population data and historical estimates of world population growth from United Nations (1999), available at http://www.un .org/esa/population/publications/sixbillion/sixbilpart1.pdf); and the U.S. Bureau of the Census, available at http://www.census.gov/ipc/www/worldpop.html and http://www .census.gov/ipc/www/worldhis.html.

reached 2 billion, and within an additional quarter-century, 4 billion (see Figure 9.1).

Demographic studies help us to see that where population growth is occurring is critical to our understanding of the future. Most industrialized nations now have population declines, no population growth, or very slow population growth. The enormous increases in population expected to occur in the next decades will take place almost entirely in African, Asian, and South American countries. Although these developing nations currently use only about a quarter of the earth's resources, their rapid population growth and industrialization may combine to dramatically change that. In this section we will look at the basics of population change.

Elements in Population Change

All population change within a society can be reduced to three factors: the birth rate, the death rate, and the migration rate into or out of the society. In 2003 the population of the United States stood at 291.5 million, with a projected population of 351.1 million in 2025 and 421.8 million in 2050 (Haub, 2003).

Birth Rate.   The **crude birth rate** is the number of live births per 1,000 members of a population in a given year. In 2003 the crude birth rate for the United States was 14.1 per 1,000, while in the countries where population growth is increasing rapidly it is much higher. In western Africa, Niger has a crude birth rate of 55 per 1,000, and Uganda in eastern Africa has a crude birth rate of 47 (Haub, 2003). The measure is called "crude" because it obscures important differences among races, ethnic groups, classes, age groups, and other categories within the population by lumping all births within a single figure.

The **general fertility rate** indicates the annual number of live births per 1,000 women age 15 to 44. Demographers also calculate **age-specific fertility,** or the number of live births per 1,000 women in a specific age group. Fertility rates provide us with information regarding the actual reproductive patterns of a society. By contrast, the potential number of children that could be born if every woman of childbearing age bore all the children she possibly could is called **fecundity.**

The annual number of births among women in the United States fell from just over 4.0 million in 1964 to 3.1 million in 1973 and then began rising again in the late 1970s. In 1990, 4,179,000 babies were born in the United States, but the figure fell to 4.08 million in 2003. The number of births rose as the large generation born during the baby boom of the 1950s reached adulthood. However, the average number of children born to women of childbearing age in recent years has been nearly half of what it was three decades earlier. Childbearing is also up sharply among women in their 30s who postponed having babies until their schooling was completed and their careers were begun.

It takes an average of 2.1 children per woman of childbearing age for a modern population to replace itself without immigration; this is the level of **zero population growth** (ZPG). In 1990, for the first time since 1971, births in the United States surpassed the population-replacement rate of 2.1. The nation's birth rates would be lower if all births represented planned births; some 35 percent of all births to currently and formerly married women, however, are unintended.

Death Rate.   The rapid world population growth we are currently experiencing is not caused by any dramatic increase in birth rate; rather, it is caused by dramatic decreases in death rate. The **crude death rate** is the number of deaths per 1,000 members of a population in a given year. In 2003 the crude death rate for Americans was 9 per 1,000. Death rates vary substantially around the world, from 2 per

1,000 in Kuwait to 28 per 1,000 in Mozambique in 2003 (Haub, 2003). Death rates primarily reflect the age distribution of a country's population, although the infection of more than 30 million people in sub-Saharan Africa with HIV, the virus that causes AIDS, has dramatically increased death rates and decreased life expectancies in those countries (McFalls, 2003). As in the case of birth rates, demographers are interested in **age-specific death rate,** or the number of deaths per 1,000 individuals in a specific age group. At ages 24 to 45, the disparity in death rates between minorities and whites is highest: 2.5 times greater for African Americans, 1.8 times higher for Native Americans, and 1.25 times greater for Hispanics. The major reason is that homicide and accidental death rates are substantially higher for these minorities than for whites.

The **infant mortality rate** is the number of deaths among infants under one year of age per 1,000 live births. In 2003 the infant mortality rate in the United States was 6.9 per 1,000, approximately 5.8 deaths per 1,000 live births for whites versus 14.6 deaths for African Americans (U.S. Census Bureau, 2003). Many industrialized nations report even lower infant mortality rates: Hong Kong, 2.6; Iceland, 2.7; Japan, 3.0; Finland, 3.2; Sweden, 3.7; Norway, 3.9; France, 4.2; and others. We have mentioned that a decrease in the death rate results in population increases; likewise, as the infant mortality rate of developing nations drops, population growth increases rapidly. A high birth rate does not add a large number of people to the population if many of those born do not live past their first birthdays. When the number of surviving babies increases, so does the number of children who grow up to have children themselves.

The life expectancy of Americans reached 77 years in 2003, but significant gender and race differences remain. White men born in 1999 could expect to live 74.6 years, compared with a life expectancy of 67.8 years for African-American men. The life expectancy for white women born in 1999 is 79.9 years, and for African-American women, 74.7 years (U.S. Census Bureau, 2003). Overall, human life expectancy is nearly twice as long as it was in 1840, and research done in Sweden shows that the rate of increase in maximum life span has accelerated from 0.44 year per decade before 1969 to 1.11 years per decade since then (Wilmoth et al., 2000). A number of other developed nations have higher average life expectancies than the United States. Japan, with a life expectancy of 81 years, holds the lead among large developed countries, closely followed by Australia and Italy (80 years); Canada, France, and Spain (79 years); and Belgium and the United Kingdom (78 years) (Haub, 2003). Some of the lowest life expectancy figures are for African countries, for example, Botswana and Lesotho, 37 years; Malawi, 39; Rwanda and Angola, 40; Zambia and Zimbabwe, 41; and Ethiopia, 42. The spread of AIDS has drastically reduced life expectancy in some countries. In general, life expectancy and population growth rates increase in developing nations along with improvements in education, nutrition, sanitation, income, and medicine (Oeppen and Vaupel, 2002).

Migration Rate.

The **net migration rate** is the increase or decrease per 1,000 members of the population in a given year that results from people entering (immigrants) or leaving (emigrants) a society. Migration is the product of two factors. There are forces—*push* factors—that encourage people to leave a habitat they already occupy. And there are other forces—*pull* factors—that attract people to a new habitat.

Movement of people from one nation to another is called **international migration.** Only a small percentage of the world's population ever moves across national boundaries. In only a few nations, including Cuba, Afghanistan, Haiti, and El Salvador, have as much as one-tenth of a national population emigrated in recent decades (Kalish, 1994). The United States was the destination for 849,800 immigrants in 2000 (U.S. Census Bureau, 2003).

People also move about within a nation. **Internal migration** has resulted in a majority of the U.S. population residing in the South and West, with population increases continuing in those regions. In 2003 Arizona, Nevada, Florida, Texas, and Idaho were the fastest-growing states in terms of percent growth (State Demographics, 2004). Boom states gain political clout nationally because congressional seats are allocated on the basis of population. And although rapid population growth often fuels economic growth, it simultaneously strains municipal and state services.

Growth Rate.

The **growth rate** of a society is the difference between births and deaths, plus the difference between immigrants and emigrants, per 1,000 population. In recent years the growth rate of the United States has been roughly 1 percent. The **rate of natural increase** is simply the difference between the birth and death rates. For world population growth, we look only at the rate of natural increase, as immigration and emigration do not affect the total world population. It takes a population with an annual rate of increase of 1 percent 69 years to double its population; a 4 percent annual rate increase leads to a doubling of the population in 17 years. In 2003 the rate of natural increase for the world was 1.3 percent (Haub, 2003). Although that rate is lower than it had been previously, world population will expand enormously in coming years. This "momentum of population growth" is fueled by the huge population of children approaching their childbearing years. The United Nations has projected that world population will be 8.9 billion by 2050, assuming continued declines in fertility (McFalls, 2003).

The rate of natural increase is now negative for a number of countries, including Germany, Romania, Russia, Hungary, Bulgaria, and Ukraine. This means that the number of deaths in these countries exceeds the number of births. Without immigration, the population of these countries will decrease.

Population Composition

Births, deaths, and migration affect population *size*. Sociologists also are interested in the *composition* or characteristics of a population. Among these characteristics are gender, age, rural or urban residence, race, religion, national origin, marital status, income, education, and occupation. The sex composition of a population is measured by the *sex ratio*—the number of males per 100 females. At birth, there are roughly 105 males for every 100 females. However, males have higher mortality rates than females. During childhood and adolescence this differential is primarily due to accidents, homicide, and suicide, which are more common among males. The result is that at around age 21 or so, women begin to outnumber men, and the trend accelerates as people grow older because men also have higher rates of illness for disorders that are the leading causes of death, such as cancer, heart disease, and stroke.

The greater longevity of women in the United States has resulted in a ratio of three women for every two men over the age of 65; in the over-85 bracket, the margin is higher than two to one. Why are sex ratios of interest to sociologists? Let's take a look at China, where there are now many more male children than female children. Finding a wife will be a serious problem for men in the future (Johansson and Nygren, 1991). And because marriage is one of the main ways societies have of controlling the behavior of males, China may face serious social problems resulting from so many unattached males.

Another important population characteristic is age composition. A population heavily concentrated in the 20- to 65-year range has a large labor force relative to its nonproductive population. Its dependency burdens tend to be light. In contrast, a population concentrated at either extreme of the age distribution—either under 20, over 65, or both—has a heavy dependency ratio (a large number of nonproductive individuals relative to its productive population). We can gain an appreciation for the social significance of sex and age composition by examining population pyramids.

Population Pyramids.   The age and sex composition of a population can be portrayed by a **population pyramid.** It is based either on absolute numbers or on proportions. Age groupings are placed in order on a vertical scale, with the youngest age group located at the bottom and the oldest age group at the top of the pyramid. The numbers or proportions that each specified age group represents of the total are plotted on the horizontal axis. The sum or portion corresponding to the male segment is placed to the left of the central dividing line and that comprising the female segment is placed to the right of it. The pyramid itself represents the entire population. Demographers use population pyramids to visualize age and gender distributions. Sociologists use them to analyze trends in fertility, mortality, and migration. Businesses often use them to gain a better understanding of their markets.

The U.S. pyramids shown in Figure 9.2 illustrate the projected shape of the age structure of the United States from 1990 through 2050 as the baby-boom generation grows older; the size of future cohorts can only be estimated.

The population projections contained in Figure 9.2 presume fluctuating fertility patterns characterized by "booms" and "busts." The complicating ramifications of migration are not considered here. Let's look at some specific aspects of these pyramids:

1. The *baby-boom cohort* can be seen in all the pyramids. Demographers use the term "baby boom" to refer to the 19-year period (1946–1964) of high fertility following World War II. In 1990 the cohort extends across the middle section (ages 25 to 44); and by 2025 it constitutes the protruding bands of individuals age 60 to 79.

   The baby-boom generation has had an enormous impact upon American life. In the 1950s the baby boomers made the United States a child-oriented society of new schools, suburbs, and station wagons. They watched *The Mickey Mouse Club*, listened to rock and roll, went to Woodstock and Vietnam, and fueled the student, civil rights, and peace movements of the 1960s and early 1970s. By the year 2030 one out of every five Americans will be 65 years of age or older and dependent on a Social Security and Medicare system that must be supported by the smaller generations behind them. The Social Security dependency ratio—the number of workers compared with the number of recipients—was five to one in 1965, but it will drop to two to one by 2035.

2. The *baby-bust cohort* stands in sharp relief to the baby boomers. The baby bust began in the early 1970s when fertility dropped rapidly, reaching its lowest level in 1976 and remaining very low until the mid-1980s. This cohort can be seen in the indentation just above the base of the 1990 pyramid.

3. It in turn is succeeded by the *baby-boom-echo*, sometimes called the "echo boom" or "baby boomlet." These are the children of

Figure 9.2   Population Pyramids in the United States 1990–2050

The pyramids trace the demographic impact of the baby boom cohort (born 1946–1964), the baby-bust cohort (born 1970–1979), and the baby-boom echo cohort (born 1985–1995).

Sources: For 1990, National Estimates Program; for 2000, 2025, and 2050, National Projections Program, Population Division, U.S. Census Bureau, available at http://www .census.gov/population/www/projections/natchart.html.

the baby boomers. Not until 2025 when a rising mortality rate takes its toll of baby boomers will the echo cohort catch up to the baby-boom cohort in size.

4. If we can use past fertility to predict future fertility, we might predict that a baby-bust echo will follow the baby-boom echo, but we won't know for sure about this until it occurs.

Malthus and Marx: Two Views of Population Growth

The relationship between population growth and the level of a nation's welfare has long been a central concern for those interested in population problems. In this section we will consider two classic arguments, those of Thomas Robert Malthus and Karl Marx. In the environment section of this chapter we will discuss other views.

Malthus.

In 1798 the English economist and cleric Thomas Malthus (1766–1834) published *An Essay on the Principle of Population*. Many of the issues he raised are still debated today. Malthus asserted that human populations tend to increase at a more rapid rate than the food supply needed to sustain them. Human beings, Malthus said, confront two unchangeable and antagonistic natural laws: (1) the "need for food" and (2) the "passion between the sexes." He contended that, whereas agricultural production tends to increase in arithmetic fashion (1-2-3-4-5-6-7-8), population has a tendency to increase in geometric fashion (1-2-4-8-16-32-64-128). Population will invariably catch up with progress and literally "eat away" higher levels of living. Malthus considered famine, war, and pestilence to be the chief deterrents to excessive population growth. As an ordained minister, Malthus either did not consider that people might use birth control, or he viewed birth control as a sin and beneath human dignity. But he did believe people could use what he called "moral restraint," postpone marriage, and refrain from sexual relations when not married.

Was Malthus Right?

Malthus failed to appreciate the full possibilities of the Industrial Revolution and its ability to expand productive capacities to an extent unknown in his time. We now know that it is not true that food always and everywhere can increase only at an arithmetic rate. For example, within the United States the application of technology—farm machinery, irrigation, fertilizers, pesticides, and hybrid plants and animals—has resulted in the food supply growing faster than the population. And as previously noted, Malthus did not foresee the possibility of new birth control methods or their application within the context of a value system favoring small families.

Those who agree with many of Malthus's ideas but who disagree with his "moral restraint" approach to population control—they favor contraception instead—are termed neo-Malthusians. Like Malthus, they believe that ultimately population will be limited in one of two ways: decreasing births or increasing deaths. They recognize that economic growth has sustained larger populations in some parts of the world in recent times, but they predict that population growth will eventually wipe out these economic gains.

In the 1970s neo-Malthusian and biologist Paul Ehrlich made some central points in his book *The Population Bomb*: There are too many people in the world, there is too little food, and the environment is being degraded. He reminded readers that those who have enough food still suffer the effects of ecosystem destruction and pollution. Neo-Malthusians point out that 0.5 million people are chronically undernourished and that people die of hunger every day; that is, there is already not enough food now (Weeks, 1989).

Marx.   Karl Marx (1867/1906) took issue with many Malthusian notions and formulations. He insisted that an excess of population, or more particularly of the working class, depends on the availability of employment opportunities, not a fixed supply of food. Marx believed that a deepening crisis of the capitalist system would inevitably force increasing numbers of workers into the ranks of the unemployed, leading some individuals to conclude that society is overpopulated. Indeed Marx believed there was enough wealth to go around; it merely needed to be redistributed.

Under socialism, Marx argued, there would be no population problem because all workers would be integrated into the economy and there would be no unemployment. Through proper use of technology, a socialist economy would produce enough food for all. Thus, he traced the problems associated with population growth to capitalist society and sought cures in a fundamental restructuring of the social and economic order. In sum, whereas Malthus looked primarily to the individual to restrain population growth through self-control, Marx looked to collective action to refashion institutional life.

Demographic Transition

A number of social scientists have employed the idea of demographic transition to map out the population growth characteristic of the modern era (Davis, 1945; Chesnais, 1992). Viewed as history, the notion seeks to explain what has happened in European nations over the past 200 years. Viewed as theory, it has been used to predict what will happen in developing nations in the future. **Demographic transition theory** holds that the process of modernization is associated with three stages in population change (see Figure 9.3).

Stage 1: High Potential Growth.   Societies untouched by industrialization and urbanization are characterized by a high birth rate and a high death rate. As a result, the population remains relatively stable. The stage is described as having "high potential growth" because once the societies gain control over their death rates, their growth is likely to be rapid.

Stage 2: Transitional Growth.   Modernization has its initial impact on mortality levels. Improved housing, better levels of nutrition, and improvements in health and sanitary measures bring about a steady decline in death rates. Since a decisive reduction in the death

Figure 9.3   Trends in Birth and Death Rates According to Demographic Transition Theory

rate has traditionally been associated with a marked drop in the infant mortality rate, a larger proportion of the huge yearly crop of babies survives and in time themselves become parents. Thus, a drop in the death rate, while the birth rate of a population remains unchanged, results in a marked increase in the rate of population growth. As time passes, however, couples begin to realize that with lower infant mortality rates, fewer births are required to produce the same number of surviving children, and they adjust their fertility accordingly. Moreover, the costs and benefits associated with children change as modernization progresses, making small families economically advantageous. The second stage ends when the birth rate sinks toward the death rate.

Stage 3: Population Stability.

Modernization both provides effective birth control techniques and undermines religious proscriptions against their use. The result, according to demographic transition theorists, is that modern societies come to be characterized by low mortality and low fertility, a situation approximating zero population growth.

Demographic Transition Theory Evaluated.

Social scientists are not sure that the stages represent an accurate portrayal of European demographic history; the theory also may have limited usefulness in predicting population change in developing nations. Declines in infant mortality and increases in life expectancy can develop very rapidly in today's technologically advanced world and outpace a society's evolution of new attitudes about family size. When children have always been considered an economic asset, it may take a significant period of time to decrease a country's average family size. Although demographic transition theory has a number of underlying problems, recent research provides some qualified support for the theory. Cren-

China's one-child policy is stipulated by law, enforced by the government, and encouraged by propaganda.

shaw, Christenson, and Oakey (2000) studied determinants of fertility in 64 developing countries from 1965 to 1990. Consistent with demographic transition theory, they found that reductions in child mortality were related to decreased fertility. They also found that growth of a service economy was related to fertility decline. Service sector dominance tends to reduce fertility because it employs many women and because complex service jobs are not appropriate for children, thus reducing the economic value of large families. Crenshaw, Christenson, and Oakey (2000) also found that independent of the effects of child mortality, service sector dominance, and other variables, family planning programs played an important role in reducing fertility in developing countries over the 1965 to 1990 period.

Population Policies

For countries that want to control population growth, what are the alternatives? There are three basic schools of thought relating to fertility reduction policies. In this section, we will discuss family planning, the developmentalist strategy, and the societalist perspective. We will consider the use of coercion to control fertility and the problems faced by countries whose population is decreasing instead of increasing.

Family Planning.   Proponents of *family planning* contend that if contraceptives are made readily available and information regarding the value and need for birth planning is disseminated throughout a society, people will reduce their fertility. In turn, a reduction in fertility will allow investment in economic development. Contemporary Bangladesh provides a good illustration of a nation that is cutting its birth rate significantly by aggressively promoting the adoption of modern contraceptive methods—without first waiting for the reduction that customarily comes with higher living standards.

But even the best family planning technique will not be employed unless people want to use it. For instance, while modern contraception makes it easier for Kenyans to limit family size, they have not responded (Passell, 1994). For people in many parts of the world, children are still their chief protection against the buffetings of life, providing care when they are unemployed, sick, or elderly.

The Developmentalist Strategy.

A second approach entails a *developmentalist* strategy, based on demographic transition theory. According to this school of thought, fertility is a pattern of behavior tied closely to the institutional and organizational structure of society. "Development is the best contraception" was a popular slogan of the 1970s. Although modernization often has been associated with a decline in fertility, as we discussed in the section on demographic transition theory, the relation is not clear-cut enough to justify a simple causal link between industrialization and smaller families.

The Societalist Perspective.

A third approach involves a *societalist* perspective in which the government fashions policies designed to produce changes in demographic behavior. Demographer Kingsley Davis (1971:403) suggested a number of social reforms that would reduce fertility by rewarding low fertility and penalizing high fertility, including tax, housing, and other advantages for single people; education and career opportunities for women; and free birth control and abortion services.

Coercion.

In recent years, China has instituted harsh methods to curb population growth, including punishing couples who have two or more children and fining a woman pregnant with a second child 20 percent of her pay if she refuses to have an abortion (Yu, 1994). Chinese officials have reported that in recent years there have been about 50 abortions for every 100 births (Tien, 1992). Such programs have aroused considerable indignation among many citizens in Western nations.

Because male children are valued more highly than female children in China, as in many other countries, the one-child policy has resulted in an imbalance in the sex ratio. In China there are now many more male children than female children. The causes of this are not completely clear; female infanticide and selective abortion are two possibilities.

For the most part, population planners in many nations have focused on how to keep the world's poorest women from having more babies. Some women's groups argue that birth rates in poorer nations will decline only after the status, health, education, and economic opportunities for women improve—in brief, when women gain more control over their lives (Chira, 1994). Overall, it is clear that programs for reducing fertility remain controversial, in terms of both their effectiveness and their morality.

Population Loss.   In some nations, population loss is of more concern than population growth. In Spain and Italy, traditionally nations of large families, the fertility rate has fallen to 1.2 children per woman, and population growth has dropped accordingly. The fertility rate for all of Europe is only 1.4, and its rate of natural increase is –0.2 percent. That is, without immigration, the European population is decreasing. Deaths exceeded births in 17 European countries in 2003 (McFalls, 2003). In some countries, fertility rates have been below replacement level for so long that the countries have negative growth momentum—even if fertility should rise to two children per woman, the population will continue to decline for decades.

Loss of population can create problems in the specific countries in which it occurs. For example, as the population ages, there may not be a sufficiently large cohort of workers to maintain the institutions of society and to support the retired and elderly cohort.

The Urban Environment

Cities are one of the most striking features of our modern era. A **city** is a relatively dense and permanent concentration of people who secure their livelihood chiefly through nonagricultural activities. The influence of the urban mode of life extends far beyond the immediate confines of a city's boundaries. Many of the characteristics of modern societies, including the problems, derive from an urban existence.

In this section we will consider the origin and growth of cities, patterns of city growth, ecological processes at work in cities, and urban crisis.

The Origin and Evolution of Cities

Cities constitute a relatively recent development in human history. The domestication of plants and the husbandry of animals were critical innovations that allowed human beings to live together in larger groups. When human beings could "produce" food, population expanded in settled communities.

We will examine the earliest preindustrial cities, move on to industrial-urban centers, and discuss metropolitan cities.

Preindustrial Cities.

Early Neolithic communities were more small villages than cities. A number of innovations were required for towns to evolve. Between 6000 and 4000 BC, the invention of the ox-drawn plow, the wheeled cart, the sailboat, metallurgy, irrigation, and the cultivation of new plants allowed for new ways of living. These innovations resulted in an economy that could sustain the concentration of people in one place.

Among the early centers of urban development were Mesopotamia, the Nile River valley of Egypt, the Indus River valley of India, and the Yellow River basin of China (Davis, 1955, 1967). However, a productive economy was not by itself sufficient to bring about the growth of cities. New forms of social organization also were required. Bureaucratic structures and stratification systems arose that enabled government officials, religious personnel, merchants, and artisans to appropriate for themselves part of the produce grown by cultivators (see Chapters 3 and 5).

For the most part, preindustrial cities did not exceed 10 percent of the population of an area. Their sizes were limited by poor transportation, the difficulty of securing larger areas from outside threats, unsanitary conditions, and a feudal social structure that tied potential migrants to the land. Cities of 100,000 or more were rare, although under favorable social and economic conditions some cities surpassed this size.

Industrial-Urban Centers.

Urbanization has proceeded quite rapidly during the past two centuries. In 1800, 3 percent of the world's population lived in urban areas; 100 years later, 14 percent of the world's population was urban, and 100 years beyond that brings us to the present, with almost half of the world's population living in urban areas (Population Reference Bureau, 2003). In 1950, just eight urban agglomerations had populations of 5 million or more, and most of the largest urban agglomerations in the world were European and North American metropolitan cities that evolved out of industrial urban centers of the 19th century. By 2000, there were 41 urban agglomerations of that size, and more than half were in the developing world. By 2015, demographers predict the seven largest urban areas in the world will be Tokyo, Bombay, Lagos (Nigeria), Dhaka (Bangladesh), São Paulo, Karachi (Pakistan), and Mexico City (United Nations, 2001). Most early urban communities were city-states, from which many modern nations have evolved.

Both social factors and technological innovations contributed to the acceleration of urban growth. Organizational changes permitted greater complexity in the division of labor (see Chapter 3). The use of steam as a source of energy promoted the widespread use of machines. Widespread by the mid- to late-19th century, power-driven machines accelerated social trends that were moving manufacturing out of the home into centralized factories. As the factory system expanded, increasing numbers of people moved to cities to find jobs. This Industrial Revolution is a part of American and European history and is now occuring elsewhere around the world.

Metropolitan Cities.   Industrial-urban centers typically had only tenuous economic and social relations with the surrounding areas. More recently, metropolitan cities—central cities and suburbs—have emerged. This phase in urban development represents a widening and deepening of urban influences in every area of social life.

Steam and belt-and-pulley power techniques had produced great congestion in urban areas by the beginning of the 20th century. A movement outward was made technologically possible by electric power, rapid transit, the automobile, and the telephone. The result has been the development of satellite and suburban areas—broad, ballooning urban bands linked by beltways—that constitute cities in their own right. In population, jobs, investment, construction, and shopping facilities, the suburbs rival the old inner cities. They are the sites of industrial plants, corporate offices and office towers, fine stores, independent newspapers, theaters, restaurants, superhotels, and big-league stadiums.

In many cases the rural interstices between metropolitan centers have filled with urban development, making a "strip city" or **megalopolis**. The northeastern seaboard is a good illustration of this process. A gigantic megalopolis lies along a 600-mile axis from southern New Hampshire to northern Virginia, encompassing 10 states, 117 counties, 32 cities larger than 500,000 people, and embracing nearly a fifth of the U.S. population. Urban projections suggest that by the year 2050, if not sooner, another urbanized strip will extend from New York State through Pennsylvania, Ohio, northern Indiana and Illinois to Green Bay, Wisconsin, and Minneapolis–St. Paul.

Patterns of City Growth

Human ecologists and urban sociologists are interested in understanding the spatial patterning of people's relationships and activities. They provide a number of models that attempt to capture the ecological patterns and structures of city growth. Here we present three classic models: the concentric circle model, the sector theory, and the multiple nuclei theory (see Figure 9.4). Probably no city has grown in exactly the way any of these models suggest. However, each model emphasizes important processes that help us understand city growth.

Concentric Circle Model.   In the period between the two world wars, sociologists at the University of Chicago viewed Chicago as a social laboratory and subjected it to intensive study. The **concentric circle model** enjoyed a prominent place in much of this work (Park,

Concentric Zone Theory

Sector Theory

Multiple Nuclei Theory

1. Central Business District
2. Wholesale Light Manufacturing
3. Low-Class Residential

4. Medium-Class Residential
5. High-Class Residential
6. Heavy Manufacturing

7. Outlying Business District
8. Residential Suburb
9. Industrial Suburb
10. Commuters' Zone

Figure 9.4   Theoretical Patterns of Urban Structure

Urban areas (numbered 1 through 10) are indicated in each structure.

Source: Reprinted from "The Nature of Cities" by Chauncey D. Harris and Edward L. Ullman from *The Annals of the American Academy of Political and Social Science,* vol. 242, 1945. Reprinted by permission.

Burgess, and McKenzie, 1925). The Chicago group held that the modern city assumes a pattern of concentric circles, each with distinctive characteristics. At the center of the city—the *central business district*— are retail stores, financial institutions, hotels, theaters, and businesses. Next is an area of residential deterioration caused by the encroachment of business and industry—the *zone in transition.* The zone in transition shades into the *zone of workingmen's homes* that contains two-flats, old single dwellings, and inexpensive apartments inhabited largely by blue-collar workers and lower-paid white-collar workers. Beyond the zone occupied by the working class are *residential zones* composed primarily of small business proprietors, professional people, and managerial personnel. The outermost ring is small cities, towns, and hamlets, the *commuters' zone.*

Critics point out that the approach is more descriptive of cities at the beginning of the 20th century and that many cities have never approximated the concentric circle pattern (Davie, 1937).

The Sector Model.   Homer Hoyt (1939) portrayed large cities as made up of a number of sectors rather than concentric circles—the **sector model** (see Figure 9.4). Low-rent districts often assume a wedge shape and extend from the center of the city to its periphery. In contrast, as a city grows, high-rent areas move outward, although remaining in the same sector. Districts within a sector that are abandoned by upper-income groups become obsolete and deteriorate. Thus, instead of forming a concentric zone around the periphery of the city, Hoyt contended that the high-rent areas typically locate on the outer edge of a few sectors. Furthermore, industrial areas evolve along river valleys, watercourses, and railroad lines rather than forming a concentric circle around the central business district. But the sector model, like the concentric circle model, does not fit a number of urban communities.

The Multiple Nuclei Model.

Another model—the **multiple nuclei model**—depicts the city as having not one center but several (Harris and Ullman, 1945). Each center specializes in some activity and gives its distinctive cast to the surrounding area. For example, the central business district has as its focus commercial and financial activities. Other centers include the "bright lights" (theater and recreation) area, "automobile row," a government center, a wholesaling center, a heavy-manufacturing district, and a medical complex. Multiple centers evolve for a number of reasons. First, certain activities require specialized facilities; for example, the retail district needs to be accessible to all parts of the city. Second, similar activities often benefit from being clustered together; for example, a retail district profits by drawing customers for a variety of shops. Third, dissimilar activities are often antagonistic to one another; for example, affluent residential development tends to be incompatible with industrial development. Finally, some activities (e.g., bulk wholesaling and storage) cannot afford high-rent areas and hence locate in low-rent districts. The multiple nuclei model is less helpful in discovering universal spatial patterns in all cities than in describing how unique patterns in particular communities developed.

Ecological Processes: Segregation and Gentrification

Some sociologists have applied the theories and vocabulary of ecology to human populations. "Human ecology" looks at the relationships between humans and their human environment and institutions. City development can be seen as the result of economic and social competition for urban space.

Segregation.

One "ecological" process sociologists are interested in is **segregation**—a process of clustering wherein individuals and groups are sifted and sorted out in space based on their sharing of certain traits or activities in common. This clustering takes place voluntarily when people find that close spatial proximity is advantageous, and the resulting segregated areas have been termed **natural areas** because they do not result from any official planning by government units. For example, the multiple nuclei model of city growth suggests that certain similar activities profit from the cohesion provided by a segregated district.

Of course, segregation also may be involuntary. Residential neighborhoods frequently attempt to exclude incompatible commercial and industrial activities through zoning ordinances. Ethnic and racial groups may systematically exclude other groups from their neighborhoods. These processes have produced an urban America that is highly segregated racially. African Americans are the most segregated minority group in the United States, followed in turn by Hispanics, Asians, and Native Americans. While racial and ethnic segregation is declining over time, the changes from 1980 to 2000 were very small (Iceland, Weinberg, and Steinmetz, 2002).

Racial segregation supports continuing segregation, as the quantity and quality of white contacts with blacks are determined primarily by physical proximity: If whites don't live near blacks, they simply don't interact, and thus have no opportunity to discard negative stereotypes and build positive attitudes (Sigelman et al., 1996).

Class segregation—the separation of the rich from the poor—increased about 26 percent from 1970 to 1990 (Morin, 1998). The poor in the United States are increasingly concentrated in high-poverty city neighborhoods. Between 1970 and 1990, the number of Americans living in poverty increased by 50 percent, but the number of poor neighborhoods has more than doubled (Jargowsky, 1997). At the same time, affluent people are increasingly living in affluent neighborhoods (Morin, 1998). Local politics are significantly affected by such segregation, with entire political jurisdictions increasingly becoming "poor" or "rich" and providing services accordingly.

Invasion and Succession.   Invasion and succession are critical ecological processes and are concepts that have been "borrowed" by sociologists and applied to urban development. **Invasion** takes place when a new type of people, institution, or activity encroaches on an area occupied by a different type. Should the invasion continue until the encroaching type displaces the other, **succession** is said to have occurred. When people with very different backgrounds come to share or compete for urban neighborhoods, issues of race, class, and culture often become highlighted and lead to social conflict (Winnick, 1991; Wysocki, 1991).

Urban gentrification—the return of the middle class, usually young, white, childless professionals (sometimes called "yuppies," for young urban professionals) to older neighborhoods—is happening in large cities throughout the United States: Haight-Ashbury in San Francisco; Queen Village in Philadelphia; Mount Adams in Cincinnati; New Town in Chicago; German Village in Columbus, Ohio; and the East Village and SoHo in New York. Gentrification typically culminates in the displacement of the poor and minorities from these neighborhoods by upwardly mobile whites with financial resources and clout. Many older cities count on urban gentrification to counteract their eroding population and tax bases. However, gentrification also adds to urban problems when it displaces the poor and pushes them into adjoining neighborhoods.

Urban Crisis: Cities in Decline

The long-term trend toward urbanization continues. More than half of all Americans now live in 49 large metropolitan areas, each with a population of more than 1 million (U.S. Census Bureau, 2003). What is happening in these large cities? Let's take a closer look at urban crisis in the United States.

"Doughnut" Development.

The "doughnut structure" is an apt description of the course of metropolitan development in many U.S. cities since World War II. The hole in the doughnut is the decaying central city, and the ring is a prosperous and growing suburban and exurban (beyond the city and suburbs) region. In some cases, such as New York City's Manhattan, the hole is a core area that is being revitalized, and the ring is a surrounding part of the city that is becoming progressively blighted. A number of trends have contributed to the phenomenon, including the rapid growth of suburbs and exurbs and the return of urban growth to coastal regions. People tend to follow jobs and migrate to areas where they believe better employment opportunities exist.

Descriptive and Functional Decline.

Urban decline can be descriptive or functional. *Descriptive decline* has to do with the loss of population or jobs. It occurs as people who have the resources to leave the city do, while those who are poor have little choice but to remain. The proportion of poor residents increases as their number is swelled by recent migrants who also are poor. Urban ills are thus aggravated and require an increasing share of a city's resources. Life in the city then becomes less agreeable and more costly for middle- and upper-income residents, who move out of the city. This cycle hurts the city and complicates its ability to be responsive to people's needs and results in increasing isolation of poor and immigrant populations.

Functional decline refers to a deterioration in city services and the social amenities of urban life. It is reflected in the decay of the urban infrastructure in older industrial cities—the network of roads, bridges, sewers, rails, and mass transit systems. Currently half of all U.S. communities cannot expand because their water treatment systems are at or near capacity. According to the Environmental Protection Agency, many of the nation's water and waste-water facilities have water quality or public health problems; additionally, some cities lose as much as 30 percent of their daily water supply as a result of leaky pipes. Many roads and bridges are bearing far greater burdens than they were designed to accommodate, and many are deteriorating. Increases in population lead to increases in traffic, with heavier use of roads that are already in poor condition. In response to the fiscal crises of past decades, many local and state officials balanced budgets by canceling preventive maintenance and deferring necessary repairs of public works, adding to the functional decline of cities.

The Ecological Environment

We have learned how demographers measure population growth and have looked at humans in their urban environments. What is the effect of human populations on the natural environment of the planet Earth? As you might guess, humans have an enormous impact on the environment: Indeed, most of earth's ecosystems are now dominated by humans.

Let's take a look at the big picture. By living beyond their means, people have changed the atmosphere, depleted fisheries, jeopardized water supplies, reduced soil fertility, and scattered pollutants everywhere (McMichael, Butler, and Folke, 2003). The species extinction rate has changed in one century from a loss of 10 or fewer species per year to a loss of 1,000 species per year (Tuxhill, 1999). Approximately half of the world's land surface has been transformed by human use, and more than half of all the accessible surface fresh water in the world has been put to use by humans (Vitousek et al., 1997). Nearly half the world's population has inadequate sanitation (Nash and De Souza, 2002). Scientists warn that major climate change can now be avoided only by drastically reducing carbon dioxide emissions—and soon (Hasselmann et al., 2003).

The United States bears a heavy share of the responsibility for the fix the world is in. For example, 24 percent of the world's carbon dioxide emissions comes from the United States. Each U.S. citizen daily uses more than *five times* the amount of energy calculated to be the worldwide average per capita. The U.S. population comprises about 4 percent of the world population, yet its citizens are responsible for 25 percent of the total energy consumed worldwide. Likewise, the United States produces more waste and pollutants than other countries, some of which is shipped abroad (see Box 9.1).

Why discuss the environment in a sociology book? Scientists understand the problems the planet faces and, in many cases, what people ought to do to solve them. But implementing solutions is a human and social endeavor. The social sciences can help biologists, engineers, ecologists, and environmental managers to "identify what is socially acceptable and politically feasible, and to understand the social mechanisms and processes by which [ecosystem] restoration and management occur" (Hull and Robertson, 2000:306). Sociologist John Bellamy Foster does a good job of summing up the role of sociology: "Ecological analysis, devoid of sociological insight, is incapable of

Toxic Trash? Ship It to Another Country

How many computers have you or your family gone through in the past 10 years? How about televisions? Cell phones? Stereos? If you're like many Americans, you buy a new computer or other piece of electronic equipment as soon as new technology makes the one you own seem out of date. Computers in otherwise good working order that cannot handle new graphics-intensive games and other advanced software are given "early retirement" to make way for the new generation. The average life span of a computer is now only two years; experts estimate that between 1997 and 2007, 500 million computers will become obsolete in the United States (Puckett et al., 2002).

What do you do with your old electronic equipment when you buy something new? E-waste, or electronic waste, is currently the most rapidly growing waste problem in the world, with amounts of e-waste increasing nearly three times more quickly than amounts of other municipal wastes. And e-waste is toxic waste: computers and other electronic equipment contain lead, mercury, cadmium, barium, chromium, beryllium, PCBs, dioxins, and other pollutants. Consumers and business users have to pay recyclers to take e-waste off their hands.

Recycling materials from electronic equipment is time consuming and unprofitable—at least in industrialized nations. So Americans ship it to other countries. In *Exporting Harm: The High-Tech Trashing of Asia* (Puckett et al., 2002), investigators documented the toxic waste trade that makes Asian countries the recipients of as much as 80 percent of the e-waste collected by recyclers in the United States. Although the export of all hazardous wastes from rich to poor countries was banned through the Basel Convention in 1994, the United States never ratified the treaty and continues to export e-waste, even to China, which passed its own ban on e-waste imports in 2002.

It is environmental, health, and safety regulations that make recycling e-waste unprofitable in the United States. It is the lack of such regulations in other countries that make recycling e-waste prof-

itable—and dangerous. For example, in Guiyu, China, about 100,000 men, women, and children are employed in taking computers apart—mostly by hand—and extracting copper from wiring, gold from capacitors, and other valuable products. Employees work with no protection for their hands, eyes, skin, and respiratory systems. Plastics are burned in the open air, acids are poured into canals and rivers, and lead-laden monitor glass and other components are dumped where heavy metals can leach into groundwater.

Global inequality is at the root of e-waste exportation. In the wealthy industrialized United States, protected by multiple layers of regulations, wastes are generated and exported. In developing nations with few or no environmental and health regulations, poor people are willing and eager to work for $1.50 a day to handle toxic materials. As the *Exporting Harm* authors point out, people only do such dangerous work when they have no alternative:

> E-waste exports to Asia are motivated entirely by brute global economics. Market forces, if left unregulated, dictate that toxic waste will always run "downhill" on an economic path of least resistance. If left unchecked, the toxic effluent of the affluent will flood towards the world's poorest countries where labor is cheap and occupational and environmental protections are inadequate. A free trade in hazardous wastes leaves the poorer peoples of the world with an untenable choice between poverty and poison—a choice that nobody should have to make (Puckett et al., 2002:1).

Questions for Discussion

1. What policies or strategies might the United States adopt to reduce the export of toxic trash?

2. Does the United States protect itself from pollution by exporting toxic wastes?

dealing with the contemporary crisis of the earth—a crisis that has its source and its meaning ultimately in society itself" (Foster, 1999:400).

Human–Environment Interactions: A Closer Look

One impact of humans on the environment is based on the use of natural resources and the production of wastes and contaminants. Another is based on the space human populations take up; every area taken over by humans is unavailable for use by most of the original plant and animal inhabitants.

Sociologists are interested in the relationships between population size, human organizations, environment, and technology. The management of fisheries provides a good example of human factors in environmental problems (Botsford, Castilla, and Peterson, 1997). A major goal of fisheries is sustainability: to limit catches so that fish populations are never damaged or depleted. Overfishing results in the loss of jobs for the 200 million people employed in fisheries globally and a loss of food for the world's population; fisheries account for 19 percent of the total human consumption of animal protein. But the goal of sustainability has never been reached. Researchers have assessed the sociopolitical pressures that interfere with sound fisheries management (Botsford, Castilla, and Peterson, 1997:512):

> Managers, under constant political pressure for greater harvests because of their short-term benefits to society (jobs and profits), allow harvests to increase when fishery scientists cannot specify with certainty that the next increase will lead to overfishing and collapse . . . the burden of proving whether higher harvests are harmful falls on the fishery managers, not the fishing industry. The result is a continuous, unidirectional increase in fishing effort, and in some cases fishery collapse.

The end result? Approximately two-thirds of major marine fisheries have been depleted, overexploited, or fully exploited (Lubchenco, 1998).

Just as humans can overexploit their natural resources, so can they protect them. A number of programs aimed at recovering populations of species at the brink of extinction have been successful; for example, the last six condors living in the wild were captured in 1986, and a captive breeding program has produced 12 to 20 fledglings per year since 1991 (Pimm, 2000). Restoration ecology—restoring land altered by human activity—is increasingly successful and has benefits beyond the reclamation of damaged ecosystems. Restoration projects often involve large groups of volunteers, and those who work to restore ecosystems better understand and respect their complexity (Hull and Robertson, 2000).

The Functionalist Perspective

Functionalist theorists approach the ecological environment by examining the interconnections between the various parts composing the ecosystems (Faia, 1989). They see the ecosystem as exhibiting a tendency toward equilibrium, in which its components maintain a delicately balanced relationship with one another. The perspective is nicely captured by the notion of Spaceship Earth—the idea that our planet is a closed system with finite resources that, if destroyed or depleted, cannot be replaced. Life exists only in the biosphere, a thin skin of air, soil, and water on the surface of the planet. Functionalists stress that our survival depends on our ability to maintain the precarious balance among the living and nonliving components comprising the biosphere. They fear that our pollution of the environment and our depletion of the earth's natural resources are jeopardizing the very environment that is the basis for life.

A graphic example of the reciprocal ties that bind human beings and their physical environment is provided by the sub-Saharan region of Africa. The tragedy of the region has been captured in recent years by television portrayals of deserts haunted by starving people, infant bellies swollen by want, and dead cattle. An estimated 35 million people in Africa live on the interfaces of deserts and arable land and are constantly threatened by hunger.

The desert is growing. Much of this "desertification" is not attributable to basic climatic change, but to the overworking of marginal lands for crops, grazing, and firewood. The introduction of Western techniques, such as irrigation, deep plowing, and the use of chemical fertilizers, has compounded the region's problems (Tucker, Dregne, and Newcomb, 1991).

When people intensify their exploitation of the land in order to compensate for desertification, problems increase, including more desertification. Functionalists emphasize that to avoid this type of damage to the ecosystem, human beings must become more sensitive to both the manifest and latent consequences of their actions on the environment.

The Conflict Perspective

As is true for many other issues, the conflict perspective does not offer a unified point of view on environmental matters. Some conflict theorists depict environmental problems as due more to the distribution of the world's resources than to a limited amount of resources available in the world. They say that the basic issue is not one of how much is available but one of which individuals and groups will secure a disproportionate share of what is available. Hence, the critical decisions that affect the environment are made not in the interests of present and future generations but in the interests of those groups that can impose their will on others.

Conflict theorists also point out that people tend to be separated into two camps on environmental issues. On one side are those who favor economic development and growth even if it results in some measure of environmental damage. On the other side are those who see environmental preservation as their primary goal and who believe that the environment must take precedence over economic goals. The two groups are at odds and contest each other in the political arena.

Conflict theorists see many of the same circumstances in Africa as the functionalists, but come to somewhat different conclusions. Desertification is not blamed for the region's problems; rather, conflict theorists say that growing indebtedness exerted pressure on African governments to promote cash crops for export rather than food crops for their people. Complicating matters, much of the money provided by Western aid agencies was diverted to highly visible projects, such as roads, port facilities, airports, and office buildings, while small African farmers were neglected. Moreover, when Western nations have provided food to African governments, they have found an outlet for surplus food in need of a market, which has benefited U.S. and European farmers. Finally, assistance is often rendered to African governments that are friendly toward the donor nations; in the process, the existing regimes are stabilized (Farnsworth, 1990).

The Interactionist Perspective

Symbolic interactionists give environmental issues a somewhat different twist, focusing their sociological eye upon "people behaviors." Here we will look at two issues of interest to interactionists: the difference between people's attitudes and their actions and the difference between expert and public perceptions of risk.

Are You Ready for Action?   Apparently many Americans believe that they are devoted to preserving the environment. But Americans are deeply divided over how to do it and at what cost to taxpayers, businesses, and national economic interests. Two-thirds of survey respondents say they would avoid using a product that was thought to be the cause of harm to the environment, and three-quarters say they recycle regularly (Public Agenda, 2004). Yet the percent of Americans identifying themselves as "environmentalists" dropped from 73 percent in 1990 to fewer than half in 2000, and in 2002 survey respondents ranked protecting the environment as a lower legislative priority than terrorism, the economy, education, and five other issues (Public Agenda, 2004). Americans are not alone; a 1997 survey of attitudes about the environment in 24 countries revealed a considerable gap between those who think environmental protection should take priority over economic growth and those who would be willing to help pay to prevent environmental pollution (Environics Research Group, 1997).

Public versus Expert Perceptions of Risk.

Interactionists also have provided significant insight on the socially constructed understandings and myths people have about the environment. For example, a considerable gap often exists between public and expert perceptions of risk. Public opinion surveys show that oil spills, hazardous waste, underground storage tanks, and releases of radioactive materials arouse high public emotions. But in terms of the actual magnitude of the risk they pose, scientists advising the Environmental Protection Agency rate these threats near the bottom. By contrast, global warming ranks relatively low in public concerns, but scientists see it as a top concern because its long-term potential consequences are so damaging and its effects so widespread and difficult to reverse.

We should not conclude that the public necessarily disregards "risk hazards" determined by scientists. Rather, people use the information in combination with information about the social, political, and ethical characteristics of a risk to make decisions about its acceptability, or what have been called "risk outrage" factors. Risks are more acceptable to the public when they are voluntary, natural, familiar, detectable, and fairly distributed among the population. The public's perception of risk, then, is in some ways as important as is the reality of risk. Some research suggests that when people see no viable solutions to problems, they show less concern and spend less time thinking about the issue (Immerwahr, 1999). Citizens may be convinced that the problem is serious, but also—especially when scientists disagree about solutions and when the underlying problem seems to be "rampant selfishness and greed"—that it is too complex to be solvable.

In sum, symbolic interactionists point out that environmental issues qualify for the adjective "social" because they involve human judgments, decisions, and choices. Environmental issues are also social issues because they entail the exercise of power. For example, the poor and minorities are much more exposed than other citizens to the dangers of natural and technological hazards, or what is termed *environmental racism*. Indeed, much risk is actually politically negotiated—a network of government agencies, corporations, and public-interest groups grapple daily with selected hazards.

The New Millennium

Scientists have been warning for years that human beings are overly dependent on fossil fuels, that people are changing the climate, that they are endangering their own lives as they push more and more species of animals over the brink to extinction, and that human inhabitants must change their ways to survive. Now humankind stands poised to add nearly 3 billion people to the world in the next 50 years—half again as many as currently live on earth—and the race to organize a sustainable society is underway. Sustainable fisheries are managed in such a way that fish populations are never damaged or depleted. That concept can be extended to all earth's resources: "For human populations, sustainability means transforming our ways of living to maximize the chances that environmental and social conditions will indefinitely support human security, well-being, and health" (McMichael, Butler, and Folke, 2003).

Americans use far more than their "fair share" of energy and other resources and generate more waste and pollutants than people elsewhere in the world. If developing nations model themselves on the United States, complete disaster will result. Look at only a single aspect of U.S. life: Americans love cars. The U.S. car population is 774 vehicles per 1,000 people, the highest rate in the world; the world average is only 176 vehicles per 1,000 people, and the U.S. rate is literally hundreds of times higher than that of many other countries (Nash and De Souza, 2002). A world modeled after the United States would have nearly 7 billion cars by 2050, causing traffic jams, spewing pollutants, and using fossil fuels at an unsupportable rate.

This disparity between wealthy industrialized nations and poor developing nations whose populations are growing rapidly is a critical problem. Though population growth is stable in industrialized nations, the American contribution to environmental problems stems from a wealthy and overconsuming lifestyle. Poor people in developing countries, on the other hand, contribute to environmental problems because they are struggling to survive, and that struggle includes cutting trees, growing crops, and grazing livestock in ecologically vulnerable and unstable environments.

The planet's environmental problems are increasingly global in nature. Climate change, radiation from nuclear reactor accidents, species extinction, depleted fisheries, ocean pollution, drifts of atmospheric particulate matter—all are problems with no political boundaries. It is thus increasingly clear that creating a sustainable world society will require a global effort.

Global cooperation, however, has not been one of the strong points of the United States. For example, climate change is a phenomenon that scientists agree is one of the most important environmental issues facing society worldwide (Watson, 2003). What will global warming bring? Some of the milder effects include "scorching summers, fiercer storms, altered rainfall patterns, and shifting species"; more serious effects include complete destruction of coral reefs, the spread of deserts, and major shifts in ocean currents bringing cold weather to warm climates and vice versa (Appenzeller, 2004). Impacts on humans will include adverse changes in the availability of drinking water, fish, and forest and agricultural products, and the most adversely affected will be the poorest people in developing countries (Watson, 2003).

In 1997 more than 160 nations forged an agreement known as the Kyoto Protocol, which called for a reduction of carbon emissions—the primary culprit in global warming—by 5 to 10 percent for industrialized nations (Watson, 2003). But far greater reductions are needed; in fact, emissions need to be reduced to a tiny fraction of current emissions. Nevertheless, the United States, Russia, and Australia refused to ratify the Kyoto Protocol. The United States argued that there were scientific uncertainties; that complying would hurt the U.S. economy; that the Protocol was unfair because developing nations were not yet required to cut emissions; and that the Protocol would be ineffective because of its allowances for developing nations (Watson, 2003).

Neo-Malthusianism maintains that the world has too many people, too little food, and an environment that is being degraded. Perhaps the political leaders in the United States who refused to participate in the Kyoto Protocol sided with the late economist Julian L. Simon, who disagreed with the neo-Malthusians. The central assertion of Simon's book, *The State of Humanity*, is that things are getting better all the time and will continue to do so (Simon, 1995). Simon promoted leaving the world more or less to its own devices, especially to the operation of unimpeded market forces. Yet many Americans apparently agree: between 31 percent and 64 percent (depending on age) of survey respondents say they believe the environment will be better than it is now, or at least the same, in the next century (Public Agenda, 2004).

Other analysts also see a role for market forces. Although environmentalism has been primarily a process of grassroots groups pushing for change and governments following behind (Hertsgaard, 1998), some researchers believe that corporations may now lead the way in reducing resource consumption. Their interest in profit provides a strong motivation to recycle, reduce costs caused by planned obsolescence, trade wastes with other companies, and find alternative energy sources (Gardner and Sampat, 1999).

The ability of various social scientists, biologists, economists, and other experts to arrive at different conclusions leads us again to the insight supplied by symbolic interactionists that social problems (including environmental problems) are matters of social definition. But the views presented above can all be seen as "true": It can be true that humans have dealt successfully with many problems in the past *and* that humans need to work hard to deal with the problems we face now and will be facing in the future. A question of interest to sociologists is, Which individuals and groups will be able to translate their vision of reality into official public policy? The answer may determine much about how we approach the future.

Key Terms

concentric circle model, 263

crude birth rate, 250

crude death rate, 250

demographic transition theory, 257

demography, 248

ecology, 248

ecosystem, 248

environment, 248

fecundity, 250

general fertility rate, 250

growth rate, 252

infant mortality rate, 251

internal migration, 252

international migration, 252

invasion, 266

megalopolis, 263

multiple nuclei model, 265

natural areas, 265

net migration rate, 252

population pyramid, 253

rate of natural increase, 252

sector model, 264

segregation, 265

succession, 266

urban gentrification, 266

zero population growth, 250

Review Questions

1. What is demography?
2. What three factors account for all population change?
3. Describe the populations depicted in the population pyramids presented in this chapter.
4. Compare the views of Marx and Malthus on population growth.
5. What is demographic transition theory?
6. List and describe three population policies.
7. What is a city? How do cities grow?
8. Describe each of the following urban processes: segregation, gentrification, decline, and the growth of edge cities.
9. How does population growth relate to the natural environment?
10. What does sociology have to offer with regard to environmental problems?
11. How do functionalists, conflict theorists, and interactionists see environmental problems?
12. Describe global warming and U.S. policy on climate change.

Chapter 10

Social Change

A World of Change

Collective Behavior

Social Movements

Looking to the Future

When the World's Columbian Exposition opened in Chicago in 1893, 74 prominent Americans tried their hands at forecasting the future. What would the world be like 100 years later? One expressed the prevailing view that in 1993 the railroad would still be the fastest means of travel. Another was convinced that mail in 1993 would still travel by stagecoach and horseback rider. A few forecasters enthused about air travel—or, more precisely, "balloon travel." None of the 1893 forecasters apparently anticipated the automobile, let alone the cell phone, the Internet, a world of 6 billion people, the publication of a map of the human genome, or the globalization of both our economy and our environmental problems.

Then, as now, forecasters fell victim to two fundamental problems in attempting to predict the future. First, change is so much a part of our lives that we take it for granted, oblivious to or unimpressed by much of it; during the 1880s a number of Europeans had already produced experimental gasoline-powered cars, but the 1893 forecasters either did not know about the primitive "horseless carriages" or did not think they were important. Second, a "rearview-mirror effect" operates in which recent events color and dominate our thinking about the future; the railroads were developing feverishly in the 1880s and 1890s, so it took little imagination to predict

277

that they would become faster and more widespread in the future (Cornish, 1993).

The study of social change is an attempt to understand and predict changes in the world. In this chapter, we will look at sources of social change and at social change in both the United States and developing countries. We will consider collective behavior, including explanations of crowd behavior. We will examine types and causes of social movements, and we will end with a look into the future.

A World of Change

Sociologists refer to fundamental alterations in the patterns of culture, structure, and social behavior over time as **social change.** It is a process by which society becomes something different while remaining in some respects the same. Consider the enormous transformations that have taken place across American life over the past 70 years. We have restyled many of our most basic values and norms: racial upheaval, a sexual revolution, computer and communications breakthroughs, and a new national identity as a world power have remolded our national life (Manchester, 1993). In the early 1930s, the U.S. population was less than half its present size. Rural America lacked electricity, and its roads were dirt. In foreign affairs we were an insular, second-class power, although Americans themselves were an ardently patriotic people. Welfare and divorce were shameful. Pregnancy made even married women uncomfortably self-conscious, and maternity clothes were designed to "keep your secret." Manliness was prized, and patriarchal authority was vested in men as heads of families. Had there been a watchword then, it would have been "duty."

Today that watchword would more likely be "self" or "identity." This cultural shift from "duty" to "self" produces the contemporary emphasis on self-esteem and ethnic identity and is partly responsible for high rates of divorce and religious switching. People's concerns about what the institutions of marriage and religion can do for them have increased relative to their commitments to the traditional duties prescribed by those institutions.

Social change has a tremendous impact on our lives. Let us begin our discussion of it by examining some of its sources. We will go on to consider perspectives on social change and to describe social change in the United States and developing nations.

Sources of Social Change

Social change confronts people with new situations and compels them to fashion new forms of action. Many factors interact to generate changes in people's behavior and in the culture and structure of their society. Sociologists identify a number of particularly critical factors, the impact of which differs with the situation and the time and place. In this section we will consider the physical environment, population, conflict over resources and values, supporting norms and values, innovation, diffusion, and the mass media.

Physical Environment.   If humans are to survive, they must achieve a working relationship with their environment. Among the chief adaptive mechanisms available to a population are social organization and technology. Hunting and gathering, horticultural, agricultural, and industrial societies all present different types of adaptations. Should the environment change for any reason, those who have evolved a given type of adaptation must respond by making appropriate institutional changes, fashioning new forms of social organization and new technologies. Droughts, floods, epidemics, earthquakes, and other forces of nature are among the ever-present realities that alter people's lives. Additionally, as we noted in Chapter 9, human beings have a tremendous impact on their physical environment.

Population.   Changes in the size, composition, and distribution of a population also affect culture and social structure. In Chapter 9 we discussed the implications of population growth. Nearly all such growth will occur in developing nations in the coming decades, with resource use in those parts of the world also increasing astronomically. The graying of the population is a principal factor in the United States, with Social Security, Medicaid, and health care costs soaring; those 85 and over are the fastest-growing part of the population.

Clashes over Resources and Values.   Conflict is a basic source of social change. The end result of conflict is not a simple quantitative mixing of the groups in conflict, but a completely new entity. Who could have foretold in 1870 the South that eventually emerged from the contest between the Reconstructionists and their opponents? Who could have foretold in 1965 the nation that would emerge 35 years later after a decade of social turbulence? And who can foretell today the ultimate form of the societies that arose in eastern Europe and the former Soviet empire following the collapse of communism? Old orders continually erode and new ones arise.

Supporting Values and Norms.   A society's values and *norms* act as "watchdogs" or "censors" permitting, stimulating, or inhibiting certain innovations. It is interesting to compare our readiness to accept technological innovations with our resistance to changes in religion or the family. For example, we continuously debate changes in sexual behavior norms, while resistance to the lightbulb, the automobile, and the airplane disappeared almost immediately. Our use of the word *inventor* reflects this cultural bias. The inventor is one who innovates in material things, whereas the inventor of intangible ideas is often called a "revolutionary" or "radical," words with sometimes odious connotations.

Innovation.

A **discovery** represents an addition to knowledge, whereas an **invention** uses existing knowledge in some novel form. Thus, a discovery constitutes the perception of a relationship or fact that had not previously been recognized or understood. Einstein's theory of relativity and Mendel's theory of heredity were discoveries. In contrast, the automobile—an invention—was composed of six old elements in a new combination: a liquid gas engine, a liquid gas receptacle, a running-gear mechanism, an intermediate clutch, a driving shaft, and a carriage body.

Innovations—both discoveries and inventions—are not single acts but combinations of existing elements plus new elements. The greater the number of cultural elements from which innovators may draw, the greater the frequency of discovery and invention. For example, glass gave birth to lenses, costume jewelry, drinking goblets, windowpanes, and many other products. Lenses in turn gave birth to eyeglasses, magnifying glasses, telescopes, cameras, searchlights, and so on. Such developments reflect the *exponential principle*—as the cultural base increases, its possible uses tend to grow exponentially.

Diffusion.

Diffusion is the process by which cultural traits spread from one social unit to another. Diffusion is a people process and hence is expedited or hindered by the social environment. Simply because a trait is functionally superior does not necessarily ensure that individuals will adopt it. Much depends on the network of relationships that tie people together in patterns of meaningful communication and influence (Strang and Tuma, 1993).

Diffusion is often overlooked. We point with pride to what other societies have acquired from us, but we often neglect to note what we have gained from them. Yet a global economy combined with the fact that our society is composed almost entirely of immigrant groups means that everything we use and do can be traced to other societies or cultures. As an illustration, consider the following now classic account of the cultural content in the life of a "100 percent" American written as satire by anthropologist Ralph Linton (1937:427–29):

> [D]awn finds the unsuspecting patriot garbed in pajamas, a garment of East Indian origin; and lying in a bed built on a pattern which originated in either Persia or Asia Minor. He is muffled to the ears in un-American materials: cotton, first domesticated in India; linen, domesticated in the Near East; wool from an animal native to Asia

Minor; or silk whose uses were first discovered by the Chinese. . . .

If our patriot is old-fashioned enough to adhere to the so-called American breakfast, his coffee will be accompanied by an orange, domesticated in the Mediterranean region. He will follow this with a bowl of cereal made from grain domesticated in the Near East. . . . As a side dish he may have the egg of a bird domesticated in Southeastern Asia or strips of the flesh of an animal domesticated in the same region. . . .

The Mass Media.

Diffusion is facilitated by the instant flooding of information across national, class, ethnic, and economic boundaries by means of the mass media. According to one view, the media functions as a kind of giant hypodermic needle, discharging endless propaganda into the passive body of the population. Another view depicts the media as affording a "marketplace of ideas" in which an enlightened public carefully and rationally sifts and winnows a variety of attitudes and behaviors. Yet the media is not nearly as simple as the proponents of either view would have us believe. Most efforts at mass communication merely confirm the beliefs that people already hold. People typically expose themselves to mass communications that are congenial or favorable to their existing opinions and interests. Selective perception also operates so that people tend to misperceive and misinterpret persuasive communications in accordance with their existing opinions.

Nevertheless, the mass media have not-so-minimal effects. We typically think of news coverage as the media bringing to public attention the "important" happenings of the day by reporting on an objective reality "out there." But as symbolic interactionists point out, "news" is *constructed*—some selected occurrences come to be translated into "public events" for a mass constituency while others are ignored (Epstein, 1973). With round-the-clock news channels and Internet news sites, "news" has become an always-available commodity. Much of what is broadcast is repetitive, with little "new news" to flesh out the stories, yet the mere fact of their repetition lends them a significance beyond their actual importance. Sensational murders and celebrity news particularly fall into this category.

The media also perform other functions, including what social scientists call "agenda setting." The media sets the agenda of issues and concerns we spend our time thinking about and discussing with others. Some communications experts argue that fictional media presentations

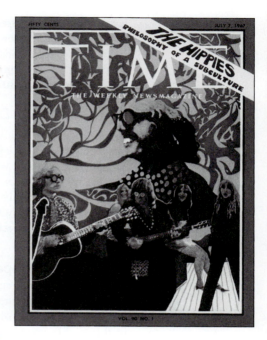

The values, behaviors, and expressive symbolism of the hippie movement of the 1960s diffused quickly from San Francisco throughout the United States by means of media portrayals, such as this cover story in *Time* magazine in 1967, facilitating many social changes during that era.

have a "cultivation effect" in which images are provided that influence public attitudes and behavior about such social policies as crime, violence, and welfare (Gerbner et al., 1978), though it is not always clear exactly what television and other media are cultivating in the minds of viewers (Hughes, 1980).

Perspectives on Social Change

The founders of sociology, particularly Auguste Comte and Herbert Spencer, looked to the grand sweep of history, searching for an understanding of how and why societies change. Many contemporary sociologists continue to be intrigued by these "big questions." The major sociological perspectives on social change, which we will consider in this section, fall within four broad categories: evolutionary perspectives, cyclical perspectives, functionalist perspectives, and conflict perspectives.

Evolutionary Perspectives.
The doctrine of social progress and a search for underlying evolutionary laws dominated much sociological thinking during the 19th century. According to Social Darwinists like Spencer, social evolution resembles biological evolution and results in the world's growing progressively better. In his theory of unilinear evolution, Spencer contended that change has persistently moved society from homogeneous and simple units toward progressively heterogeneous and interdependent units. He viewed the "struggle for existence" and "the survival of the fittest" as basic natural laws. Spencer equated this struggle with "free competition." If unimpeded by outside intervention, particularly government, those individuals and social institutions that are "fit" will survive and proliferate, while those that are "unfit" will in time die out.

As we pointed out in Chapter 1, Spencer's Social Darwinism mirrored the orientation of laissez-faire capitalism. Social Darwinism was a doctrine well suited to imperialism and provided a justification for Western colonialism. The white race and its cultures were extolled as the highest forms of humanity and civilization. Other peoples and cultures were "lower" in evolutionary development, and so it was only proper that Europeans, being "fitter," should triumph in the struggle for existence. However, such blatant ethnocentrism did not stand the test of scientific research. Anthropologists demonstrated that non-Western societies—and many European nations as well—did not pass through the same sequence of stages. In brief, there is no one scenario, but many scenarios of social change.

Contemporary approaches take a *multilinear* view of evolution. Their proponents recognize that change does not necessarily imply progress, that change occurs in quite different ways, and that change proceeds in many different directions. Talcott Parsons (1966, 1977), a leading structure-function sociologist, suggested that societies tend to become increasingly differentiated in their structures and functions, leading to *adaptive upgrading.*

Sociologist Gerhard Lenski (1966; Lenski and Lenski, 1987) held that evolution depends largely on changes in a society's level of technology and its mode of economic production. These changes, in turn, have consequences for other aspects of social life, including stratification systems, the organization of *power,* and family structures. According to Lenski, there is an underlying continuum in terms of which all societies can be ranked: hunting and gathering societies, simple horticultural societies, advanced horticultural societies, agrarian societies, and industrial societies. More specialized evolutionary bypaths include herding societies and hybrid societies such as fishing and maritime societies.

Cyclical Perspectives.

Cyclical theorists look at the rise and fall of civilizations. Their objective is to predict the course of a civilization or society, including its demise. Cyclical theorists compare societies in a search for generalizations regarding their stages of growth and decline.

The German scholar Oswald Spengler (1880–1936) contended that culture passes through the same stages of growth and decline as individuals: a period of development, followed by maturity, eventual decline, and death. Based on his examination of eight cultures, Spengler said that each culture possesses a life span of approximately 1,000 years. Western culture, he held, emerged about A.D. 900, and therefore its end is close at hand.

English historian Arnold J. Toynbee (1934/1954) also sought to depict uniformities in the growth and decline of civilization and to identify the principles that underlie this development. Toynbee said that civilizations arise in response to some challenge, such as severe climate or warlike neighbors. A civilization grows and flourishes when the challenge is not too severe and when a creative minority (an intelligent elite) finds an adequate response to the challenge. When the creative minority fails to find a response adequate to a challenge, the civilization breaks down and disintegrates.

Archaeologists have previously cited combinations of social, political, and economic factors as the root causes of societal collapse, but new research has allowed researchers to conclude that the primary agent in prehistoric and early historic societal collapses was abrupt and highly disruptive climate change (Weiss and Bradley, 2001). Floods, droughts, and changes in the availability of the resources exploited by hunting and gathering societies have been identified with climate changes that have driven societal collapses. Because human contributions of carbon to the atmosphere have been predicted to cause major climate changes in the future, our own societies may be forced to adapt and change rapidly.

Functionalist Perspectives.

As we saw in Chapter 1, the concept of system is central to the structure-function model of society. A system is a set of elements or components related in a more-or-less stable fashion over a period of time. One of the features of a system stressed by structure-function theorists is its tendency toward *equilibrium.*

As we pointed out earlier in the chapter, structure-function sociologists like Parsons (1966, 1977) have introduced the notion of evolution to the perspective to broaden the concept of equilibrium to include both developing and self-maintaining properties. The social group is portrayed as living in a state of dynamic or moving equilibrium. The equilibrated social system adjusts itself to disturbances that occur, accommodating them within the functioning structure and establishing a new level of equilibrium. Hence, even though society changes, it remains stable through new forms of social integration.

Sociologist William F. Ogburn (1922) drew upon evolutionary models to fashion a functionalist approach to social change. He distinguished between *material* and *nonmaterial* culture and located the source of change in material invention—tools, weapons, and technical processes. Nonmaterial culture—values, norms, beliefs, and institutions—must adapt or respond to changes in material culture, resulting in an adjustment gap Ogburn called **cultural lag.** Although the notion of cultural lag contains a valuable insight, it vastly oversimplifies matters. No single factor is capable of explaining social change; in real-life situations a vast array of forces converge in complex interaction with one another to give society its dynamic properties.

Social life abounds with examples of an uneven rate of change resulting in social dislocation. For instance, the automobile fostered a whole host of changes. It spurred tremendous growth in the oil, tire, glass, and accident insurance industries. It promoted suburban development, degradation of the natural environment, and an exodus of the central city's affluent population. Cultural lag is evident today in the many problems associated with the use of the Internet, including hacking, the spread of computer viruses, Internet pornography, Internet scams, and the Napster controversy. We can expect that our society also will require a significant amount of cultural adjustment as a result of the sequencing of the human genome (Jeffords and Daschle, 2001).

Conflict Perspectives.

Conflict theorists hold that tensions between competing groups are the basic source of social change. Nowhere does one find a clearer exposition of the conflict perspective than that provided by Karl Marx, particularly as it finds expression in his notion of the *dialectic.* As we saw in Chapter 1, the dialectic depicts the world in dynamic terms as a world of *becoming* rather than *being.* According to Marxian *dialectical materialism,* every economic order grows to a state of maximum efficiency, at the same time developing internal contradictions or weaknesses that contribute to its decay. Class conflict is a particularly powerful source of change, and Marx saw it as the key to understanding human history. Marx said that all change is the product of a constant conflict between opposites. All development—social, economic, or human—proceeds through the resolution of existing contradictions and the eventual emergence of new contradictions. The outcome of the clash between opposing forces is not a compromise (an averaging out of the differences among them), but an entirely new product, one born of struggle. In this manner both individuals and societies change. It is a dynamic process of complex interchanges between all facets of social life. As Marx (1867/1906) observed, "By acting on the external world and changing it, he [the individual] at the same time changes his own nature."

Not all conflict theorists agree with Marx that "all history is the history of class conflict." Other types of conflict may be equally or in some instances more important than class conflict, including conflict between nations, ethnic groups, religions, and economic interest groups (Coser, 1956, 1957; Dahrendorf, 1958).

Social Change in the United States

In this section we will examine one aspect of change, that associated with the rapid introduction of technology into American life. Sociological models depict technological innovations as a reweaving of the social fabric—a reshaping of the norms, roles, relationships, groups, and institutions that make up society. Today we hear a good deal about the construction of "information highways" and "information infrastructures." The building of another highway system—the interstate system—reminds us of the vast impact that changes can have. The system was inspired by a wish to improve commerce, foster physical and social mobility, and bolster national defense. But the interstate system also had many unanticipated consequences that permanently changed the nation's social landscape. It fostered the rapid growth of strip and edge cities and magnified the split between outlying communities and inner cities. Are "information highways" having both positive and negative effects?

The Information Revolution.

The Industrial Revolution was a revolution because the steam engine, the cotton gin, the locomotive and rails, and the power loom were agents for great social change. They took people out of the fields and brought them into factories. They gave rise to mass production and, through mass production, to a society in which wealth was not confined to the few.

In a similar fashion, computers are revolutionizing the structure of American life—what some have termed the *information revolution*. Two-thirds of the U.S. population had computers in 2001, and 54 percent had Internet access (U.S. Department of Commerce, 2002). We can read the newspaper; access government data; order books, CDs, and groceries; check on class assignments; read lectures; and exchange messages with friends or strangers in virtually any part of the world—all on the Internet. In 2002 Internet use was growing by 2 million new users per month, and children and teenagers were using computers and the Internet more than any other age group, with 90 percent of 5- to 17-year-olds using computers and the Internet (U.S. Department of Commerce, 2002).

A number of issues have been repeatedly raised about the social impact of computers. First, the computer automates workplace activities that have been performed by people. The Industrial Revolution centered on the supplementation and ultimate replacement of the muscles of humans and animals by introducing mechanical methods. The information revolution goes beyond this to supplement and replace some aspects of the minds of human beings by electronic methods. But it seems that job creation accompanies job destruction, with the highest rates of both occurring in the most technologically advanced sectors of the economy where overall employment is increasing (International Labor Organization, 2001).

Second, information is a source of power, and computers mean information. The centralized accumulation of data permits the concentration of considerable power in those who have access to computers. These are most likely to be people who already have more power and advantages than others. While recent increases have occurred in all economic, racial, and ethnic groups, and the gender gap in Internet use has disappeared, important differences remain (see Figure 10.1). For example, African Americans and Hispanics are less than half as likely as whites and Asian Americans to have household Internet access; female-headed households are half as likely to have Internet access as two-parent households; and Internet use is strongly correlated with family income and educational attainment (U.S. Census Bureau, 2003). But in 2001 Internet use among these lower-use groups was growing more rapidly than among any other group (U.S. Department of Commerce, 2002). And although in the Western world many of us take Internet access for granted, only 6 percent of the world's population has ever logged on (International Labor Organization, 2001).

Third, computers alter the way people relate to one another (see Box 10.1). On a telephone, we hear the other person's voice. In face-to-face contact, we see people smile, frown, and nod. But computer exchanges offer no such feedback. Thus, computers may have consequences for our sense of individuality. Computer exchanges differ in other ways. People are less likely to hold back strong feelings when communicating by computer. And as with any piece of writing, how clearly ideas are communicated depends on the writer's skill.

Fourth, computers have implications for individual privacy and the confidentiality of our communications and personal data. The

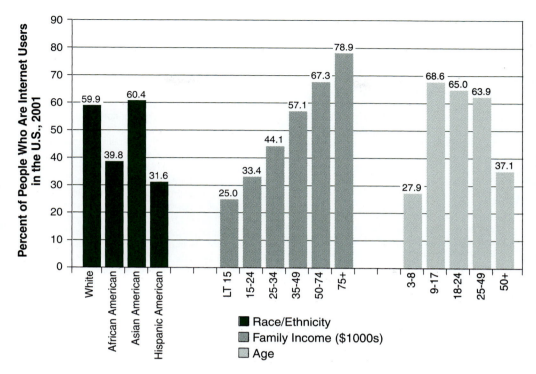

Figure 10.1   The Digital Divide

Although the gender gap in Internet use has disappeared, differences remain in economic, racial, ethnic, and age groups. Data for computer use follow the same patterns.

Source: Figure generated by the authors using data from the U.S. Department of Commerce, 2002.

growing use of computers to collect data and store information provides the technical capability for integrating several information files into networks of computerized data banks. With such networks, personal data that we provide for one purpose can potentially be accessed for other purposes. Thus, as people handle more and more of their activities through electronic instruments—mail, banking, shopping, entertainment, and travel plans—it becomes technically feasible to monitor these activities with unprecedented ease.

Finally, computers and the Internet provide new means and opportunity for crime and deviance. People have found innovative ways to use the Internet to commit fraud and identity theft (O'Harrow, 2003), to solicit for prostitution, to prey upon the vulnerable, and to buy and sell illegal goods and pornography (e.g., Durkin and Bryant, 1995). We should expect more such innovation until means are developed to eliminate or reduce crime and deviance in this new medium of communication.

Blogging Our Way to Intimacy

Hey everyone ever. Stop making fun of people. It really is a sucky thing to do, especially if you hate being made fun of yourself. . . . This has been a public service announcement. You may now resume your stupid hypocritical, lying lives.

Blog entry of 15-year-old boy (Nussbaum, 2004)

Web logs, or blogs—online diaries—are growing rapidly in popularity. Free accounts are available, and site design requires almost no technical know-how. Half of all bloggers are 13- to 19-years-old and 90 percent are between 13 and 29. Some 10 million blogs were expected to be broadcasting their users' thoughts, experiences, and feelings by the end of 2004 (Nussbaum, 2004).

Blogs are one of many ways to communicate that the Internet has made possible. E-mail exchanges, instant messaging, chat rooms on every conceivable interest, and now blogs—a way to post private journal entries for all the world to see. What is the social impact of all this communication? Do we know one another better? Feel closer? Understand and sympathize with the feelings expressed in blogs? Social psychologists Robert Kraut and Sara Kiesler (2003) have spent nearly a decade studying the influence of Internet use on social relationships.

Kraut and Kiesler began their research in 1995, when in-home Internet access was quite new. Their early studies were primarily descriptive and focused on how people integrated computers and Internet access into their lives. Later they attempted a true experiment, in which they would compare people without Internet access to those with access, but Internet use was growing so rapidly that their "without" group became members of the "with" group even while their study was underway. Nevertheless, they ended up with many years of longitudinal data on Internet use and social relationships. What did they conclude?

Using the Internet seems to increase the size of people's social circles, their face-to-face (or "offline") communication, and their trust in people. On the other hand, it also seems to increase stress, perhaps by introducing more activities and social obligations into users' lives. It also is associated with a decline in users' knowledge of and commitment to their local area (Kraus and Kiesler, 2003). But these conclusions were not clear-cut. For extraverts, using the Internet was linked to increases in community involvement and self-esteem, while for introverts the opposite was true. And their most recent findings indicate that using the Internet for social purposes is associated with a decline in some measures of social engagement.

Why such complicated findings? Perhaps their results are complex because it is increasingly difficult to define the nature of the communication made possible by the Internet. As Emily Nussbaum comments in her article on blogging (2004:34), "If this new technology has provided a million ways to stay in touch, it has also acted as both an amplifier and a distortion device for human intimacy. The new forms of communication are madly contradictory: anonymous, but traceable; instantaneous, then saved forever." Kraut and Kiesler see use of the Internet as a continuously evolving phenomenon, and the norms and effects of use change as the purposes of use change (2003:10–11): "The Internet of today is not the Internet of 1996, and the Internet of tomorrow will not be the Internet of today . . . as these changes take place, people will find new ways to use this technology, and its social impact will change once again."

Questions for Discussion

1. How would the structure of young people's lives be different if they did not have access to the Internet, with its chat rooms, instant messaging, e-mail, and blogs?

2. In the early years of Internet use, people thought that the Internet would increase solidarity in towns and communities. Research shows that this has not been a result of Internet use. What do you think accounts for this?

What the Information Revolution Cannot Do.

While the changes to come in this still-very-young revolution will probably be dramatic, there also are clear limits to the impact the Internet will have on our lives. First, as we have mentioned, the "digital divide" effectively excludes much of the world, and significant portions of the United States, from participating in Internet-related activities. As the number of people who routinely use the Internet rises, those who have no access are at an increasing disadvantage. Second, how the Internet changes our lives depends entirely on how we use it. In 2001, the biggest use of the Internet was for sending and receiving e-mail. U.S. citizens also were using it to make online purchases (39 percent of users), to search for product and service information (36 percent of users), and to search for health information (35 percent of users) (U.S. Department of Commerce, 2002). To the extent that such activities reduce our use of paper, transportation, and other consumers of resources and energy, using the Internet can be seen as environmentally friendly. On the other hand, an assessment of energy consumption concluded that 8 percent of the electricity used in the United States is now attributable to computer use (*The Economist*, 2000b). And when the end result of convenient order placing is increased consumption and delivery of goods, we are not helping the environment.

Neither, some analysts think, are we likely to significantly improve international relations and understanding via the Internet. In the mid-1850s, when the first transatlantic telegraph was sent, technology enthusiasts predicted that it would eradicate "old prejudices and hostilities" (*The Economist*, 2000b). Likewise, the ease of communication offered by the Internet might be thought to have the potential to improve our understanding of those in other cultures. But some pin the blame for war and conflict on human nature, which remains unchanged by the information revolution: "Despite the claims of the technoprophets, humanity cannot simply invent away its failings. The Internet is not the first technology to have been hailed as a panacea—and it will certainly not be the last" (*The Economist*, 2000b:12). It may be that an intelligently structured and wisely applied computer technology might help a society to raise its standard of literacy, education, and general knowledgeability. But there is no automatic, positive link between knowledge and its enlightened use.

Social Change in Developing Nations

It is difficult today to read a newspaper or watch the news without noticing the changes that continually affect the world. The Middle East, Central America, southern Africa, and countless other global centers may conjure up images of boiling cauldrons of social transition and transformation. Sociologists have approached social change in developing nations from two somewhat different perspectives: modernization and world system.

Modernization.

Modernization describes the process by which a society moves from traditional or preindustrial social and economic arrangements to those characteristic of industrial societies. Implicit in the notion of modernization is the assumption that there is basically one predominant course of development—namely, that followed by advanced Western nations and Japan. Viewed in this manner, modernization entails patterns of convergence in which societies become increasingly urban, industry overshadows agriculture, the population increases in size and density, the division of labor becomes more specialized, and the knowledge base grows larger and more complex. East Asia, including Taiwan, South Korea, Hong Kong (now part of China), and Singapore, is the showcase of modernization theories.

The momentum for change derives from internal forces and processes. The chances that a developing country will evolve in the direction of liberal Western democracies are thought to be enhanced when a nation's economy provides for literacy, education, and communication; creates a pluralistic rather than a centrally dominated social order; and prevents extreme inequalities among the various social strata. Efficient systems of communication and a diversity of social groups and organizations are believed to distribute political resources and skills among multiple segments of the community and provide the foundation of effective opposition parties.

World System or Dependency.

World system (and dependency) approaches view the social structures of developing nations as shaped by the historical experience of colonialism, the timing and manner of their incorporation into the global capitalist economy, and the perpetuation of their dependency through political domination, multinational corporations, and unfavorable exchange arrangements.

According to world system and dependency analysis, developing nations cannot recapitulate the developmental trajectory of Western nations and Japan. An unequal exchange takes place between core and periphery nations (see Chapter 8), with development in core nations occurring at the cost of underdevelopment in periphery nations (London and Williams, 1990; Walton and Ragin, 1990; Chase-Dunn and Hall, 1993). More particularly, specialization in the production and export of raw materials is said to be detrimental to the long-term growth prospects of developing nations. Such specialization distorts these nations' economies because they become responsive to the demands of the world market rather than to internal developmental needs; development is shaped primarily by external forces and processes. Further, investments in the production or mining of raw materials monopolize capital to the detriment of other types of investment. And class formation in the dependent nations results in a small elite whose economic interests are linked to foreign investors in the core countries (Berberoglu, 1987; Bradshaw, 1988). Dependency theorists see Latin America and Africa as affording stark evidence of the limits that dependency imposes on nations.

In sum, whereas modernization approaches look to convergences in political and economic development, world system and dependency analysis looks to divergences. And while modernization theories view direct, private foreign investment as an asset in the development of developing nations, world system and dependency approaches consider foreign investment as the prime culprit in many Third World social ills. Overall, those in advantaged international positions tend to favor explanations that emphasize the internal features of development (modernization approaches), and those in disadvantaged positions prefer explanations that look to external factors (world system or dependency approaches).

Fast-moving world events also have impacted the sociological study of change in developing nations (Firebaugh, 1992; Bollen and Appold, 1993; Moaddel, 1994). The field is in flux because it is confronting a host of new issues: Will an information age enable developing nations to leapfrog stages in economic development? How will rapid population growth, AIDS, and women's issues affect development policies?

Collective Behavior

Rapid social change and the upheavals that result from it also make it more likely that people will engage in **collective behaviors**—ways of thinking, feeling, and acting that develop among a large number of people and that are relatively spontaneous and unstructured. And collective behaviors can result in social change. From earliest recorded times people have thrown themselves into a great many types of mass behavior, including social unrest, riots, manias, fads, panics, mass flights, lynchings, religious revivals, and rebellions. Accordingly, no discussion of social change can neglect collective behavior.

Varieties of Collective Behavior

Collective behavior comes in a great many forms. To gain a better appreciation for the impact such behavior has on our lives, let us consider a number of varieties of collective behavior at greater length.

Rumors.   A **rumor** is a difficult-to-verify piece of information transmitted from person to person in relatively rapid fashion. We often think of rumors as providing false information, and in many cases this is true. But they also may be accurate or, at the very least, contain a kernel of truth. Rumors typically arise in situations in which people lack information or distrust the official sources of information. Rumors are both a form of collective behavior and an important element in most other forms of collective behavior.

Periods of anxiety and tension provide an environment in which rumors proliferate. After the September 11, 2001, terrorist attacks, rumors flew about a wide range of topics, including the sorts of biological and chemical weapons terrorists might unleash to the best antidotes to such weapons. Official information competed with rapidly circulating advice about sealing doors and windows with duct tape and laying in supplies of gas masks, food, water, and medicines.

Rumors tend to evolve and take on new details as people interact and talk, and with the Internet they can spread around the world in the time it takes to walk to your neighbor's house to gossip. The Internet also can be used to try to control rumors. A high school student who is the subject of gossip may use a Web log—an online journal—to try to set the story straight or at least to provide readers with an alternate view of the story (Nussbaum, 2004).

One type of rumor that is particularly common involves alleged contamination. In 2003 the Centers for Disease Control issued a list of currently circulating hoaxes and rumors that included e-mails about tainted cola products, poisonous perfume samples that arrive in the mail, underarm antiperspirants and deodorants that cause breast cancer, a child who died of a heroin overdose from a needle found on a playground, and online offers for antibiotics that protect users against bioterrorism (Centers for Disease Control, 2003).

Fashion and Fads.   The uniformity of dress on college campuses is sometimes so extreme as to make it appear that students are required to wear certain uniforms. Black clunky-heeled platform shoes and black dresses are in for women one year; jeans, hiking boots, and flannel shirts another. Contemporary society is full of both fashions and fads. What is the difference?

A **fashion** is a folkway that lasts for a short time and enjoys widespread acceptance within society. Fashion finds expression in styles of clothing, automobile design, and home architecture.

A **fad** is a folkway that lasts for a short time and enjoys acceptance among only a segment of the population. Fads often appear in amusements, new games, popular tunes, dance steps, health practices, movie idols, and slang. Adolescents are particularly prone toward fads; the fads provide a sense of identity and belonging, with aspects of dress and gesture serving as signs of an *in-group* or *out-group* status (Erikson, 1968).

Some fads become all-consuming passions. Such fads are called **crazes.** Financial speculation at times assumes craze proportions (Chatzky, 1992). In the famous Holland tulip mania in the 17th century, the value of tulip bulbs came to exceed their weight in gold; the bulbs were not planted, but bought and sold among speculators.

Mass Hysteria.   **Mass hysteria** refers to the rapid dissemination of behaviors involving contagious anxiety, usually associated with some mysterious force. For instance, medieval witch hunts rested on the belief that many social ills were caused by witches. Likewise, some "epidemics" of assembly-line illness—*mass psychogenic illness*—derive from hysterical contagion. In recent years episodes of mass psychogenic illness have occurred in U.S. plants packing frozen fish, punching computer cards, assembling electrical switches, sewing shoes, making dresses, and manufacturing lawn furniture. In most cases the workers complain of headache, nausea, dizziness, weakness, and breathing difficulty. However, health authorities, including physicians, industrial hygienists, and toxicologists, find no bacteria, virus, toxic material, or other pathogenic agent to explain the symptoms. Mass psychogenic illness is usually a collective response to severe stress.

Panic.   **Panic** involves irrational and uncoordinated but collective actions among people induced by the presence of an immediate, severe threat. For example, people commonly flee from a catastrophe such as a fire or flood. The behavior is collective because social interaction intensifies people's fright.

As with other forms of collective behavior, panics can be greatly amplified by modern information technologies. When the SARS epidemic spread from China to other countries in 2003, an "information epidemic" fueled a panic that affected the lives of millions of people (Rothkopf, 2003). Although the total number of people who died from SARS worldwide was smaller than the number of people who die from choking on small objects every year in the United States, the panic about the disease resulted in economic losses in Asia of an estimated $30 billion. As Rothkopf explained the situation, "A few facts, mixed with fear, speculation and rumor, amplified and relayed swiftly worldwide by modern information technologies, . . . affected national and international economies, politics and even security in ways that are utterly disproportionate with the root realities." Rothkopf traces the cause of an information epidemic to mainstream media, specialist media, and Internet sites combined with "informal" media, including pagers, e-mail, faxes, cell phones, and text messaging, all of which may be transmitting rumor, interpretation, propaganda, or fact. Other information epidemics fueling panics and having significant economic consequences in recent years were associated with the sniper attacks in Washington, D.C.; the effect of the threat of another Gulf war on travel in that area; and the Enron company financial scandal.

Crowds.   The **crowd** is one of the most familiar and at times spectacular forms of collective behavior. It is a temporary, relatively unorganized gathering of people in close physical proximity. Because a wide range of behavior is encompassed by the concept, sociologist Herbert Blumer (1946; see also McPhail, 1989) distinguishes four basic types of crowd behavior. The first, a **casual crowd,** is a collection of people who have little in common except that they may be viewing a common event, such as looking through a department store window, visiting a museum, or attending a movie. The second, a **conventional crowd,** entails a number of people who have assembled for some specific purpose and who typically act in accordance with established norms, such as people attending a baseball game or a concert. The third, an **expressive crowd,** is an aggregation of people who have gotten together for self-stimulation and personal gratification, such as occurs at a religious revival or a rock festival. And fourth, an **acting crowd** is an excited, volatile collection of people who are engaged in rioting, looting, or other forms of aggressive behavior in which established norms carry little weight.

Although crowds differ from one another in many ways, they also share a number of characteristics:

1. *Suggestibility.* The behavior of crowd members is not guided by conventional norms. Individuals are usually more susceptible to images, directions, and propositions emanating from others.

2. *Deindividualization.* **Deindividualization** is a psychological state of diminished identity and self-awareness (Zimbardo, 1969). People feel less inhibited in committing disapproved acts in a group.

3. *Invulnerability.* In crowd settings, individuals often acquire a sense that they are more powerful and invincible than they are in routine, everyday settings. Moreover, they feel that social control mechanisms are less likely to be applied to them as individuals, resulting in an increase in behavior not normally approved by society, such as aggression, risk taking, self-enhancement, stealing, vandalism, and the uttering of obscenities (Dipboye, 1977; Mann, Newton, and Innes, 1982).

Let us now consider several theories of crowd behavior.

Explanations of Crowd Behavior

Although crowd members differ in a great many ways, their behavior seems to derive from a common impulse and to be dominated by a single spirit. What happens in the course of crowd behavior? What processes fashion people's behavior under crowd conditions? Three somewhat different answers have been supplied by sociologists to these questions.

Contagion Theory.   **Contagion theory** emphasizes the part that rapidly communicated and uncritically accepted feelings, attitudes, and actions play in crowd settings. Its proponents assume that unanimity prevails within a crowd; crowd members often seem to act in identical ways and to be dominated by a similar impulse. Thus, a crowd is often spoken of in the singular, as if it were a real thing—"the crowd roars" and "the angry mob surges forward." This view of the crowd is embodied in the influential work of the 19th-century French writer Gustave Le Bon (1896:23–24), who set forth the "law of the mental unity of crowds."

Le Bon's contagion theory depicted the crowd as characterized by a "mob mind" that overpowers and submerges the individual. A uniform mood and imagery evolve contagiously through three mechanisms: *imitation*—the tendency for one person to do the same thing that others are doing; *suggestibility*—a state in which individuals become susceptible to images, directions, and propositions emanating from others; and *circular reaction*—a process whereby the emotions of others elicit the same emotions in oneself, in turn intensifying the emotions of others in a reciprocal manner. However, Le Bon's concept of the crowd mind as some sort of supraindividual entity—one that is endowed with thinking processes and a capacity for feeling and believing—is rejected by most social scientists (Milgram and Toch, 1969). Only individual human beings are capable of thought and emotion.

Convergence Theory.
Whereas contagion theorists see normal, decent people being transformed under crowd influence, **convergence theory** proposes that a crowd consists of a highly unrepresentative body of people who assemble because they share the same predispositions. For instance, social psychologist Hadley Cantril (1941) studied a Leeville, Texas, lynching and contended that the active members came chiefly from the lowest economic bracket and several had previous police records. As a class, poor whites were most likely to compete for jobs with African Americans and were most likely to find their own status threatened by the presence of successful African Americans. These individuals provided a reservoir of people who were ready for a lynching with a minimum of provocation.

Emergent-Norm Theory.
The **emergent-norm theory** stresses the lack of unanimity in many crowd situations and the differences in motives, attitudes, and actions that characterize crowd members. They may be impulsive, suggestible, opportunistic, passive supporters, cautious activists, or passers-by. The approach denies that people find themselves spontaneously infected with the emotions of others to the extent that they want to behave as others do (Turner, 1964; Turner and Killian, 1972; Shibutani, 1986).

Instead, emergent-norm theory draws upon the work of psychologists Muzafer Sherif (1936) and Solomon Asch (1952) that deals with social conformity in ambiguous situations (see Chapter 3). Collective behavior entails an attempt by people to find meaning in an uncertain social setting (Turner and Killian, 1972). Individuals search for cues to appropriate and acceptable behavior. Like the subjects in Sherif's experiments, who developed group norms that were different from the standards they developed when they were alone, crowd members collectively evolve new standards for behavior. Crowd members then proceed to enforce the norm: They reward behavior consistent with it, inhibit behavior contrary to it, justify proselytizing, and institute actions that restrain dissenters. Since the new behavior differs from that in noncrowd situations, the norm must be specific to the situation—hence, an *emergent* norm.

Assessing the Perspectives.   The three perspectives provide differing views of crowd behavior. Even so, they are not mutually exclusive. Consider what happens at a homecoming football game. Contagion contributes to the excitement through a process of circular reaction. Convergence operates since loyal alumni and football enthusiasts are selected out from the larger population and come together in the stadium. Finally, an emergent norm defines what constitutes an appropriate response to a particular event and suppresses incongruous behavior. Each perspective affords a useful tool for understanding crowd behavior.

Social Movements

Sociologists view a **social movement** as a more-or-less persistent and organized effort on the part of a relatively large number of people to bring about or resist change. The civil rights movement mobilized 200,000 people to march in Washington, D.C., in 1963 and many more to demonstrate across the country and resulted in an end to segregated schools and other public facilities. The women's movement has transformed our society from one in which women are relegated to the kitchen to one in which women work alongside men in almost every type of career. Like collective behavior, social movements often appear in times of rapid social change. Both frequently provide an impetus to social change. Indeed, both occur outside the institutional framework that forms everyday life and break through the familiar web of ordered expectations. But while collective behavior is characterized by spontaneity and a lack of internal structure, social movements possess a considerable measure of internal order and purposeful orientation. This organizational potential allows social movements to challenge established institutions.

Central to the concept of social movement is the idea that people intervene in the process of social change. Rather than responding passively to the flow of life or to its troubling aspects, people seek to alter the course of history. Of equal significance, they undertake joint activity. Individuals consciously act together with a sense of engaging in a common enterprise. Christianity, the Crusades, the Reformation, the American Revolution, the antislavery movement, the labor movement,

Zionism, and fascism—like other social movements—have profoundly affected the societies they have touched.

Causes of Social Movements

What social factors produce social movements, and what leads people to join and persist in social movements? Social movements may arise from social misery and, more particularly, in social and economic deprivation. They also require resources and organizations.

Deprivation Approaches.

As noted in earlier chapters, Karl Marx held that capitalist exploitation leads to progressive impoverishment of the working class. He expected that over time conditions would become so abominable that workers would be compelled to recognize the social nature of their misery and overthrow their oppressors. However, Marx also recognized that the suffering of the underclasses can be so intense and their resulting alienation so massive that all social and revolutionary consciousness is deadened. Marx also recognized a type of **relative deprivation,** a discontent associated with the gap between what people actually have and what they have come to expect and feel to be their just due. He foresaw that the working class could become better off as capitalism advanced, but the gap between owners and workers would widen and produce among the latter deepening feelings of comparative disadvantage (Giddens, 1973; Harrington, 1976).

A number of sociologists have suggested that a major factor in the evolution of the African-American protest in the 1960s was the emergence among African Americans of a growing sense of relative deprivation (Geschwender, 1964; Gurr, 1970). The prosperity of the 1950s and 1960s gave many African Americans a taste of the affluent society. They gained enough to arouse realistic hopes for more. Hence, grievances related to squalid housing, limited job opportunities, persistent unemployment, low pay, and police brutality were felt as severely frustrating. The civil rights movement arose not so much as a protest fed by despair as one fed by rising expectations.

Sociologist James Davies (1962, 1969, 1974) found that relative deprivation also may be fostered under another condition—that characterized by his "rise-and-drop," or "J-curve," hypothesis (see Figure 10.2). He contended that revolutions are most likely to take place when a prolonged period of social and economic betterment is followed by a period of sharp reversal. People fear that the gains they achieved with great effort will be lost, and their mood becomes revolutionary.

Resource Mobilization Approaches.

According to the resource mobilization school, social discontent is more or less constant and thus

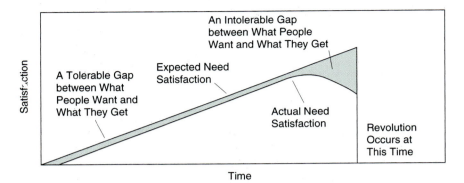

Figure 10.2   Davies's *J*-Curve Theory of Revolution

The figure illustrates Davies's theory that revolutions are often fostered when a period of social and economic betterment is succeeded by sharp reversals, fueling concern that the gains will be lost.

Source: Adapted from James C. Davies, "Toward a Theory of Revolution," *American Sociological Review,* vol. 27, February 1962, fig. 1, p. 6.

endemic within all modern societies (Tilly, 1978; Taylor, 1989; Walton and Ragin, 1990). They emphasize the importance of structural factors, such as the availability of resources for pursuing particular goals and the network of interpersonal relationships that serve as the focus for membership recruitment. People are seen as participating in a social movement not as the result of deprivation but as a response to a rational decision-making process whereby they weigh the costs and benefits of participation. Consequently, conditions of political opportunity—for instance, support from established elites, contemporary models of successful political activism, and preexisting organizational networks and organizations—play a critical part in the development of social movements.

In many cases, resources and organizations outside the protest group are crucial in determining the scope and outcomes of collective action. External support is especially critical for movements of the poor. Sociologist J. Craig Jenkins (1985) contrasted the unsuccessful attempt to organize farmworkers by the National Farm Labor Union from 1946 to 1952 with the successful organization of Mexican farmworkers by the United Farm Workers from 1965 to 1972. Jenkins argued that the United Farm Workers succeeded because internal divisions in government neutralized opposition elites, while the support of the liberal-labor coalition during the reform years of the 1960s and early 1970s turned the tide in favor of the farmworkers. Hence, the success or failure of a social movement derives from strategic factors and the political processes in which it becomes enmeshed (Burstein, 1991; Morris, 1993).

What keeps people involved in social movements? The rational choice model suggests that people get involved because of what they perceive the movements can do for them (Hechter, 1987). But once people are involved, how should leaders of the movements keep members actively participating and contributing and prevent them from engaging in "free ridership"; that is, being members in name but not actually contributing anything to the cause?

One answer is that leaders must get members and potential members to believe in the cause, to be committed to it out of personal, fervent belief. In addition, social mechanisms are required to control behavior and to maintain commitment to the movement for reasons beyond personal belief in its inherent worth.

Rosabeth Kanter (1968) showed that successful communal groups were more likely to have used mechanisms promoting commitment than unsuccessful groups. John Hall found that four factors were strongly associated with a group's long-term success (1988):

- A common ethnic background and/or a foreign language spoken by the group's members.

- A spiritual hierarchy, with those in authority being of higher moral status than other members.

- Obligatory confession, in which one's transgressions might be pointed out before confession by other members or leaders.

- The wearing of uniforms, or special clothes that set group members apart from the rest of society.

An example might help make those characteristics more concrete: The Amish, a group that speaks German, has church leaders and elders, and dresses very differently than the "English," as Amish call non-Amish persons. Children are not taught to speak English until they attend school. If one transgresses in Amish society, the punishment can be shunning, in which the transgressor is cast out from Amish society and cut off from friends and family.

Hall found that in the groups that were the oldest and survived intact the longest, researchers found continuing high levels of control mechanisms. Hall's study shows that the mechanisms of social control are more important than other factors in maintaining group solidarity and promoting the longevity of social movements and groups.

Types of Social Movements

A set of ideas—an **ideology**—is critical to a social movement. An ideology provides individuals with conceptions of the movement's purposes, its rationale for existence, its indictment of existing conditions or arrangements, and its design for action (Moaddel, 1992). It functions as a kind of glue that joins people together in a fellowship of belief. But an ideology not only binds together otherwise isolated and separated individuals, it unites them with a cause. In so doing it prepares them for self-sacrifice on behalf of the movement—at times even to lay down their lives for the "True God," "the New Nation," or "the Revolution."

Some movements pursue objectives that aim to change society through challenging fundamental values; others seek modifications within the framework of the existing value scheme. In the former case, **revolutionary movements** advocate replacement of the existing value scheme; in the latter, **reform movements** pursue changes that will implement the existing value scheme more adequately. The civil rights movement identified with the leadership of the Reverend Martin Luther King Jr. had a reform emphasis. It sought to extend values already acknowledged as inherent in political democracy to the African-American population of the United States. In contrast, a number of African-American nationalist groups that arose in the late 1960s had a revolutionary emphasis. They sought to institute basic changes in the republican form of government in the United States, to rearrange the class structure, and to inaugurate a system of greater African-American autonomy.

Organized efforts called **resistance movements** arise not only for the purpose of instituting change but also to block change or to eliminate a previously instituted change. Thus, the movement for civil rights in the South unleashed a white counterattack beginning in the 1950s that found expression in the organization of white citizens' councils and Ku Klux Klan groups (Vander Zanden, 1965, 1983).

Still other types of movements—**expressive movements**—are less concerned with institutional change than with a renovating or renewing of people from *within*, frequently with the promise of some future redemption. Pentecostal and holiness religious sects are the most common examples of expressive movements. Less common are expressive movements that appeal primarily to the middle class, such as Zen Buddhism and *est* (Erhard Seminars Training) that were popular in the United States in the 1970s and 1980s (Tipton, 1982). Although most expressive movements arise among the underprivileged, they do not seek comprehensive social change nor do they aim to save the world. Their goal is to save individuals from a world that is becoming progressively degenerate or oppressive.

Social Revolution

A **social revolution** involves the overthrow of a society's state and class structures and the creation of new social arrangements. Revolutions are most likely to occur under certain conditions. First, a good deal of political power is concentrated in the state, so there is a centralized governing apparatus. Accordingly, the state can become the focus for collective anger and attack. Second, the military's allegiance to the established regime is weakened so that the army is no longer a reliable tool for suppressing domestic disorder. Where army officers are drawn from elites in conflict with the central government, or when troops sympathize with their civilian counterparts, the unreliability of the army increases the vulnerability of the state. Third, political crises—often associated with long-term international conflicts that result in military defeat—weaken the existing regime and contribute to the collapse of the state apparatus. And fourth, a substantial segment of the population must mobilize in uprisings that bring a new elite to power. Peasant revolts usually stem from landlords' taking over peasant lands, substantial increases in taxation or rents, or famines. Urban uprisings commonly derive from sharp jumps in food prices and unusually high levels of unemployment (Skocpol, 1979; Goldstone, 1991).

A number of historians and sociologists have surveyed important Western revolutions in search of common stages and patterns in their development. From this work have stemmed a number of observations regarding the sequence of events that typically unfold in the course of major social revolutions, an approach called the **natural history of revolutions.**

Prior to the revolution, intellectuals—journalists, poets, playwrights, essayists, lawyers, and others—withdraw support from the existing regime and demand major reforms. Under increasing attack, the state attempts to meet the criticisms by instituting a number of reforms (e.g., the reforms of Louis XVI in France). The onset of the revolution is heralded by a weakening or paralysis of the state, usually brought on by the government's inability to deal with a major military, economic, or political problem. The collapse of the old regime brings to the forefront divisions among conservatives who attempt to minimize change, radicals who seek fundamental change, and moderates who try to steer a middle course. Coups or civil war often ensue. The first to gain the reins of power are usually moderate reformers.

The moderates seek to reconstruct governmental authority on the basis of limited reform, often employing organizational structures left over from the old regime. Simultaneously, radical centers of mass mobilization spring up with new organizations. The moderates, saddled with the same problems and liabilities that felled the old regime, are replaced by the radicals. The disorder that follows the revolution and the seizure of power by the radicals results in coercive rule. This is the stage of "terror" that characterized the guillotine days of the French Revolution. Turmoil persists and allows military leaders to

U.S. interest in and concern about terrorism accelerated rapidly with the September 11, 2001, attacks on Washington, D.C., and New York City.

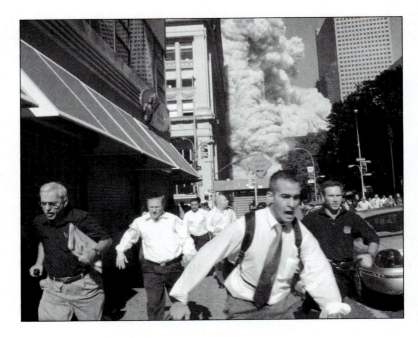

move into ascendancy. Finally, radicalism gives way to a phase of prag-matism and the consolidation of a new status quo. The "excesses" of the revolution are condemned, and the emphasis falls on the fashion-ing of stable institutions. Although not all revolutions pass through the identical sequence of stages, there are recurrent patterns in the unfold-ing of revolutionary activity.

Terrorism

The September 11, 2001, attacks in New York City and Washington, D.C., alerted the United States to its vulnerability to terrorists. Although no one definition of **terrorism** is universally accepted, the U.S. Department of State offers this: "premeditated, politically moti-vated violence perpetrated against noncombatant targets by subna-tional groups or clandestine agents, usually intended to influence an audience" (Atran, 2003). The U.S. Congress defines acts of terror as acts that appear to be intended "(i) to intimidate or coerce a civilian population; (ii) to influence the policy of a government by intimidation or coercion; or (iii) to affect the conduct of a government by assassina-tion or kidnapping." Familiar to all of us in the 21st century is suicide terrorism, the use of self-destructing humans to commit terrorist acts.

    In practice, what constitutes terrorism is a matter of social defini-tion, with one side labeling people as "terrorists" while another side labels the same people "freedom fighters." Similarly, whether an action is "aid to terrorists" as opposed to "covert support of friendly forces" is a matter of perspective, as illustrated by the Reagan administration's controversial support of the Nicaraguan contras, or counter-revolutionary fighters, in the mid-1980s.

A Media Event.

Very often terrorism is aimed at a media audience, not the actual victims. The "theater of terror" becomes possible only when the media afford the stage and access to a worldwide audience. The act of media coverage also often enhances the importance of the issue that allegedly led to the terrorist activities. Newspaper readers and television viewers see the issue as of substantially greater importance and as justifying resolution by national or international action. As one analyst noted, "The primary target is not those actually killed or injured in the attack, but those made to witness it. The enemy's own information media amplify the attack's effects to the larger target population" (Atran, 2003).

Terrorists and Social Change.

Although terrorists have sometimes been profiled as poor, uneducated, and politically powerless, research has shown that suicide terrorists are as educated and economically well-to-do as those in the surrounding populations (Atran, 2003). And although political and social change may be what the terrorists' leaders are seeking, those who carry out the missions are motivated primarily by their group commitment. According to psychologists who studied the September 11 attacks, the 19 men who carried out the plans of Al-Qaida were motivated less by religious zeal and hatred for the United States than by peer pressure—the commitment each had made to the others to go forward with the plan (Vedantam, 2001).

With terrorism a grim fact of contemporary life, some analysts are calling for incorporating the potential for terrorist acts into disaster planning. Although the causes of disaster differ, plans for relief, development of backup systems, and the incorporation of disaster resistance into new communication, energy, water supply, and other systems are equally useful for dealing with natural disasters and large-scale acts of terrorism (Kennedy, 2002).

In an assessment of the root causes of and preventive measures for suicide terrorism, Scott Atran (2003) recommends sociological and psychological research on how terrorist institutions form and on recruitment and retention procedures. The first line of defense, he says, is to reduce the receptivity of potential recruits to recruiting organizations—but that cannot be done until planners understand more about the mix of community and institutional factors that make so many people eager to take part in terrorist groups. Atran also recommends that the United States respond to terrorist acts by addressing the grievances of terrorist organizations: "Our society can ill afford to ignore either the consequences of its own actions or the causes behind the actions of others" (Atran, 2003).

Looking to the Future

We undertake many of our daily activities in anticipation of the future. We carry out our job responsibilities in the expectation that we will be paid at the end of the week or the month. We invest our money, energy, and time in an education based on the assumption that there will be a job payoff down the road. We involve ourselves in environmental, civil rights, antinuclear, or women's movements to have a voice in the shaping of tomorrow's world.

And yet we can only speculate on what the future will bring. We will probably have little more success anticipating the century ahead than did our compatriots 100 years ago at the future-oriented World's Columbian Exposition in Chicago, which we discussed in the introduction to the chapter. For the most part the forecasts provided by 74 prominent Americans not only turned out to be wrong but hilariously wrong.

However, some social phenomena can be predicted fairly accurately. Selling insurance is based on mostly accurate estimates of the risk of loss the company will incur due to illness, death, accidents, crime, and other things. Economists can predict that if the price of a product is doubled, fewer people will buy it. Sociologists can predict the persistence of educational inequality. But social scientists do not do well in predicting major social changes (Hechter, 1995).

Many years ago, philosopher Karl Popper distinguished between *scientific predictions,* which are conditional (e.g., a prediction that specific changes in a system will result in specific changes in outcomes), and *unconditional historical prophecies.* The characteristics required to make accurate predictions for a system are that it be well isolated, stationary, and recurrent—characteristics that simply do not apply to societies. Societies can change, new social situations that we have never experienced before can arise, the growth of technology and knowledge can shift things in directions we are unable now to anticipate (Hechter, 1995).

As a consequence, social scientists cannot predict with any accuracy major social phenomena such as revolution. But as Hechter pointed out, the utility of the physical and social sciences "may not rest in their ability to accurately forecast events"; rather, as Karl Popper said, the role of science in social life is "the modest one of helping us to understand even the more remote consequences of possible actions, and thus of helping us to choose our actions more wisely" (Popper, 1963:343).

As we have noted throughout this textbook, sociology invites us to scrutinize our prosaic world and notice what we otherwise often ignore, neglect, or take for granted. It looks behind the outer reaches of the social experience and discerns its inner structure and processes—suspending the belief that things are simply as they seem. As such, sociology is uniquely suited to fostering the skills necessary for living in an ever-changing world filled with countless choices and seemingly endless uncertainty. The challenges we confront in the 21st century may well inspire you to pursue a sociological career.

Key Terms

acting crowd, 294

casual crowd, 293

collective behavior, 291

contagion theory, 294

conventional crowd, 294

convergence theory, 295

craze, 292

crowd, 293

cultural lag, 284

deindividualization, 294

diffusion, 280

discovery, 280

emergent-norm theory, 295

expressive crowd, 294

expressive movement, 300

fad, 292

fashion, 292

ideology, 299

invention, 280

mass hysteria, 292

modernization, 290

natural history of revolutions, 301

panic, 293

reform movement, 300

relative deprivation, 297

resistance movement, 300

revolutionary movement, 300

rumor, 291

social change, 278

social movement, 296

social revolution, 300

terrorism, 302

world system, 290

Review Questions

1. What is social change? Give one example of a major social change that has taken place in the past 100 years. What were some of the factors responsible for that change?

2. Describe the major theories of social change.

3. How have computer use and Internet access affected life in the United States?

4. Compare the modernization and world system approaches to social change in developing nations.

5. What is collective behavior? List and define some of its forms.

6. What are the major explanations of crowd behavior?

7. What is a social movement? What causes a social movement?

8. What are the differences among revolutionary, reform, resistance, and expressive movements?

9. How does a social revolution occur?

10. What is terrorism?

Glossary

achieved status: A status that individuals secure on the basis of choice and competition.

acting crowd: An excited, volatile collection of people who are engaged in rioting, looting, or other forms of aggressive behavior in which established norms carry little weight.

age-specific death rate: The number of deaths per 1,000 individuals in a specific age group.

age-specific fertility: The number of live births per 1,000 women in a specific age group.

aggregate: A collection of anonymous individuals who are in one place at the same time.

animism: A belief in spirits or otherworldly beings.

anomie: A social condition in which people find it difficult to guide their behavior by norms they experience as weak, unclear, or conflicting.

anticipatory socialization: The process in which people think about, experiment with, and try on the behaviors associated with a new role.

archival research: The use of existing records that have been produced or maintained by persons or organizations other than the researcher.

asceticism: A way of life characterized by hard work, sobriety, thrift, restraint, and the avoidance of earthly pleasures.

ascribed status: A status assigned to an individual by a group or society.

assimilation: Those processes whereby groups with distinctive identities become culturally and socially fused.

authoritarianism: A political system in which the government tolerates little or no opposition to its rules but permits nongovernmental centers of influence and allows debate on issues of public policy.

authority: Legitimate power.

bilineal: An arrangement based on reckoning descent and transmitting property through both the father and the mother.

body language: Physical motions and gestures that provide social signals.

bureaucracy: A social structure made up of a hierarchy of statuses and roles that is prescribed by explicit rules and procedures and based on a division of function and authority.

capital punishment: The application of the death penalty for a capital crime.

capitalist economy: An economic system relying primarily on free markets and privately held property.

casual crowd: A collection of people who have little in common with one another except that they may be viewing a common event, such as looking through a department store window.

category: A collection of people who share a characteristic that is deemed to be of social significance.

charismatic authority: Power that is legitimated by the extraordinary superhuman or supernatural attributes people attribute to a leader.

church: A religious organization that considers itself uniquely legitimate and enjoys a positive relationship with the dominant society.

city: A relatively dense and permanent concentration of people who secure their livelihood chiefly through nonagricultural activities.

civil society: A social realm of mediating groups, networks, and institutions that sustains public life outside the worlds of the state and the economy.

class conflict: The view of Karl Marx that society is divided into those who own the means of producing wealth and those who do not, giving rise to struggles between classes.

closed system: A stratification system in which people have great difficulty changing their status.

coercive organization: A formal organization that people become members of against their will.

collective behavior: Ways of thinking, feeling, and acting that develop among a large number of people and that are relatively spontaneous and unstructured.

communication: The process by which people transmit information, ideas, attitudes, and mental states to one another.

complementary needs: Two different personality traits that are the counterparts of each other and that provide a sense of completeness when they are joined.

concentric circle model: The approach to city growth stating that the modern city assumes a pattern of concentric circles, each with distinctive characteristics.

conditioning: A form of learning in which the consequences of behavior determine the probability of its future occurrence.

constructed reality: Our experience of the world. Meaning is not something that inheres in things; it is a property that derives from, or arises out of, the interaction that takes place among people in the course of their daily lives.

contagion theory: An approach to crowd behavior that emphasizes the part played in crowd settings by rapidly communicated and uncritically accepted feelings, attitudes, and actions.

control group: The group that affords a neutral standard against which the changes in an experimental group can be measured.

conventional crowd: A number of people who have assembled for some specific purpose and who typically act in accordance with established norms, such as people attending a baseball game or concert.

convergence theory: An approach to crowd behavior stating that a crowd consists of a highly unrepresentative body of people who assemble because they share the same predispositions.

core regions: Geographical areas that dominate the world economy and exploit the rest of the system.

correlation: A change in one variable associated with a change in another variable.

correspondence principle: The notion set forth by Samuel Bowles and Herbert Gintis that the social relations of work find expression in the social relations of the school.

counterculture: A subculture whose norms and values are substantially at odds with those of the larger society.

craze: A fad that becomes an all-consuming passion.

credentialism: The requirement that a worker have a degree that does not provide skills needed for the performance of a job.

crime: An act prohibited by law.

criminal justice system: The reactive agencies of the state that include the police, courts, and prisons.

crowd: A temporary, relatively unorganized gathering of people who are in close physical proximity.

crude birth rate: The number of live births per 1,000 members of a population in a given year.

crude death rate: The number of deaths per 1,000 members of a population in a given year.

cult: A religious movement that represents a new and independent religious tradition.

cultural lag: The view that immaterial culture must constantly "catch up" with material culture, resulting in an adjustment gap between the two forms of culture.

cultural relativism: A value-free or neutral approach that views the behavior of a people from the perspective of their own culture.

cultural universals: Patterned and recurrent aspects of life that appear in all known societies.

culture: The social heritage of a people; those learned patterns for thinking, feeling, and acting that are transmitted from one generation to the next, including the embodiment of these patterns in material items.

culture of poverty: The view that the poor possess self-perpetuating lifeways characterized by weak ego structures, lack of impulse control, a present-time orientation, and a sense of resignation and fatalism.

definition of the situation: A concept, formulated by William I. Thomas, that refers to the interpretation or meaning people give to their immediate circumstances.

deindividualization: A psychological state of diminished identity and self-awareness.

democracy: A political system in which the powers of government derive from the consent of the governed and in which regular constitutional avenues exist for changing government officials.

demographic transition theory: A view of population change that holds that the process of modernization passes through three stages: high potential growth, transitional growth, and population stability.

demography: The science dealing with the size, distribution, composition, and changes in population.

denomination: A religious organization that accepts the legitimacy of other religious groups and enjoys a positive relationship with the dominant society.

dependent variable: The variable that is affected in an experimental setting.

deviance: Behavior that a considerable number of people in a society view as reprehensible and beyond the limits of tolerance.

dialectical materialism: The notion in Marxist theory that development depends on the clash of contradictions and the creation of new, more advanced structures out of these clashes.

differential association: The notion that the earlier, the more frequent, the more intense, and the longer the duration of the contacts people have in deviant settings, the greater the probability that they, too, will become deviant.

diffusion: The process by which culture traits spread from one social unit to another.

discovery: An addition to knowledge.

discrimination: The arbitrary denial of privilege, prestige, and power to members of a minority group whose qualifications are equal to those of members of the dominant group.

disease: A condition in which an organism does not function properly because of biological causes.

dramaturgical approach: The sociological perspective, associated with Erving Goffman, that views the performances staged in a theater as an analytical analogy and tool for depicting social life.

dual labor market: An economy characterized by two sectors. The primary, or core, sector offers "good jobs," and the secondary, or periphery, sector offers "bad jobs."

duties: The actions that others can legitimately insist that we perform.

dyad: A two-member group.

dysfunctions: Observed consequences that lessen the adaptation or adjustment of a system.

ecology: The study of the interrelations between the living and nonliving components of an ecosystem.

economic determinist: A believer in the doctrine that economic factors are the primary determinants of the structure of societies and social change.

ecosystem: A relatively stable community of organisms that have established interlocking relationships and exchanges with one another and their natural habitat.

education: The transmission of particular attitudes, knowledge, and skills to the members of a society through formal, systematic training.

egalitarian authority: An arrangement in which power and authority are equally distributed between husband and wife.

emergent-norm theory: An approach to crowd behavior stating that crowd members evolve new standards for behavior in a crowd setting and then enforce the expectations in the manner of norms.

endogamy: The requirement that marriage occur within a group.

environment: All the surrounding conditions and influences that affect an organism or group of organisms.

environmental racism: The practice of deliberately locating incinerators and other types of hazardous waste facilities in or next to minority communities.

ethic: The perspective and values engendered by a religious way of thinking.

ethnic groups: Groups identified chiefly on cultural grounds—language, religion, folk practices, dress, gestures, mannerisms.

ethnocentrism: The tendency to judge the behavior of other groups by the standards of one's own culture.

exchange theory: The view proposing that people involved in a mutually satisfying relationship will exchange behaviors that have low cost and high reward.

exogamy: The requirement that marriage occur outside a group.

experiment: A technique in which researchers work with two groups that are identical in all relevant respects. They introduce a change in one group, but not in the other group. The procedure permits researchers to test the effects of an independent variable on a dependent variable.

experimental group: The group in which researchers introduce a change in an experimental setting.

expressive crowd: An aggregation of people who have gotten together for self-stimulation and personal gratification, such as occurs at a religious revival or a rock festival.

expressive movement: A movement that is less concerned with institutional change than with a renovating or renewing of people from within.

expressive ties: Social links formed when we emotionally invest ourselves in and commit ourselves to other people.

extended family: A family arrangement in which kin—individuals related by common ancestry—provide the core relationship; spouses are functionally marginal and peripheral.

fad: A folkway that lasts for a short time and enjoys acceptance among only a segment of the population.

family: Traditionally defined as a social group whose members are related by ancestry, marriage, or adoption and who live together, cooperate economically, and care for the young.

family life course: Changes and realignments related to the altered expectations and requirements imposed on a husband and a wife as children are born and grow up.

family of orientation: A nuclear family that consists of oneself and one's father, mother, and siblings.

family of procreation: A nuclear family that consists of oneself and one's spouse and children.

fashion: A folkway that lasts for a short time and enjoys widespread acceptance within society.

fecundity: The potential number of children that could be born if every woman of childbearing age bore all the children she possibly could.

folkways: Norms people do not deem to be of great importance and to which they exact less stringent conformity.

force: Power whose basis is the threat or application of punishment.

formal organization: A group formed deliberately for the achievement of specific objectives.

functions: Observed consequences that permit the adaptation or adjustment of a system.

gender: The sociocultural distinction between males and females.

gender identities: The conceptions we have of ourselves as being male or female.

gender roles: Sets of cultural expectations that define the ways in which the members of each sex should behave.

general fertility rate: The annual number of live births per 1,000 women ages 15 to 44.

generalized other: The term George Herbert Mead applied to the social unit that gives individuals their unity of self. The attitude of the generalized other is the attitude of the larger community.

genocide: The deliberate and systematic extermination of a racial or ethnic group.

government: Those political processes that have to do with the authoritative formulating of rules and policies that are binding and pervasive throughout a society.

group: Two or more people who share a feeling of unity and who are bound together in relatively stable patterns of social interaction.

group marriage: The marriage of two or more husbands and two or more wives.

groupthink: A decision-making process found in highly cohesive groups in which the members become so preoccupied with maintaining group consensus that their critical faculties are impaired.

growth rate: The difference between births and deaths, plus the difference between immigrants and emigrants per 1,000 population.

health: As defined by the World Health Organization, "a state of complete physical, mental, and social well-being and not merely the absence of disease or infirmity."

hidden curriculum: A complex of unarticulated values, attitudes, and behaviors that subtly fit children in the image of the dominant institutions.

homogamy: The tendency of like to marry like.

homosexuality: A preference for an individual of the same sex as a sexual partner.

horizontal mobility: Movement from one social status to another that is approximately equivalent in rank.

hypothesis: A proposition that can be tested to determine its validity.

ideology: A set of ideas that provides individuals with conceptions of the purposes of a social movement, a rationale for the movement's existence, an indictment of existing conditions, and a design for action.

impression management: The term Erving Goffman applied to the process whereby we present ourselves to others in ways that will lead them to view us in a favorable light.

incest taboos: Rules that prohibit sexual intercourse with close blood relatives.

income: The amount of money people receive.

independent variable: The variable that causes an effect in an experimental setting.

index crimes: Crimes reported by the Federal Bureau of Investigation in its Uniform Crime Reports. These offenses consist of four categories of violent crime against people—murder, rape, robbery, and assault—and four categories of crime against property—burglary, theft, motor vehicle theft, and arson.

infant mortality rate: The number of deaths among infants under one year of age per 1,000 live births.

informal organization: Interpersonal networks and ties that arise in a formal organization but that are not defined or prescribed by it.

in-group: A group with which we identify and to which we belong.

institutional discrimination: The functioning of the institutions of society in a way that produces unequal outcomes for different groups.

institutions: The principal instruments whereby the essential tasks of living are organized, directed, and executed.

instrumental ties: Social links formed when we cooperate with other people to achieve some goal.

interest groups: Organizations of people who share common concerns or points of view.

interests: People who share common concerns or points of view.

intergenerational mobility: A comparison of the social status of parents and their children at some point in their respective careers.

internal migration: Population movement within a nation.

internalization: The process by which individuals incorporate within their personalities the standards of behavior prevalent within the larger society.

international migration: Population movement between nations.

intragenerational mobility: A comparison of the social statuses of a person over an extended period of time.

invasion: A new type of people, institution, or activity that encroaches on an area occupied by a different type.

invention: The use of existing knowledge in a new form.

iron law of oligarchy: The principle that states that bureaucracies invariably lead to the concentration of power in the hands of a few individuals who use their offices to advance their own fortunes and self-interests.

language: A socially structured system of sound patterns (words and sentences) with specific and arbitrary meanings.

language acquisition device: The view associated with Noam Chomsky that human beings possess an inborn language-generating mechanism. The basic structure of language is seen as biologically channeled, forming a sort of prefabricated filing system to order the words and phrases that make up human languages.

latent functions: Consequences that are neither intended nor recognized by the participants in a system.

laws: Rules that are enforced by a special political organization composed of individuals who enjoy the right to use force.

learning: A relatively permanent change in behavior or capability that results from experience.

legal-rational authority: Power that is legitimated by explicit rules and rational procedures that define the rights and duties of the occupants of given positions.

life chances: The likelihood that individuals and groups will enjoy desired goods and services, fulfilling experiences, and opportunities for living healthy and long lives.

life course: The interweave of age-graded trajectories with the vicissitudes of changing social conditions and future options that characterize the life span from conception through old age and death.

lifestyle: The overall pattern of living that people evolve to meet their biological, social, and emotional needs.

looking-glass self: The term that Charles Horton Cooley applied to the process by which we imaginatively assume the stance of other people and view ourselves as we believe they see us.

macrosociology: The study of large-scale and long-term social processes.

mana: The notion that there is in nature a diffuse, impersonal, supernatural force operating for good or evil.

manifest functions: Consequences that are intended and recognized by the participants in a system.

marriage: A socially approved sexual union between two or more individuals that is undertaken with some idea of permanence.

mass hysteria: The rapid dissemination of behaviors involving contagious anxiety, usually associated with some mysterious force.

master status: A key or core status that carries primary weight in a person's interactions and relationships with others.

matching hypothesis: The notion that we typically experience the greatest payoff and the least cost when we select partners who have a degree of physical attractiveness similar to our own.

matriarchal authority: A family arrangement in which power is vested in women.

matrilineal: An arrangement based on reckoning descent and inheritance through the mother's side of the family.

matrilocal residence: The residence pattern in which a bride and groom live in the household or community of the wife's family.

medicine: An institution providing an enduring set of cultural patterns and social arrangements responsible for problems of health and disease.

megalopolis: A strip city formed when the rural interstices between metropolitan centers fill with urban development.

microsociology: The detailed study of what individuals say, do, and think moment by moment as they go about their daily lives.

minority group: A racially or culturally self-conscious population, with hereditary membership and a high degree of in-group marriage, that suffers oppression at the hands of a dominant segment of a nation-state.

modernization: The process by which a society moves from traditional or preindustrial social and economic arrangements to those characteristic of industrial societies.

monogamy: The marriage of one husband and one wife.

monotheism: The belief in one god.

mores: Norms to which people attach a good deal of importance and exact strict conformity.

mortification: A procedure in which rituals employed by coercive organizations render individuals vulnerable to institutional control, discipline, and resocialization.

multinational corporations: Firms that have their central office in one country and subsidiaries in other countries.

multiple nuclei model: The approach to city growth that assumes a city has several centers, each of which specializes in some activity and gives its distinctive cast to the surrounding area.

natural areas: Geographic areas with distinctive characteristics.

natural history of revolutions: The view that social revolutions pass through a set of common stages and patterns in the course of their development.

negotiated order: The fluid, ongoing understanding and agreements people reach as they go about their daily activities.

neolocal residence: The residence pattern in which newlyweds set up a new place of residence independent of either of their parents or other relatives.

net migration rate: The increase or decrease per 1,000 members of the population in a given year that results from people entering (immigrants) or leaving (emigrants) a society.

norm of legitimacy: The rule that children not be born out of wedlock.

norms: Social rules that specify appropriate and inappropriate behavior in given situations.

nuclear family: A family arrangement in which the spouses and their offspring constitute the core relationship; blood relatives are functionally marginal and peripheral.

objective method: An approach to the identification of social classes that employs such yardsticks as income, occupation, and education.

observational learning: Learning that occurs when people reproduce the responses they observe in other people, either real or fictional; also referred to as modeling or imitation.

open system: A stratification system in which people can change their status with relative ease.

organized crime: Large-scale bureaucratic organizations that provide illegal goods and services in public demand.

out-group: A group with which we do not identify and to which we do not belong.

panic: Irrational and uncoordinated but collective action among people that is induced by the presence of an immediate, severe threat.

paralanguage: Nonverbal cues surrounding speech—voice, pitch, volume, pacing of speech, silent pauses, and sighs—that provide a rich source of communicative information.

Parkinson's law: The principle that states that work expands so as to fill the time available for its completion.

participant observation: A technique in which researchers engage in activities with the people that they are observing.

patriarchal authority: A family arrangement in which power is vested in men.

patriarchy: A system of social organization in which men have a disproportionate share of power.

patrilineal: An arrangement based on reckoning descent and inheritance through the father's side of the family.

patrilocal residence: The residence pattern in which a bride and groom live in the household or community of the husband's family.

periphery regions: Geographical areas that provide raw materials to the core and are exploited by it.

personal efficacy: The belief that one can overcome obstacles and achieve goals.

pluralism: A situation where diverse groups coexist side by side and mutually accommodate themselves to their differences.

political power: Power that is organized and wielded by the state.

politics: The processes by which people and groups acquire and exercise power.

polyandry: The marriage of two or more husbands and one wife.

polygyny: The marriage of one husband and two or more wives.

polytheism: The belief in many gods with equal or relatively similar power.

population pyramid: A graphic representation of the age and sex composition of a population.

power: The ability of individuals and groups to realize their will in human affairs even if it involves the resistance of others.

prejudice: Attitudes of aversion and hostility toward the members of a group simply because they belong to it and hence are presumed to have the objectionable qualities ascribed to it.

prestige: The social respect, admiration, and recognition associated with a particular social status.

primary deviance: Behavior that violates social norms but usually goes unnoticed by the agents of social control.

primary group: Two or more people who enjoy a direct, intimate, cohesive relationship with one another.

profane: Those aspects of social reality that are everyday and commonplace.

Protestant ethic: The Calvinist ethos that embodied the spirit of capitalism.

proxemics: The way we employ social and personal space to transmit messages.

race: A population that differs from other populations in the incidence of various hereditary traits.

racism: The belief that some racial groups are naturally superior and others are inferior.

random sample: A sampling procedure in which researchers select subjects on the basis of chance so that every individual in the population has the same opportunity to be chosen.

rate of natural increase: The difference between the birth rate and the death rate.

recidivism: Relapse into criminal behavior.

reference group: A social unit we use for appraising and shaping our attitudes, feelings, and actions.

reflected appraisals: Appraisals of ourselves that we see reflected in the behavior of others.

reflexive behavior: Actions through which people observe, interpret, evaluate, communicate with, and attempt to control themselves.

reform movement: A social movement that pursues changes that will implement the existing value scheme of a society more adequately.

relationship: An association that lasts long enough for two people to become linked together by a relatively stable set of expectations.

relative deprivation: Discontent associated with the gap between what people actually have and what they believe they should have.

religion: Those socially shared and organized ways of thinking, feeling, and acting that concern ultimate meanings and assume the existence of the supernatural or "beyond" and that are centered in beliefs and practices related to sacred things.

reputational method: An approach to identifying social classes that involves asking people how they classify others.

resistance movement: A social movement that arises to block change or eliminate a previously instituted change.

resocialization: A process by which a person's old roles and identities are stripped away and new ones are created.

revolutionary movement: A social movement that advocates the replacement of a society's existing value scheme.

rights: Actions that we can legitimately insist that others perform.

rituals: Social acts prescribed by rules that dictate how human beings should comport themselves in the presence of the sacred.

role: A set of expectations (rights and duties) that define the behavior people view as appropriate and inappropriate for the occupant of a status.

role conflict: The situation in which individuals are confronted with conflicting expectations stemming from their simultaneous occupancy of two or more statuses.

role performance: The actual behavior of the person who occupies a status.

role set: The multiple roles associated with a single status.

role strain: The situation in which individuals find the expectations of a single role incompatible, so that they have difficulty performing the role.

romantic love: The strong physical and emotional attraction between two people.

rumor: A difficult-to-verify piece of information that is transmitted from person to person in relatively rapid fashion.

sacred: Those aspects of social reality that are set apart and forbidden.

secondary deviance: Deviance that individuals adopt in response to the reactions of other individuals.

secondary group: Two or more people who are involved in an impersonal relationship and have come together for a specific, practical purpose.

sect: A religious organization that stands apart from the dominant society but is rooted in established religious traditions.

sector model: The approach to city growth that assumes that large cities are made up of sectors—wedge-shaped areas—rather than concentric circles.

segregation: A process of clustering wherein individuals and groups are sifted and sorted out in space based on their sharing certain traits or activities in common.

self: The set of concepts we use in defining who we are.

self-conception: An overriding view of ourselves; a sense of self through time.

self-esteem: The belief that one is a good and valuable person.

self-image: A mental conception or picture we have of ourselves that is relatively temporary; it changes as we move from one context to another.

self-placement method: An approach to identifying social classes that involves self-classification.

sex: A reference to whether one is genetically male or female; determines the biological role that one will play in reproduction.

sexism: The set of cultural and social processes that justify and promote disadvantage for women.

sick role: A set of cultural expectations that define what is appropriate and inappropriate behavior for people with a disease or health problem.

significant other: The term George Herbert Mead applied to a social model, usually an important person in an individual's life.

social change: Fundamental alterations in the patterns of culture, structure, and social behavior over time.

social comparisons: Comparing one's performance, ability, or characteristics with those of others and rating oneself as positive, neutral, or negative.

social control: Methods and strategies that regulate behavior within society.

Social Darwinism: The application of evolutionary notions and the concept of survival of the fittest to the social world.

social differentiation: The process by which a society becomes increasingly specialized over time.

social dynamics: Those aspects of social life that pattern institutional development and have to do with social change.

social facts: Those aspects of social life that cannot be explained in terms of the biological or mental characteristics of the individual. People experience the social fact as external to themselves in the sense that it has an independent reality and forms a part of their objective environment.

social mobility: The process in which individuals or groups move from one level (stratum) to another in the stratification system.

social movement: A more-or-less persistent and organized effort on the part of a relatively large number of people to bring about or resist change.

social revolution: The overthrow of a society's state and class structures and the fashioning of new social arrangements.

social statics: Those aspects of social life that have to do with order and stability and that allow societies to hold together and endure.

social stratification: The structured ranking of individuals and groups; their grading into hierarchical layers or strata.

social structure: The interweaving of people's interactions and relationships in more or less recurrent and stable patterns.

social-emotional specialist: A leadership role that focuses on overcoming interpersonal problems in a group, defusing tension, and promoting solidarity.

social imagination: The ability to see our private experiences and personal difficulties as entwined with the structural arrangements of our society and the historical times in which we live.

socialist economy: An economic system relying primarily on state planning and publicly held property.

socialization: A process of social interaction by which people acquire the knowledge, attitudes, values, and behaviors essential for effective participation in society.

society: A group of people who live within the same territory and share a common culture.

socioeconomic life cycle: A sequence of stages that begins with birth into a family with a specific social status and proceeds through childhood, socialization, schooling, job seeking, occupational achievement, marriage, and the formation and functioning of a new family unit.

sociology: The scientific study of social interaction and social organization.

spurious correlation: The apparent relationship between two variables produced by a third variable that influences the original variables.

state: An arrangement that consists of people who exercise an effective monopoly in the use of physical coercion within a given territory.

status: A position within a group or society; a location in a social structure.

stratified random sample: A sampling procedure in which researchers divide a population into relevant categories and draw a random sample from each of the categories.

style of life: The magnitude and manner of people's consumption of goods and services.

subculture: A group whose members participate in the main culture of a society while simultaneously sharing a number of unique values, norms, traditions, and lifestyles.

succession: Invasion that continues until the encroaching type of people, institution, or activity displaces the previous type.

survey: A method for gathering data on people's beliefs, values, attitudes, perceptions, motivations, and feelings. The data can be derived from interviews or questionnaires.

symbolic racism: A form of racism in which whites feel that blacks are too aggressive, do not play by the rules, and have negative characteristics.

symbols: Acts or objects that have come to be socially accepted as standing for something else.

task specialist: A leadership role that focuses on appraising the problem at hand and organizing people's activity to deal with it.

terrorism: The use of force or violence against persons or property to intimidate or coerce a government, a formal organization, or a civilian population in furtherance of political, religious, or social objectives.

theism: A religion centered in a belief in gods who are thought to be powerful, to have an interest in human affairs, and to merit worship.

Thomas theorem: The notion that our definitions influence our construction of reality; as stated by William I. Thomas and Dorothy S. Thomas: "If [people] define situations as real, they are real in their consequences."

total institutions: Places of residence where individuals are isolated from the rest of society.

totalitarianism: A "total state" in which the government undertakes to control all parts of the society and all aspects of social life.

traditional authority: Power that is legitimated by the sanctity of age-old customs.

trained incapacity: The term Thorstein Veblen applied to the tendency within bureaucracies for members to rely on established rules and regulations and to apply them in an unimaginative and mechanical fashion.

triad: A three-member group.

unobtrusive observation: A technique in which researchers observe the activities of people without intruding or participating in the activities.

urban gentrification: The return of the middle class—usually young, white, childless professionals—to older urban neighborhoods.

utilitarian organization: A formal organization set up to achieve practical ends.

value-free sociology: The view of Max Weber that sociologists must not allow their personal biases to affect the conduct of their scientific research.

values: Broad ideas regarding what is desirable, correct, and good that most members of a society share.

variable: A concept that can take on different values; the term scientists apply to something they think influences (or is influenced by) something else.

Verstehen: An approach to the study of social life developed by Max Weber in which sociologists mentally attempt to place themselves in the shoes of other people and identify what they think and how they feel; translates roughly as "understanding."

vertical mobility: Movement of individuals from one social status to another of higher or lower rank.

victimless crime: An offense in which no one involved is considered a victim.

voluntary organization: A formal organization that people enter and leave freely.

wealth: What people own.

white-collar crime: Crime committed by relatively affluent persons, often in the course of business activities.

world system: An approach that views development as involving an unequal exchange between core and periphery nations, with development at the former end of the chain coming at the cost of underdevelopment at the other end.

zero population growth: The point at which a modern population replaces itself without immigration—2.1 children per woman.

References

Abbott, Pamela, and Claire Wallace. 1997. *An introduction to sociology: Feminist perspectives*. London: Routledge.

Acker, Joan. 1992. Gendered institutions. *Contemporary Sociology*, 21:565–69.

Adam, Barbara, and Stuart Allen, eds. 1995. *Theorizing culture: An interdisciplinary critique after postmodernism*. New York: New York University Press.

Adams, Mary. 1998. *Marital status and happiness, 1972–1996*. Paper presented in the Colloquium Series. Department of Sociology, Virginia Polytechnic Institute and State University, Blacksburg, VA 24060-0137, September.

Adler, Freda, Gerhard O. W. Mueller, and William S. Laufer. 2004. *Criminology and the criminal justice system*. New York: McGraw-Hill.

Adler, Patricia A., and Peter Adler. 1989. The gloried self: The aggrandizement and the constriction of self. *Social Psychological Quarterly*, 52:299, 310.

Adler, Stephen J. 1991. Suits over sexual harassment prove difficult due to issue of definition. *The Wall Street Journal* (October 9):B1.

Agger, Ben. 1991. Critical theory, poststructuralism, postmodernism: Their sociological relevance. *Annual Review of Sociology*, 17:105–31.

Ahlburg, Dennis, and Carol J. De Vita. 1992. New realities of the American family. *Population Bulletin*, 47: No. 2.

Aizcorbe, Ana M., Arthur B. Kennickell, and Kevin B. Moore. 2003. Recent changes in U.S. family finances: Evidence from the 1998 and 2001 Survey of Consumer Finances. *Federal Reserve Bulletin*, 89 (January):1–32.

Allport, Gordon W. 1954. *The nature of prejudice*. Boston: Beacon Press.

Amato, Paul R., and Juliana M. Sobolewski. 2001. The effects of divorce and marital discord on adult children's psychological well-being. *American Sociological Review*, 66:900–21.

American Academy of Pediatrics. 2001. Childhood, adolescents, and television. *Pediatrics*, 107(2):423–26.

American Anthropological Association. 1997. *American Anthropological Association response to OMB Directive 15: Race and ethnic standards for federal statistics and administrative reporting*. Arlington, VA: American Anthropological Association.

American Sociological Association. 1989. Code of ethics. Washington, DC: American Sociological Association.

Amnesty International. 2004. *Starved of rights*. http://www.amnesty.org/library/Index/ENGASA 240032004?open&of =ENG-PRK.

Anderson, Elijah. 2001. Urban ethnography. In Neil J. Smelser and Paul B. Baltes, eds., *International encyclopedia of the social and behavioral sciences*. New York: Elsevier.

Anderson, Craig A., and Brad J. Bushman. 2002. The effects of media violence on society. *Science*, 295:2377–79.

Appenzeller, Tim. 2004. The case of the missing carbon. *National Geographic* (February):88–117.

Apple, Michael W. 1982. *Education and power*. London: Routledge & Kegan Paul.

Appy, Christian G. 1993. *Working-class war: American combat soldiers and Vietnam*. Chapel Hill: University of North Carolina Press.

Armas, Genaro C. 2003. Study: Rents up by one-third. Associated Press (September 9).

Aronson, Eliot. 1994. *The social animal*. New York: W. H. Freeman.

Arrillaga, Pauline. 2000. Putting polygamy on trial in Utah. *Washington Post* (December 8):A49.

Arrow, Kenneth, Samuel Bowles, and Steven Durlauf, eds. 2000. *Meritocracy and economic inequality.* Princeton, NJ: Princeton University Press.

Asch, Solomon. 1952. *Social psychology.* Englewood Cliffs, NJ: Prentice Hall.

Associated Press. 2003. Gay-rights group compares gay couples to others. *Washington Post* (May 18):A7.

Association of American Medical Colleges. 2003. http://www.aamc.org/data/facts/2003/2003 school.htm.

Atran, Scott. 2003. Genesis of suicide terrorism. *Science,* 299:1534–39.

Axinn, William G., and Jennifer S. Barber. 1997. Living arrangements and family formation attitudes in early adulthood. *Journal of Marriage and the Family,* 59:595–611.

Bachu, Amara. 1997. Fertility of American women: June 1995 (update). *Current Population Reports,* P20-499, Washington, DC: U.S. Bureau of the Census.

Baer, Ellen D. 1991. The feminist disdain for nursing. *New York Times* (February 23):17.

Baker, David P., and Deborah Perkins Jones. 1993. Creating gender equality: Cross-national gender stratification and mathematical performance. *Sociology of Education,* 66:91–103.

Baker, Stephen. 1993. The owners vs. the boss at Weirton Steel. *Business Week* (November 15):38.

Bales, Robert F. 1970. *Personality and interpersonal behavior.* New York: Holt, Rinehart and Winston.

Bandura, Albert. 1965. Influence of models' reinforcement contingencies on the acquisition of imitative responses. *Journal of Personality and Social Psychology,* 1:589–95.

Bandura, Albert. 1971. *Psychological modeling: Conflicting theories.* Chicago: Aldine-Atherton.

Bandura, Albert. 1973. *Aggression: A social learning analysis.* Englewood Cliffs, NJ: Prentice Hall.

Bane, Mary Jo. 1997. Welfare as we might know it. *The American Prospect,* No. 30 (January–February):47–53.

Bane, Mary Jo, and David T. Ellwood. 1994. *Welfare realities: From rhetoric to reform.* Cambridge, MA: Harvard University Press.

Bank, Lew, Marion S. Forgatch, Gerald R. Patterson, and Rebecca A. Fetrow. 1993. Parenting practices of single mothers: Mediators of negative contextual factors. *Journal of Marriage and the Family,* 55:371–84.

Barak, Gregg, ed. 1991. *Crimes by the capitalist state. An introduction to state criminality.* Albany: State University of New York Press.

Barnes, Jessica S., and Claudette Bennett. 2002. The Asian Population 2000. U.S. Census Bureau C2KBR/01-16. Washington, DC: U.S. Government Printing Office.

Barnet, Richard J., and John Cavanagh. 1994. *Global dreams: Imperial corporations and the new world order.* New York: Simon and Schuster.

Barringer, Felicity. 1993. Sex survey of American men finds 1% are gay. *New York Times* (April 15):A1, A9.

Barrow, Clyde W. 1990. *Universities and the capitalist state: Corporate liberalism and the reconstruction of American higher education, 1894–1928.* Madison: University of Wisconsin Press.

Bartol, Kathryn M., and David C. Martin. 1998. *Management.* 3rd ed. New York: McGraw-Hill.

Bartollas, Clemens. 2003. *Juvenile delinquency.* Boston: Allyn and Bacon.

Bass, Bernard M. 1981. *Stogdill's handbook of leadership.* New York: Free Press.

Baxter, Janeen. 1994. Is husband's class enough? Class location and class identity in the United States, Sweden, Norway, and Australia. *American Sociological Review,* 59:220–35.

Beck, E. M., Patrick Horan, and Charles Tolbert. 1980. Social stratification in industrial society: Further evidence for a structural alternative. *American Sociological Review,* 45:712–19.

Becker, Howard S. 1963. *Outsiders: Studies in the sociology of deviance.* New York: Free Press.

Beeghley, Leonard. 2000. *The structure of social stratification in the United States.* Boston. Allyn and Bacon.

Begley, Sharon. 2003. Scientifically, race is only skin deep and not very useful. *The Wall Street Journal* (August 1):B1.

Bell, Alan P., and Martin S. Weinberg. 1978. *Homosexualities: A study of diversity among men and women.* New York: Simon and Schuster.

Bell, Alan P., Martin S. Weinberg, and Sue K. Hammersmith. 1981. *Sexual preference: Its development in men and women.* Bloomington: Indiana University Press.

Belsky, Jay, and Michael Rovine. 1990. Patterns of marital change across the transition to parenthood: Pregnancy to three years postpartum. *Journal of Marriage and the Family,* 52:5–19.

Bem, Sandra. 1981. Gender schema theory: A cognitive account of sex typing. *Psychological Bulletin,* 88:354–64.

Bennett, Amanda. 1990. Quality programs may be shoddy stuff. *The Wall Street Journal* (October 4):B1.

Berberoglu, Berch. 1987. *The internationalization of capital: Imperialism and capitalist development on a world scale.* New York: Praeger.

Berger, Peter L. 1963. *Invitation to sociology.* Garden City, NY: Anchor Books.

Berger, Peter L. 1967. *The sacred canopy: Elements of a sociological theory of religion.* Garden City, NY: Doubleday.

Berger, Peter L. 1986. *The capitalist revolution.* New York: Basic Books.

Bergman, Mike. 2003. Women edge men in high school diplomas, breaking 13-year deadlock. *U.S. Department of Commerce News* (March 21). U.S. Census Bureau.

Berk, Richard A., and Phyllis J. Newton. 1985. Does arrest really deter wife battery? An effort to replicate the findings of the Minneapolis spouse abuse experiment. *American Sociological Review,* 50:253–62.

Berkowitz, Leonard. 1989. Frustration-aggression hypothesis: Examination and reformulation. *Psychological Bulletin,* 106:59–73.

Bernard, Jessie. 1987. *The female world from a global perspective.* Bloomington: Indiana University Press.

Berns, Nancy. 1999. "My problem and how I solved it": Domestic violence in women's magazines. *Sociological Quarterly,* 40(1):85–108.

Bertrand, Marianne, and Sendhil Mullainathan. 2003. Are Emily and Greg more employable than Lakisha and Jamal? A field experiment on labor market discrimination. *National Bureau of Economic Research.* Working Paper No. w9873.

Best, Steven, and Douglas Kellner. 1991. *Postmodern theory: Critical interrogations.* New York: Guilford Press.

Beylotte, Frank. 2003. Genes and behavior take center stage. *Psychological Science Agenda,* 16(3):14.

Bianchi, Suzanne M. 1999. Feminization and juvenilization of poverty: Trends, relative risks, causes, and consequences. *Annual Review of Sociology,* 25:307–33.

Biderman, Albert D., and James P. Lynch. 1991. *Understanding crime incidence statistics: Why the UCR diverges from the NCS.* New York: Springer-Verlag.

Bierstedt, Robert. 1950. An analysis of social power. *American Sociological Review,* 15:730–38.

Biersteker, Thomas J. 1987. *Multinationals, the state and control of the Nigerian economy.* Princeton, NJ: Princeton University Press.

Birdwhistell, Raymond L. 1970. *Kinesics and context.* Philadelphia: University of Pennsylvania Press.

Birkett, Dea. 1997. *Serpent in paradise: Among the people of the Bounty.* New York: Doubleday.

Bittman, Michael, Paula England, Liana Sayer, Nancy Folbre, and George Matheson. 2003. When does gender trump money? Bargaining and time in household work. *American Journal of Sociology,* 109(1):186–214.

Blackwell, Brenda Sims. 2000. Perceived sanction threats, gender, and crime: A test and elaboration of power-control theory. *Criminology,* 38(2):439–88.

Blasi, Joseph R. 1988. *Employee ownership: Revolution or rip-off?* Cambridge, MA: Ballinger.

Blau, Judith R., and Eric S. Brown. 2001. Du Bois and diasporic identity: The *Veil* and the *Unveiling* project. *Sociological Theory,* 19:219–33.

Blau, Peter M., and Otis Dudley Duncan. 1972. *The American occupational structure.* 2nd ed. New York: John Wiley.

Block, N. J., and Gerald Dworkin, eds. 1976. *The IQ controversy: Critical readings.* New York: Pantheon.

Bluhm, Carey, Thomas A. Widiger, and Gloria M. Miele. 1990. Interpersonal complementarity and individual differences. *Journal of Personality and Social Psychology,* 58:464–71.

Blum, Deborah. 1997. *Sex on the brain: The biological differences between men and women.* New York: Viking Penguin.

Blumer, Herbert. 1946. *Collective behavior.* In A. M Lee, ed., *New outline of the principles of sociology.* New York: Barnes & Noble.

Blumer, Herbert. 1958. Race prejudice as a sense of group position. *Pacific Sociological Review,* 1:3–7.

Blumer, Herbert. 1969. *Symbolic interaction: Perspective and method.* Englewood Cliffs, NJ: Prentice Hall.

Blumstein, Philip, and Pepper Schwartz. 1983. *American couples.* New York: Morrow.

Bobo, Lawrence. 1983. Whites' opposition to busing: Symbolic racism or realistic group conflict. *Journal of Personality and Social Psychology,* 45:1196–210.

Boesch, Christophe. 2003. Is culture a golden barrier between human and chimpanzee? *Evolutionary Anthropology,* 12:82–91.

Bok, Derek. 1993. *The cost of talent: How executives and professionals are paid and how it affects America.* New York: Free Press.

Bollen, Kenneth A., and Stephen J. Appold. 1993. National industrial structure and the global system. *American Sociological Review,* 58:283–301.

Bonacich, Edna, and John Modell. 1980. *The economic basis of ethnic solidarity.* Berkeley: University of California Press.

Bonczar, Thomas P., and Allen J. Beck. 1997. Lifetime likelihood of going to state or federal prison. NCJ-160092. Washington, DC: U.S. Department of Justice.

Bonger, William A. 1936. *An introduction to criminology.* London: Methuen.

Boodman, Sandra G. 2000. Second thoughts: Think the arrival of your first child changed your life? Just wait until number two joins the family. *Washington Post Health Magazine* (November 28):6.

Boswell, Terry. 1989. Colonial empires and the capitalist world-economy: A time series analysis of colonization, 1640–1960. *American Sociological Review,* 54:180–96.

Botsford, Louis W., Juan Carlos Castilla, and Charles H. Peterson. 1997. The management of fisheries and marine ecosystems. *Science,* 277:509–15.

Bouchard, Thomas J. 1994. Genes, environment, and personality. *Science,* 264:1700–01.

Bouchard, Thomas J., David T. Lykken, Matthew McGue, Nancy L. Segal, and Auke Tellegen. 1990. Sources of human psychological differences. The Minnesota study of twins reared apart. *Science,* 250:223–28.

Bowles, Samuel, and Herbert Gintis. 1976. *Schooling and capitalist America.* New York: Basic Books.

Bradshaw, York W. 1988. Reassessing economic dependency and uneven development: The Kenyan experience. *American Sociological Review,* 53:693–708.

Brand-Williams, Oralandar. 1997. Tiger's comments stir up racial-designation debate. *Detroit News* (April 25):Metro.

Brenner, Lynn. 2003. How did you do? *Parade: The Sunday Newspaper Magazine* (March 2):4–7.

Brown, Dee. 1971. *Bury my heart at Wounded Knee.* New York: Holt, Rinehart, and Winston.

Brown, Lester R., and Christopher Flavin. 1999. A new economy for a new century. In *State of the world 1999: A Worldwatch Institute report on progress toward a sustainable society.* New York: Norton.

Bumiller, Elisabeth. 2003. Why America has gay marriage jitters. *New York Times* (August 10):Week in Review.

Bumpass, Larry L., and Hsien-Hen Lu. 2000. Trends in cohabitation and implications for children's family contexts in the United States. *Population Studies,* 54:19–41.

Bumpass, Larry L., James A. Sweet, and Andrew Cherlin. 1991. The role of cohabitation in declining rates of marriage. *Journal of Marriage and the Family,* 53:913–27.

Bunzel, John H. 1988. Choosing freshmen: Who deserves an edge? *The Wall Street Journal* (February 1):22.

Burawoy, Michael. 1979. *Manufacturing consent.* Chicago: University of Chicago Press.

Burchard, Esteban Gonzalez, Elad Ziv, Natasha Coyle, Scarlett Lin Gomez, Hua Tang, Andrew J. Kartner, Joanna L. Mountain, Eliseo J. Perez-Stable, Dean Sheppard, and Neil Risch. 2003. The importance of race and ethnic background in biomedical research and clinical practice. *New England Journal of Medicine,* 348:1170–75.

Bureau of Justice Statistics. 2003. U.S. Department of Justice Office of Justice Programs. Available at http://www.ojp.usdoj.gov/bjs/correct.htm.

Bureau of Labor Statistics. 1997. *Labor force statistics from the Current Population Survey, October 1997, third quarter statistics.* Washington, DC: U.S. Department of Labor.

Burkett, Steven R., and Mervin White. 1974. Hellfire and delinquency: Another look. *Journal for the Scientific Study of Religion,* 13:455–62.

Burr, Chandler. 1996. *A separate creation: The search for the biological origins of sexual orientation.* New York: Hyperion.

Burstein, Paul. 1991. Legal mobilization as a social movement tactic: The struggle for equal employment opportunity. *American Journal of Sociology,* 96:1201–25.

Butterfield, Fox. 1986. Why Asians are going to the head of the class. *New York Times* (August 3):Education 18–23.

Buzawa, E. S., and C. G. Buzawa. 1990. *Domestic violence.* Newbury Park, CA: Sage.

Byfield, Joanne. 2001. Home is where the smarts are. *Report/Newsmagazine,* 28(23):43–44.

Cacioppo, John T., Gary G. Bernston, John F. Sheridan, and Martha K. McClintock. 2000. Multilevel integrative analyses of human behavior: Social neuroscience and the complementing nature of social and biological approaches. *Psychological Bulletin,* 126:829–43.

Campbell, Donald T. 1965. Ethnocentric and other altruistic motives. In Robert Levine, ed., *Nebraska symposium on motivation.* Lincoln: University of Nebraska Press.

Cantril, Hadley. 1941. *The psychology of social movements.* New York: John Wiley.

Caplow, Theodore, Howard M. Babr, Bruce A. Chadwick, Reuben Hill, and Margaret H. Williamson. 1982. *Middletown families: Fifty years of change and continuity.* Minneapolis: University of Minnesota Press.

Carmichael, Stokely, and Charles Hamilton. 1967. *Black power.* New York: Random House.

Carmona, Richard. 2003. A preventive defense. *Washington Post* (March 11):F1.

Casey, B. J. 2002. Windows into the human brain. *Science,* 296:1408–09.

Caspi, Avshalom, Joseph McClay, Terrie E. Moffitt, Jonathan Mill, Judy Martin, Ian W. Craig, Alan Taylor, and Richie Poulton. 2002. Role of genotype in the cycle of violence in maltreated children. *Science,* 297:851–54.

Cast, A. D., and P. J. Burke. 2002. A theory of self-esteem. *Social Forces,* 80(3):1041–68.

Catalyst. 2003. *Women in U.S. Corporate Leadership: 2003.* http://www.catalystwomen.org.

Centers for Disease Control. 2003. Health related hoaxes and rumors. Available at http://www.cdc.gov/ hoax_rumors.htm.

Cernkovich, Steven A., and Peggy Giordano. 1987. Family relationships and delinquency. *Criminology,* 25:295–319.

Cernkovich, Steven A., and Peggy Giordano. 1992. School bonding, race, and delinquency. *Criminology,* 30:261–91.

Chambliss, William J. 1973. The Saints and the Roughnecks. *Society,* 2 (November):24–31.

Chase-Dunn, Christopher. 1989. *Global formation: Structure of the world-economy.* Cambridge, MA: Blackwell.

Chase-Dunn, Christopher, and Thomas D. Hall. 1993. Comparing world-systems: Concepts and working hypotheses. *Social Forces,* 71:851–86.

Chatzky, Jean Sherman. 1992. A brief history of stock fads. *Forbes* (September 14):253–68.

Chen, Li-Hui, Susan P. Baker, Elisa R. Braver, and Guohua Li. 2000. Carrying passengers as a risk factor for crashes fatal to 16- and 17-year-old drivers. *Journal of the American Medical Association,* 283:1578–82.

Cherlin, Andrew. 1978. Remarriage as an incomplete institution. *American Journal of Sociology,* 84:634–50.

Cherlin, Andrew J. 1997. A reply to Glenn: What's most important in a family textbook. *Family Relations,* 46:209–11.

Cherlin, Andrew J. 2002. *Public and private families: An introduction.* New York: McGraw-Hill.

Chesnais, Jean-Claude. 1992. *The demographic transition: Stages, patterns and economic implications: A longitudinal study of sixty-seven countries.* Trans. Elizabeth and Philip Kreager. New York: Clarendon.

Chesney-Lind, Meda, and Randall G. Shelden. 1998. *Girls, delinquency, and juvenile justice.* Belmont, CA: West-Wadsworth.

Childe, V. Gordon. 1941. *Man makes himself.* London: Watts.

Chira, Susan. 1994. Study confirms worst fears on U.S. children. *New York Times* (April 12):A1, A11.

Chomsky, Noam. 1957. *Syntactic structures.* The Hague: Mouton.

Chomsky, Noam. 1980. *Rule and representations.* New York: Columbia University Press.

Clinard, Marshall B. 1990. *Corporate corruption: The abuse of power.* New York: Praeger.

Clinard, Marshall B., and Robert F. Meier. 1995. *Sociology of deviant behavior.* 9th ed. Fort Worth, TX: Harcourt Brace.

Clinard, Marshall B., and Peter C. Yeager. 1980. *Corporate crime.* New York: Free Press.

Cochran, John K., Mitchell B. Chamlin, Peter B. Wood, and Christine S. Sellers. 1999. Shame, embarrassment, and formal sanction threats. Extending the deterrence/rational choice model to academic dishonesty. *Sociological Inquiry,* 69(1):91–105.

Cohen, Albert K. 1955. *Delinquent boys.* New York: Free Press.

Cohen, Jean L., and Andrew Arato. 1992. *Civil society and political theory.* Cambridge, MA: MIT Press.

Cohen, Jere. 1980. Rational capitalism in Renaissance Italy. *American Journal of Sociology,* 85:1340–55.

Cole, Stephen. 1972. *The sociological method.* Chicago: Markham.

Coleman, James S., E. Q. Campbell, C. J. Hobson, J. McPartland, A. M. Mood, F. D. Weinfeld, and R. L. York. 1966. *Equality of educational opportunity.* Washington, DC: U.S. Government Printing Office.

Coleman, James W. 1987. Toward an integrated theory of white-collar crime. *American Journal of Sociology,* 93:406–39.

Coleman, Richard D., and Lee Rainwater. 1978. *Social standing in America.* New York: Basic Books.

Collins, Nancy L., and Stephen J. Read. 1990. Adult attachment, working models, and relationship quality in dating couples. *Journal of Personality and Social Psychology,* 58:644–63.

Collins, Randall. 1975. *Conflict sociology.* New York: Academic Press.

Collins, Randall. 1976. Review of "Schooling in capitalist America." *Harvard Educational Review,* 46:246–51.

Collins, Randall. 1977. Some comparative principles of educational stratification. *Harvard Educational Review,* 47:1–27.

Collins, Randall. 1979. *Credential society.* New York: Academic Press.

Collins, Randall. 1981. *Sociology since mid-century: Essays in theory cumulation.* New York: Academic Press.

Collins, Randall. 1988a. *Sociology of marriage and the family.* 2nd ed. Chicago: Nelson Hall.

Collins, Randall. 1988b. *Theoretical sociology.* San Diego: Harcourt Brace Jovanovich.

Collins, W. Andrew, Eleanor E. Maccoby, Laurence Steinber, E. Mavis Hetherington, and Marc H. Bornstein. 2000. Contemporary research on parenting: The case for nature *and* nurture. *American Psychologist,* 55:218–32.

Cooley, Charles Horton. 1902/1964. *Human nature and the social order.* New York: Scribner's.

Coontz, Stephanie. 1992. *The way we never were: American families and the nostalgia trap.* New York: Basic Books.

Cooper, Richard S., Jay. S. Kaufman, and Ryk Ward. 2003. Race and genomics. *New England Journal of Medicine,* 348:1166–70.

Copp, Terry, and Bill McAndrew. 1990. *Battle exhaustion: Soldiers and psychiatrists in the Canadian army, 1939–1945.* Montreal and Kingston: McGill-Queen's University Press.

Corcoran, Mary, Sandra K. Danziger, Ariel Kalil, and Kristin S. Seefeldt. 2000. How welfare reform is affecting women's work. *Annual Review of Sociology,* 26:241–69.

Cornish, Edward. 1993. 1993 as predicted in 1893: If they could see us now! *The Futurist* (May–June):41–42.

Coser, Lewis A. 1956. *The functions of social conflict.* New York: Free Press.

Coser, Lewis A. 1957. Social conflict and the theory of social change. *British Journal of Sociology,* 8:170–83.

Coughlin, Ellen K. 1988. Worsening plight of the "underclass" catches attention of researchers. *Chronicle of Higher Education* (March 30):A1.

Crenshaw, E. M., M. Christenson, and D. R. Oakey. 2000. Demographic transition in ecological focus. *American Sociological Review,* 65(3):371–91.

Crispell, Diane. 1993. Sex surveys: Does anyone tell the truth? *American Demographics,* 15 (July):9–10.

Crittenden, Ann. 2001. *The price of motherhood. Why the most important job in the world is still the least valued.* New York: Henry Holt and Company.

Crocker, Jennifer, and Rila Luhtanen. 1990. Collective self-esteem and ingroup bias. *Journal of Personality and Social Psychology,* 58:60–67.

Cross, Susan E., and Laura Madson. 1997. Models of the self: Self-construals and gender. *Psychological Bulletin,* 122:5–37.

Crosset, Todd W., J. Ptacek, M. A. McDonald, and J. R. Benedict. 1996. Male student-athletes and violence against women: A survey of campus judicial affairs offices. *Violence Against Women,* 2:163–79.

Crutchfield, Robert D., and Susan R. Pitchford. 1997. Work and crime: The effects of labor stratification. *Social Forces,* 76:93–118.

Dahrendorf, Ralf. 1958. Toward a theory of social conflict. *Journal of Conflict Resolution,* 2:170–83.

Dahrendorf, Ralf. 1959. *Class and class conflict in industrial society.* Stanford, CA: Stanford University Press.

Dandeker, Christopher. 1990. *Surveillance, power and modernity: Bureaucracy and discipline from 1700 to the present day.* New York: St. Martin's Press.

Daniels, Arlene Kaplan. 1987. Invisible work. *Social Problems,* 34:403–15.

Darnton, Nina. 1991. The pain of the last taboo. *Newsweek* (October 7):70–72.

Davidow, William H., and Michael S. Malone. 1993. *The virtual corporations: Structuring and revitalizing the corporation for the 21st century.* New York: Harper Business.

Davie, Maurice R. 1937. The patterns of urban growth. In George P. Murdock, ed., *Studies in the science of society*. New Haven, CT: Yale University Press.

Davies, James. 1962. Toward a theory of revolution. *American Sociological Review,* 27:5–19.

Davies, James. 1969. The *J*-curve of rising and declining satisfactions as a cause of some great revolutions and a contained revolution. In H. D. Graham and T. R. Gurr, eds., *The history of violence in America*. New York: Bantam.

Davies, James. 1974. The *J*-curve and power struggle theories of collective violence. *American Sociological Review,* 39:607–10.

Davis, Allison, B. B. Gardner, and M. R. Gardner. 1941. *Deep South*. Chicago: University of Chicago Press.

Davis, F. James. 1991. *Who is black? One nation's definition*. University Park: Pennsylvania State University Press.

Davis, James. 1982. Up and down opportunity's ladder. *Public Opinion*, 5 (June–July): 11–15ff.

Davis, Kingsley. 1945. The world demographic transition. *Annals of the American Academy of Political and Social Science,* 237:1–11.

Davis, Kingsley. 1949. *Human society*. New York: Macmillan.

Davis, Kingsley. 1951. Introduction. In William J. Goode, *Religion among the primitives*. New York: Free Press.

Davis, Kingsley. 1955. The origin and growth of urbanization in the world. *American Journal of Sociology,* 60:429–37.

Davis, Kingsley. 1959. The myth of functional analysis as a special method in sociology and anthropology. *American Sociological Review,* 24:757–72.

Davis, Kingsley. 1967. The urbanization of the human population. In *Cities*. New York: Knopf.

Davis, Kingsley. 1971. The world's population crisis. In Robert K. Merton and Robert A. Nisbet, eds., *Contemporary social problems,* 3rd ed. New York: Harcourt Brace Jovanovich.

Davis, Kingsley, and Wilbert Moore. 1945. Some principles of stratification. *American Sociological Review,* 10:242-49.

Davis, Nancy J., and Robert V. Robinson. 1988. Class identification of men and women in the 1970s and 1980s. *American Sociological Review,* 53:103–12.

Dawidowicz, Lucy S. 1975. *The war against the Jews 1933–1945*. New York: Holt, Rinehart, and Winston.

Dawson, R. J. M. 1995. The "unusual episode" data revisited. *Journal of Statistics Education* [Online], 3(3), http://www.amstat.org/publications/jse/v3n3/datasets.dawson.html.

DeBruine, Lisa. 2002. Facial resemblance enhances trust. *Proceedings of the Royal Society of London B,* 269:1307–12.

Deegan, Mary Jo. 1991. *Women in sociology: A bio-bibliographical sourcebook*. Westport, CT: Greenwood Press.

Deegan, Mary Jo. 2003. Textbooks, the history of sociology, and the sociological stock of knowledge. *Sociological Theory,* 21:298–305.

Deininger, Klaus, and Lyn Squire. 1996. A new data set measuring income inequality. *World Bank Economic Review,* 10(3):565–91.

DeMaris, Alfred, and K. Vaninadha Rao. 1992. Premarital cohabitation and subsequent marital stability in the United States: A reassessment. *Journal of Marriage and the Family,* 54:178–90.

Demos, Vasilikie. 1990. Black family studies in the *Journal of Marriage and the Family,* and the issue of distortion: A trend analysis. *Journal of Marriage and the Family,* 52:603–12.

Denton, Nancy A., and Douglas S. Massey. 1989. Racial identity among Caribbean Hispanics: The effect of double minority status on residential segregation. *American Sociological Review,* 54:790–808.

DeParle, Jason. 1992. Report, delayed months, says lowest income group grew sharply. *New York Times* (May 12):A7.

Devine, Patricia G. 1989. Stereotypes and prejudice: Their automatic and controlled components. *Journal of Personality and Social Psychology,* 56:518.

Dillman, Don A. 2000. *Mail and Internet surveys: The tailored design method.* 2nd ed. New York: John Wiley.

Dillman, Don A., and Lisa R. Carley-Baxter. 2001. *Structural determinants of mail survey response rates over a 12-year period, 1988–1999.* 2000 Proceedings of American Statistical Association Survey Methods Section, Alexandria, VA.

Dionne, E. J., Jr. 1980. Abortion poll: Not clear-cut. *New York Times* (August 10):A15.

Dipboye, Robert L. 1977. Alternative approaches to deindividualization. *Psychological Bulletin,* 84:1057–75.

Dixon, William J., and Terry Boswell. 1996. Dependency, disarticulation, and denominator effects: Another look at foreign capital penetration. *American Journal of Sociology,* 102:543–62.

Du Bois, W. E. B. 1903/1990. *The souls of black folk.* New York: Vintage.

Dugger, Celia W. 1992. U.S. study says Asian Americans face widespread discrimination. *New York Times* (February 29):1, 5.

Duncan, Greg. 1984. *Years of poverty, years of plenty.* Ann Arbor: Institute for Social Research, University of Michigan.

Duncan, Greg J. 1987. On the slippery slope. *American Demographics,* 9 (May):30–35.

Duncan, Greg J., Martha S. Hill, and Saul D. Hoffman. 1988. Welfare dependence within and across generations. *Science,* 239:467–71.

Duneier, Mitchell. 1992. *Slim's table.* Chicago: University of Chicago Press.

Dunn, Ashley. 1994. Southeast Asians highly dependent on welfare in U.S. *New York Times* (May 19):A1, A13.

Dunn, J. R., and M. V. Hayes. 2000. Social inequality, population health, and housing: A study of two Vancouver neighborhoods. *Social Science and Medicine,* 51(4):563–87.

Dunn, William. 1993. Educating diversity. *American Demographics,* 15 (April):38–43.

Durkheim, Émile. 1893/1964. *The division of labor in society.* New York: Free Press.

Durkheim, Émile, 1897/1951. *Suicide.* New York: Free Press.

Durkheim, Émile. 1912/1965. *The elementary forms of religious life.* New York: Free Press.

Durkin, Keith F., and Clifton D. Bryant. 1995. "Log on to sex": Some notes on the carnal computer and erotic cyberspace as an emerging research frontier. *Deviant Behavior,* 16:179–200.

Durr, Virginia Foster. 1985. *Outside the magic circle: The autobiography of Virginia Foster Durr.* Tuscaloosa: University of Alabama Press.

Eagly, A. H., M. C. Johannesen-Schmidt, and M. L. van Engen. 2003. Transformational, transactional, and laissez-faire leadership styles: A meta-analysis comparing women and men. *Psychological Bulletin,* 129(4):569–91.

Economist, The. 2000a. The disaffected. (December 23): 9.

Economist, The. 2000b. What the Internet cannot do. (August 19):11–12.

Edin, Kathryn. 2000. What do low-income single mothers say about marriage? *Social Problems,* 47(1):112–33.

Edwards, Richard. 1978. The social relations of production at the point of production. *Insurgent Sociologist,* 8:109–25.

Edwards, Richard. 1979. *Contested terrain.* New York: Basic Books.

Eichar, Douglas M. 1989. *Occupation and class consciousness in America.* New York: Greenwood Press.

Ekman, Paul, Wallace V. Friesen, and John Bear. 1984. The international language of gesture. *Psychology Today,* 18 (May): 64–67.

Ekman, Paul, Wallace V. Friesen, and Maureen O'Sullivan. 1988. Smiles when lying. *Journal of Personality and Social Psychology,* 54:414–20.

Elder, Glenn H., Jr. 1983. Families, kin, and the life course. In R. Parke, ed., *The family.* Chicago: University of Chicago Press.

Elder, Glenn H., Jr., and Elizabeth C. Clipp. 1988. Wartime losses and social bonding: Influences across 40 years in men's lives. *Psychiatry,* 51:177–97.

Elias, Marilyn. 1994. Poverty impacts children's IQ. *USA Today* (May 9):D1.

Ellyson, Steve I., John F. Dovidio, Randi L. Corson, and Debbie L. Vinicur. 1980. Visual dominance behavior in female dyads. *Social Psychology Quarterly,* 43:328–36.

Emerson, Richard M. 1962. Power-dependence relations. *American Sociological Review,* 27:31–41.

Engels, Friedrich. 1884/1902. *The origin of the family, private property, and the state.* Chicago: Kerr.

England, Paula. 1993. Work for pay and work at home: Women's double disadvantage. In Craig Calhoun and George Ritzer, eds., *Social Problems—Primis.* New York: McGraw-Hill. Revised version published 1997.

Environics Research Group Ltd. 1997. *The Environmental Monitor, 1997, Cycle 4.* Toronto: Environics.

Epstein, Edward J. 1973. *News from nowhere.* New York: Random House.

Erikson, Erik. 1968. *Identity: Youth and crisis.* New York: Norton.

Erikson, Kai T. 1962. Notes on the sociology of deviance. *Social Problems,* 9:307–14.

Erikson, Kai T. 1966. *Wayward Puritans: A study in the sociology of deviance.* New York: Wiley.

ESOP Association. 2003. ESOP facts and figures. Available at http://www .esopassociation.org/pubs/stats.html.

Espiritu, Yen Le. 1992. *Asian American panethnicity: Bridging institutions and identities.* Philadelphia: Temple University Press.

Etzioni, Amitai. 1975. *A comparative analysis of complex organizations.* New York: Free Press.

Ezzati, Majid, Alan D. Lopez, Anthony Rodgers, Stephen Vander Hoorn, and Christopher J. L. Murray. 2002. Selected major risk factors and global and regional burden of disease. *The Lancet,* 360:1347–1360.

Fagot, Beverly I., Mary D. Leinbach, and Cherie O'Boyle. 1992. Gender labeling, gender stereotyping, and parenting behaviors. *Developmental Psychology,* 28:225–30.

Faia, Michael A. 1989. Cultural materialism in the functionalist mode. *American Sociological Review,* 54:658–60.

Farnsworth, Clyde H. 1990. Report by World Bank sees poverty lessening by 2000 except in Africa. *New York Times* (July 16):A3.

Fassinger, Polly A. 1989. Becoming the breadwinner: Single mothers' reactions to changes in their paid work lives. *Family Relations,* 38:404–11.

Fay, R. E., Charles F. Turner, A. D. Klassen, and John H. Gagnon. 1989. Prevalence and patterns of same-gender contact among men. *Science,* 243:338–48.

Feingold, Alan. 1988. Matching for attractiveness in romantic partners and same-sex friends: A meta-analysis and theoretical critique. *Psychological Bulletin,* 104:226–35.

Feingold, Alan. 1990. Gender differences in effects of physical attractiveness on romantic attraction: A comparison across five research paradigms. *Journal of Personality and Social Psychology,* 59:981–93.

Feldman, Marcus W., Richard C. Lewontin, and Mary-Clare King. 2003. A genetic melting-pot. *Nature,* 424:374.

Feldman, Marcus W., Sarah P. Otto, and Freddy B. Christiansen. 2000. Genes, culture and inequality. In Kenneth Arrow, Samuel Bowles, and Steven Durlauf, eds., *Meritocracy and economic inequality.* Princeton, NJ: Princeton University Press.

Fennema, Meinhert. 1982. *International networks of banks and industry.* Boston: Martinius Nijhoff.

Ferree, Myra Marx. 1990. Beyond separate spheres: Feminism and family research. *Journal of Marriage and the Family,* 52: 866–84.

Ferree, Myra Marx, and Elaine J. Hall. 2000. Gender stratification and paradigm change. *American Sociological Review,* 65(3): 475–81

Fetissov, S. O., J. Hallman, L. Oreland, B. af Klinteberg, E. Grenback, A. Hulting, and T. Hokfelt. 2002. Autoantibodies against—α-MSH, ACTH and LHRH in anorexia and bulimia nervosa patients. *Proceedings of the National Academy of Sciences,* 99:17155–160.

Fiedler, Fred E., and Joseph E. Garcia. 1987. *New approaches to effective leadership: Cognitive resources and organizational performance.* New York: John Wiley.

Fields, Jason. 2003. Children's living arrangements and characteristics: March 2002. *Current Population Reports,* P20-547. Washington, DC: U.S. Census Bureau.

Fields, Jason, and Lynne M. Casper. 2001. America's families and living arrangements. *Current Population Reports: Population Characteristics,* P20-537. Washington, DC: U.S. Census Bureau.

Fields, Suzanne. 1993. Rape as sport: The culture is at the root. *Insight on the News,* 9 (May 3):19–20.

Fine, Gary Alan. 1993. The sad demise, mysterious disappearance, and glorious triumph of symbolic interactionism. *Annual Review of Sociology,* 19:61–87.

Finkelhor, David. 1979. *Sexually victimized children.* New York: Free Press.

Firebaugh, Glenn. 1992. Growth effects of foreign and domestic investment. *American Journal of Sociology,* 98:105–30.

Firebaugh, Glenn. 1996. Does foreign capital harm poor nations? New estimates based on Dixon and Boswell's measures of capital penetration. *American Journal of Sociology,* 102:563–75.

Firebaugh, Glenn, and Kevin Chen. 1995. Vote turnout of Nineteenth Amendment women: The enduring effect of disenfranchisement. *American Journal of Sociology,* 100(4):972–96.

Firebaugh, Glenn, and Kenneth E. Davis. 1988. Trends in anti-black prejudice, 1972–1984: Region and cohort effects. *American Journal of Sociology,* 94:251–72.

Fischer, Claude S., Michael Hout, Martin Sanchez Jankowski, Samuel R. Lucas, Ann Swidler, and Kim Voss. 1996. *Inequality by design: Cracking the bell curve myth.* Princeton, NJ: Princeton University Press.

Fisher, Bonnie S., Franels T. Cullen, and Michael G. Turner. 2000. *The sexual victimization of college women.* National Institute of Justice. Bureau of Justice Statistics.

Fitzgerald, Louise F. 1993. Sexual harassment. *American Psychologist,* 48:1070–76.

Fletcher, Michael A. 2002. Rocky start in "cyber" classrooms. *Washington Post* (February 26):A1.

Flynn, James R. 2000. IQ trends over time: Intelligence, race, and meritocracy. In Kenneth Arrow, Samuel Bowles, and Steven Durlauf, eds., *Meritocracy and economic inequality.* Princeton, NJ: Princeton University Press.

Ford, C. S., and F. A. Beach. 1951. *Patterns of sexual behavior.* New York: Harper & Row.

Foster, John Bellamy. 1999. Marx's theory of metabolic rift: Classical foundations for environmental sociology. *American Journal of Sociology,* 105(2):366–405.

Foster, Terry. 1997. Woods correctly pays tribute to his heritage, but still has much to learn as a minority trailblazer. *Detroit News* (June 12):Sports.

Fowler, Floyd J., Jr. 2001. *Survey research methods.* Thousand Oaks, CA: Sage.

Freud, Sigmund. 1930/1961. *Civilization and its discontents.* London: Hogarth.

Friedman, Andrew. 1977. *Industry and labor: Class struggle at work and monopoly capitalism.* New York: Macmillan.

Fuller, C. J. 1976. *The Nayars today.* Cambridge, MA: Cambridge University Press.

Furstenberg, Frank F., Jr., and Andrew J. Cherlin. 1991. *Divided families.* Cambridge, MA: Harvard University Press.

Gaertner, Lowell, and Chester A. Insko. 2000. Intergroup discrimination in the minimal group paradigm: Categorization, reciprocation, or fear? *Journal of Personality and Social Psychology,* 79:77–94.

Gaither, Avalaura L., and Eric C. Newburger. 2000. The emerging American voter: An examination of the increase in the black vote in November 1998. U.S. Census Bureau Population Division Working Paper No. 44. Washington, DC: U.S. Government Printing Office.

Gallup, George, Jr. 1997. Many women cite spousal abuse; job performance affected. *Gallup Poll.*

Gans, Herbert J. 1972. The positive functions of poverty. *American Journal of Sociology,* 78:275–89.

Gardner, Gary, and Payal Sampat. 1999. Forging a sustainable materials economy. In

State of the world 1999: A Worldwatch Institute report on progress toward a sustainable society. New York: Norton.

Gecas, Viktor, and Michael L. Schwalbe. 1983. Beyond the looking-glass self: Social structure and efficacy-based self-esteem. *Social Psychology Quarterly,* 46:77–88.

Gelles, Richard J., Murray A. Strauss, and John W. Harrop. 1988. Has family violence decreased? *Journal of Marriage and the Family,* 50:286–91.

Gerald, Debra E., and William J. Hussar. 2002. *Projections of education statistics to 2012.* NCES 2002–030. Washington, DC: U.S. Department of Education, National Center for Education Statistics. Available at http://nces.ed.gov/ pubs2002/2002030.pdf.

Gerbner, George, Larry Gross, Michael F. Eleey, Marilyn Jackson-Beeck, Suzanne Jeffries-Fox, and Nancy Signorielli. 1978. Cultural indicators: Violence profile no. 9. *Journal of Communication,* 28:176–207.

Geschwender, James A. 1964. Social structure and the Negro revolt: An examination of some hypotheses. *Social Forces,* 43:248–56.

Gibbs, Jack P. 1989. *Control: Sociology's central notion.* Urbana: University of Illinois Press.

Giddens, Anthony. 1973. *The class structure of the advanced societies.* New York: Harper & Row.

Giddens, Anthony. 1985. *A contemporary critique of historical materialism.* Vol. 2: *The nation-state and violence.* Berkeley: University of California Press.

Gittleman, Maury, and Mary Joyce. 1995. Earnings mobility in the United States, 1967–91. *Monthly Labor Review,* September 3–11.

Glassman, Ronald M., William H. Swatos Jr., and Paul L. Rosen, eds. 1987. *Bureaucracy against democracy and socialism.* Westport, CT: Greenwood Press.

Glenn, Norval D. 1992. What does family mean? *American Demographics,* 14 (June): 30–37.

Glenn, Norval D. 1997. A critique of twenty family and marriage and family textbooks. *Family Relations,* 46:197–208.

Glenn, Norval D., and C. N. Weaver. 1981. The contribution of marital happiness to global happiness. *Journal of Marriage and the Family,* 43:161–68.

Glenn, Norval D., and Charles N. Weaver. 1988. The changing relationship of marital status to reported happiness. *Journal of Marriage and the Family,* 50:317–24.

Goffman, Erving. 1959. *The presentation of self in everyday life.* Garden City, NY: Doubleday.

Goffman, Erving. 1961a. *Encounters.* Indianapolis: Bobbs-Merrill.

Goffman, Erving. 1961b. *Asylums: Essays on the social situation of mental patients and other inmates.* Garden City, NY: Anchor Books.

Goldberg, Jeffrey. 2003. The unknown: The C.I.A. and the Pentagon take another look at Al Qaeda and Iraq. *The New Yorker* (February 10):40–47.

Goldhagen, Daniel Jonah. 1996. *Hitler's willing executioners: Ordinary Germans and the Holocaust.* New York: Knopf.

Goldin-Meadow, Susan, and Carolyn Mylander. 1984. Gestural communication in deaf children. *Monographs of the Society for Research in Child Development,* 49, no. 207.

Goldstein, Sidney. 1992. Profile of American Jewry: Insights from the 1990 National Jewish Population Survey. In *American Jewish Yearbook 1992.* New York: American Jewish Committee.

Goldstone, Jack A. 1991. *Revolution and rebellion in the early modern world.* Berkeley: University of California Press.

Goleman, Daniel. 1992. Family rituals may promote better emotional adjustment. *New York Times* (March 11):B6.

Goodall, Jane. 1990. *Through a window: My thirty years with the chimpanzees of Gombe.* Boston: Houghton Mifflin.

Goode, William J. 1959. The theoretical importance of love. *American Sociological Review,* 24:38–47.

Goode, William J. 1972. The place of force in human society. *American Sociological Review,* 37:507–19.

Gordon, Milton M. 1964. *Assimilation in American life: The role of race, religion, and national origins.* New York: Oxford University Press.

Gordon, Suzanne. 1997. *Life support: Three nurses on the front lines.* Boston: Little, Brown.

Gornick, Vivian, and B. K. Moran. 1971. *Women in sexist society.* New York: New American Library.

Gottdiener, Mark, and Ray Hutchison. 2000. *The new urban sociology.* New York: McGraw-Hill.

Gove, Walter R. 1987. Sociobiology misses the mark: An essay on why biology but not sociobiology is very relevant to sociology. *American Sociologist,* 18:258–77.

Gove, Walter R. 1994. Why we do what we do: A biopsychosocial theory of human motivation. *Social Forces,* 73:363–94.

Gove, Walter R., Michael Hughes, and Michael Geerken. 1985. Are Uniform Crime Reports a valid indicator of the index crimes? An affirmative answer with minor qualifications. *Criminology,* 23: 451–500.

Gove, Walter R., Michael Hughes, and Carolyn Briggs Style. 1983. Does marriage have positive effects on the psychological well-being of the individual? *Journal of Health and Social Behavior,* 24(June):122–31.

Gove, Walter R., Carolyn Briggs Style, and Michael Hughes. 1990. The effect of marriage on the well-being of adults. *Journal of Family Issues,* 11(March):4–35.

Grant, Don Sherman, and Ramiro Martinez. 1997. Crime and the restructuring of the U.S. economy: A reconsideration of the class linkages. *Social Forces,* 75:769–99.

Gray, Bradford H. 1991. *The profit motive and patient care: The changing accountability of doctors and hospitals.* Cambridge, MA: Harvard University Press.

Greenwood, Peter W. 1982. *Selective incapacitation.* Santa Monica, CA: Rand Corporation.

Grimes, Michael D. 1991. *Class in twentieth-century American sociology: An analysis of theories and measurement strategies.* New York: Praeger.

Grimsley, Kirstin Downey. 1997. Avon calling . . . on a man: Board bypasses staff, names former Duracell chief next CEO. *Washington Post* (December 12):G1.

Groves, Robert M., Don A. Dillman, John Eltinge, and Roderick J. A. Little, eds. 2002. *Survey nonresponse.* New York: Wiley-Interscience.

Gubrium, Jaber F., and James A. Holstein. 1990. *What is family?* Mountain View, CA: Mayfield.

Guida, Nancy. 2003. Despite women's gains in business, their representation on America's corporate boards barely improves. *Catalyst* press release, December 4.

Guo, G. 1998. The timing of the influences of cumulative poverty on children's cognitive ability and achievement. *Social Forces,* 77(1):257–87.

Gurr, Ted R. 1970. *Why men rebel.* Princeton, NJ: Princeton University Press.

Hagan, John. 1989. *Structural criminology.* New Brunswick, NJ: Rutgers University Press.

Hagan, John, and Alberto Palloni. 1999. Sociological criminology and the mythology of Hispanic immigration and crime. *Social Problems,* 46(4):617–32.

Hall, Edward T. 1966. *The hidden dimension.* Garden City, NY: Doubleday.

Hall, John R. 1988. Social organization and pathways of commitment: Types of communal groups, rational choice theory, and the Kanter thesis. *American Sociological Review,* 53:679–92.

Halpern, Diane F. 1992. *Sex difference in cognitive abilities.* 2nd ed. Hillsdale, NJ: Erlbaum.

Hamper, Ben Rivethead. 1991. *Tales from the assembly line.* New York: Warner.

Haney, C., C. Banks, and Phillip Zimbardo. 1973. Interpersonal dynamics in a simulated prison. *International Journal of Criminology and Penology,* 1:69–97.

Hareven, Tamara K. 1982. *Family time and industrial time.* New York: Cambridge University Press.

Harrington, Michael. 1976. *The twilight of capitalism.* New York: Simon and Schuster.

Harris, Chauncey D., and Edward L. Ullman. 1945. The nature of cities. *Annals of the*

American Academy of Political and Social Science, 242:7–17.

Harris, Judith Rich. 1998. *The nurture assumption: Why children turn out the way they do.* New York: Free Press.

Hartmann, Heidi, and Vicky Lovell. 2003. *The gender wage gap: Progress of the 1980s fails to carry through.* Institute for Women's Policy Research IWPR #C353.

Hasselmann, K., M. Latif, G. Hooss, C. Azar, O. Edenhofer, C. C. Jaeger, O. M. Johannessen, C. Kemfert, M. Welp, and A. Wokaun. 2003. The challenge of long-term climate change. *Science,* 302:1923–25.

Haub, Carl. 2003. *World population data sheet.* Washington, DC: Population Reference Bureau.

Hauser, Marc D., Noam Chomsky, and W. Tecumseh Fitch. 2002. The faculty of language: What is it, who has it, and how did it evolve? *Science,* 298:1569–79.

Haynie, D. L. 2001. Delinquent peers revisited: Does network structure matter? *American Journal of Sociology,* 106(4):1013–57.

Haynie, Dana L., and Bridget K. Gorman. 1999. A gendered context of opportunity: Determinants of poverty across urban and rural labor markets. *Sociological Quarterly,* 40(2):177–97.

Hechter, Michael. 1987. *Principles of group solidarity.* Los Angeles: University of California Press.

Hechter, Michael. 1995. Symposium on prediction in the social sciences: Introduction: Reflections on historical prophecy in the social sciences. *American Journal of Sociology,* 100(6):1520–27.

Heckathorn, Douglas D. 1988. Collective sanctions and the emergence of prisoner's dilemma. *American Journal of Sociology,* 94:535–62.

Heckathorn, Douglas D. 1990. Collective sanctions and compliance norms: A formal theory of group-mediated social control. *American Sociological Review,* 55:366–84.

Heilbroner, Robert. 1993. *21st century capitalism.* New York: Norton.

Hepworth, Joseph T., and Stephen G. West. 1988. Lynchings and the economy: A time-series reanalysis of Hovland and Sears (1940). *Journal of Personality and Social Psychology,* 55:239–47.

Herman, Judith, and Lisa Hirschman. 1981. Families at risk for father-daughter incest. *American Journal of Psychiatry,* 138:967–70.

Herrnstein, Richard J., and Charles Murray. 1994. *The bell curve: Intelligence and class structure in American life.* New York: Free Press.

Hersey, Paul, and Kenneth H. Blanchard. 1988. *Management of organizational behavior: Utilizing human resources.* Englewood Cliffs, NJ: Prentice Hall.

Hertsgaard, Mark. 1998. *Earth odyssey: Around the world in search of our environmental future.* New York: Broadway Books.

Hewitt, John P. 2003. *Self and society.* Boston: Allyn and Bacon.

Hill, Martha S., and W. Jean Young. 1999. How has the changing structure of opportunities affected transitions to adulthood? In Alan Booth, Ann C. Crouter, and Michael J. Shanahan, eds., *Transitions to adulthood in a changing economy: No work, no family, no future?* Westport, CT: Praeger.

Hilts, Philip J. 1994. 6% of pregnant women say they were battered. *New York Times* (March 4):A8.

Hirschi, Travis. 1969. *Causes of delinquency.* Berkeley: University of California Press.

Hirschi, Travis, and Rodney Stark. 1969. Hellfire and delinquency. *Social Problems,* 17:202–13.

Hirschman, Charles, and Morrison G. Wong. 1986. The extraordinary educational attainment of Asian Americans: A search for historical evidence and explanations. *Social Forces,* 65:1–27.

Hodge, Robert, and Donald Treiman. 1968. Class identification in the United States. *American Journal of Sociology,* 73:535–47.

Hoebel, E. A. 1958. *Man in the primitive world.* 2nd ed. New York: McGraw-Hill.

Hoecker-Drysdale, Susan. 1994. *Harriet Martineau: First woman sociologist.* New York: Berg Press.

Hoffman, Curt, and Nancy Hurst. 1990. Gender stereotypes: Perception or rationalization? *Journal of Personality and Social Psychology,* 58: 197–208.

Holden, Constance. 2002. Last word on El Dorado. *Science,* 297:333.

Hondagneu-Sotelo, Pierrette. 2001. *Domestica: Immigrant workers cleaning and caring in the shadows of affluence.* Berkeley: University of California Press.

Horowitz, Carl. 1994. What's environmental racism? *Investor's Business Daily* (March 2):1–2.

Horowitz, Helen Lefkowitz. 1987. *Campus life: Undergraduate cultures from the end of the eighteenth century to the present.* New York: Knopf.

Hostetler, John A. 1980. *Amish society.* Baltimore: Johns Hopkins University Press.

House, James. 1995. Introduction: Social structure and personality: Past, present, and future. In Karen S. Cook, Gary Alan Fine, and James S. House, eds., *Sociological perspectives on social psychology.* Boston: Allyn and Bacon.

Hoyt, Homer. 1939. *The structure and growth of residential neighborhoods in American cities.* Washington, DC: Federal Housing Administration.

Huesmann, L. Rowell, Jessica Moise-Titus, Cheryl-Lynn Podolski, and Leonard D. Eron. 2003. Longitudinal relations between children's exposure to TV violence and their aggressive and violent behavior in young adulthood: 1977–1992. *Developmental Psychology,* 39(2):201–21.

Hughes, Michael. 1980. The fruits of cultivation analysis: A reexamination of some effects of television watching. *Public Opinion Quarterly,* 44:289–302.

Hughes, Michael. 1989. Parenthood and psychological well-being among the formerly married: Are children the primary source of psychological distress. *Journal of Family Issues,* 10:163–81.

Hughes, Michael. 1997. Symbolic racism, old fashioned racism, and whites' opposition to affirmative action. In Steven A. Tuch and Jack K. Martin, eds., *Racial attitudes in the 1990s: Continuity and change.* Westport, CT: Praeger.

Hull, R. Bruce, and David P. Robertson. 2000. Which nature? In Paul H. Gobster and R. Bruce Hull, eds., *Restoring nature: Perspectives from the social sciences and humanities.* Washington, DC: Island Press.

Hurst, Charles E. 1998. *Social inequality: Forms, causes, and consequences.* Boston: Allyn and Bacon.

Hutter, Mark. 1998. *The changing family.* 3rd ed. Boston: Allyn and Bacon.

Hyde, Janet Shibley. 1991. Half the human experience: The psychology of women. Lexington, MA: Heath.

Hyde, Janet S., Elizabeth Fennema, and Susan J. Lamon. 1990. Gender differences in mathematics performance: A meta-analysis. *Psychological Bulletin,* 107:139–55.

Hyman, Herbert H., and Eleanor Singer. 1968. Introduction. In H. H. Hyman and E. Singer, eds., *Readings in reference group theory and research.* New York: Free Press.

Iceland, John, Daniel H. Weinberg, and Erika Steinmetz. 2002. *Racial and ethnic residential segregation in the United States: 1980–2000.* U.S. Census Bureau, Series CENSR-3. Washington, DC: U.S. Government Printing Office.

Immerwahr, John. 1999. Waiting for a signal: Attitudes toward global warming. Available at http://www.agu.org.

Inglehart, Ronald, et al. 2000. *World values surveys and European values surveys, 1981–1984, 1990–1993, and 1995–1997* [Computer file]. ICPSR version. Ann Arbor, MI: Institute for Social Research.

International Labor Organization. 2001. *World employment report 2001: Life at work in the information economy.* International Labor Organization Web site, http://www.ilo.org.

International Telecommunication Union. 2003. *World telecommunication development report 2003: Access indicators for the information society.* Geneva, Switzerland: International Telecommunication Union. Summary available at http://www.itu.int/ITU-D/ict/publications/wtdr_03/.

Intons-Peterson, Margaret Jean. 1988. *Gender concepts of Swedish and American youth.* Hillsdale, NJ: Erlbaum.

Jackendoff, Ray. 2002. *Foundations of language: Brain, meaning, grammar, evolution.* New York: Oxford University Press.

Jackman, Mary R., and Robert W. Jackman. 1983. *Class awareness in the United States.* Berkeley: University of California Press.

Jackson, Walter A. 1990. *Gunnar Myrdal and America's conscience: Social engineering and racial liberalism, 1938–1987.* Chapel Hill: University of North Carolina Press.

Jacobs, David, and Ronald E. Helms. 1996. Toward a political model of incarceration: A time-series examination of multiple explanations for prison admission rates. *American Journal of Sociology,* 102:323–57.

Jacobs, David, and Ronald E. Helms. 1997. Testing coercive explanations for order: The determinants of law enforcement strength over time. *Social Forces,* 75:1361–92.

Jaffee, David. 2001. *Organization theory: Tension and change.* New York: McGraw-Hill.

Janis, Irving. 1972. *Victims of groupthink.* Boston: Houghton Mifflin.

Janis, Irving L. 1982. *Groupthink.* 2nd ed. Boston: Houghton Mifflin.

Janis, Irving L. 1989. *Crucial decisions: Leadership in policymaking and crisis management.* New York: Free Press.

Jargowsky, Paul A. 1997. *Poverty and place.* New York: Russell Sage Foundation.

Jeffords, James M., and Tom Daschle. 2001. Political issues in the genome era. *Science,* 291:1249–51.

Jencks, Christopher. 1992. *Rethinking social policy: Race, poverty, and the underclass.* Cambridge: Harvard University Press.

Jencks, Christopher, and Meredith Phillips. 1998. *The black-white test score gap.* Washington, DC: Brookings Institution Press.

Jenkins, J. Craig. 1985. *The politics of insurgency: The farm worker movement in the 1960s.* New York: Columbia University Press.

Jensen, Gary F., and Dean G. Rojek. 1992. *Delinquency and youth crime.* Prospect Heights, IL: Waveland.

Johansson, S., and O. Nygren. 1991. The missing girls of China. *Population and Development Review,* 17:35–52.

Johnson, Hayes. 1988. Hispanics, blacks are dropping out. *USA Today* (March 23):D3.

Johnson, James Weldon. 1927/1989. *The autobiography of an ex-coloured man.* New York: Vintage Books.

Johnson, Jeffrey G., Patricia Cohen, Elizabeth M. Smailes, Stephanie Kasen, and Judith S. Brook. 2002. Television viewing and aggressive behavior during adolescence and adulthood. *Science,* 295:2468–71.

Johnson, Miriam. 1993. Functionalism and feminism: Is estrangement necessary? In Paula England, ed., *Theory on gender/feminism on gender.* New York: Aldine de Gruyter.

Johnson, Robert. 1990. Heavenly gifts: Preaching a gospel of acquisitiveness, a showy sect prospers. *Wall Street Journal* (December 11):A1, A6.

Johnston, David Cay. 2003. Very richest's share of wealth grew even bigger, data show. *New York Times* (June 26):A1.

Jones, Arthur F., and Daniel H. Weinberg. 2000. The changing shape of the nation's income distribution. *Current Population Reports* P60-204 (June). Washington, DC: U.S. Census Bureau.

Jones, Jacqueline. 1992. *The dispossessed: America's underclasses from the Civil War to the present.* New York: Basic Books.

Kain, Edward L. 1984. Surprising singles. *American Demographics,* 6 (August): 16–19ff.

Kain, Edward L. 1990. *The myth of family decline: Understanding families in a world of rapid social change.* Lexington, MA: Lexington Books.

Kalish, Susan. 1994. International migration: New findings on magnitude, importance. *Population Today,* 22:1–3.

Kamolnick, Paul. 1988. *Classes: A Marxist critique.* Dix Hills, NY: General Hall.

Kanter, Rosabeth M. 1968. Commitment and social organization: A study of commitment mechanisms in utopian communities. *American Sociological Review,* 46:141–58.

Keister, Lisa A., and Stephanie Moller. 2000. Wealth inequality in the United States. *Annual Review of Sociology,* 26:63–81.

Kendall-Tackett, Kathleen A., Linda Meyer Williams, and David Finkelhor. 1993. Impact of sexual abuse on children: A review and synthesis of recent empirical studies. *Psychological Bulletin,* 113:164–80.

Kennedy, Donald. 2002. Science, terrorism, and natural disasters. *Science,* 295:405.

Kennedy, Edward M. 2002. In *Out of reach: America's growing wage-rent disparity.* National Low Income Housing Coalition.

Kennickell, Arthur B. 2000. An examination of changes in the distribution of wealth from 1989 to 1998. Evidence from the Survey of Consumer Finances. *Summary 9* (Fall) Working Paper No. 307, http://www.levy.org/docs/summary/sumfall00.html.

Kennickell, Arthur B. 2003. A rolling tide: Changes in the distribution of wealth in the U.S., 1989–2001. Board of Governors of the Federal Reserve System (March 3). Available at http://www.federalreserve.gov/pubs/oss/ oss2/scfindex.html.

Kerbo, Harold. 2003. *Social stratification and inequality: Class conflict in historical, comparative, and global perspective.* 5th ed. New York: McGraw-Hill.

Kertzer, David. 1991. Household history and sociological theory. *Annual Review of Sociology,* 17:155–79.

Kessler, Ronald C., Amanda Sonnega, Evelyn Bromet, Michael Hughes, and Christopher B. Nelson. 1995. Posttraumatic stress disorder in the National Comorbidity Survey. *Archives of General Psychiatry,* 52: 1048–60.

Kessler-Harris, Alice. 1990. *A woman's wage: Historical meanings and social consequences.* Lexington: University Press of Kentucky.

Kiecolt, K. Jill. 1994. Stress and the decision to change oneself: A theoretical model. *Social Psychology Quarterly,* 57:49–63.

Kilborn, Peter T. 1992. Sad distinction for the Sioux: Homeland is no. 1 in poverty. *New York Times* (September 20):1, 14.

Kim, Jae-On. 1987. Social mobility, status inheritance, and structural constraints: Conceptual and methodological considerations. *Social Forces,* 65:783–805.

Kinder, Donald R., and Lynn M. Sanders. 1996. *Divided by color: Racial politics and democratic ideals.* Chicago: University of Chicago Press.

Kinder, Donald R., and David O. Sears. 1981. Prejudice and politics. Symbolic racism versus racial threats to the good life. *Journal of Personality and Social Psychology,* 40:414–31.

Kinsey, Alfred C., Wardell B. Pomeroy, and Clyde E. Martin. 1948. *Sexual behavior in the human male.* Philadelphia: Saunders.

Kirkpatrick, R. C. 2000. The evolution of human homosexual behavior. *Current Anthropology,* 41(3):385–413.

Kitson, Gay C., and William M. Holmes. 1992. *Portrait of divorce: Adjustment to marital breakdown.* New York: Guilford.

Klass, Perri. 1987. When the doctor-patient relationship breaks down. *Discover,* 8(March):16.

Klaus, Patsy A. 2002. *Crime and the nation's households, 2000.* NCJ-194107.Washington, DC: U.S. Department of Justice.

Klein, Katherine J. 1987. Employee stock ownership and employee attitudes: A test of three models. *Journal of Applied Psychology,* 72:319–32.

Klineberg, Otto. 1986, SPSSI and race relations in the 1950s and after. *Journal of Social Issues,* 42:53–59.

Kluckhohn, Clyde. 1960. *Mirror for man.* Greenwich, CT: Fawcett.

Knottnerus, J. David. 1991. Status attainment's image of society: Individual factors, structural effect, and the transformation of the class structure. *Sociological Spectrum,* 11:147–76.

Kohlberg, Lawrence. 1966. A cognitive-developmental analysis of children's sex-role concepts and attitudes. In Eleanor F. Maccoby, ed., *The development of sex differences.* Stanford, CA: Stanford University Press.

Kohlberg, Lawrence. 1969. Stage and sequence: The cognitive-developmental approach to socialization. In D. A. Goslin, ed., *Handbook of socialization theory and research*. Chicago: Rand McNally.

Kohlberg, Lawrence, and D. Z. Ullian. 1974. Stages in the development of psychosexual concepts and attitudes. In R. C. Friedman, R. N. Richart, and R. L. Van de Wiele, eds., *Sex differences in behavior*. New York: John Wiley.

Kolbert, Elizabeth. 1991. Sexual harassment at work is pervasive, survey suggests. *New York Times* (October 11):A1, A11.

Konner, Melvin. 1993. *Medicine at the crossroads: The crisis in health care*. New York: Pantheon.

Kornhauser, William. 1959. *The politics of mass society*. New York: Free Press.

Koss, Mary P., and J. A. Gaines. 1993. The prediction of sexual aggression by alcohol use, athletic participation and fraternity affiliation. *Journal of Interpersonal Violence*, 8:94–108.

Koss, Mary, Christine A. Gidycz, and Nadine Wisniewski. 1987. The scope of rape: Incidence and prevalence of sexual aggression and victimization in a national sample of higher education students. *Journal of Consulting and Clinical Psychology*, 55:162–70.

Krasikov, Sana. 2001. Group recalculates living wage. *Cornell Daily Sun* (March 12).

Kraut, Robert, and Sara Kiesler. 2003. The social impact of Internet use. *Psychological Science Agenda*, 16(3):8–11.

Kuhn, Manford. 1964. Major trends in symbolic interaction theory in the past twenty-five years. *Sociological Quarterly*, 5:61–84.

Kurdek, Lawrence A. 1993. The allocation of household labor in gay, lesbian, and heterosexual married couples. *Journal of Social Issues*, 49:127–39.

Kuttner, Robert. 1994. Pat Moynihan's blarney on health care. *Business Week* (February 14):18.

LaFree, Gary. 1999. Declining violent crime rates in the 1990s: Predicting crime booms and busts. *Annual Review of Sociology*, 25:145–68.

Lane, Charles. 2003. Ruling is landmark victory for gay rights. *Washington Post* (June 27):A1.

Langan, Patrick A., and David J. Levin. 2002. *Recidivism of prisoners released in 1994*.

NCJ-193427. Washington, DC: U.S. Department of Justice.

Lantz, Paula M., James S. House, James M. Lepkowski, David R. Williams, Richard P. Mero, and Jieming Chen. 1998. Socioeconomic factors, health behaviors, and mortality: Results from a nationally representative prospective study of U.S. adults. *Journal of the American Medical Association*, 279(21):1703–708.

Lareau, Annette. 2002. Invisible inequality: Social class and childrearing in black families and white families. *American Sociological Review*, 67(5):747–76.

Lareau, Annette. 2003. *Unequal childhoods: Class, race, and family life*. Berkeley: University of California Press.

Larson, Jan. 1992. Understanding stepfamilies. *American Demographics*, 14 (July):36–40.

Laslett, Peter. 1974. *Household and family in past time*. New York: Cambridge University Press.

Laslett, Peter. 1976. Societal development and aging. In R. Binstock and E. Shanas, eds., *Handbook of aging and the social sciences*. New York: Van Nostrand/Reinhold.

Lasswell, Harold. 1936. *Politics: Who gets what, when and how*. New York: McGraw-Hill.

Lauer, Robert H., and Jeanette C. Lauer. 2000. *Marriage and family: The quest for intimacy*. New York: McGraw-Hill.

Laumann, Edward O., John H. Gagnon, Robert T. Michael, and Stuart Michaels. 1994. *The social organization of sexuality: Sexual practices in the United States*. Chicago: University of Chicago Press.

Lawler, Edward J., Cecilia Ridgeway, and Barry Markovsky. 1993. Structural social psychology and the micro-macro problem. *Sociological Theory*, 11:269–90.

Lawler, Edward J., and Jeongkoo Yoon. 1993. Power and the emergence of commitment behavior in negotiated exchange. *American Sociological Review*, 58:465–81.

Leary, Mark R., and Robin M. Kowalski. 1990. Impression management: A literature review and two-component model. *Psychological Bulletin*, 107:34–47.

Le Bon, Gustav. 1896. *The crowd: A study of the popular mind*. London: Ernest Benn.

Lehman, Edward W. 1988. The theory of the state versus the state of theory. *American Sociological Review,* 53:807–23.

Leitenberg, H., and H. Saltzman. 2000. A statewide survey of age at first intercourse for adolescent females and age of their male partners: Relation to other risk behaviors and statutory rape implications. *Archives of Sexual Behavior,* 29(3):203–15.

Lemert, Charles. 2002. *Social things.* Lanham, MD: Rowman & Littlefield.

Lemert, Edwin M. 1951. *Social pathology: A systematic approach to the theory of socio- pathic behavior.* New York: McGraw-Hill.

Lemert, Edwin M. 1972. *Human deviance, social problems and social control.* 2nd ed. Englewood Cliffs, NJ: Prentice Hall.

Lengermann, Patricia Madoo, and Jill Niebrugge-Brantley. 2000a. Early women sociologists and classical sociological the- ory: 1830–1930. In George Ritzer, *Classi- cal sociological theory.* New York: McGraw-Hill.

Lengermann, Patricia Madoo, and Jill Niebrugge-Brantley. 2000b. Contemporary feminist theory. In George Ritzer, *Sociologi- cal theory.* New York: McGraw-Hill.

Lenski, Gerhard E. 1966. *Power and privilege.* New York: McGraw-Hill.

Lenski, Gerhard E., and Jean Lenski. 1987. *Human societies: An introduction to macrosociology.* 5th ed. New York: McGraw-Hill.

LeVay, Simon. 1991. A difference in hypo- thalmic structure between heterosexual and homosexual men. *Science,* 253:1034–37.

LeVay, Simon. 1996. *Queer science: The use and abuse of research into homosexuality.* Cambridge, MA: MIT Press.

Lewin, Kurt, Ronald Lippitt, and Ralph K. White. 1939. Patterns of aggressive behav- ior in experimentally created "social cli- mates." *Journal of Social Psychology,* 10:271–99.

Lewis, Oscar. 1966. *La vida: A Puerto Rican family in the culture of poverty, San Juan and New York.* New York: Random House.

Lewontin, R. C., Steven Rose, and Leon J. Kamin. 1984. *Not in our genes.* New York: Pantheon.

Lichter, Daniel T., and Rukamalie Jayakody. 2002. Welfare reform: How do we measure success? *Annual Review of Sociology,* 28:117–41.

Lichter, Daniel T., Deborah Roempke Graefe, and J. Brian Brown. 2003. Is marriage a panacea? Union formation among economi- cally disadvantaged unwed mothers. *Social Problems,* 50(1):60–86.

Liebow, Elliot. 1967. *Tally's corner.* Boston: Little, Brown.

Liebow, Elliot. 1967/2003. *Tally's corner.* Lan- ham, MD: Rowman & Littlefield Publishers.

Liker, Jeffrey K., Carol J. Haddad, and Jen- nifer Karlin. 1999. Perspectives on technol- ogy and work organization. *Annual Review of Sociology,* 25:575–96.

Lindblom, Charles E. 1990. *Inquiry and change: The troubled attempt to under- stand and shape society.* New Haven: Yale University Press.

Lindorff, Dave. 1992. *Marketplace medicine: The rise of the for-profit hospital chains.* New York: Bantam Books.

Lindsey, Robert. 1987. Colleges accused of bias to stem Asians' gain. *New York Times* (January 19):8.

Linton, Ralph. 1936. *The study of man.* New York: Appleton-Century-Crofts.

Linton, Ralph. 1937. One hundred per cent American. *American Mercury,* 40 (April):427–29.

Lipset, Seymour Martin. 1994. The social req- uisites of democracy revisited. *American Sociological Review,* 59:1–22.

Liska, Allen E. 1986. *Perspectives on deviance.* Englewood Cliffs, NJ: Prentice Hall.

Liska, Allen E., and Steven F. Messner. 1999. *Perspectives on crime and deviance.* Upper Saddle River, NJ: Prentice Hall.

Litan, Robert E., and Alice M. Rivlin. 2001. *Beyond the dot.coms: The economic prom- ise of the Internet.* Washington, DC: Brookings.

Loftus, Jeni. 2001. America's liberalization in attitudes toward homosexuality, 1973–1998. *American Sociological Review,* 66:762–82.

London, Bruce, and Bruce A. Williams. 1990. National political, international dependency, and basic needs provision: A cross-national analysis. *Social Forces,* 69:565–84.

Lubchenco, Jane. 1998. Entering the century of the environment: A new social contract for science. *Science,* 279:491–97.

Lucal, Betsy. 1994. Class stratification in introductory textbooks: Relational or distributional models? *Teaching Sociology,* 22:139–50.

Lugaila, Terry A. 2003. A child's day: 2000 (Selected indicators of child well-being). *Current Population Reports* P70-89. Washington, DC: U.S. Census Bureau.

Lundman, Richard J., and Robert L. Kaufman. 2003. Driving while black: Effects of race, ethnicity, and gender on citizen self-reports of traffic stops and police actions. *Criminology,* 41(1):195–220.

Ly, Phuong. 2003. Girls teach teen cyber gab to FBI agents: MD students help catch pedophiles on the Internet. *Washington Post* (June 4):A1.

Lyman, Peter, and Hal R. Varian. 2000. How big is the information explosion? *iMP magazine* (November). Available at http://www.cisp.org/imp/november_ 2000/11 _00lyman.htm.

Lynd, Robert S., and Helen Merrill Lynd. 1929. *Middletown: A study in American culture.* New York: Harcourt, Brace & World.

Lynd, Robert S., and Helen Merrill Lynd. 1937. *Middletown in transition: A study in cultural conflicts.* New York: Harcourt, Brace & World.

Maccoby, Eleanor E., and Carol N. Jacklin. 1974. *The psychology of sex differences.* Stanford, CA: Stanford University Press.

Malinosky-Rummell, Robin, and David J. Hansen. 1993. Long-term consequences of childhood physical abuse. *Psychological Bulletin,* 114:68–79.

Manchester, William. 1993. A world lit only by change. *U.S. News & World Report* (October 25):69.

Mann, James. 1983. One-parent family: The troubles and the joys. *Newsweek* (November 28):57–62.

Mann, Leon, James W. Newton, and J. M. Innes. 1982. A test between deindividuation and emergent norm theories of crowd aggression. *Journal of Personality and Social Psychology,* 12:260–72.

Maranto, Robert. 2003. Lobbying in disguise: The American Federation of Teachers "studies" charter schools. *Education Next,* Winter:79–84.

Marger, Martin N. 2003. *Race and ethnic relations: American and global perspectives.* 6th ed. Belmont, CA: Wadsworth.

Marks, Carole. 1991. The urban underclass. *Annual Review of Sociology,* 17:445–66.

Marsh, Herbert W. 1986. Global self-esteem: Its relation to specific facets of self-concept and their importance. *Journal of Personality and Social Psychology,* 51:1224–36.

Martin, Carol Lynn, and Jane K. Little. 1990. The relation of gender understanding to children's sex-typed preferences and gender stereotypes. *Child Development,* 61:1427–39.

Martin, Laura. 1983. "Eskimo words for snow": A case study in the genesis and decay of an anthropological example. *American Anthropologist,* 88:418–23.

Martin, Patricia Yancey, and Robert A. Hummer. 1995. Fraternities and rape on campus. In Alex Thio and Thomas C. Calhoun, eds., *Readings in deviant behavior.* New York: HarperCollins.

Marx, Karl. 1844/1960. Estranged labour: Economic and philosophic manuscripts of 1844. In C.W. Mills, ed., *Images of man.* New York: Braziller.

Marx, Karl. 1867/1906. *Capital.* Vol. 1. New York: Modern Library.

Marx, Karl. 1970. *Critique of Hegel's "philosophy of right."* Trans. A. O'Malley and J. O'Malley. London: Cambridge University Press.

Marx, Karl, and Friedrich Engels. 1848/1955. *The communist manifesto.* S. H. Beer, ed. New York: Appleton Century Crofts.

Massey, Douglas S. 1990. American apartheid: Segregation and the making of the underclass. *American Journal of Sociology,* 96:329–57.

Matsueda, Ross L. 1988. The current state of differential association theory. *Crime and Delinquency,* 34:277–306.

Maynard, Douglas W., and Steven E. Clayman. 1991. The diversity of ethnomethodology. *Annual Review of Sociology,* 17:385–418.

Mazur, Allan. 1985. A biosocial model of status in face-to-face primate groups: Social groups. *Social Forces,* 64:377–402.

MCCD. 2003. Housing costs climb in Maryland. *Maryland Center for Community Development.* Available at http://www.mccd.org.

McConahay, John B. 1986. Modern racism, ambivalence, and the modern racism scale. In John F. Dovidio and Samuel Gaertner, eds., *Prejudice, discrimination, and racism.* Orlando, FL: Academic Press.

McFalls, Joseph A., Jr. 2003. *Population: A lively introduction.* Washington, DC: Population Reference Bureau.

McGee, Reece. 1975. *Points of departure.* Hinsdale, IL: Dryden Press.

McGuire, Meredith B. 1981. *Religion: The social context.* Belmont, CA: Wadsworth.

McKinnon, Jessie. 2003. *The black population in the United States: March 2002.* Current Population Reports P20-541. Washington, DC: U.S. Census Bureau.

McLanahan, Sara, and Julia Adams. 1987. Parenthood and psychological well-being. *Annual Review of Sociology,* 13:237–57.

McLaughlin, Steven D., Barbara D. Melber, John O. G. Billy, Denise M. Zimmerle, Linda D. Winges, and Terry R. Johnson. 1988. *The changing lives of American women.* Chapel Hill: University of North Carolina Press.

McManus, Patricia A., and Thomas A. DiPrete. 2001. Losers and winners: The financial consequences of separation and divorce for men. *American Sociological Review,* 66:246–68.

McMichael, A. J., C. D. Butler, and Carl Folke. 2003. New visions for addressing sustainability. *Science,* 302:1919–20.

McPhail, Clark. 1989. Blumer's theory of collective behavior: The development of a non-symbolic interaction explanation. *Sociological Quarterly,* 30:401–23.

Mead, George Herbert. 1934/1962. *Mind, self, and other.* Chicago: University of Chicago Press.

Mead, Lawrence M. 1992. *The new politics of poverty: The nonworking poor in America.* New York: Basic Books.

Medlin, Richard G. 2000. Home schooling and the question of socialization. *Peabody Journal of Education,* 75:107–24.

Mehrabian, Albert. 1968. Communication without words. *Psychology Today,* 2 (September):53–55.

Merton, Robert. 1968. *Social theory and social structure.* Rev. ed. New York: Free Press.

Merton, Robert K. 1995. The Thomas theorem and the Matthew Effect. *Social Forces,* 74:379–422.

Messner, Steven F., and Marvin D. Krohn. 1990. Class, compliance structures, and delinquency: Assessing integrated structural-Marxist theory. *American Journal of Sociology,* 96:300–28.

Messner, Steven F., and Richard Rosenfeld. 1997a. *Crime and the American dream.* 2nd ed. Belmont, CA: Wadsworth.

Messner, Steven F., and Richard Rosenfeld. 1997b. Political restraint of the market and levels of criminal homicide: A cross-national application of institutional-anomie theory. *Social Forces,* 75:1393–416.

Michael, Robert T., John H. Gagnon, Edward O. Laumann, and Gina Kolata. 1994. Applying theories of deviance to academic cheating. *Social Science Quarterly,* 70:870–85.

Michaels, James W., and Terance D. Miethe. 1989. Applying theories of deviance to academic cheating. *Social Science Quarterly,* 70:870–85.

Michels, Robert. 1911/1966. *Political parties.* New York: Free Press.

Mickelson, Roslyn Arlin. 1990. The attitude-achievement paradox among black adolescents. *Sociology of Education,* 63:44–61.

Milgram, Stanley. 1963. Behavioral study of obedience. *Journal of Abnormal and Social Psychology,* 67(4):371–78.

Milgram, Stanley, and Hans Toch. 1969. Collective behavior: Crowds and social movements. In G. Lindzey and E. Aronson, eds., *The handbook of social psychology,* 2nd ed., Vol. 2. Reading, MA: Addison Wesley.

Mills, C. Wright. 1959. *The sociological imagination*. New York: Oxford University Press.

Milner, Murray, Jr. 1987. Theories of inequality: An overview and a strategy for synthesis. *Social Forces*, 65:1053–89.

Mirowsky, John, and Catherine E. Ross. 2003. *Education, social status, and health*. New York: Aldine de Gruyter.

Mischel, Walter. 1970. Sex-typing and socialization. In P. H. Mussen, ed., *Carmichael's manual of child psychology*. 3rd ed. Vol. 2. New York: John Wiley.

Moaddel, Mansoor. 1992. Ideology as episodic discourse: The case of the Iranian revolution. *American Sociological Review*, 57:353–79.

Moaddel, Mansoor. 1994. Political conflict in the world economy: A cross-national analysis of modernization and world-system theories. *American Sociological Review*, 59:276–303.

Moffitt, Terrie E., Robert F. Krueger, Avshalom Caspi, and Jeff Fagan. 2000. Partner abuse and general crime: How are they the same? How are they different? *Criminology*, 38(1):199–232.

Moller, Stephanie, Evelyne Huber, John D. Stephens, David Bradley, and Francois Nielsen. 2003. Determinants of relative poverty in advanced capitalist democracies. *American Sociological Review*, 68:22–51.

Molm, Linda D. 1991 Affect and social exchange: Satisfaction in power-dependence relations. *American Sociological Review*, 56:475–93.

Molnar, Stephen. 1997. *Human variation*. Upper Saddle River, NJ: Prentice Hall.

Morin, Richard. 1998. The new great divide: More and more, where you live depends on what you're worth. *Washington Post Magazine* (January 18):14.

Morin, Richard, and Alan Cooperman. 2003. Majority against blessing gay unions. *Washington Post* (August 14):A1.

Morris, Aldon D. 1993. Birmingham confrontation reconsidered: An analysis of the dynamics and tactics of mobilization. *American Sociology Review*, 58:621–36.

Morrison, Donna Ruane, and Amy Ritualo. 2000. Routes to children's economic recovery after divorce: Are cohabitation and remarriage equivalent? *American Sociological Review*, 65:560–80.

Mortenson, Thomas G., and Zhijun Wu. 1991. *High school graduation and college participation of young adults by family income backgrounds 1970 to 1989*. Iowa City, IA: American College Testing, Educational and Social Research.

Mortimer, Jeylan T., and Roberta G. Simmons. 1978. Adult socialization. *Annual Review of Sociology*, 4:421–54.

Moskowitz, Breyne Arlene. 1978. The acquisition of language. *Scientific American*, 239 (November):92–108.

Mouzelis, Nicos. 1992. The interaction order and the micro-macro distinction. *Sociological Theory*, 10:122–28.

Moynihan, Daniel Patrick. 1985. *Family and nation*. Cambridge, MA: Harvard University Press.

Mura, David. 1992. Bashed in the U.S.A. *New York Times* (April 2):A15.

Murdock, George P. 1934. *Our primitive contemporaries*. New York: Macmillan.

Murdock, George P. 1935. Comparative data on the division of labor by sex. *Social Forces*, 15:551–53.

Murdock, George Peter. 1949. *Social structure*. New York: Macmillan.

Murdock, George Peter. 1967. *Ethnographic atlas*. Pittsburgh: University of Pittsburgh Press.

Murphy, Caryle. 1997. U.S. Catholic bishops urge acceptance of gay orientation. *Washington Post* (October 1):A1.

Murray, Charles. 1994. Does welfare bring more babies? *American Enterprise*, 5 (January–February):52–59.

Murstein, Bernard I. 1972. Physical attractiveness and marital choice. *Journal of Personality and Social Psychology*, 22:8–12.

Murstein, Bernard I. 1976. *Who will marry whom?* New York: Springer.

Musick, Kelly, and Larry Bumpass. 1999. How do prior experiences in the family affect transitions to adulthood? In Alan Booth, Ann C. Crouter, and Michael J. Shanahan, eds., *Transitions to adulthood in a changing economy: No work, no family, no future?* Westport, CT: Praeger.

Myrdal, Gunnar. 1944. *An American dilemma.* New York: Harper.

Nagel, Joane. 1994. *American Indian ethnic renewal: Red power and the transformation of identity and culture.* New York: Oxford University Press.

Nakao, Keiko, Robert W. Hodge, and Judith Treas. 1990. On revising prestige scores for all occupations. GSS Methodological Report No. 69. Chicago: National Opinion Research Center.

Nanda, Serena, and Richard L. Warms. 2002. *Cultural anthropology.* 7th ed. Wadsworth: Thomson Learning.

Nash, Jonathan G., and Roger-Mark De Souza. 2002. *Making the link: Population, health, environment.* Washington, DC: Population Reference Bureau.

Neff, Robert. 1994. The many faces of free enterprise. *Business Week,* (January 24):17–18.

Nelson, Mariah Burton. 1994. *The stronger women get, the more men love football: Sexism and the American culture of sports.* New York: Harcourt Brace.

Nelson, Sandi, Rebecca L. Clark, and Gregory Acs. 2001. *Beyond the two-parent family: How teenagers fare in cohabiting couple and blended families.* Washington, DC: The Urban Institute. New Federalism: National Survey of America's Families, No. B-31.

Neuhouser, Kevin. 1992. Democratic stability in Venezuela: Elite consensus or class compromise? *American Sociological Review,* 57:117–35.

Newcomb, Theodore M. 1950. *Social psychology.* New York: Holt, Rinehart and Winston.

Nisbett, Richard E. 1998. Race, genetics, and IQ. In Christopher Jencks and Meredith Phillips, eds., *The black-white test score gap.* Washington, DC: Brookings Institution Press.

Noble, Kenneth B. 1989. Low commodity prices vex life in Ivory Coast. *New York Times* (November 19):6.

Noel, Donald L. 1968. A theory of the origin of ethnic stratification. *Social Problems,* 16:157–62.

Noel, Donald M. 1972. *The origins of American slavery and racism.* Columbus, OH: Charles E. Merrill.

Nolan, Martin F. 1997. Tiger's racial multiplicity. *Boston Globe* (April 26):A11.

Nolan, Patrick, and Gerhard E. Lenski. 1999. *Human societies: An introduction to macro sociology.* 8th ed. New York: McGraw-Hill.

Nussbaum, Emily. 2004. My so-called blog. *New York Times Magazine* (January 11):32–37.

O'Connor, Alice. 2000. Poverty research and policy for the post-welfare era. *Annual Review of Sociology,* 26:547–62.

Oeppen, Jim, and James W. Vaupel. 2002. Broken limits to life expectancy. *Science,* 296:1029–31.

Ogburn, William F. 1922. *Social change.* New York: Hoebsch.

Ogunwole, Stella U. 2002. *The American Indian and Alaska Native population: 2000.* U.S. Census Bureau C2KBR/01–15. Washington, DC: U.S. Government Printing Office.

O'Hare, William P., and Judy C. Felt. 1991. Asian Americans: America's fastest growing minority group. *Population Trends and Public Policy.* Population Reference Bureau, no. 19.

O'Harrow, Robert, Jr. 2003. Identity crisis. *Washington Post Magazine* (August 10):14–18, 23–29.

Olson, David H., and John DeFrain. 1997. *Marriage and the family: Diversity and strengths.* 2nd ed. Mountain View, CA: Mayfield Publishing.

Olzak, Susan. 1992. *The dynamics of ethnic competition and conflict.* Stanford, CA: Stanford University Press.

Orcutt, James D. 1987. Differential association and marijuana use: A closer look at Sutherland (with a little help from Becker). *Criminology,* 25:341–58.

Page, Clarence. 1997. Grappling with the "one-drop" rule. *Chicago Tribune* (April 27):C19.

Page, Jake. 2003. *In the hands of the Great Spirit: The 20,000 year history of American Indians.* New York: Free Press.

Pager, Devah. 2003. The mark of a criminal record. *American Journal of Sociology,* 108(5):937–75.

Paisano, Edna L. 2003. *The American Indian, Eskimo, and Aleut population.* Available at http://www.census.gov/population/www/pop-profile/amerind.html.

Palen, J. John. 1997. *The urban world.* New York: McGraw-Hill.

Palmer, Louann Bierlein, and Rebecca Gau. 2003. *Charter school authorizing: Are states making the grade?* Washington, D.C.: Thomas B. Fordham Institute.

Park, Robert E., Ernest W. Burgess, and Roderick D. McKenzie. 1925. *The city.* Chicago: University of Chicago Press.

Parker, Stephen. 1990. *Informal marriage, cohabitation and the law, 1750–1989.* New York: St. Martin's Press.

Parkinson, C. Northcote. 1962. *Parkinson's law.* Boston: Houghton Mifflin.

Parsons, Talcott. 1949. *The structure of social action.* 2nd ed. New York: McGraw-Hill.

Parsons, Talcott. 1951. *The social system.* New York: Free Press.

Parsons, Talcott. 1966. *Societies: Evolutionary and comparative perspectives.* Englewood Cliffs, NJ: Prentice Hall.

Parsons, Talcott. 1977. On building social system theory: A personal history. In Talcott Parsons, ed., *Social systems and evolution of action theory.* New York: Free Press.

Parsons, Talcott, and Robert F. Bales. 1955. *Family socialization and interaction process.* New York: Free Press.

Passell, Peter. 1994. Controlling world population growth: Where to put the money. *New York Times* (April 21):C2.

Pastore, Ann L., and Kathleen Maguire, eds. 2003. *Sourcebook of criminal justice statistics.* Available at http://www.albany.edu/sourcebook/.

Paternoster, Raymond. 1989. Absolute and restrictive deterrence in a panel of youth: Explaining the onset, persistence/desistance, and frequency of delinquent offending. *Social Problems,* 36:289–309.

Patterson, Orlando. 1991. *Freedom.* Vol. 1: *Freedom in the making of western culture.* New York: Basic Books.

Perrow, Charles. 1982. Disintegrating social sciences. *Phi Delta Kappan,* 63:684–88.

Perrow, Charles. 1986. *Complex organizations.* New York: Random House.

Perry, Susan, and Joseph H. Manson. 2003. Traditions in monkeys. *Evolutionary Anthropology,* 12:71–81.

Peterson, Richard A. 1979. Revitalizing the culture concept. *Annual Review of Sociology,* 5:137–66.

Petterson, Stephen M. 1997. Are young black men really less willing to work? *American Sociological Review,* 62:605–13.

Pettigrew, Thomas J. 1967. Social evaluation theory: Convergences and applications. *Nebraska Symposium on Motivation.* Lincoln: University of Nebraska Press.

Piaget, Jean. 1926/1955. *The language and thought of the child.* New York: New American Library.

Pill, Cynthia J. 1990. Stepfamilies: Redefining the family. *Family Relations,* 39:186–93.

Pimm, Stuart L. 2000. Against triage. *Science,* 289:2289.

Pinker, Steven. 2002. *The blank slate: The modern denial of human nature.* New York: Viking.

Pipher, Mary. 1994. *Reviving Ophelia: Saving the selves of adolescent girls.* New York: Ballantine Books.

Pipher, Mary. 1997. *The shelter of each other.* New York: Ballantine Books.

Pope, Whitney. 1976. *Durkheim's* Suicide: *A classic analyzed.* Chicago: University of Chicago Press.

Popenoe, David. 1993. American family decline, 1960–1990: A review and appraisal. *Journal of Marriage and the Family,* 55:527–55.

Popper, Karl. 1963. *Conjectures and refutations: The growth of scientific knowledge.* London: Routledge & Kegan Paul.

Population Reference Bureau. 2003. *Human population: Fundamentals of growth patterns of world urbanization.* Washington, DC: Population Reference Bureau.

Portes, Alejandro, and Robert L. Bach. 1985. *Latin journey: Cuban and Mexican immigrants in the United States.* Berkeley: University of California Press.

Portes, Alejandro, and Kenneth L. Wilson. 1976. Black-white differences in educational attainment. *American Sociological Review,* 41:414–31.

Pressler, Margaret. 2003. Cost and robbers: Shoplifting and employee thievery add dollars to price tags. *Washington Post* (February 16):H5.

Proctor, Bernadette D., and Joseph Dalaker. 2003. *Poverty in the United States: 2002.* U.S. Census Bureau, Current Population Reports, P60-219. Washington, DC: U.S. Government Printing Office.

Public Agenda. 2004. The environment: people's chief concerns. Available at http://www.publicagenda.org/issues/pcc.cfm?issue_type=environment.

Puckett, Jim, Leslie Byster, Sarah Westervelt, Richard Gutierrez, Sheila Davis, Asma Hussain, and Madhumitta Dutta. 2002. *Exporting harm: The high-tech trashing of Asia.* The Basel Action Network and Silicon Valley Toxics Coalition (www.svtc.org).

Quadagno, Jill S. 1982. *Aging in early industrial society.* New York: Academic Press.

Quinney, Richard. 1974. *Criminal justice in America.* Boston: Little, Brown.

Quinney, Richard. 1980. *Class, state, and crime.* New York: Longman.

Radelet, Michael L., and Marian J. Borg. 2000. The changing nature of death penalty debates. *Annual Review of Sociology,* 26:43–61.

Ramirez, Roberto R., and G. Patricia de la Cruz. 2002. *The Hispanic population in the United States: March 2002.* Current Population Reports, P20-545. Washington, DC: U.S. Census Bureau.

Rank, M. R., and T. A. Hirschl. 2002. Welfare use as a life course event: Toward a new understanding of the U.S. safety net. *Social Work,* 47(3):237–48.

Reckless, Walter C. 1961. A new theory of delinquency and crime. *Federal Probation,* 25:42–46.

Reckless, Walter C. 1967. *The crime problem.* 4th ed. New York: Appleton-Century-Crofts.

Rector, Robert. 1990. Poverty in U.S. is exaggerated by census. *The Wall Street Journal* (September 25):A18.

Reeves, Terrance, and Claudette Bennett. 2003. *The Asian and Pacific Islander population in the United States: March 2002.* Current Population Reports, P20-540. Washington, DC: U.S. Census Bureau.

Regoli, Robert M., and John D. Hewitt. 2000. *Delinquency in society.* New York: McGraw-Hill.

Rennison, Callie. 2002a. Criminal victimization 2001: Changes 2000–01 with trends 1993–2001. Washington, DC: U.S. Department of Justice. NCJ-194610.

Rennison, Callie. 2002b. *Rape and sexual assault: Reporting to police and medical attention, 1992–2000.* NCJ-194530. Washington, DC: U.S. Department of Justice.

Reno, Raymond R., Robert B. Cialdini, and Carl A. Kallgren. 1993. The transsituational influence of social norms. *Journal of Personality and Social Psychology,* 64:104–12.

Reynolds, J. R., and C. E. Ross. 1998. Social stratification and health: Education's benefit beyond economic status and social origins. *Social Problems,* 45(2): 221–47.

Richardson, Laurel, Verta Taylor, and Nancy Whittier. 1997. *Feminist frontiers IV.* New York: McGraw-Hill.

Richburg, Keith. 1997. North Korea near economic collapse: Spreading famine and hardship reflect system no longer functioning. *Washington Post* (October 19):A1.

Richburg, Keith. 2003. Gay marriage becomes routine for Dutch. *Washington Post* (September 23):A20.

Ridgeway, C. L., and L. Smith-Lovin. 1999. The gender system and interaction. *Annual Review of Sociology,* 25:191–216.

Ritch, Ellie. 2002. Prison experiment repeated for ratings. *The Stanford Daily* (February 5). Available at http://www.stanforddaily.com.

Ritzer, George. 1995. *Expressing America: A critique of the increasingly global credit card society.* Thousand Oaks, CA: Sage.

Ritzer, George. 1997. *Postmodern social theory.* New York: McGraw-Hill.

Ritzer, George. 2000. *Sociological theory*, 5th ed. New York: McGraw-Hill.

Roethlisberger, Fritz J., and William J. Dickson. 1939. *Management and the worker*. Cambridge, MA: Harvard University Press.

Rohan, Meg J. 2000. A rose by any name: The values construct. *Personality and Social Psychology Review*, 4:255–77.

Roig-Franzia, Manuel. 2003. In Miami, a bus stop for broken marriages. *Washington Post* (May 4):D1.

Roper Starch Worldwide. 2000. Roper Reports Worldwide Global Consumers 2000 Study.

Rosen, George. 1963. The hospital: Historical sociology of a community institution. In E. Freidson, ed., *The hospital in modern society*. New York: Free Press.

Rosenau, Pauline. 1992. *Post modernism and the social sciences*. Princeton, NJ: Princeton University Press.

Rosenberg, Morris. 1973. Which significant others? *American Behavioral Scientist*, 16:829–60.

Rosenberg, Morris. 1981. The self-concept: Social product and social force. In Morris Rosenberg and Ralph H. Turner, eds., *Social psychology: Sociological perspectives*. New York: Basic Books.

Rosenberg, Noah A., Jonathan K. Prichard, James L. Weber, Howard M. Cann, Kenneth, K. Kidd, Lev A. Zhivotovsky, and Marcus W. Feldman. 2002. Genetic structure of human populations. *Science*, 298:2381–85.

Rosenthal, Elisabeth. 1993. Medicine suffers as fewer doctors join front lines. *New York Times* (May 24):A1, A11.

Ross, Andrew. 2003. *No-collar: The humane workplace and its hidden costs*. New York: Basic Books.

Rossi, Alice S. 1973. *The feminist papers*. New York: Columbia University Press.

Rossi, Alice S., and Peter H. Rossi. 1990. *Of human bonding: Parent child relations across the life course*. New York: Aldine de Gruyter.

Rothbart, Myron, and Oliver P. John. 1993. Intergroup relations and stereotype change: A social cognitive analysis and some longitudinal findings. In Paul M. Sniderman, Philip E. Tetlock, and Edward G. Carmines, eds., *Prejudice, politics, and the American dilemma*. Stanford, CA: Stanford University Press.

Rothchild, John. 1993. Sacred cows. *Worth* (December–January):55–58.

Rothkopf, David J. 2003. When the buzz bites back. *Washington Post* (May 11):B1.

Rudner, Lawrence M. 1999. Scholastic achievement and demographic characteristics of home school students in 1998. *Education Policy Analysis Archives*, 7(8).

Ruggles, Patricia. 1992. Measuring poverty. University of Wisconsin, Institute for Research on Poverty, *Focus*, 14:2.

Ruggles, Steven. 1987. *Prolonged connections: The rise of the extended family in nineteenth-century England and America*. Madison: University of Wisconsin Press.

Saad, Lydia. 1996. Americans growing more tolerant of gays. *Gallup Poll*.

Sagarin, Edward. 1975. *Deviants and deviance*. New York: Praeger.

Sakamoto, Arthur, and Meichu D. Chen. 1991. Inequality and attainment in a dual labor market. *American Sociological Review*, 56:295–308.

Sampson, Robert J., and W. Byron Groves. 1989. Community structure and crime: Testing social-disorganization theory. *American Journal of Sociology*, 94:774–802.

Samuelsson, Kurt. 1961. *Religion and economic action: A critique of Max Weber*. Trans. E. G. French. New York: Harper Torchbooks.

Sanchez, Rene. 1996. Math-science study faults U.S. teaching, curricula. *Washington Post* (November 21):A1.

Sanchez, Rene. 1997. Popularity grows for alternatives to public schools: Some districts reacting to threat of competition. *Washington Post* (October 1):A1.

Sanchez, Rene, and Clay Chandler. 1997. Education aid at what cost?: Clinton's $50 billion plan has skeptics even on campus. *Washington Post* (February 3):A1.

Sanday, Peggy Reeves. 1981. The socio-cultural context of rape: A cross-cultural study. *Journal of Social Issues,* 37:5–27.

Sanday, Peggy Reeves. 1996. Rape-prone versus rape-free campus cultures. *Violence Against Women,* 2:191–208.

Sapir, Edward. 1949. *Selected writings in language, culture, and personality.* Berkeley: University of California Press.

Saporito, Bill. 1986. The revolt against "working smarter." *Fortune* (July 21):58–65.

Satchell, Michael. 1993. Trashing the reservations? *U.S. News & World Report* (January 11):24–25.

Savin-Williams, R. C., and K. G. Esterberg. 2000. Lesbian, gay, and bisexual families. In D. H. Demo, K. R. Allen & M. A. Fine, eds., *Handbook of family diversity* (pp. 197–215). New York: Oxford University Press.

Scales-Trent, Judy. 1995. *Notes of a white black woman: Race, color, and community.* University Park: Pennsylvania State University Press.

Scanzoni, John. 1997. A reply to Glenn: Fashioning families and policies for the future—not the past. *Family Relations,* 46:213–17.

Schoen, Robert, and Robin M. Weinick. 1993. Partner choice in marriages and cohabitations. *Journal of Marriage and the Family,* 55:408–14.

Schorr, Alvin L. 1984. Redefining poverty levels. *New York Times* (May 9):27.

Schuman, Howard, Charlotte Steeh, Lawrence Bobo, and Maria Krysan. 1997. *Racial attitudes in America.* Cambridge, MA: Harvard University Press.

Schur, Edwin. 1965. *Crimes without victims.* Englewood Cliffs, NJ: Prentice Hall.

Schwartz, Martin D. 1995. Date rape on college campuses. In Alex Thio and Thomas C. Calhoun, eds., *Readings in deviant behavior.* New York: HarperCollins.

Schwartz, Martin D., and Walter S. DeKeseredy. 1997. *Sexual assault on the college campus: The role of male peer support.* Thousand Oaks, CA: Sage.

Schwendinger, Herman, and Julia Siegel Schwendinger. 1985. *Adolescent subcultures and delinquency.* New York: Praeger.

Scott, John. 1991. Networks of corporate power: A comparative assessment. *Annual Review of Sociology,* 17:181–203.

Searle, John R. 1995. *The construction of social reality.* New York: Free Press.

Sears, David O., Jim Sidanius, and Lawrence Bobo, eds. 2000. *Racialized politics: The debate about racism in America.* Chicago: University of Chicago Press.

Seelye, Katharine Q., and Janet Elder. 2003. Strong support is found for ban on gay marriage. *New York Times* (December 21).

Selin, Helaine. 2002. An inclusive perspective. *Science,* 298:969–70.

Selltiz, Claire, Lawrence S. Wrightsman, and Stuart W. Cook. 1976. *Research methods in social relations.* 3rd ed. New York: Holt, Rinehart and Winston.

Selz, Michael. 1994. Testing self-managed teams, entrepreneur hopes to lose job. *The Wall Street Journal* (January 11):B1–B2.

Serbin, Lisa A., and Carol Sprafkin. 1986. The salience of gender and the process of sex typing in three- to seven-year-old children. *Child Development,* 57:1188–99.

Sewell, William H., Jr. 1992. A theory of structure: Duality, agency, and transformation. *American Journal of Sociology,* 98:1–29.

Sewell, William H., Archibald O. Haller, and George W. Ohlendorf. 1970. The educational and early occupational status attainment process: Replication and revision. *American Sociological Review,* 35:1014–27.

Sewell, William H., and Robert M. Hauser. 1975. *Education, occupation, and earnings: Achievement in early career.* New York: Academic Press.

Shaw, Clifford R. 1930. *Natural history of a juvenile career.* Chicago: University of Chicago Press.

Shaw, Clifford R., and Henry McKay. 1942. *Juvenile delinquency in urban areas.* Chicago: University of Chicago Press.

Sherif, Muzafer. 1936. *The psychology of social norms.* New York: Harper & Row.

Sherif, Muzafer, O. J. Harvey, B. Jack White, William R. Hood, and Carolyn W. Sherif. 1961. *Intergroup conflict and cooperation:*

The Robbers' Cave experiment. Norman: University of Oklahoma Book Exchange.

Sherman, Lawrence W., Douglas A. Smith, Janell D. Schmidt, and Dennis P. Rogan. 1992. Crime, punishment, and stake in conformity: Legal and informal control of domestic violence. *American Sociological Review,* 57:680–90.

Shibutani, Tamotsu. 1986. *Social processes: An introduction to sociology.* Berkeley: University of California Press.

Shibutani, Tamotsu, and Kian M. Kwan. 1965. *Ethnic stratification.* New York: Macmillan.

Shoemaker, Donald J. 2000. *Theories of delinquency.* New York: Oxford University Press.

Sica, Alan. 1996. Review essay: Sociology as worldview. *American Journal of Sociology,* 102:252–55.

Sigelman, Lee, Timothy Bledsoe, Susan Welch, and Michale W. Combs. 1996. Making contact? Black-white social interaction in an urban setting. *American Journal of Sociology,* 101:1306–32.

Simmel, Georg. 1908/1955. *Conflict and the web of group affiliations.* New York: Free Press.

Simmel, Georg. 1908/1959. How is society possible? In Kurt Wolff, ed., *Essays in sociology, philosophy, and aesthetics.* New York: Harper & Row.

Simmel, Georg. 1950. *The sociology of George Simmel.* Ed. and trans. Kurt Wolff. New York: Free Press.

Simon, David R., and D. Stanley Eitzen. 1993. *Elite deviance.* Boston: Allyn and Bacon.

Simon, Julian, ed. 1995. *The state of humanity.* Cambridge, MA: Blackwell.

Simon, Robin W. 1998. Assessing sex differences in vulnerability among employed parents: The importance of marital status. *Journal of Health and Social Behavior,* 39:38–54.

Simons, Ronald L., Jay Beaman, Rand D. Conger, and Wei Chao. 1993. Stress, support, and antisocial behavior trait as determinants of emotional well-being and parenting practices among single mothers. *Journal of Marriage and the Family,* 55:385–98.

Simons, Ronald L., Christine Johnson, Jay Beaman, and Rand D. Conger. 1993. Explaining women's double jeopardy: Factors that mediate the association between harsh treatment as a child and violence by a husband. *Journal of Marriage and the Family,* 55:713–23.

Singer, Eleanor. 1981. Reference groups and social evaluations. In Morris Rosenberg and Ralph H. Turner, eds., *Social psychology: Sociological perspectives.* New York: Basic Books.

Skinner, B. F. 1953. *Science and human behavior.* New York: Macmillan.

Sklair, Leslie. 1991. *Sociology of the global system.* Baltimore: Johns Hopkins University Press.

Skocpol, Theda. 1979. *States and social revolution.* Cambridge, MA: Cambridge University Press.

Skolnick, Arlene. 1991. *Embattled paradise: The American family in an age of uncertainty.* New York: Basic Books.

Skolnick, Arlene. 1997. A reply to Glenn: The battle of the textbooks: Bringing in the culture war. *Family Relations,* 46:219–22.

Smedley, Brian D., Adrienne Y. Stith, and Alan R. Nelson, eds. 2003. *Unequal treatment: Confronting racial and ethnic disparities in health care.* Washington, DC: National Academy Press.

Smock, Pamela J. 2000. Cohabitation in the United States: An appraisal of research themes, findings, and implications. *Annual Review of Sociology,* 26:1–20.

Snell, Tracy L., and Laura M. Maruschak. 2002. *Capital punishment 2001.* NCJ 197020. Washington, DC: U.S. Department of Justice.

Snipp, C. Matthew. 1989. *American Indians: The first of this land.* New York: Russell Sage Foundation.

Snizek, William E. 1995. Virtual offices: Some neglected considerations. *Communications of the ACM,* 38:15–17.

Sobel, Richard. 1989. *The white-collar working class: From structure to politics.* New York: Praeger.

Sommer, Robert. 1969. *Personal space.* Englewood Cliffs, NY: Prentice Hall.

Sørensen, Aage B. 2000. Toward a sounder basis for class analysis. *American Journal of Sociology,* 105:1523–58.

Sorokin, Pitirim. 1959. *Social and cultural mobility.* New York: Free Press.

Soupiset, Mark F. 2003. Striking back at fraud. *USAA Magazine* (August):14–18.

South, Scott J., and Glenna Spitze. 1994. Housework in marital and nonmarital households. *American Sociological Review,* 59:327–47.

South, Scott J., and Katherine Trent. 1988. Sex ratios and women's roles: Cross-national analysis. *American Journal of Sociology,* 93:1096–115.

Spates, James L. 1983. The sociology of values. *Annual Review of Sociology,* 9:27–49.

Sperber, Murray. 2000. *Beer and circus: How big-time college sports is crippling undergraduate education.* New York: Henry Holt.

Spiegel, David. 1994. Compassion is the best medicine. *New York Times* (January 10):A11.

Spohn, Cassia C. 2000. Thirty years of sentencing reform: The quest for a racially neutral sentencing process. *Criminal Justice 2000* 3 (National Institute of Justice).

Spraggins, Renee E. 2003. *Women and men in the United States: March 2002.* U.S. Census Bureau. Washington, DC: Government Printing Office.

Sprey, Jetse. 1979. Conflict theory and the study of marriage and the family. In Wesley R. Burr, Reuben Hill, F. Ivan Nye, and Ira L. Reiss, eds., *Contemporary theories about the family,* Vol. 2. New York: Free Press.

Stacey, Judith. 1996. *In the name of the family: Rethinking family values in the postmodern age.* Boston: Beacon Press.

Stacey, Judith, and Timothy J. Biblarz. 2001. (How) does the sexual orientation of parents matter? *American Sociological Review,* 66:159–83.

Stack, John F., Jr., ed. 1986. *The primordial challenge: Ethnicity in the contemporary world.* Westport, CT: Greenwood Press.

Stark, Rodney, and William S. Bainbridge. 1979. Of churches, sects, and cults: Preliminary concepts for a theory of religious movements. *Journal for the Scientific Study of Religion,* 18:117–33.

Stark, Rodney, and William S. Bainbridge. 1987. *A theory of religion.* New York: Peter Lang.

Starr, Paul. 1982. *The social transformation of American medicine.* New York: Basic Books.

State Demographics. 2004. Available at http://demog.state.nc.us/demog/stgr13b.html.

Stearns, Peter N. 1977. *Old age in European society.* London: Croom Helm.

Steffensmeier, Darrell, and Emilie Allan. 1996. Gender and crime: Toward a gendered theory of female offending. *Annual Review of Sociology,* 22:459–87.

Steinberg, Stephen. 1989. *The ethnic myth: Race, ethnicity, and class in America.* Updated and expanded ed. New York: Atheneum.

Steinmetz, George, and Erik Olin Wright. 1989. The fall and rise of the petty bourgeoisie: Changing patterns of self-employment in the postwar United States. *American Journal of Sociology,* 94:973–1018.

Stephens, William N. 1963. *The family in cross-cultural perspective.* New York: Holt, Rinehart and Winston.

Stepp, Laura Sessions. 2003. In La. school, son of lesbian learns "gay" is a "bad wurd." *Washington Post* (December 3):C1.

Stevenson, Betsey, and Justin Wolfers. 2003. Bargaining in the shadow of the law: Divorce laws and family distress. *National Bureau of Economic Research Working Paper 10175.*

Stevenson, David Lee. 1991. Deviant students as a collective resource in classroom control. *Sociology of Education,* 64:127–33.

Stokes, Randall G., and Andy B. Anderson. 1990. Disarticulation and human welfare in less developed countries. *American Sociological Review,* 55:63–74.

Stone, Arthur A., Jaylan S. Turkkan, Christine Bachrach, Jared B. Jobe, Howard S. Kurtzman, and Virginia S. Cain, eds. 1999. *The science of self-report: Implications for* research and practice. Mahwah, NJ: Lawrence Erlbaum Associates.

Stone, Katherine. 1974. The origins of job structures in the steel industry. *Review of Radical Economics,* 6:61–97.

Strang, David, and Nancy Brandon Tuma. 1993. Spatial and temporal heterogeneity in diffusion. *American Journal of Sociology,* 99:614–39.

Straus, Murray A., and Richard J. Gelles. 1986. Societal change and change in family violence from 1975 to 1985 as revealed by two national surveys. *Journal of Marriage and the Family,* 48:465–79.

Straus, Murray A., and Richard J. Gelles. 1990. *Physical violence in American families: Risk factors and adaptations to violence in 8,145 families.* New Brunswick, NJ: Transaction.

Straus, Murray A., David B. Sugarman, and Jean Giles-Sims. 1997. Spanking by parents and subsequent antisocial behavior of children. *Archives of Pediatrics and Adolescent Medicine,* 151:761–67.

Strauss, Anselm, Leonard Schatzman, Rue Bucher, Danuta Ehrlich, and Melvin Sabshin. 1964. *Psychiatric ideologies and institutions.* New York: Free Press.

Stryker, Robin. 1994. Rules, resources, and legitimacy processes: Some implications for social conflict, order, and change. *American Journal of Sociology,* 99:847–910.

Sumner, William Graham. 1906. *Folkways.* Boston: Ginn.

Sunstein, Cass R. 2003. Sober lemmings. *The New Republic* (April 14):34–37.

Super, David A., Sharon Parrott, Susan Steinmetz, and Cindy Mann. 1996. *The new welfare law—Summary.* Washington, DC: Center on Budget and Policy Priorities.

Sutherland, Edwin H. 1939. *Principles of criminology.* Philadelphia: Lippincott.

Sutherland, Edwin H. 1949. *White-collar crime.* New York: Dryden Press.

Szymanski, Albert. 1981. *The logic of imperialism.* New York: Praeger.

Taylor, Verta. 1989. Social movement continuity: The women's movement in abeyance. *American Sociological Review,* 54:761–75.

Teachman, J. 2003. Premarital sex, premarital cohabitation, and the risk of subsequent marital dissolution among women. *Journal of Marriage and the Family,* 65(2):444–55.

Thio, Alex. 1998. *Deviant behavior.* 5th ed. New York: Longman.

Thistle, Susan. 2000. The trouble with modernity: Gender and the remaking of social theory. *Sociological Theory,* 18:275–88.

Thoits, Peggy A. 1995. Identity-relevant events and psychological symptoms: A cautionary tale. *Social Forces,* 36:72–82.

Thomas, William I., and Dorothy S. Thomas. 1928. *The child in America: Behavior problems and programs.* New York: Knopf.

Thrasher, Frederic M. 1927. *The gang.* Chicago: University of Chicago Press.

Tien, H. Yuan. 1992. China's demographic dilemmas. *Population Bulletin,* 47(1) (June).

Tierney, Patrick. 2000. *Darkness in El Dorado: How scientists and journalists devastated the Amazon.* New York: Norton.

Tilly, Charles. 1978. *From mobilization to revolution.* Reading, MA: Addison-Wesley.

Tilly, Charles. 1990. *Coercion, capital, and European states, AD 990–1990.* Cambridge, MA: Blockwell.

Tipton, Steven M. 1982. *Getting saved from the sixties.* Berkeley and Los Angeles: University of California Press.

Tittle, Charles R., and Raymond Paternoster. 2000. *Social deviance and crime: An organizational and theoretical approach.* Los Angeles, CA: Roxbury Publishing Company.

Tittle, Charles R., and Alan R. Rowe. 1974. Certainty of arrest and crime rates: A further test of the deterrence hypothesis. *Social Forces,* 52:455–62.

Tittle, Charles R., and Michael R. Welch. 1983. Religiosity and deviance: Toward a contingency theory of constraining effects. *Social Forces,* 61:653–82.

Toynbee, Arnold J. 1934/1954. *A study of history.* 10 vols. New York: Oxford University Press.

Tracy, Paul E., Marvin E. Wolfgang, and Robert M. Figlio. 1990. *Delinquency careers in two birth cohorts.* New York: Plenum.

Trafford, Abigail. 2001. The hill tunes in to nurses' lament. *Washington Post* (February 27):8.

Tuch, Steven A., and Michael Hughes. 1996. Whites' racial policy attitudes. *Social Science Quarterly*, 77:723–45.

Tucker, Compton J., Harold E. Dregne, and Wilbur W. Newcomb. 1991. Expansion and contraction of the Sahara Desert from 1980 to 1990. *Science*, 253:299–301.

Tucker, Joan S., Joseph E. Schwartz, Carol Tomlinson-Keasey, Howard S. Friedman, Michael H. Criqui, Deborah L. Wingard, and Leslie R. Martin. 1997. Parental divorce: Effects on individual behavior and longevity. *Journal of Personality and Social Psychology*, 73(2):381–91.

Tucker, Neely. 2000. A matter of violent death and little girls. *Washington Post* (December 31):C1.

Tumin, Melvin M. 1953. Some principles of stratification: A critical analysis. *American Sociological Review*, 18:387–94.

Turkheimer, Eric, and Mary Waldron. 2000. Nonshared environment: A theoretical, methodological, and quantitative review. *Psychological Bulletin*, 126:78–108.

Turner, Bryan S. 1987. *Medical power and social knowledge*. Bevery Hills, CA: Sage.

Turner, Ralph H. 1964. Collective behavior. In R. E. L. Faris, ed., *Handbook of modern sociology*. Chicago: Rand McNally.

Turner, Ralph H. 1968. The self-conception in social interaction. In C. Gordon and K. J. Gergen, eds., *The self in social interaction*. New York: John Wiley.

Turner, Ralph H., and Lewis M. Killian. 1972. *Collective behavior*, 2nd ed. Englewood Cliffs, NJ: Prentice Hall.

Tuxhill, John. 1999. Appreciating the benefits of plant biodiversity. In *State of the world 1999: A Worldwatch Institute report on progress toward a sustainable society*. New York: W.W. Norton & Company.

Tyler, Tom R. 1990. *Why people obey the law*. New Haven, CT: Yale University Press.

Udry, J. Richard. 1995. Sociology and biology: What biology do sociologists need to know? *Social Forces*, 73:1267–78.

Udry, J. Richard. 2000. Biological limits of gender construction. *American Sociological Review*, 65:443–57.

Uggen, Christopher. 2000. Class, gender, and arrest: An intergenerational analysis of workplace power and control. *Criminology*, 38(3):835–62.

Uggen, Christopher, and Jeff Manza. 2002. Democratic contraction? Political consequences of felon disenfranchisement in the United States. *American Sociological Review*, 67:777–803.

United Nations. 1999. *The world at six billion*. New York: United Nations. Available at http://www.un.org/esa/population/publications/sixbillion/sixbilpart1.pdf.

United Nations. 2001. *World urbanization prospects: The 1999 revision*. New York: United Nations.

U.S. Census Bureau. 1996. *Statistical abstract of the United States*. Washington, DC: U.S. Government Printing Office.

U.S. Census Bureau. 1999. *Statistical abstract of the United States: 1999*. Washington, DC: U.S. Government Printing Office.

U.S. Census Bureau. 2000. *Coming from the Americas: A profile of the nation's Latin American foreign born*. Census Brief CENBR/00-3. Washington, DC: U.S. Government Printing Office.

U.S. Census Bureau. 2003. *Statistical abstract of the United States: 2002*. Washington, DC: U.S. Government Printing Office.

U.S. Department of Commerce. 2002. *A nation online: How Americans are expanding their use of the Internet*. Washington, DC: U.S. Government Printing Office.

U.S. Department of Health and Human Services. 1996. *Vital statistics of the United States 1988: Volume III—marriage and divorce*. Hyattsville, MD: U.S. Department of Health and Human Services.

U.S. Department of Health and Human Services. 2000a. *Blueprint for action on breastfeeding*. Washington, DC: U.S. Government Printing Office.

U.S. Department of Health and Human Services. 2000b. *Healthy people 2010: Understanding and improving health*. 2nd ed.

Washington, DC: U.S. Government Printing Office.

U.S. Department of Health and Human Services. 2003. *Child maltreatment 2001.* Washington, DC: U.S. Government Printing Office.

U.S. Department of Health, Education, and Welfare. 1973. *100 years of marriage and divorce statistics: United States, 1867–1967.* Rockville, MD: Health Resources Administration, National Center for Health Statistics.

U.S. Department of Labor. 2003. Bureau of Labor Statistics, Annual Averages 2002. Available at http://www.dol.gov.

Vago, Steven. 2003. *Law and society.* 7th ed. Upper Saddle River, NJ: Prentice Hall.

Valente, Judith. 1991. A century later, Sioux still struggle, and still are losing. *The Wall Street Journal* (March 25):A1, A12.

Valentine, Charles. 1968. *Culture and poverty.* Chicago: University of Chicago Press.

van den Berghe, Pierre. 1963. Dialectic and functionalism: Toward a theoretical synthesis. *American Sociological Review,* 28:695–705.

Vander Zanden, James W. 1965. *Race relations in transition.* New York: Random House.

Vander Zanden, James W. 1983. *American minority relations.* 4th ed. New York: Knopf.

Vander Zanden, James W. 1993. *Human development.* 5th ed. New York: McGraw-Hill.

van Schaik, Carel P., Marc Ancrenaz, Gwendolyn Borgen, Birute Galdikas, Cheryl D. Knott, Ian Singleton, Akira Suzuki, Sri Suci Utami, and Michelle Merrill. 2003. Orangutan cultures and the evolution of material culture. *Science,* 299:102–05.

Veblen, Thorstein. 1899. *The theory of the leisure class.* New York: Viking.

Veblen, Thorstein. 1921. *Engineers and the price system.* New York: Viking.

Vedantam, Shankar. 2001. Peer pressure spurs terrorists, psychologists say. *Washington Post* (October 16):A16.

Ventura, Stephanie J., and Christine A. Bachrach. 2000. Nonmarital childbearing in the United States, 1940–99. *National Vital Statistics Reports,* 48(16):October 18. Atlanta: Centers for Disease Control.

Visgaitis, Gary. 1994. A look at Native Americans across the USA. *USA Today* (April 28):7A.

Vitousek, Peter M., Harold A. Mooney, Jane Lubchenco, and Jerry M. Melillo. 1997. Human domination of Earth's ecosystems. *Science,* 277:494–99.

von Drehl, David. 2003. Gay marriage is a right, Massachusetts court rules. *Washington Post* (November 19):A1.

Vroom, Victor H., and Arthur G. Jago. 1988. *The new leadership: Managing participation in organizations.* Englewood Cliffs, NJ: Prentice Hall.

Waddoups, Jeffrey, and Djeto Assane. 1993. Mobility and gender in a segmented labor market: A closer look. *American Journal of Economics and Sociology,* 52:399–411.

Wagley, Charles, and Marvin Harris. 1964. *Minorities in the New World.* New York: Columbia University Press.

Waite, Linda J., and Maggie Gallagher. 2000. *The case for marriage: Why married people are happier, healthier, and better off financially.* New York: Doubleday.

Waitzkin, Howard. 1983. *The second sickness: Contradictions of capitalist health care.* New York: Free Press.

Waldo, Gordon P., and Theodore G. Chiricos. 1972. Perceived penal sanction and self-reported criminality: A neglected approach to deterrence research. *Social Problems,* 19:522–40.

Wallerstein, Immanuel. 1974. *The modern world-system: Capitalist agriculture and the origins of the European world economy in the 16th century.* New York: Academic Press.

Wallerstein, Immanuel. 1980. *The modern world-system II: Mercantilism and the consolidation of the European world-economy, 1600–1775.* New York: Academic Press.

Wallerstein, Immanuel. 1989. *The modern world-system III: The second era of great expansion of the capitalist world-economy, 1730–1840.* New York: Academic Press.

Walmsley, Roy. 2003. *World prison popula-tion list.* 5th ed. London: United Kingdom Home Office Research, Development and Statistics Directorate.

Walton, John, and Charles Ragin. 1990. Global and national sources of political protest: Third World responses to the debt crisis. *American Sociological Review,* 55:876–90.

Warner, W. Lloyd. 1949. *Democracy in Jonesville.* New York: Harper & Row.

Warner, W. Lloyd, and Paul S. Lunt. 1941. *The social life of the modern community.* New Haven, CT: Yale University Press.

Warner, W. Lloyd, and Paul S. Lunt. 1942. *The status system of a modern community.* New Haven, CT: Yale University Press.

Warren, John Robert, Robert M. Hauser, and Jennifer T. Sheridan. 2002. Occupational stratification across the life course: Evidence from the Wisconsin Longitudinal Study. *American Sociological Review,* 67:432–55.

Washington Post. 2003. Canadian government proposes bill offering definition of marriage. (July 18):A15.

Watson, Robert T. 2003. Climate change: The political situation. *Science,* 302:1925–26.

Weber, Max. 1904/1958. *The Protestant ethic and the spirit of capitalism.* New York: Scribner's.

Weber, Max. 1916/1964. *The religion of China: Confucianism and Taoism.* New York: Macmillan.

Weber, Max. 1917/1958. *The religion of India: The sociology of Hinduism and Buddhism.* New York: Free Press.

Weber, Max. 1921/1968. *Economy and society.* 3 vols. Totowa, NJ: Bedminster Press.

Weber, Max. 1946. *The theory of social and economic organization.* Ed. and trans. A. M. Henderson and Talcott Parsons. New York: Macmillan.

Weber, Max. 1947. *From Max Weber: Essays in sociology.* Ed. and trans. Hans H. Gerth and C. Wright Mills. New York: Oxford University Press.

Weeden, Kim A. 2002. Why do some occupations pay more than others? Social closure and earnings inequality in the United States. *American Journal of Sociology,* 108(1):55–101.

Weeks, John R. 1989. *Population: An intro-duction to concepts and issues.* Belmont, CA: Wadsworth.

Weiss, Harvey, and Raymond S. Bradley. 2001. What drives societal collapse? *Science,* 291:609–10.

Weiss, Rick. 1997. Psychologists' society adopts resolution seeking to limit gay "conversion" therapy. *Washington Post* (August 15):A14.

Wells, Thomas. 1999. Changes in occupational sex segregation during the 1980s and 1990s. *Social Science Quarterly,* 80(2):370–80.

Western, Bruce. 2002. The impact of incarceration on wage mobility and inequality. *American Sociological Review,* 67:526–46.

White, Lynn, and John N. Edwards. 1990. Emptying the nest and parental well-being: An analysis of national panel data. *American Sociological Review,* 55:235–42.

White, Ralph K., and Ronald O. Lippitt. 1960. *Autocracy and democracy.* New York: Harper & Row.

White, T. D., B. Asfaw, D. DeGusta, H. Tilbert, G. D. Richards, G. Suwa, and F. C. Howell. 2003. Pleistocene Homo sapiens from Middle Awash, Ethiopia. *Nature,* 423:742–47.

WHO. 2000. Database on violence against women, 2000. In *The World's Women 2000: Trends and Statistics* (United Nations). http://unstats.un.org/unsd/demographic/ww2000/table6c.htm.

Whorf, Benjamin L. 1956. *Language, thought, and reality.* Cambridge, MA: MIT Press.

Whyte, Martin King. 1990. *Dating, mating, and marriage.* New York: Aldine de Gruyter.

Wiggins, James A., Beverly B. Wiggins, and James Vander Zanden. 1994. *Social psychology.* New York: McGraw-Hill.

Williams, Redford B. 1998. Lower socioeconomic status and increased mortality. Early childhood roots and the potential for successful interventions. *Journal of the American Medical Association,* 279(21):1745–46.

Williams, Robin M., Jr. 1964. *Strangers next door.* Englewood Cliffs, NJ: Prentice Hall.

Williams, Robin M., Jr. 1970. *American society.* 3rd ed. New York: Knopf.

Wilmoth, J. R., L. J. Deegan, H. Lundstrom, and S. Horiuchi. 2000. Increase of maximum life-span in Sweden, 1861–1999. *Science,* 289:2366–68.

Wilson, Bryan R. 1990. *The social dimensions of sectarianism: Sects and new religious movements in contemporary society.* New York: Oxford University Press.

Wilson, Edward O. 2002. *The future of life.* New York: Knopf.

Wilson, James Q. 1990. *What government agencies do and why they do it.* New York: Basic Books.

Wilson, James Q. 1993. Mr. Clinton, meet Mr. Gore. *The Wall Street Journal* (October 28):A18.

Wilson, Peter J. 1988. *The domestication of the human species.* New Haven, CT: Yale University Press.

Wilson, William Julius. 1987. *The truly disadvantaged: The inner city, the underclass, and public policy.* Chicago: University of Chicago Press.

Wilson, William Julius. 1991. Studying inner-city social dislocations: The challenge of public agenda research. *American Sociological Review,* 56:1–14.

Wilson, William J. 1996. *When work disappears.* New York: Knopf.

Winch, Robert F. 1958. *Mate selection: A study of complementary needs.* New York: Harper & Row.

Winnick, Louis. 1991. *New people in old neighborhoods.* New York: Russell Sage Foundation.

Wiseman, Alan E. 2000. *The Internet economy: Access, taxes, and market structure.* Washington, DC: Brookings Institution Press.

Wolfinger, Nicholas H. 1999. Trends in the intergenerational transmission of divorce. *Demography,* 36:415–20.

Wolfinger, Nicholas H. 2003. Parental divorce and offspring marriage. Early or late? *Social Forces,* 82(1):337–53.

Wolfgang, Marvin E., Robert M. Figlio, and Thorsten Sellin. 1972. *Delinquency in a birth cohort.* Chicago: University of Chicago Press.

Woodard, Michael D. 1987. Voluntary association membership among black Americans: The post-civil-rights era. *Sociological Quarterly,* 28:285–301.

Wright, Erik Olin. 1985. *Classes.* New York: Schocken.

Wright, Erik Olin. 1993. Typologies, scales, and class analysis: A comment on Halaby and Weakliem's "Ownership and authority in the earnings function." *American Sociological Review,* 58:31–34.

Wright, Erik Olin. 2000. Working-class power, capitalist-class interests, and class compromise. *American Journal of Sociology,* 105:957–1002.

Wright, Erik Olin. 2002. The shadow of exploitation in Weber's class analysis. *American Sociological Review,* 67:832–53.

Wright, John Paul, and Francis T. Cullen. 2000. Juvenile involvement in occupational delinquency. *Criminology,* 38(3):863–96.

Wrigley, Julia. 1995. *Other people's children.* New York: Basic Books.

Wrigley, Julia. 2003. Review of "Domestica: Immigrant workers cleaning and caring in the shadows of affluence." *Gender and Society,* 17:326–28.

Wysocki, Bernard, Jr. 1991. Influx of Asians brings prosperity to Flushing, a place for newcomers. *The Wall Street Journal* (January 15):A1, A10.

Yablonsky, Lewis, and Martin R. Haskell. 1988. *Juvenile delinquency.* 4th ed. New York: Harper & Row.

Yamaguchi, Kazuo, and Yanatao Wang. 2002. Class identification of married employed women and men in America. *American Journal of Sociology,* 108(2):440–75.

Young, Robert L. 2004. Guilty until proven innocent: Conviction orientation, racial attitudes, and support for capital punishment. *Deviant Behavior,* 25:151–167.

Yu, P. 1994. China's experience in population matters: An official statement. *Population and Development Review,* 20:488–91.

Zigli, Barbara. 1984. Asian-Americans beat others in academic drive. *USA Today* (April 25): D1.

Zimbardo, Philip G. 1969. The human choice: Individuation, reason, and order versus deindividualization, impulse, and chaos. In W. Arnold and D. Levine, eds., *Nebraska Symposium on Motivation,* 17:237–307.

Zingraff, Matthew T., Jeffrey Leiter, Matthew C. Johnson, and Kristen A. Myers. 1994. The mediating effect of good school performance on the maltreatment-delinquency relationship. *Journal of Research in Crime and Delinquency,* 31:62–91.

Photo Credits

Index